ICONS OF DEMOCRACY

American Leaders as Heroes, Aristocrats, Dissenters, and Democrats

BRUCE MIROFF

BasicBooks
A Division of HarperCollins*Publishers*

Designed by Ellen Levine

Library of Congress Cataloging-in-Publication Data

Miroff, Bruce.
    Icons of democracy : American leaders as heroes, aristocrats, dissenters, and
democrats / Bruce Miroff.
        p.   cm.
    Includes bibliographical references and index.
    ISBN 0–465–08747–7 (cloth)
    ISBN 0–465–03261–3 (paper)
    1. Political leadership—United States—History. 2. Statesmen—United
States—History.   3.   Dissenters—United   States—History. 4.   United
States—Politics and government. 5. Heroes—United States—History.   I.
Title.
E183.M69   1993
973'.099—dc20   92–53245
                                                                       CIP

94 95 96 97 ♦/RRD 9 8 7 6 5 4 3 2 1

For Melinda and Nick

C O N T E N T S

PREFACE

THIS BOOK HAS ITS ROOTS IN PERSONAL HISTORY. IN THE SUMMER OF 1965, at the age of twenty, I went south as a civil rights volunteer for the Southern Christian Leadership Conference (SCLC) and witnessed a memorable American story of democracy and leadership. The story began in Atlanta, with an orientation for the student volunteers. The speakers were heroic figures fresh from the dramatic events at Selma, Alabama, only a few months earlier: Martin Luther King, Jr., Hosea Williams, James Bevel, and Andrew Young among others. Their words took on the weight of their personal stature: these were exemplary leaders living out a blazing moral vision with commitment, courage, and grace.

My group of volunteers from Berkeley was assigned to work in Charleston County, South Carolina. The man to whom we reported, Esau Jenkins, offered me yet another model of leadership. Esau, then in his sixties, was a prosperous motel and tavern owner. He was also a pioneer in the civil rights struggle: since the late 1940s, he had been working with tireless determination to register Charleston County blacks to vote. Esau had none of the dramatic flair of the principal SCLC leaders. He was quiet, undemonstrative, sometimes gruff. Impressed by the heroic figures I had seen in Atlanta, I was inclined at first to question his leadership ability. But by the end of that summer

I had developed enormous respect for his tenacious commitment, tactical insight, and quiet wisdom. Esau Jenkins was not famous and had no taste for the heroic—but he was a superb democratic leader.

The most poignant memories from that summer were, however, of followers rather than leaders. The unsung followers who responded to the civil rights movement and its remarkable leadership suggested the redemptive powers of democratic action. The movement and its leaders spoke to people previously excluded from public life—consigned to passivity and public insignificance. It offered them the chance not only to vote but also to act; seizing that chance, ordinary black citizens found new personal powers, achieved a profound sense of dignity, and undertook countless small acts of quiet courage. I have vivid memories of two such unsung followers.

The first was a farmer in his sixties, who through long and difficult efforts had made a good living from his piece of land. With grown children who were equally hardworking and successful, he was a pillar of his rural black community on James Island, South Carolina. But he was illiterate and he could not vote (this was before passage of the Voting Rights Act). He showed up at our voter-education school and asked us to teach him to read and write so that he could register to vote. It was painful to watch this proud man place himself in the position of a child, as he grappled with the elementary forms of language. But it was also intensely moving to see his commitment to registering to vote to complete his sense of personal dignity.

The second was a woman with a severe nervous condition. Charleston County only permitted voter registration at the county courthouse during three consecutive days early in the month. The woman took a bus into Charleston on the first of these days and attempted to register. When we talked to her after her return, she was extremely agitated. The registrar had harassed and intimidated her, and she had broken down. She was in tears as she told us how he had rejected her application. At the end of her tale, however, she pulled herself together, and said: "I'm going back tomorrow to try again."

In the years since 1965 I have read, taught, and written about political leadership in America. I have developed a long-standing scholarly interest in the subject. But the genesis of this book owes at least as much to that summer in the South as to the subsequent years of scholarship. That summer, I learned something important about what kinds of democratic leadership and followership might be possible in America. I have been troubled ever since by the fact that leadership and citizenship in America so seldom fulfill that sense of possibility. Too often, American leaders pursue personal mastery and monopolize public attention, while citizens become passive onlookers to spectacles in which they can play no meaningful parts.

This book is an exploration of the puzzle of leadership and democracy in America. It aims to approach the subject with the care and depth of the scholar. It also aims to remain faithful to the sense of possibility that I first grasped during a few sweltering Southern months of the struggle for democracy.

In the ten years that I have been working on this book, I have been fortunate to receive the friendship, encouragement, and thoughtful advice of a number of individuals. For their commentary and criticisms on one or two chapters, I wish to thank friends, colleagues, and several scholars who were gracious enough to read the work of someone whom they had never met: G. J. Barker-Benfield, Philip Cooper, Don E. Fehrenbacher, Greil Marcus, Richard Nathan, Michael Rogin, Nick Salvatore, Robert Scigliano, Raymond Seidelman, Stephen Skowronek, and Marion Smiley. Special thanks go to two friends who helped me with large chunks of the manuscript: Jim Miller and Todd Swanstrom.

Travel funds for research trips were provided by the State University of New York at Albany. Michael Gizzi, my graduate assistant, helped me explore the literature on political leadership.

I have been doubly fortunate to have Steve Fraser as an editor. Along with his exceptional editorial acumen, he has brought to this project the insights and instincts of a fine historian. The final shape that this book has taken owes much to his sense of possibility.

My son, Nick, has long known this book as something of a mystery. When I began it he was a preschooler; as I finish it he stands taller than I after his first year in high school. But his companionship and love have been a constant in my life.

My deepest and most abiding debt is to Melinda Lawson. She has lived with and anguished over this book almost as much as I have. Her knowledge and talent as a historian have enriched every chapter. Even more important to me, though, have been her love, her patience, and her trust.

INTRODUCTION

In the representative system, the reason for everything must publicly appear. Every man is a proprietor in government, and considers it a necessary part of his business to understand. . . . [A]bove all, he does not adopt the slavish custom of following what in other governments are called leaders.
—THOMAS PAINE, *The Rights of Man*, 1792

To wish is passive; to will is active. Followers wish. Leaders will.
—RICHARD NIXON, *Leaders*, 1982

L
EADERSHIP HAS RARELY FIT COMFORTABLY WITH DEMOCRACY IN America. The claim of leaders to political precedence violates the equality of democratic citizens. The most committed democrats have been suspicious of the very idea of leadership. When Thomas Paine railed against the "slavish custom" of following leaders, he expressed a democrat's deepest anxiety. Having won the struggle to free themselves from hereditary authority and to claim their natural and political rights, would Americans proceed to subordinate themselves to masters of their own creation? Paine's assertion of citizens' independence, competence, and political activism functioned as a democratic talisman, warding off a return to mass passivity and deference in a new guise.[1]

On the other hand, American political thought has not lacked admirers of leadership. Richard Nixon's words serve his own sense of personal drama, but they also encapsulate a prominent strain of American belief. Americans have been no less preoccupied than other peoples with political "greatness," no less prone to communicate their collective experience through the history making of a few famous leaders. Nixon states explicitly what most American admirers of leadership only dare to hint: that the counterpart of the leader as masterful hero is a passive citizenry.[2]

Although Paine and Nixon express two long-standing and characteristic American perspectives on leadership, neither of these perspectives successfully comes to terms with the tension between leadership and democracy. The committed democrats' skepticism toward leadership safeguards them against the dependence of hero-worship. It also leaves them ill equipped to understand the pervasiveness of leadership in American political life. More important, it impedes any effort to develop forms of leadership that might foster a more democratic politics in America. The elitist perspective on leadership attends more closely to how it operates in American politics. But the devotees of elite leadership also tend to reduce politics to a handful of actors atop an inert mass. They work to undermine democratic public life, even as they proclaim their loyalty to it.

If both of these perspectives deny the compatibility of leadership with democracy, is there yet another terrain, in which leadership and democracy can coexist in fruitful tension? What are the possibilities in the space between a Paine's fear of leadership and a Nixon's secret scorn for democracy?

This is a book about the rich variety of forms that American political leadership has taken. I examine nine emblematic figures from the era of the American founding to the present. Through a study of these figures, I differentiate four types of American leadership: aristocratic, democratic, heroic, and dissenting. The depiction of these figures and the delineation of these types will occupy me for most of the book. But my overarching concern is normative: to distinguish those types of American leadership that foster democratic political life from other types—often more prominent and heralded—that undermine it.

The standard for genuinely democratic leadership that underlies my analyses of American leaders should be made clear. I take democratic leadership to require a respect for followers, rooted in a recognition of what Herman Melville called the "democratic dignity" of every individual. Democratic leaders want for followers what they want for themselves; their goals are egalitarian rather than exclusionary. Committed to the democratic belief in self-government, they understand that leadership must aim at engagement with followers rather than mastery. Yet engagement is a far cry from pandering; to nurture the democratic possibilities of citizenship, democratic leaders must be willing to question, challenge, even defy common conventions. In the face of the conventional antithesis between power and education, democratic leadership raises the possibility that dialogue between leader and followers can be mutually empowering.[3]

Genuinely democratic leadership may be rarer in America than we think. It is rendered problematic by enduring characteristics of American thought and practice. A mechanistic institutionalism, for example, conditions Americans to rely on the structures of governance established by the Founding Fathers. Political actors are directed into well-established institutional channels, where, in a scenario principally associated with James Madison, their talents are effectively utilized and their propensities for aggrandizement are checked and balanced. Indeed, mechanistic institutionalism has largely fulfilled its promise of stability and safety, but it has also undermined Americans' recognition of the need explicitly to define and develop democratic leadership.

The practices and values of American capitalism pose a different kind of threat to democratic leadership. A society imbued with commercial principles regards economic success as the principal signpost of worth, while relegating political attainments to a secondary place. Consequently, political leaders are entrusted with authority over economic decisions of considerable significance but are not easily insulated from the attractions and temptations of money. They are also threatened by corruption in a more subtle sense: the corruption of public discourse when economic categories drive out political categories, when political leaders are transformed into entrepreneurs, and citizens, into consumers.

A further impediment to democratic leadership has been confusion over its meaning. In contemporary American politics fear of declining economic power has given rise to widespread calls for a new leadership. Hopes for the revival of American fortunes have focused upon a recrudescence of masterful leaders. In our desire for leadership that is both strong and democratic, however, we shy away from facing the tensions between the two. In this climate, power is confused with virtue, and dominance is mistaken for democracy.

Confusion about democratic leadership has taken a number of forms in the American experience. Since the downfall of the Hamiltonian Federalists, all types of leadership in America have claimed the name and mantle of democracy. Democratic leadership has often been skillfully simulated. Hence, it is essential to distinguish the genuine from the spurious. On the track of democratic leadership, we will gain instruction and inspiration from some unexpected figures, and we will find disturbing implications in the stories of some familiar American heroes.

Studying American Political Leadership

Leadership has attracted growing scholarly interest in recent years. James MacGregor Burns finds its essence in the leader-follower relationship. Leaders, he writes, are purposeful individuals who mobilize their personal and political resources "so as to arouse, engage, and satisfy the motives of followers." Taking issue with Burns, Robert C. Tucker argues that the relationship with followers is only one aspect of the leadership role. For Tucker, a political leader is one who "gives direction, or meaningfully participates in the giving of direction, to the activities of a political community."[4]

Both definitions are serviceable for my purposes: Tucker's will be employed as a generic definition, while Burns's highlights the most critical element in democratic leadership. I am not concerned in this book with postulating and developing yet another theoretical perspective on leadership. Rather, I seek to plumb the resources of American historical experience in order to see what leadership has meant—and can mean—in this society. In this book, I set out to examine and decipher the leadership of nine major figures in the American political tradition, seeking clues from their stories as to what we might do and what we ought to avoid if we hope to arrive at a fuller understanding and practice of democratic leadership. Robert Bellah and his colleagues speak in *Habits of the Heart* of the need to reappropriate American tradition, "finding sustenance in tradition and applying it actively and creatively to our present realities." Democratic leadership today requires this kind of sustenance and creativity.[5]

My approach to the rich store of American images of political leadership is selective and interpretive. I concentrate on individuals who, through their writings and actions, have projected compelling images of leadership. Some of these figures (for example, Alexander Hamilton, Abraham Lincoln, and Franklin Roosevelt) played signal roles in giving shape to the American understanding of leadership. Others, such as John Adams and Elizabeth Cady Stanton, are worth exploring in spite of their limited influence, because they inquired so deeply into the forms leadership might assume in American political life.

While concentrating on what such figures reveal about enduring features of political leadership in America, I still treat them historically, in the context of their times, relating their leadership to biographical facts, political dilemmas, prevailing conventions of discourse. I develop a typology of American political leadership drawn not from abstract or caricatured portraits but rather from nine often frustratingly complex and ambiguous historical actors. Working, therefore, with historical complexity on one side and theoretical relevance on the other, I attempt to do justice to both. If the generalizations that emerge from this study of American political leadership are sometimes saddled with tensions and ambiguities, it is because they cannot be detached from the historical realities upon which they have been based.[6]

Icons of Democracy

The book begins in the founding era with two rival versions of aristocratic leadership in America. Alexander Hamilton, the subject of chapter 1, developed a powerful mode of aristocratic leadership that survived his downfall and lived on in democratic disguise. Believing that democracy cast up base leadership, exemplified at its most frightening by the "embryo-Caesar" Aaron Burr, Hamilton saw the aristocratic statesman as the savior of the Republic. He presented himself as the model statesman, whose classical desire for fame, "the ruling passion of the noblest minds," had been placed in the service of a distinctively modern vision. Hamilton yoked his personal dreams to a dynamic economy, finding the material for national greatness in a capitalist spirit of enterprise rather than a civic spirit of republican virtue. Standing on what he conceived to be a superior eminence, he set out to tame the democratic passions of the American masses, while utilizing the avaricious passions of American men of business to fulfill his vision. Military power complemented economic power for Hamilton, as he sought to build a national government that would "appear like a *Hercules* and inspire respect by the display of strength." But the realist fell victim to a fantasy of destiny, a premature pioneer of American empire.

John Adams, the subject of chapter 2, punctured Hamilton's imperial fantasy. Steeped in a republican tradition that feared the corrupting influence of commerce and wealth, Adams envisioned a classical (Roman) political aristocracy of "virtue, talents, and services." Building on his psychological premise that the spring of human action was a "passion for distinction," he sought a republic that could gratify this passion in its most able men through resplendent symbolic honors and turn it to public advantage. But Adams was doomed to frustration and ridicule. Sabotaged in his political career by those he labeled "intriguers," outshone by those he decried for their "impostures," he let his own passion lead him into "weaknesses and fopperies" that earned him a dubious distinction for egregious vanity. His version of aristocratic leadership, unlike Hamilton's, was buried with his defeat at the hands of Jefferson. Yet Adams remains an intriguing figure, both as an acerbic critic of the forces that would distort and corrupt American leadership and as a passionate advocate of the genuinely political motives upon which any conception of democratic leadership must build.

Chapter 3 finds many of the best possibilities of democratic leadership fulfilled in America's favorite icon of democracy, Abraham Lincoln. Driven by a passion for distinction whose dangerous potential he brilliantly articulated, Lincoln struggled to give a democratic shape to his ambition. He was candid about his desire to attain "high eminence"—but it must be "so reached that the oppressed of my species might [share] with me in the elevation." Rising to political prominence and power, he attempted to remain close to the people, while educating them to the demands of American liberty. Carefully crafting words for which he was prepared to be "responsible through time and in eternity," he revealed with his remarkable wartime speeches the potential power of democratic language. A traditional politician, Lincoln made himself into a new kind of democratic character. Combining qualities that American culture conventionally has dichotomized along lines of gender, he developed what I will call a masculine/feminine political temperament. His substantive vision sometimes fell short of his democratic style of leadership, and his uses of emergency powers provided dangerous precedents for men who lacked his temperament or principles. But he remains an inescapable subject for a student of democratic leadership in America—the teacher whose example of "charity for all" haunts the imagination.

Some of the most important leaders in American democratic experience have located themselves not within the normal institutional channels but outside and against the prevailing order. Elizabeth Cady Stanton, Eugene V. Debs, and Martin Luther King, Jr., serve as my exemplars of dissenting leadership. Rebelling against confinement to the sphere of domesticity, Stanton, the subject of chapter 4, shaped a new kind of politics out of the outrage of women's exclusion from public life. "Woman alone," she proclaimed at the Seneca Falls Convention that launched a women's rights movement in the United States, "can understand the height, the depth, the length, and the breadth of her own degradation." Stanton made of herself not only a public voice but also a dramatic embodiment of the nineteenth-century feminist vision. Committed to the faith that political education could overcome prejudice and awaken Americans to the demands of justice, she unlocked the democratic potential of America's classical political idiom. She argued with great force that the republican ideal was a false one unless woman can "stand on an even pedestal with man [and] look him in the face as an equal." Stanton's career was not without disturbing episodes; the pain of women's exclusion led her, on occasion, to outbursts of racist and nativist sentiments. Nevertheless, her career provides a feminist image of American political leadership that has too often been neglected.

The heroic leader who assumes the mantle of democratic champion to pursue a self-aggrandizing role that jeopardizes democratic public life is exemplified in this book by Theodore Roosevelt and John F. Kennedy. Chapter 5 details how Roosevelt conceived of democratic politics as a theater of the ego. His favorite persona was the muscular reformer, not only "unselfish" and "disinterested," but also "vigorous in mind and body, . . . able to suffer punishment without flinching and, at need, to repay it in kind with full interest." In substituting energy for education and drama for discourse, Roosevelt redefined the American public as spectators for his heroic contests. He scorned the masculine/feminine balance of democratic leadership that Lincoln represented and returned to the Hamiltonian standard wherein the masculine accomplishments of economic organization and imperial expansion were the keys to American happiness. Through the masculine spectacle of his leadership, Roosevelt proclaimed America's readiness "to stand among the great races" and bid for glory on the stage of world history.

Chapter 6 takes up a dissenting leader on the far borders of American political life. Eugene V. Debs frequently lamented his prominence in the socialist cause, insisting that he would have preferred "to remain in the ranks, . . . fighting unnamed and unhonored side by side with my comrades." But in rejecting the power of leadership as inherently corrupting, Debs tended to evade hard questions of organizational and ideological conflict. He preferred instead to float above the sectarian fray as a symbol of both protest against industrial capitalism and hope for the coming of democratic socialism. Nonetheless, Debs was a genuine leader as well as a symbol—at his best, the kind of "true leader [who] uses all his power, not to rule others, but to impart the power and intelligence to them to rule themselves." Few American leaders have ever matched his ability to incorporate the experiences of followers into his own. Few have ever matched his exploration of the radical democratic meanings in the American republican tradition. If in his role as a prophet of impending social revolution, Debs appears as something of an archaic figure, in his role as a dissenting leader he stands as an abiding American icon of "democratic dignity."

Franklin D. Roosevelt, the subject of chapter 7, personifies the dilemmas of democratic leadership in the modern American state. Taking a different path from that followed by Lincoln, Roosevelt too arrived at a masculine/feminine balance, becoming in his prime an often perplexing combination of ego, political cunning, humane nurturance, and democratic faith. In the dispiriting circumstances of the Great Depression, he exuberantly assumed the task of the political educator. Announcing that "the greatest duty of a statesman is to educate," he revitalized old and somewhat forgotten American idioms of cooperation and community. Both the moral and the economic objectives of the New Deal legitimated his proud assertion that "in a world which in many places has gone undemocratic, we have gone more democratic." Yet Roosevelt's impact on American democratic life was rife with paradox. He was blithe about power so long as it was under his control, but the very instruments of national power that he developed to serve democratic ends also tended to dwarf democratic citizens. The circumstances of war gave Roosevelt a second chance to rally and mobilize the American people, but in his preoccupation with winning the war, he permitted the democratic spirit of the New Deal to falter and oversaw the restoration of corporate power and the establishment of a militarized state.

If democratic leadership is caught up in the paradoxes of the modern state, heroic leadership finds the modern age of television admirably suited to its purposes. Chapter 8 portrays a heroic leader less strident and more charming than Theodore Roosevelt: with a graceful persona—and the assistance of skilled manufacturers of heroic imagery—John F. Kennedy ascended to the top of American politics as rapidly as the Rough Rider. Proclaiming a rebirth of political excellence in America, Kennedy mastered the modern media; on television, the heroic leader could be at once engaging and familiar yet remote and superior. The modern hero's stage for excellence was global. Eager "to seize the burden and the glory of freedom," Kennedy led the nation into what he had predicted would be "its hour of maximum danger." In the terrifying days of the Cuban missile crisis, his prophecy was fulfilled and his apotheosis was assured. Dominant though he was abroad, however, the hero encountered unexpected challenges at home—from a business community that reminded him who had the decisive power over the economy and from a civil rights movement that compelled him to take a moral stand at odds with the politician's cautious calculations.

Chapter 9 depicts the journey of Martin Luther King, Jr., from a hopeful idealism to a haunted and tragic political wisdom. Elaborating his dissenting leadership through an integration of religious and political traditions and of black and white discourses, King was the most celebrated leader of a multifaceted civil rights movement that both followed and resisted him. Through rhetoric that evoked the powerful music of African American "freedom songs," he challenged the white majority to practice its democratic faith. More than Elizabeth Cady Stanton or Eugene V. Debs, King realized that dissenting leadership must not turn away from political prudence in its moral fervor; he became a political man who knew how to move American institutions toward racial justice. Yet when he left behind the Southern terrain where the struggle for desegregation had triumphed and took on the larger targets of racism, economic inequality, and imperialism, he met defeat and tasted scorn. Still, King would not abandon his dream of racial reconciliation, as he told his followers: "There have been too many hymns of hope, too many anthems of expectation, too many deaths, too many dark days of standing over graves of those who fought for integration for us to turn back now." Pursued by forces that he knew were determined to destroy him, he testified at the end of his life to the deepest task of dissenting leadership: the democratic redemption of the American people.

The nine American leaders considered in this book have been, to a greater or lesser extent, icons of democracy. Some of these leaders provide alluring images that turn out to jeopardize a democratic public life. From others, however, we can draw ideas, images, and examples of leadership that advance democratic ends. In an era when American leadership seems sunk in petty power struggles and shallow media spectacles, some of our icons have much to teach us about the forms of leadership that can still speak to the democratic possibilities of the American people.

Alexander Hamilton

The Aristocratic Statesman and the Constitution of American Capitalism

S HORTLY AFTER ALEXANDER HAMILTON RESIGNED HIS POSITION AS SEC-
retary of the treasury and returned to New York to resume the
practice of law, a close friend, Robert Troup, wrote to him
about a potentially lucrative business venture. Troup and Hamilton
were being solicited by a group of foreign investors to provide "advice
and assistance" for land speculation in the Northwest Territory.
Troup suggested that his friend's role in the venture could be kept
confidential and, anticipating Hamilton's objections, insisted that
there would be no impropriety in his involvement. "Why should you
object to making a little money in a way that cannot be reproachful?
Is it not time for you to think of putting yourself in a state of independence?"[1]

Hamilton agreed that there was no "indelicacy in the thing" but
would not even consider the proposition. Despite his return to private
life, he was still preoccupied with the reverberations of the French
Revolution and the war in Europe: "I think there is at present a great
crisis in the affairs of mankind which may in its consequences involve
this country in a sense most affecting to every true friend to it." Intent
on keeping himself prepared for this crisis, Hamilton would not risk
even the faintest taint of speculation. Others might legitimately obtain
wealth in this fashion, but for him—"because there must be some
public fools who sacrifice private to public interest at the certainty of
ingratitude and obloquy—because my *vanity* whispers I ought to be

one of those fools and ought to keep myself in a situation the best calculated to render service—because I don't want to be rich"—such
schemes were out of the question. Besides, Hamilton saw himself as
gambling for higher stakes: "The game to be played may be a most important one. It may be for nothing less than true liberty, property,
order, religion, and, of course, *heads*. I will try, Troup, if possible, to
guard yours and mine."[2]

Hamilton liked to portray himself as an exemplar of aristocratic
leadership in a country whose increasingly democratic sentiments
brought him misunderstanding and abuse. As used here, aristocratic
leadership does not imply hereditary authority. Rather, it rests on the
explicit affirmation of a political elite that stands apart from the people as a whole. This elite boasts of its superior talents and wisdom. Its
claim to political authority is predicated on the assumption that it
knows best how to advance the public good.

Hamilton put forward his image of aristocratic leadership in the
teeth of democratic and egalitarian passions unleashed by the American Revolution. In overturning British authority, Americans had called
into question all authority not immediately rooted in the sovereign
people. The most radical republicans, such as Thomas Paine, voiced
suspicions about any who viewed themselves as superior to the
masses. But economic conflict and political disillusionment in the
decade between the Declaration of Independence and the Constitution
revived yearnings for authority and leadership, especially among members of the gentry. The most powerful conceptions of leadership that
emerged in the founding era reflected an aristocratic sensibility, as the
gentry struggled to stay atop a novel and explosively democratic political world.[3]

Most of the Constitution makers of 1787 hoped that skillful institutional design and the remoteness of the national government would
dampen democratic passions. But Hamilton believed that leadership
was more critical than any mechanical contrivances. Seeing in the
French Revolution only the mob and the Reign of Terror, Hamilton
insisted that only his kind of aristocratic leadership could defend a
free yet ordered society against an American version of the radical,
bloody-minded Jacobins. The talents of the "statesman," who valued
lasting fame over popularity or power, were essential to overmaster
the "demagogue," whose skill lay in the manipulation and exploitation
of mass discontent.

Hamilton's aristocratic leadership was uniquely American. The
order he set out to defend was not steeped in tradition and obsessed
with stability; it was a fluid order that needed to be protected from
democratic frenzies so that it could foster a dynamic economy. Where

classical aristocratic virtues pitted themselves against the disruptive vices of avarice and ambition, Hamilton's aristocratic leadership, while holding itself superior to these vices, sought to use them as its raw materials. Hamilton's concern was not to produce active citizens whose civic commitments would sustain the republic but rather to produce capitalists whose enterprise and energy would help the republic to thrive. Taming a people whose rage for an unfettered liberty jeopardized "true liberty" as well as order, property, and religion, he sought to show Americans how they might be prosperous and powerful and, thereby, happy.

Hamilton propelled the new national government to establish institutions that would promote a dynamic capitalist economy. He was successful as well in developing a strong national executive who could contain democratic turbulence while nurturing economic and military power. But his eventual defeat by the Jeffersonians seemed to relegate his kind of aristocratic leadership to a predemocratic era. Nevertheless, Hamilton's type of leadership has continued to lead a subterranean life in American politics. His heirs have been careful to cloak their desire for mastery and fame in the garb of democracy, exploiting the very rhetoric and rituals of democracy that Hamilton had disdained. Still, the Hamiltonian vision of the leader is apparent beneath many later disguises.

The Young Publius

What appalled the Jeffersonians—and what impressed later commentators who prided themselves on their "realistic" view of human nature—was Hamilton's determination to rest the success of the American republican experiment on selfish passions rather than the potential for civic virtue. Hamilton himself had not always viewed the American future in this manner. As a young officer in the Revolutionary army he had excoriated signs of American avarice and passionately affirmed a classical republican politics of virtuous action. The young Hamilton is a poignant figure—and an interesting contrast to the mature statesman. A brief look at this young man, who called himself Publius long before *The Federalist Papers*, will highlight the contrast.

The three letters sent to a New York newspaper in the fall of 1778 under the pseudonym of Publius were Hamilton's first public writings since the outbreak of the war. It was the case of Samuel Chase that stirred him to pick up his pen. Chase had used his official knowledge as a delegate to the Continental Congress to monopolize the supply of flour that Congress intended to purchase for the French fleet and then to more than double its price. In censuring Chase's behavior, Hamilton set out in dramatic terms his conception of the struggle between republican virtue and corruption.

In the then-familiar scheme of classical republican thought, a virtuous people, whose commitment to the public good transcended their concern for private advantages, could be corrupted by the spirit of commerce and profit seeking. Eagerness for wealth and luxury would not only detract from public involvement; it would reverse the proper relationship between public and private ends. This was the language used by the young Publius in his condemnation of Chase, whom he depicted as a member of "that tribe who, taking advantage of the times, have carried the spirit of monopoly and extortion, to an excess, which scarcely admits of a parallel." Unless this spirit was effectively countered, it would destroy everything that the Revolution was hoping to accomplish. In voicing these fears, Publius used the same kind of language that would be employed only a decade and a half later to condemn Secretary of the Treasury Hamilton: "When avarice takes the lead in a State, it is commonly the forerunner of its fall."[4]

Chase was loathsome to the young Hamilton not only for his behavior but as a character type. A man of mediocre talents and sordid qualities, he had won office by deceptive words that ingratiated him with the public. A man whose overpowering greed had won out over a "natural timidity," he had no scruples about bilking the people: "No man will suspect you of the folly of public spirit; a heart notoriously selfish exempts you from any charge of this nature." That men like Chase were starting to appear on the public stage did not bode well for a young republic. "We begin to emulate the most veteran and accomplished states in the art of corruption."[5]

Publius's final letter eloquently depicted a public figure whose motives and actions were the opposites of Chase's avarice and corruption. It set out a code of political conduct that Hamilton would continue to apply to himself, even as he grew skeptical of the capacity of others to adhere to it:

> The station of a member of Congress is the most illustrious and important of any I am able to conceive. He is to be regarded not only as a legislator, but as the founder of an empire. A man of virtue and ability, dignified with so precious a trust, would rejoice that fortune had given him birth at a time, and placed him in circumstances so favorable for promoting human happiness. He would esteem it not more the duty, than the privilege and ornament of his office, to do

good to mankind; from this commanding eminence, he would look down with contempt upon every mean or interested pursuit.[6]

If Chase represented a disturbing sign of corruption in the American cause, Hamilton was still confident that avarice could be kept under control by heroic legislators of the type he portrayed. The American people had only to be made aware of the situation to rally to the standard of virtue. The young Publius thus confidently predicted Chase's downfall (little imagining that Chase would someday be a Federalist justice of the United States Supreme Court, detested by Jeffersonians almost as much as they despised Hamilton). "I have too good an opinion of the sense and spirit, to say nothing of the virtue of your countrymen, to believe they will permit you any longer to abuse their confidence, or trample upon their honor."[7]

Classical republican thought provided the young Publius with both a language of condemnation and a vision of virtuous leadership and citizenship. But as Hamilton's frustrations with the ineptitude of Congress and the precarious situation of the army mounted, his classical republican sentiments came to feed a disenchanted view of both his country's fortunes and his own, a topic on which he dwelled in correspondence with John Laurens, a fellow officer who had become his closest friend. The congressional controversy over Silas Deane, the profiteering American envoy in France, prompted Hamilton to comment, "I hate money making men." Laurens's proposal to recruit black slaves into the Revolutionary army and to reward their services with emancipation brought from Hamilton not only a prediction that Southern self-interest would block such a scheme but also a scathing denunciation of American avarice and corruption. "Every hope of this kind, my friend, is an idle dream. Everything will convince you that there is no virtue in America—that commerce which presided over the birth and education of these states has fitted their inhabitants for the chain, and that the only condition they sincerely desire is that it may be a golden one."[8]

Doubting that a commercial America could be virtuous, Hamilton despaired of his own prospects as a statesman. As he wrote to Laurens in January 1780, political aspirants whose merits were in no way superior to those of Hamilton were given preference over him: "I am a stranger in this country. I have no property here, no connections. If I have talents and integrity (as you say I have), these are justly deemed very spurious titles in these enlightened days, when unsupported by others more solid." His dreams of serving as the legislator and founder of a virtuous and powerful empire seemingly dashed, Hamilton could see no other path to honor and glory than a romantic death in battle: "In short, Laurens, I am disgusted with everything in this world but yourself and very few more honest fellows and I have no other wish than as soon as possible to make a brilliant exit."[9]

Within a few weeks of this letter, Hamilton would meet and begin his courtship of Elizabeth Schuyler, daughter of one of the wealthiest and most powerful patroons of the Hudson River aristocracy. Although his political disenchantment persisted for a time in his letters to Laurens, once marriage brought him into the company of New York's gentry, he would have the connections he needed to ground his "talents and integrity." The disenchanted classical republican began the process of shedding the political philosophy that had inspired his gloom. The ideals of behavior that he had articulated in his Publius letters would now be reserved for himself and a few others; for the bulk of his countrymen he would hold very different expectations. Hamilton's abandonment of classical hopes was explicit by 1782: "We may preach till we are tired of the theme, the necessity of disinterestedness in republics, without making a single proselyte. . . . It is as ridiculous to seek for models in the simple ages of Greece and Rome, as it would be to go in quest of them among the Hottentots and Laplanders."[10]

Human Nature and the American People

The harsh view of human nature that was to become so familiar a part of Alexander Hamilton's political thought was evident even in the young republican enthusiast. Perhaps it was a product of the painful circumstances—the stigmas of illegitimacy and poverty—of his childhood. Perhaps it was fueled by his youthful reading of the skeptical David Hume. Whatever its sources, one can find traces of the mature Hamilton's low opinion of his fellow human beings in his earliest writings. The precocious Whig pamphleteer of 1774–75 was given to quoting Hume to the effect that "*every man* ought to be supposed a *knave*," and to reminding his readers that "a vast majority of mankind is entirely biased by motives of self-interest." But during the early years this dark view was balanced by hopes for a redemptive republicanism: "There is a certain enthusiasm in liberty, that makes human nature rise above itself in acts of bravery and heroism."[11]

As his republican hopes faded, the Hamilton of the 1780s came to pride himself on his unflattering portrait of humankind. His prose during the era of the Constitutional Convention and *The Federalist Pa-*

pers was studded with descriptions and vignettes of human vice. He was particularly eager to demolish the remaining adherents of classical republican virtue with his demonstrations that "men are ambitious, vindictive, and rapacious." His starkest statement on human nature came at the Constitutional Convention (according to the notes of Robert Yates): "Take mankind in general, they are vicious."[12]

The grimness of Hamilton's view of human nature was not unrelieved. The phrase "in general" was meant to signal some important exceptions. Addressing a convention of distinguished men who could hardly be expected to acknowledge their own viciousness, Hamilton proceeded to sketch a political elite whose guiding motives were very different from those of the masses. "Take mankind as they are, and what are they governed by? Their passions. There may be in every government a few choice spirits, who may act from more worthy motives. . . . Perhaps a few men in a state may, from patriotic motives, or to display their talents, or to reap the advantage of public applause, step forward." Herein we find not only a self-portrait but also Hamilton's psychology of aristocratic leadership.[13]

Political virtue would be a rare phenomenon for Hamilton, the attribute of a tiny elite rather than a mass public. He also distinguished another kind of elite, one grounded in economic matters; human nature, that is, had a class dimension. As Hamilton told the New York Ratifying Convention in 1788:

> Experience has by no means justified us in the supposition that there is more virtue in one class of men than in another. Look through the rich and the poor of the community; the learned and the ignorant. Where does virtue predominate? The difference indeed consists, not in the quantity but kind of vices, which are incident to the various classes; and here the advantage of character belongs to the wealthy. Their vices are probably more favorable to the prosperity of the state, than those of the indigent; and partake less of moral depravity.[14]

Despite these qualifications, Hamilton's view of human nature seems, on the surface, to be the bleakest of the Founding Fathers'. Yet in one important respect, Hamilton was more sanguine than his colleagues about the potential uses of human nature. James Madison and John Adams, looking for a counterpoise to ambition and avarice, sought a balanced government that could neutralize the more dangerous human impulses. Hamilton, in contrast, thought less about balancing these passions than about extracting their energies and turning them to the statesman's purposes.

What Hamilton feared was the focusing of selfish passions upon the goods that the state governments could provide. The national government, he insisted, must have the means to capture such passions, a point he emphasized in the notes for his major speech at the Constitutional Convention:

> AMBITION   AVARICE
> To effect any thing PASSIONS must be turned toward
> general government?. . .
> [T]he government must be so constituted as to offer strong motives.
> In short, to interest all the *passions* of individuals.
> And turn them into that channel.[15]

A high-toned national government could supply offices and honors attractive enough for most ambitious men. The national government offered not only more eminence but also longer terms of office than the state governments. And it was not hamstrung by the radical republican provision for rotation of representatives. Hamilton believed that "the desire of reward is one of the strongest incentives of human conduct," and he was intent on channeling that desire away from the states and toward the nation.[16]

In Hamilton's vision, avarice was an even more crucial raw material than ambition. He differed most strikingly from the other Founders in his belief that avarice could be transmuted into something not only benign but even beneficial. Though Hamilton himself, the aristocratic statesman, personally disdained the pursuit of material rewards, his central project as a statesman was to banish the dream of a classical republic and to constitute in its place a modern, thriving, capitalist political economy.

The tradition of classical republican thought that the young Publius had echoed viewed avarice as weakening the state, undermining civic virtue, and promoting the pursuit of private gain at public expense. The mature Hamilton wanted the state to encourage the spirit of gain—now dubbed a spirit of "enterprise" rather than "avarice." The drives of the enterprising, a source of vitality rather than of disease, would solidify a state whose power derived from economic growth. In the political economy that Hamilton envisioned, capitalists would not be interested in raiding the public coffers. Instead, state policies would direct them to new and more profitable private endeavors. If their passion for material gain prevented them from being virtuous citizens in the classical republican mold, it made them solid citizens of a state that was carefully attuned to their interests.

Democracy and the Demagogue

Contemporary historians of the era of the American founding perceive a politics characterized by hierarchy and deference, with the
full-fledged democratization of American politics usually dated to the
1820s and 1830s. For Alexander Hamilton, however, the spirit of
American politics was already too democratic. Surveying the situation
in New York in 1782, Hamilton sounded like Plato assailing the vices
of Athenian democracy: "Here we find the general disease which in-
fects all our constitutions, an excess of popularity. . . . The inquiry
constantly is what will *please* not what will *benefit* the people. In such
a government there can be nothing but temporary expedient, fickle-
ness, and folly."[17]

Hamilton equated democracy with disorder. He complained to his
fellow delegates at the Constitutional Convention that for all their
criticisms of democratic tendencies in America, they did not grasp the
full extent of the danger. This failure stemmed from "not duly considering the amazing violence and turbulence of the democratic spirit.
When a great object of government is pursued, which seizes the popular passions, they spread like wild fire, and become irresistible."
Hamilton's portrait of democracy was drawn largely from ancient history, but the triumph of the radicals in France provided him with a
more contemporary image of democratic horror. Defending the Jay
Treaty in 1795, he argued that its settlement of American differences
with Britain had averted a war that would have brought the American
democrats to power:

> [A] considerable party among us is deeply infected with those horrid
> principles of Jacobinism which, proceeding from one excess to an-
> other, have made France a theatre of blood. . . . It was too probable
> that the direction of the war, if commenced, would have fallen into
> the hands of men of this description. The consequences of this, even
> in imagination, are such as to make any virtuous man shudder.[18]

Democracy disturbed Hamilton not only because it threatened
property and order, but because it bred the most despicable kind of
leadership. He looked with contempt upon the skills of democratic
politicians. Even when Hamilton was defeated by the Jeffersonians,
he scoffed at them as "LITTLE POLITICIANS" and confidently predicted their swift downfall: "Consummate in the paltry science of
courting and winning popular favor, they falsely infer that they have
the capacity to govern, and they will be the last to discover their

error." But this contempt sometimes gave way to a deep fear. While most of the "little politicians" were scrambling after petty rewards, the most dangerous of their tribe had more extensive ambitions. Democracy was the milieu of the demagogue.[19]

The demagogue was the specter who haunted Hamilton's political vision, indeed, a central character who reappeared in almost all of the political dramas of Hamilton's career. In the first of *The Federalist Papers,* Hamilton portrayed him as the arch foe of the new Constitution:

> A dangerous ambition more often lurks behind the specious mask of zeal for the rights of the people than under the forbidding appearance of zeal for the firmness and efficiency of government. History will teach us that the former has been found a much more certain road to the introduction of despotism than the latter, and that of those men who have overturned the liberties of republics, the greatest number have begun their career by paying an obsequious court to the people, commencing demagogues and ending tyrants.[20]

While Hamilton provided a number of general depictions of the demagogic type, his most complete and dramatic portraits were of individuals. One of these men—George Clinton—dominated New York politics and threatened Hamilton's political base. The second—Aaron Burr—posed a more profound threat, both to the nation and to Hamilton personally. In his accounts of these two, Hamilton wrote fascinating case studies of the demagogue in action.

Governor George Clinton of New York had once been Hamilton's friend and ally, but his hostility to a strong national government in the 1780s turned him into a powerful foe. Clinton's determined efforts to make New York a hotbed of opposition to the new Constitution finally led Hamilton to denounce him. The occasion was the New York election of 1789, and Hamilton's tactic, in letters printed in a newspaper under the signature of "H. G." and in an open address to the electorate, was to persuade the voters that Clinton was a demagogue.

Hamilton painted Clinton as a man lacking all of the attributes of genuine statesmanship. Unimpressive in ability, intellect, or past public service, Clinton was distinguished in only one sense. He had the essential skill of the demagogue: "he early got the character with many of being a very *artful* man. . . ." But it was not only his political methods, Hamilton insisted, that marked Clinton as a demagogue. The demagogue was a psychological as well as a political type. Clinton was one of "those who are of restless and turbulent spirits, impatient of constraint, averse to all power or superiority, which they do not themselves enjoy." Hamilton attributed to Clinton a disordered psyche, whose hostility to the authority of those with genuine ability and wisdom masked his own will to power.[21]

Hamilton castigated Clinton for resisting national authority. Equally abhorrent to him was Clinton's demagogic propensity to disrupt economic harmony. The governor had turned his back on those of substantial property and cast his lot with their enemies, a choice based not on conviction but on a political calculation that class conflict would enhance his popularity:

> It is well known that large property is an object of jealousy in republics, and that those who possess it, seldom enjoy extensive popularity. The Governor was aware that he would have risked the loss, rather than have promoted the continuance of that which he possessed, by connecting himself with men of that class; and that his purpose could be better answered by an opposite course.[22]

Governor Clinton, Hamilton warned the New York voters, was "too dangerous to be trusted at the head of the state." But Clinton paled as a threat when a far more formidable demagogue appeared on the scene. In the vice presidential contest of 1792, Hamilton preferred John Adams to Clinton, yet Clinton, he now conceded, "is a man of property, and, in private life, as far as I know, of probity." But Aaron Burr is "unprincipled both as a public and private man." Clinton's ambitions were provincial, but Burr's were far-reaching: "In a word, if we have an embryo-Caesar in the United States, 'tis Burr."[23]

Hamilton's recurring nightmare—the prospect of Burr's ascent to power—came perilously close to reality in the election of 1800. Jefferson and Burr each received the same number of electoral votes (under the original constitutional design, electors did not differentiate their ballots for president and vice president), and the choice of the chief executive was thrown into the House of Representatives. Disgruntled Federalist congressmen, seeing their longtime foe, Jefferson, about to gain power, began to look favorably upon the alternative. Burr was not addicted to Jefferson's democratic principles. Further, these Federalists supposed that Burr would be amenable to their influence if they were responsible for his selection as president.

Hamilton responded with a furious letter-writing campaign. Over the course of a single month (December 16, 1800–January 16, 1801), he wrote thirteen letters devoted in whole or in part to a dissection of Burr's character and ambitions. These letters contain the most dramatic and passionate prose of Hamilton's entire career. He exerted every effort to be persuasive—and to strike fear to the hearts of those Federalists who were leaning toward Burr. But there was also a compulsive vein in this discussion: Hamilton seemed unable to stop before he had given complete and vivid shape to his own nightmare.

If Clinton's soul had been disordered, Burr's was, Hamilton argued, positively diseased. At the core of his character was a monstrous egotism: "Burr loves nothing but himself; thinks of nothing but his own aggrandizement; and will be content with nothing, short of permanent power in his own hands." It was Hamilton's belief that Burr was after power to gratify the limitless desires of a perverted psyche: "He is in every sense a profligate; a voluptuary in the extreme, with uncommon habits of expense."[24]

A demagogue, in Hamilton's view, sought power but lacked the qualifications to legitimate it. Like Clinton, Burr was described as skillful only in the lowest and the most dangerous political arts. "As to his talents, great management and cunning are the predominant features—he is yet to give proofs of those solid abilities which characterize the statesman." Nor could Burr lay claim to having rendered valuable service to the American republic. His military career had not produced "any distinguished action," while "in civil life he has never projected nor aided in producing a single measure of important public utility." What did distinguish Burr—and make him, in Hamilton's eyes, the most dangerous demagogue in the United States—was the combination of extraordinary boldness and exceptional immorality. "He is sanguine enough to hope everything—daring enough to attempt everything—wicked enough to scruple nothing. From the elevation of such a man, heaven preserve the country!"[25]

The demagogue shared Hamilton's own contempt for democracy but professed to love it with hypocritical ardor. Of aristocratic birth and style, Burr was "a man who, despising democracy, has chimed in with all its absurdities." Secretly laughing at his followers, he "played the whole game of Jacobinism" and fueled their most radical follies. Having no principles to violate, his hypocrisy came easily:

> No mortal can tell what his political principles are. He has talked *all round the compass. At times* he has dealt in all the jargon of Jacobinism; at other times he has proclaimed decidedly the total insufficiency of the Federal Government and the necessity of changes to one far more energetic. The truth seems to be that he has no plan but that of *getting* power by *any* means and *keeping* it by *all* means. It is probable that if he has any theory, 'tis that of a simple *despotism.*[26]

Steeped in vice, Burr was a master at appealing to the vicious side of mankind that democracy gave free rein. His true following, in Hamilton's portrait, was himself writ large: "Like *Catiline,* he is indefatigable in courting the *young* and the *profligate*. He knows well the weak sides of human nature, and takes care to play in with the passions of all with whom he has intercourse." Burr would find ample material for his ambitions among the American people. He would "use the *worst* part of the community as a ladder to climb to permanent power and an instrument to crush the better part." Hamilton saw no limit to the horrors that might ensue from Burr's lust for power: "I am sure there are no means too atrocious to be employed by him."[27]

Hamilton painted a terrifying picture of a Burr presidency. "As to foreign policies," he wrote, "war will be a necessary means of power and wealth. The animosity to the British will be the handle by which he will attempt to wield the nation to that point." The Constitution would be discarded as an impediment to personal dominion: "The maintenance of the existing institutions will not suit him, because under them his power will be too narrow and too precarious." The demagoguery of Aaron Burr would destroy everything for which Hamilton had labored. It would leave in ruins his own achievements, which he saw as inseparable from the successful functioning of the American republic.[28]

Some commentators have wondered whether "Hamilton's analysis of Burr in 1801 [might be] a mirror of his own heart and personality." It is tempting to see in Hamilton's dramatic portrait of Burr the traces of his own frustrated ambition. Yet he was profoundly different from Burr, not only in personality but in his understanding of political leadership. Hamilton himself underscored the difference in the final letter of his campaign against Burr: "Let it be remembered that Mr. Burr has never appeared solicitous for fame, and that great ambition, unchecked by principle, or the love of glory, is an unruly tyrant which never can keep long in a course which good men will approve." Committed to his own vision of the nation's future and seeking his fame in the fulfillment of that vision, Hamilton viewed Burr not as his double but as his destroyer.[29]

Fearing for all that he had built, he was ready to sacrifice even his life to stop Burr. He would couch that sacrifice not in the language of self but in the name of the values that he had championed. In 1804, when Burr demanded an apology for malicious statements Hamilton had allegedly made about him in a private conversation, Hamilton refused to recant and agreed to carry the matter to the dueling field. He wrote to his wife, however, that his developing Christian scruples would not allow him to fire first and take the life of another. On the heights of Weehawken, across the Hudson from New York City, Burr fired first and inflicted a fatal wound. In 1792, facing the prospect of Burr's ascent to power, Hamilton had written, somewhat metaphorically, that "I feel it a religious duty to oppose his career." Twelve years later, a more literal reading of Christian duty led Hamilton to refrain from firing at Burr and to accept his bullet.[30]

The Statesman

Alexander Hamilton often pictured political leadership as a matter of stark alternatives: the American people could be tricked by "the cunning of a demagogue" or they could reap benefits from "the talents of a statesman." Unable to conceive of any responsible forms of popular leadership, Hamilton envisioned an aristocratic form of leadership that would serve the people's true interests while mastering their misguided passions. Images of the statesman were scattered throughout his writings and actions: while he sketched detailed likenesses of demagogues, he depicted the statesman only in fragmentary analyses—an indication, perhaps, that his notion of the statesman was more a self-portrait than a well-developed conception.[31]

The demagogue and the statesman shared in common only their unusual energy. While the demagogue's cunning masked the absence of solid talents, the statesman was a man of superb abilities. Self-controlled and prudent, he grasped the nub of public business and carried out his duties with a fine sense of order and system. Yet he was not the captive of inflexible institutions and rules; an expansive reading of the creative possibilities of governance led him to innovate as well as to preserve. Such abilities were, Hamilton believed, most often to be found among the economic and social elite. As early as 1780, he was advocating that Congress fill the chief offices of state with "men of the first abilities, property, and character in the continent." He did, however, acknowledge that the talents of a statesman might be found elsewhere. In a clearly autobiographical passage, he wrote: "There are strong minds in every walk of life that will rise superior to the disadvantages of situation and will command the tribute due to their merit."[32]

Ability was closely tied to images of strength in Hamilton's discussions of statesmanship. Words such as "energy" and "vigor" appear frequently in his prose. The personal vitality of the statesman was indispensable to a government whose capacity for action had been hindered by fragmentation of power. Strength also meant a tough-minded, unsentimental view of the realities of politics. Hamilton equated his own statesmanship with masculinity, while portraying his opponents as both misguided *and* emasculated. Describing the foreign policy views of Jefferson and Madison in 1792, he wrote: "*They have a womanish at-*

tachment to France and a womanish resentment against Great Britain."[33]

Talents and strength were prerequisites for genuine statesmanship, but they had to be placed in the service of a guiding vision. Hamilton scoffed at several of his rivals for their attachment to abstract political theories. Complaining to Rufus King about John Adams's conduct as president, Hamilton observed: "You know . . . how widely different the business of government is from the speculation of it." Mocking Thomas Jefferson's presidential proposals on public finance, Hamilton characterized his longtime rival as one of those persons "who, enveloped all their lives in the mists of theory, are constantly seeking for an ideal perfection which never was and never will be attainable in reality." The Hamiltonian statesman was too prudent and realistic to fall prey to the illusions of theory. Yet he could not forgo theory either. Responding to the claims of some of his Federalist colleagues that Burr was preferable to Jefferson because of his utter disinterest in questions of political theory, Hamilton retorted: "But is it a recommendation to have *no theory?* Can that man be a systematic or able statesman who has none? I believe not."[34]

Between Burr's unprincipled quest for self-aggrandizement and the airy speculations of Adams and Jefferson lay the realm of the statesman's vision. Hamilton was not, ultimately, concerned about the possibilities of human nature or the best form of political institutions; these issues were too hypothetical and remote from the stage of political action to capture his interest. The statesman's vision was architectonic rather than philosophical; it centered around "liberal or enlarged plans of public good." Grasping the limits imposed by the materials with which he had to work, he nonetheless followed theoretical principles sufficiently far to construct something that would partake of greatness. Free of the folly of his foes—and with a perception superior to that of his own followers—he possessed "sufficient capaciousness of views for the greatness of the occasion."[35]

The statesman's real—though unspoken—object was fame. The most revealing (and most often cited) of Hamilton's references to the desire for fame came in *The Federalist Papers*. In *Federalist 72*, Hamilton argued vigorously that restrictions upon the president's eligibility for reelection would diminish his incentives for "good behavior" and would discourage the most far-sighted executive, depriving the people of the benefits of his genius:

> Even the love of fame, the ruling passion of the noblest minds, which would prompt a man to plan and undertake extensive and arduous enterprises for the public benefit, requiring considerable time to mature and perfect them, if he could flatter himself with the

prospect of being allowed to finish what he had begun, would, on
the contrary, deter him from the undertaking, when he foresaw that
he must quit the scene before he could accomplish the work, and
must commit that, together with his own reputation, to hands
which might be unequal or unfriendly to the task.[36]

This passage is unmistakably autobiographical. The "noblest mind"
was Hamilton's own; only he among the founding generation was
planning "extensive and arduous enterprises for the public benefit."
For the Hamiltonian statesman, the path to fame lay through empire
building—a prosperous and mighty nation would revere the statesman who had laid the foundations for its ascendancy.[37]

A desire for fame was common to many of the leading figures of
the founding period. But Hamilton's drive to link personal greatness
with national greatness ran far ahead of the vision of George Washington; Hamilton had no desire to be a Cincinnatus. And it would ultimately bring him into bitter confrontation with a man who had reflected far more extensively on the subject of fame, John Adams. As
the next chapter will show, Adams had a classical republican conception of fame: For him, greatness lay in preserving the republic and its
central values from the forces that threatened to corrupt or destroy it.
Hamilton, by contrast, required a dynamic and expanding empire.
The two would clash in the crisis of 1798–1800, and their battle would
do damage to the fame of both.[38]

A man of ability, vision, and noble passion, Hamilton's statesman
stood on a commanding eminence, far above both the common people and the economic elite. From this lofty perspective he sought to
guide their conduct along those courses that were most congruent
with his plans. He felt little kinship with them, for he was plainly their
superior. Nevertheless, he could not afford to ignore their interests or
even their prejudices. Hamilton abandoned himself to the full force of
his vision on one occasion, in a remarkable speech before the Constitutional Convention. He argued that because America faced a crisis of
extraordinary proportions, "it leaves us room to dream as we think
proper." He then sketched out a plan for a high-toned government
with such features as a senate and an executive serving "during good
behavior." For this articulation of his dream, Hamilton would be repeatedly put on the defensive. Throughout the remainder of his career, he would have to answer charges that his convention speech
proved his aristocratic and monarchical leanings.[39]

Burned by dreaming too openly, Hamilton came to recognize that
the statesman had to be practical in the pursuit of his vision. In a
retrospective defense of his funding system, he cogently laid out the
case for practical statesmanship:

It was proper for him [the secretary of the treasury] to endeavor to unite two ingredients in his plan, intrinsic goodness [and] a reasonable probability of success. It may be thought that the first was his only concern—that he ought to have devised such a plan as appeared to him absolutely the best. . . . But would not this have been to refine too much? If a plan had been offered too remote from the prevailing opinions—incapable of conciliating a sufficient number to constitute a majority—what would have been the consequences? The Minister would have been defeated in his first experiment. . . . Placed in a back ground, he would have lost confidence and influence. . . . The public interest might have been still more injured.[40]

The statesman thus had to be what Hamilton called the "true politician." Whereas "political-empyric" leaders (his phrase for his Jeffersonian opponents) either restricted themselves to attacking and harassing the administration in power or else attempted "to travel out of human nature and introduce institutions and projects for which man is not fitted," the "true politician" understood and worked with the often-recalcitrant materials at hand. Taking human nature "as he finds it, a compound of good and ill qualities, . . . he will not attempt to warp or to distort it from its natural direction. . . . [H]e will favor all those institutions and plans which tend to make men happy according to their natural bent, which multiply the sources of individual enjoyment and increase those of national resources and strength."[41]

The American statesman would, of course, operate within the framework of a constitutional order. Not only was Hamilton an extremely effective publicist for the new Constitution, but he was also a powerful and influential voice on behalf of an expansive reading of constitutional powers. Clinton Rossiter has written that "we live today . . . under a Hamiltonian Constitution, a fundamental law that is interpreted in a style of which he has been the most spirited advocate in American history." That Hamiltonian Constitution was a far cry from the Constitution whose paternity is usually attributed to James Madison. Madison's document neatly arranged and balanced powers, trusting more to institutional logic than to human wisdom. Hamilton's Constitution was a platform for statesmanship.[42]

Hamilton's dependence on the executive to make the new Constitution efficacious will be discussed in the next section. What needs to be noted in the present context is Hamilton's view of the Constitution as an instrument of the statesman's plans. Hamilton elaborated constitutional justifications for each of the elements of his economic program. Challenged to find constitutional warrant for a national bank, he gave a broad reading to the "necessary and proper" clause and argued that "the powers contained in a constitution of government . . . ought to be

construed liberally, in advancement of the public good." Going even
further in his proposal for government bounties to encourage new industries in the United States, he rested his argument on the power of
Congress to provide for the "general welfare"—a phrase that was, he
insisted, "as comprehensive as any that could have been used." There
was nothing in the Constitution, at least as Hamilton interpreted it, to
stand in the way of the statesman's pursuits.[43]

Empowered more than restrained by the Constitution, the Hamiltonian statesman had to deal with two distinct constituencies: the
people and the economic elite. His relationship with the people could
take several forms. (His relationship with the economic elite will be
taken up in a later section.) Sometimes Hamilton depicted the statesman as standing firm for the public interest against the misguided
sentiments of the majority. While the demagogue would flatter the
people and exacerbate their worst errors, the statesman was a "true
patriot who never fears to sacrifice popularity to what he believes to
be the cause of public good."[44]

Nevertheless, the practical statesman had to be careful not to
arouse too much popular displeasure, for it could undermine his extensive plans. He had to hope that the people could respond to the
force of reason. Against the image of a people led astray by the
rhetoric of demagoguery, Hamilton set the image of a people receptive to the language of statesmanship. "It is to be expected that the
public ear will be . . . assailed with the commonplace topics that so
readily present themselves and are so dexterously retailed by the
traffickers in popular prejudice. But it need never be feared to submit a solid truth to the deliberate and final opinion of an enlightened and sober people." These "solid truths" spoke to the reason of
"an enlightened and sober people," but they also reached to the people's desires and fears. To the extent that the people could be impressed by prudential arguments, Hamilton spoke of prosperity, stability, and order. To the extent that they could be impressed by a
calculus of risks, he spoke of vigorous law enforcement and military
power.[45]

During the years of his political ascendancy as secretary of the treasury, Hamilton attempted to sway public opinion by reasoned, prudential argument. But as his political adversaries became increasingly
effective at mobilizing public opposition, he began to grope for more
potent material. He might despise popular prejudices, but he could
not ignore them. Against the symbols of liberty fashioned by his foes
he would have to attempt to fashion a symbolics of authority.[46]

Well aware of provincial loyalties, Hamilton nonetheless entertained the hope that the American people would begin to identify with

national power. In his newspaper war with Jefferson in 1792, Hamilton, calling himself "An American," recited all of the benefits the people derived from the strong national government that Jefferson consistently opposed. Among them was the fact that "their own importance is increased by the increased respectability of their country, which from an abject and degraded state, owing to the want of government, has, by the establishment of a wise constitution and by the measures which have been pursued under it, become a theme for the praise and admiration of mankind." Identifying with a national state, the people could vicariously enjoy foreign admiration. They could also experience power vicariously. Justifying the government's use of massive force to subdue the Whiskey Rebels, Hamilton wrote: "Ye cannot but remember that the government is YOUR OWN work—that those who administer it are but your temporary agents; that YOU are called upon not to support their power, BUT YOUR OWN POWER."[47]

National greatness and national power were images that clearly belonged to the Hamiltonian statesman rather than to his opponents. Another possible subject of symbolic appeal was religion. When tensions mounted between the United States and France in 1797, Hamilton proposed "some religious solemnity to impress seriously the minds of the people." Calling for "a day of humiliation and prayer," he suggested that a "politician will consider this as an important means of influencing opinion, and will think it a valuable resource in a contest with France to set the religious ideas of his countrymen in active competition with the atheistical tenets of their enemies." The possibilities of religious symbolism grew even more attractive to Hamilton once the Jeffersonians came to power. Proposing to James Bayard the creation of a Christian Constitutional Society, Hamilton spoke of the statesman's need for symbolic aids:

> Unluckily . . . for us, in the competition for the passions of the people our opponents have great advantage over us; for the plain reason that the vicious are far more active than the good passions. . . . Yet unless we can contrive to take hold of and carry along with us some strong feelings of the mind we shall in vain calculate upon any substantial or durable results.[48]

The most useful symbol of authority for Hamilton was George Washington. Most of Hamilton's successes were achieved under Washington's mantle. Even after Washington left the presidency, Hamilton looked for ways to exploit his symbolic stature. In 1798 he tried to enlist Washington to tour the areas most unfriendly to a belligerent stance toward France:

I have asked myself whether it might not be expedient for you to make a circuit through Virginia and North Carolina under some pretence of health. . . . This would call forth addresses, public dinners, etc., which would give you an opportunity of expressing sentiments in answers, toasts, etc., which would throw the weight of your character into the scale of the Government and revive an enthusiasm for your person that may be turned into the right channel.[49]

Hamilton's ventures into a symbolics of authority were none too successful. Washington rejected a Southern tour because its pretense was too palpable; the opposition would, he pointed out, "turn it to their own advantage, by malicious insinuations." Bayard made a similar argument in rejecting Hamilton's suggestion of a Christian Constitutional Society: "An attempt at association organized into clubs on the part of the Federalists would revive a thousand jealousies and suspicions which now begin to slumber." Brilliant at reasoned argument and prudential appeal, Hamilton was clumsy at symbolic politics. His aristocratic stance so removed him from popular feelings that he could not gauge them properly. Whatever else it might accomplish, Hamiltonian statesmanship could not win the emotional allegiance of a public for which it ultimately felt so little sympathy.[50]

More than a political handicap, aristocratic distance from the people was the core of what remains most disturbing in Hamilton's image of statesmanship. While his brilliance is undeniable and the sweep of his architectonic vision has few parallels in American history, his vision was rooted in disenchantment with and distrust of the American people. Hamiltonian leadership regarded the majority of Americans as capable only of respecting power and of reveling in prosperity, not of making good use of political freedom. His vision promised Americans a greatness comparable to that of the European powers, England and France. But it rejected the novel kind of greatness promised by the American Revolution—of republican citizens who refused to be molded and manipulated by authority because they insisted that they could govern themselves with wisdom and dignity.

The Chief Executive and the Administrative State

Hamiltonian statesmanship could be pursued from a number of vantage points, including a cabinet department and a New York law practice. But the key to statesmanship in the new national government was the presidency, and Hamilton lavished some of his most extensive theoretical and practical efforts on shaping that office. In developing and carrying out his conception of the "energetic" executive, he made a lasting contribution to American political thought and exerted enormous influence on subsequent American understandings of the possibilities of political leadership.

Hamilton never shared the American Revolutionary suspicion of magisterial power. As his friend Gouverneur Morris remarked, he was "no enemy to kings." At the Constitutional Convention, he proposed "an executive for life," whose features were copied from "the English model." This executive was to be elected in a complicated and cumbersome fashion, with the ultimate decision two stages removed from popular choice. The powers of the executive were to be substantial. Two areas where Hamilton's plan went beyond the powers eventually given to the chief executive by the convention were his provisions for an absolute veto and for sole appointment of the *"heads or chief* officers of the departments of finance, war, and foreign affairs."[51]

That the American presidency fell short of Hamilton's ideal executive did not dishearten him; he would direct his subsequent efforts to lifting the presidency toward his "high-toned" vision. These efforts would begin almost immediately, in Hamilton's extended commentary on the presidency in *The Federalist Papers*. But Hamilton would have to be careful about what Publius could say about the executive; he would have to pay obeisance to American fears. His papers on the executive thus revolved around an elaborate balancing act. On the one hand, Hamilton emphasized as much as possible the energy, strength, and dignity of the new American executive. On the other hand, he went to great lengths to deny to the public what he had advocated in the convention: the resemblance of the president to the British monarch. And he would stress the strict accountability of the president to the American people.

Publius assured his readers that the president of the United States would be a special kind of individual. Thanks to the mechanism of the electoral college, the most reputable men in the nation could weed out not only the unqualified but also the dangerous and the demagogic. The man who could survive this screening process would be exempt from the baser passions and depravities that typified most of humankind. "Talents for low intrigue, and the little arts of popularity, may alone suffice to elevate a man to the first honors in a single state; but it will require other talents and a different kind of merit to establish him in the esteem and confidence of the whole union. . . . It will not be too strong to say that there will be a constant probability of seeing the station filled by characters preeminent for ability and virtue."[52]

"Preeminent" leaders would occupy an office whose characteristics were independence, power, and, above all, energy. In *Federalist* 70 Hamilton presented his famous discourse on executive energy. His sweeping phrases underscored its centrality to the success of the new constitutional order: "Energy in the executive is a leading character in the definition of good government." They contrasted the unified and vigorous actions of the single executive with the circumspect and often divided deliberations of the legislature. Hamilton's unitary executive bore the inherent qualities of statesmanlike action: "[d]ecision, activity, secrecy, and dispatch."[53]

Executive energy was, for Hamilton, a critical counterbalance to the force of popular and legislative passions. While the president would be subject to popular appraisal every four years, rather than enjoying the protection of a lifetime tenure, the term was nonetheless long enough to permit a man "with a tolerable portion of fortitude" to act on behalf of his conception of the public good even in the face of contrary pressures from the public or the legislature. As Hamilton envisioned it, a president would not take his cues from popular desires or views. Instead, he would attempt to bring the people around to his views, so that they could perceive his course of action as being in their true interest. Four years would be "time enough . . . to make the community sensible of the propriety of the measures he might incline to pursue."[54]

In making his case for executive energy and independence, Hamilton had to reassure the public that the president would not escape their control and threaten their liberties. To do this, he had to counter "that maxim of republican jealousy which considers power as safer in the hands of a number of men than of a single man." His retort was to invert the maxim, to argue that power is safer in the hands of one man. The president, as a unitary executive, would have a keener and more clear-cut sense of responsibility than any collective body could have. The people would have an easier time holding him accountable; a president, on his unique eminence, was a highly visible figure "who, from the very circumstance of his being alone, will be more narrowly watched and more readily suspected, and who cannot unite so great a mass of influence as when he is associated with others." Hamilton's arguments were brilliant—but also somewhat disingenuous. For this visible executive would possess the capacity for secrecy and, as Hamilton would soon show, a potential for symbolic aloofness and majesty. However prominent the president might be, much about him would remain obscure even to a watchful public.[55]

While Hamilton expected the most distinguished men in America to fill the presidential office, he claimed that the executive was so well constituted that it was safe even with lesser men in charge. The provision for reeligibility offered a reward that would induce almost any kind of man to behave well. An avaricious man might be satisfied with the continuance of the office's substantial perquisites. An ambitious man would likely be contented with a renewed tenure "on the summit of his country's honors." The presidency was such a superb prize, such an "exalted eminence," that it would inspire dutiful performance even when preeminent talent and virtue were lacking. Hamilton well understood the allure that the presidency would quickly come to possess; he even saw that some men would turn into "discontented ghosts" if denied the chance to remain as president.[56]

Hamilton's conception of the presidency should not be read only from *The Federalist Papers*. As Washington's secretary of the treasury, he seized upon any opportunity to infuse the office with additional power, energy, and stature. One of his first concerns was presidential dignity. He had the perfect vehicle in Washington, the one man who could "give the requisite weight to the office in the commencement of the government." Asked by Washington for advice on presidential etiquette (Washington also consulted John Adams and John Jay), Hamilton set down his prescription for a dignified executive. While John Adams was getting himself into trouble with his impolitic call for a majestic title for the president, Hamilton was tempering his proposal for "high-toned" conduct with gestures aimed at mitigating republican suspicions. The practical statesman had to weigh carefully the symbolism he should employ:

> The public good requires as a primary object that the dignity of the office should be supported. . . . But care will be necessary to avoid extensive disgust or discontent. Men's minds are prepared for a pretty high tone in the demeanor of the Executive; but I doubt whether for so high a tone as in the abstract might be desireable. The notions of equality are yet, in my opinion, too general and too strong to admit of such a distance being placed between the President and other branches of the government as might even be consistent with a due proportion.[57]

Washington was advised to hold a levee one day a week to meet visitors. But propriety precluded dialogue between president and citizens. "The President to remain half an hour, in which time he may converse cursorily on indifferent subjects with such persons as shall strike his attention, and at the end of that half hour disappear." Despite Hamilton's desire to avoid arousing criticism, the formality of the ceremony, coupled with Washington's natural aloofness, hardly

warmed republican hearts. A description of the levee captures its awk-
wardly royal air. The president was attired

> in black velvet; his hair in full dress, powdered and gathered behind
> in a large silk bag; yellow gloves on his hands; holding a cocked hat
> with cockade in it. . . . He wore knee and shoe buckles; and a long
> sword. . . . He stood always in front of the fireplace, with his face to-
> wards the door of entrance. . . . He received his visitor with a digni-
> fied bow, while his hands were so disposed of as to indicate that the
> salutation was not to be accompanied with shaking hands.[58]

Hamilton was always better at interpreting the Constitution than at
interpreting the public's feelings. So he was more successful in winning constitutional sweep and latitude for the executive than in promoting the president's symbolic stature. His chance to make the case
for a president far more empowered than restrained by the Constitution came in the defense of Washington's Neutrality Proclamation of
1793. Writing under the pseudonym of Pacificus, Hamilton explained
the language of Article II of the Constitution in an audacious argument that would outrage James Madison, his former collaborator as
Publius, as much as it would Thomas Jefferson. According to Pacificus, the opening words of Article II bestowed upon a president a
"comprehensive grant" of executive powers; the "enumeration of particular authorities" that followed spelled out the principal, but not the
full, powers that an executive could exercise. "The general doctrine
then of our Constitution is that the EXECUTIVE POWER of the nation is vested in the President, subject only to the *exceptions* and *qualifications* which are expressed in the instrument." For Hamilton, executive energy was the key to a powerful national government, and he
was largely successful in convincing Washington that the Constitution
did not impede an energetic executive.[59]

A dignified and independent executive, armed with extensive and
ill-defined constitutional powers, could use his energies to promote
innovations as well as to protect the status quo. Hamilton wanted the
executive to take the initiative and to shape events—to be an "agenda
setter"—to use the contemporary language of presidential scholarship. The irony, of course, was that the agenda came not from the
chief executive but from his secretary of the treasury and all-purpose
adviser. Hamilton's economic program was the core of the new republic's domestic agenda. Considerable energy was to be invested in enacting and implementing this agenda. As John C. Miller observes,
Hamilton "supervised the whole process of legislation from the inception of bills to their passage, securing the appointment of committees

friendly to his plans, determining questions of strategy with prominent members of Congress, and marshaling his followers in Congress
when heads were being counted." The executive described in *The Federalist Papers* depended on the veto to "keep things in the same state
in which they may happen to be at any given period." The executive in
action used more complex and informal methods to introduce sweeping change in the economy and the society.[60]

It was equally imperative, in Hamilton's judgment, that the executive be the dominant figure in determining America's international relations. He urged Washington to be a forceful actor on the international stage. When Citizen Genet, the ambassador from revolutionary
France, outfitted a captured British vessel as a French privateer and
made plans for the ship to sail from Philadelphia in search of British
prizes, Hamilton (along with Secretary of War Knox) warned the
president of the consequences if Genet was not stopped. In language
that prefigured the cold war doctrine of credibility, he suggested that
"indecision in such a case must necessarily tend to destroy, both at
home and abroad, a due respect for the government—to weaken its
arm—to embolden the enterprises of an intriguing and daring foreign
agent."[61]

The energetic executive needed to be decisive not only in reacting
to events but also in formulating strategies to influence them. Facing
a crisis with Great Britain in 1794 that threatened war, Hamilton proposed to Washington a detailed set of measures. Arguing for "some
executive impulse" that would correspond to "the exigency of affairs,"
he prodded the president to take the lead in determining American
foreign policy.[62]

When Hamilton spoke of executive energy, he had in mind more
than the vitality of the chief executive. If the drive and efficiency of
the presidency were to have a significant impact upon society, they
needed to be magnified through institutions that carried out the presidential will. If the statesman's vision was to be put into place, he had
to shape and staff an administrative apparatus. Thus, Hamilton the
institutionalist viewed administrative system and order as essential
means to power. Indeed, he was, as Leonard White has stated, "the
greatest administrative genius of his generation in America, and one
of the great administrators of all time."[63]

Without expert public administration, an innovative executive's
"liberal or enlarged plans of public good" would come to naught.
Where Hamilton could place his own imprint on executive agencies,
as with the Treasury Department, the administrative apparatus was
extensive and effective. Where his reach did not extend, the results
often left him frustrated. At his moments of greatest frustration, he

came to suspect that it was not inadequate measures or men that undermined administrative efficiency but the republican spirit itself. "There is in a government like ours a natural *antipathy to system of every kind.*"[64]

System in administration was not to be confused with rigidity. Hamilton was a champion of administrative discretion, especially for higher officials. He believed that "if the terms of a law will bear several meanings, that is to be preferred which will best accord with convenience. . . . The business of administration requires accommodation to so great a variety of circumstances that a rigid construction would in countless instances arrest the wheels of government." Energy was not to be defeated by "an over-scrupulous adherence to general rules."[65]

An extensive, well-ordered, yet flexible corps of administrators would, Hamilton believed, win both elite and popular support for the national government in general and the chief executive in particular. Associating a participatory, democratic politics with turbulence and disorder, Hamilton thought that good administration could pacify the people—and diminish their propensity to engage in political action. In this conception of the administrative state, the people were recipients of services rather than active citizens.[66]

Through his writings and his precedent-setting actions, Hamilton established potent images of the American executive: independent, willful, decisive, energetic, visionary, even willing to stretch the constitutional fabric. Some of the heirs of these images, such as Theodore Roosevelt, would pay him homage. Others, leery of Hamilton's aristocratic reputation, admired him only in secret. All, at least after Andrew Jackson, would depart from Hamilton's conception in giving the presidency a democratic tone and asserting their championship of the people's cause. But the relationship between president and people would usually remain more symbolic than actual. The essentials of presidential activism would remain the ones laid down by Alexander Hamilton.

The Statesman and the Capitalist

"Money is, with propriety, considered as the vital principle of the body politic; as that which sustains its life and motion and enables it to perform its most essential functions." Alexander Hamilton is the only one of the Founders who could have written this statement; one cannot imagine it coming from Jefferson, Adams, or even Madison.

The national republic envisioned by Hamilton would not depend upon citizen commitments or elaborate arrangements of political power; rather it would rest upon ample fiscal powers. The state would need money, not to fill its own coffers, but to foster a new economic system. The statesman would also need therefore to be a financial founder; his measures would provide, in effect, a constitution for an emerging American capitalism.[67]

As secretary of the treasury, Hamilton introduced all of the major provisions of his economic constitution between January 1790 and December 1791. He proposed that Congress fund the unpaid national debt, assume the debts of the states, create a national bank, and provide incentives for the development of manufactures. Hamilton sought thereby to stabilize the American economy, by placing government credit on a firm footing, and to stimulate it, by establishing new sources of money that would facilitate enhanced economic activity. He justified his program as a life-giving source. A national bank, for example, would be a means for the

> augmentation of the active or productive capital of a country. Gold and silver, when they are employed merely as the instruments of exchange and alienation, have not been improperly denominated dead stock; but when deposited in banks, to become the basis of a paper circulation, . . . they then acquire life, or, in other words, an active and productive quality.[68]

Hamilton insisted that while his measures were immediately directed at public creditors, financial investors, and manufacturers, they were not designed to benefit any particular groups or sections at the expense of others. Invoking a harmony of interests, he promised a general prosperity in which the agrarian majority would abundantly share. The rise of a substantial manufacturing sector would, he predicted, be responsible for "creating, in some instances, a new, and securing in all a more certain and steady demand, for the surplus produce of the soil." Yet the obvious thrust of the Hamiltonian program of commercial and industrial development—and the immediate profits it offered for men of business in the Northern states—rapidly crystallized a potent opposition that was predominantly agrarian and Southern. While conflicting economic interests fueled the division between Hamilton and his adversaries, the division was exacerbated by the ideological terms through which the conflict came to be expressed. Hamilton's enemies saw him not as a harbinger of economic change but as the successor to the corrupting forces from which Americans had only recently freed themselves. As Lance Banning has observed, Hamilton's "funding program, from the first, stirred memories of English experience and neo-Harringtonian fears of a shift in the balance of property, which might eventually undermine the social structure that supported a republican state."[69]

The secretary of the treasury was indeed seeking to shift the balance of property away from planters and yeoman farmers and toward men of business. Nonetheless, his relationship with the business class is evocative less of the British past than of the American future. Like a number of his successors, Hamilton would sometimes court businessmen, sometimes curse them, yet always need them because they were so central to his plans. The statesman was himself governed by political rather than economic motives. But he believed that capitalist acquisitiveness could be the paramount end for most Americans and the principal means to national greatness. The statesman's success thus required the correct understanding and use of economic drives.

Hamilton believed that the hunger for wealth, which was widespread in America, had produced the virtue of entrepreneurial energy. If Americans lacked public spirit, at least some of them possessed a spirit of enterprise. In *The Defence* 11, one of a series of papers justifying the Jay Treaty, he proclaimed: "As to whatever may depend on enterprise, we need not fear to be outdone by any people on earth. It may almost be said that enterprise is our element."[70]

Entrepreneurial virtue, in Hamilton's view, was largely a matter of energy and risk taking; it also entailed a certain prudence of intellect and breadth of vision. The agrarian was bound to the traditional practices of the soil and to the narrow horizons of the locality. The entrepreneur, by contrast, could be taught to grasp the possibilities in new modes of business and an enlarged framework for economic activity. The agrarian was the prospective target for provincial democratic politicians and petty demagogues. The entrepreneur could be induced to look to the national government and to take his guidance from the statesman.

Hamiltonian political economy envisioned a partnership between political men whose motives and objectives were essentially classical and businessmen whose motives and objectives were distinctly modern. The statesman would handle public matters, while men of business devoted themselves to private affairs. But the division of labor between political and economic elites could not be sharply defined. For in the underdeveloped state of the American economy, the statesman could not be satisfied with existing levels of either capital formation or capitalist consciousness. His task was to take an immature capitalist system and rapidly bring it to maturity.[71]

Hamilton was impressed by the American spirit of enterprise, but he deplored the tendency of most businessmen to follow well-trod paths of economic endeavor. Commercial and financial efforts were abundant, but too few Americans were essaying ventures in the manufacturing sector, which Hamilton saw as the key to the future of the economy. As Tench Coxe informed Hamilton in preparing materials for the *Report on the Subject of Manufactures,* the "want of capitalists in manufactures is yet a very great difficulty." Hamilton proposed to supply this want. If confidence in the potential of manufacturing was lacking among men of business in America, the secretary of the treasury would establish that confidence:

> Experience teaches, that men are often so much governed by what they are accustomed to see and practice, that the simplest and most obvious improvements, in the most ordinary occupations, are adopted with hesitation, reluctance, and by slow gradations. The spontaneous transition to new pursuits, in a community long habituated to different ones, may be expected to be attended with proportionably greater difficulty. . . . To produce the desireable changes, as early as may be expedient, may therefore require the incitement and patronage of government.[72]

The numerous forms of government aid proposed by Hamilton to encourage manufacturing—tariffs, bounties, premiums, and others— were designed to change the habits and overcome the timidity of American businessmen. The statesman was concerned less with benefiting existing capitalists than with creating new ones and instilling in them his own confidence. By altering the structure of incentives in the American economy, he could reshape the character, understanding, and behavior of economic actors and bring them in line with his vision. If Hamiltonian statesmanship was pessimistic about the potential for political virtue, it was audacious and visionary in its claims to produce economic virtue. It would not try to educate and shape good citizens; it would, however, seek to entice and mold good capitalists.

Not only would the statesman create capitalists for the manufacturing sector, he would also create the capital with which they would work. In his report on manufacturing, Hamilton demonstrated that America already possessed the sources of capital needed to finance industrial development. He cited the growth of banks, the availability of foreign capital, and "the effect of a funded debt as a species of capital." These three pools of capital had largely flowed out of Hamilton's own prior efforts. He was the architect of the funded debt and the Bank of the United States. He had established the secure credit and promoted the dynamic economic growth that were attracting large amounts of foreign investment. Hamilton first provided the economic means and then went to work on the motives of the business class in America.[73]

A capitalist economy that added manufacturing to commerce and finance as a field for entrepreneurial energy and risk taking would be dynamic and unpredictable—it had to have a stable governmental infrastructure of credit, subsidy, tax collection, and regulation. This need, too, would be supplied by the statesman. Hamilton's organizational efforts, particularly in the Treasury Department, promoted regular and systematic procedures that were a boon to capitalist calculation. His corps of administrators was to be efficient in ways that facilitated economic vitality and also satisfied the public's desire for order.

As if it were not enough to provide incentives, sources of capital, and a dependable infrastructure for the development of manufacturing, Hamilton also set out to show men of business the possibility of manufacturing on a grand scale. The statesman would, for a moment at least, become an exemplary capitalist. Hamilton's vehicle was the Society for Establishing Useful Manufactures (commonly abbreviated as S.E.U.M.). He organized and even wrote the prospectus for this corporation, which would be capitalized at one million dollars (making it by far the largest manufacturing enterprise in the United States) and which would establish pioneering industrial facilities in what was to become Paterson, New Jersey. Although Hamilton had no financial stake of his own in S.E.U.M., the political stakes led him to employ his enormous influence, as secretary of the treasury, on behalf of the corporation.[74]

Hamilton's efforts to stimulate the growth of a capitalist economy won the applause of the business class. Fisher Ames wrote him from Boston of "the perfect confidence reposed by our opulent men in the Government. People here are full of exultation and gratitude. They know who merits the praise of it, and they are not loth to bestow it." Basking in an economic boom to which Hamilton's economic program had contributed greatly, men of business found in their secretary of the treasury the ideal statesman. Nevertheless, their admiration did not translate readily into a willingness to follow the statesman's lead on to unfamiliar economic terrain or to eschew questionable modes of money-making. The statesman would have more success at creating profits for the emerging capitalist class than at guiding their behavior along his chosen course.[75]

That most American capitalists of the day preferred quick profits through speculative activities rather than prudent enterprises that would foster economic growth was evident in the financial frenzies of

1791 and 1792. In the first instance, sales of stock in the Bank of the United States produced a speculative orgy that threatened to unhinge Hamilton's economic plans; in the second, rival schemes to manipulate the market for government bonds led to a financial panic and a brief depression. While Hamilton could take effective measures to protect the price of government securities, there was little he could do to counter the spirit of speculation. He vented his frustration in a letter to Philip Livingston:

> I observe that certain characters continue to sport with the market and with the distresses of their fellow citizens. 'Tis time there should be a line of separation between honest men and knaves; between respectable stockholders and dealers in the funds, and mere unprincipled gamblers. Public infamy must restrain what the laws cannot.[76]

These words evinced Hamilton's desire that capitalists acknowledge some measure of public responsibility. Yet his economic program had stimulated the spirit of speculation, and he had no effective means to check it. When Hamilton confronted unruly behavior on the part of citizens, he turned to law, authority, and even repression to bring it under control; faced with unruly behavior by capitalists, however, he could only summon up "public infamy." The statesman who tied his hopes to capitalist acquisitiveness was bound to be frustrated by capitalist avarice and shortsightedness. The statesman who empowered the national government found that he had scant power over the abuses of those whom he had identified as the agents of American prosperity and progress.

The most high-flying and disaster-prone of the speculators was Hamilton's former associate and a close friend. William Duer, the first assistant secretary of the treasury, exploited this position to turn confidential information into speculative profit. After leaving the government, he plunged even deeper into speculative enterprises. It was his grandiose scheme that touched off the financial panic of 1792. Hamilton's response to Duer's misdeeds stands in stark contrast to his youthful excoriation of Samuel Chase. The young Publius had been appalled by the greed and selfishness that sought to profit at the nation's expense. The secretary of the treasury would admonish his corrupt friend to restrain his boundless avarice but would regard him as a poignant fool rather than a republican pariah.[77]

If Duer was a symbol of the difficulty of transmuting avarice into economic virtue, the Society for Establishing Useful Manufactures became a symbol of America's inability, in the 1790s, to support the kind of manufacturing Hamilton envisioned. S.E.U.M. turned out to be a money-losing venture, and its manufacturing operations in Paterson were shut down in 1795. One of Hamilton's most egregious miscalculations was the selection of Duer as its governor; the latter borrowed from the corporation's stock of capital to finance his own speculative schemes. Apart from mismanagement, S.E.U.M. also suffered from the lack of manufacturing expertise and skilled labor. Perhaps the most striking source of its failure, however, was the reluctance of American investors to put their funds into manufacturing when more lucrative prospects beckoned in stock or land speculation. The refusal of Congress to adopt the Hamiltonian incentives for manufacturing may have influenced their calculations. But even if Hamilton had succeeded in enacting all of the proposals contained in his report on manufacturing, it is questionable whether American business was yet ready to live up to his premature—though prophetic—economic vision.[78]

Before the introduction of his economic program, when he was battling for the Constitution at the New York Ratifying Convention in 1788, Hamilton made what sounded like a prophetic statement:

> While property continues to be pretty equally divided, and a considerable share of information pervades the community, the tendency of the people's suffrages will be to elevate merit even from obscurity. As riches increase and accumulate in few hands, as luxury prevails in society, virtue will be in a greater degree considered as only a graceful appendage of wealth, and the tendency of things will be to depart from the republican standard. . . . It is a common misfortune, that awaits our state constitution, as well as all others.

Hamilton treated the concentration of economic and political power as inevitable in 1788. Once in office as secretary of the treasury, however, he pursued a vision that required the deliberate promotion of inequality.[79]

Hamilton did not regret that the thrust of his economic program might "depart from the republican standard." But his successors would be left with the task of reconciling capitalist inequality with republicanism. Future leaders in the Hamiltonian mold would continue to find that their relationship with men of business was one of the most problematic facets of their vocation. Their problem was different from his, however. They would not have to shape the behavior of capitalists, as Hamilton had attempted so audaciously. Rather, they would have to maintain autonomy from a business class whose growing power threatened to shape them.

The Statesman Armed

The Hamiltonian statesman was a master of the sword as well as the purse. Military power and glory were essential to his architectonic vision. Certainly they were essential components of Hamilton's own identity. In his earliest surviving letter, we can see the West Indian boy, unhappy with "the groveling and condition of a clerk," proclaiming to a friend that he wanted "to exalt my station" and concluding that "I wish there was a war." The transplanted young man got his wish in America, where he forged his new career and self in the army of the Revolution. It pained him to contemplate losing his identification with the military with the coming of peace. Writing to Washington in September 1783, he made an unusual—and unsuccessful—request. "I build a hope that I may be permitted to preserve my rank, in the peace establishment, without emoluments and unattached to any corps—as an honorary reward for the time I have devoted to the public. As I may hereafter travel, I may find it an agreeable circumstance to appear in the character I have supported in the revolution."[80]

While Hamilton went on to triumphs as a lawyer, Founding Father, and financial minister, the tug of military glory remained strong. In an unofficial military capacity, he organized and directed the massive force that marched over the mountains of Pennsylvania to scatter the Whiskey Rebels. Once war with his longtime enemy, France, seemed likely in 1798, he intrigued to become second-in-command to Washington—whose age and poor health made him only the titular chief of the army. Hard at work building an army that would bear his imprint, Hamilton entertained his most grandiose vision: himself at the head of an American force that, aided by the British navy, would drive out the Spanish and make the Anglo-Americans the commercial masters of all the Americas.

Military power had psychological appeal for Hamilton: it embodied the energy, authority, and masculine force that he had to fight so hard to infuse into political leadership. But military power was also integral to his conception of statesmanship. Among the many reasons why Hamilton found the American people such recalcitrant material—such reluctant agents of the national greatness he wanted for them—was their deep hostility to professional armed forces. Committed to militias and fearful of standing armies, Americans did not grasp, in Hamilton's view, the national government's need for an organized and expert force, if that government was to enjoy respectability abroad and secure order at home. He would undertake the task of creating the military establishment for them, just as he undertook the building of a manufacturing sector of the economy. The Hamiltonian statesman would not be left unarmed.[81]

Hamilton's conception of an American military was most fully revealed in 1798–1800, when he was in effective command of the force created after the XYZ affair. The professional army he set out to shape was to stand in dramatic contrast to the reigning militia system. Hamilton despised militias. They were state-centered, fostering parochial over national loyalties. They were politically unreliable, capable of sympathizing with disgruntled citizens rather than national authority. By keeping arms in the hands of citizens and denying them to the national government, they encouraged dangerous fantasies of popular power. And apart from their political implications, they offended Hamilton's sense of efficiency and order.

The army Hamilton envisioned for the national government would be as well organized and potent as the financial system he had crafted earlier. In his usual tireless fashion, he drew up detailed plans for its every facet. The training of a professional military required a military academy; Hamilton not only pushed hard for its establishment but also outlined its entire faculty and curriculum. He devoted himself as well to organizing a system of supplies, arranging parades, and determining the army's appropriate formations and battle tactics. Hamilton wanted American soldiers to march—literally—to his directions: "The proper measure of the *pace* is a matter of primary importance in the tactics of the infantry. The establishments of different nations differ in this particular. . . . The true standard should be found in nature. The *natural* pace of a man of medium height, say 5 feet, eight inches, would seem to me to be the true rule." (Although often thought of as short, Hamilton himself was of "medium height"—five feet, seven inches tall.)[82]

No detail was too small to escape Hamilton's scrutiny. One of his prime concerns was for an imposing military appearance. His expression of frustration at the poor quality of supplies (and the military contractors who cheated the government) provides a rare comic moment in the life of a very solemn character:

> When I came to see the hats furnished for the Twelfth Regiment, I was disappointed and distressed. The Commander in Chief recommended cocked hats. This always means hats cocked on three sides. I was assured that cocked hats were provided. I repeated the assurance to the officers. But the hats received are only capable of being cocked on one side; and the brim is otherwise so narrow as to consult neither good appearance nor utility.[83]

In Hamilton's conception, a professional army was designed for use at home as well as in conflicts with other nations. The idea that national force was the ultimate purgative for domestic political diseases was emphasized repeatedly in *The Federalist Papers*. "That there may happen cases in which the national government may be necessitated to resort to force cannot be denied. . . . [S]editions and insurrections are, unhappily, maladies as inseparable from the body politic as tumors and eruptions from the natural body." Hamilton was not troubled by the prospect of deploying armed force against rebellious citizens. Three times in the 1790s—the Whiskey Rebellion, Fries's Rebellion, and Virginia's resistance to the Alien and Sedition Acts—he was a leading advocate of military repression. He consistently proposed that massive force be mustered, not to kill rebels or insurrectionaries but to cow them. "Whenever the government appears in arms it ought to appear like a *Hercules*, and inspire respect by the display of strength." Those who challenged national authority were to be intimidated by the very sight of Hamilton's army.[84]

To Hamilton, the exemplary use of armed forces to remove a domestic "tumor" was the case of the Whiskey Rebellion. Mounting anger in western Pennsylvania over the burden of the excise tax on whiskey had produced not only inflammatory attacks on the national government in mass meetings but also violent assaults on tax collectors. Hamilton took this to be a fundamental challenge to national authority, proclaiming that "now the crisis was arrived when it must be determined whether the government can maintain itself." The challenge was personal as well: the "whiskey boys" were condemning a tax that Hamilton had devised and a funding system of which he was the architect. Perhaps this was why he seemed to inflate not only the threat to national authority posed by the rebellion but also the military danger: "The insurgents are of an enterprising character."[85]

In the face of such challenges, Hamilton "insisted upon the propriety of an immediate resort to military force." While state officials appealed for negotiations, and President Washington delayed long enough to win public support for the use of force, Hamilton was impatient to get troops on the march. His purpose was political rather than military, however. He wanted a symbolic show of force, not a sanguinary display. "The force ought, if attainable, to be an imposing one, such . . . as will deter from opposition, save the effusion of the blood of citizens, and secure the object to be accomplished."[86]

Since he had been an early and persistent advocate of military force, Hamilton requested and obtained the president's permission to accompany the troops and share in whatever dangers they encountered. When the commander in chief turned back before the arduous journey over the mountains, Hamilton was left as the de facto commander, a situation he had no doubt anticipated. The insurrection melted away as the massive force marched through western Pennsylvania. Hamilton was immensely pleased, not only at successfully cowing the malcontents but at affirming the position of his Federalists as champions of national strength. Writing to his sister-in-law, Angelica Church, in London, he adopted the facetious and lighthearted tone that he reserved for correspondence with women, but his sense of triumph was unmistakable:

> I am thus far, my dear Angelica, on my way to attack and subdue the wicked insurgents of the West. But you are not to promise yourself that I shall have any trophies to lay at your feet. A large army has cooled the courage of those madmen. . . . [T]he insurrection will do us a great deal of good and add to the solidity of everything in this country.[87]

When Hamilton contemplated the use of American military forces in international conflicts, he was inclined to be more cautious than when dealing with domestic adversaries. However much he might love military glory, he was too much the financial statesman to endorse the tenets of all-out war, so destructive to international commerce and finance. His militarism was also tempered by his recognition of America's military weakness in comparison with Britain or France. The statesman already had the means to appear as a "Hercules" to his own citizens, but with regard to the great powers of Europe America was "a Hercules in the cradle." Hamilton thus cautioned repeatedly against armed conflicts with the French or the British. The United States, he warned in 1795, should "avoid war for ten or twelve years more," until it "acquired a maturity." He had no desire to tackle the powerful armies and navies of Europe until the American people had been won over to the wisdom of a professional military and had developed the economic and organizational bases for its strength.[88]

If concern for commerce and finance and awareness of America's military immaturity restrained Hamilton's militarist urges, what finally unleashed those urges was the prospect of seizing an empire from a feeble Spain. The lure of empire was irresistible for the Hamiltonian statesman. To be sure, many of Hamilton's contemporaries were also drawn to visions of empire. But they generally looked to the West, seeking the acquisition of its immense territories. Hamilton did not want the West; he feared that accelerated westward settlement would stretch the frail fabric of centralized authority dangerously thin and, moreover, exacerbate the shortage of labor in Eastern manufacturing locales. His empire, commercial rather than continental and agrarian, lay in South America. His imperial vision was both more grandiose and more militaristic.

The dream of an American empire was a recurring motif in Hamilton's years as a statesman. His bid to actualize his dream came in 1798–99. Confident that the United States would soon be at war with France, and ensconced in the effective command of the army, he worked out a plan with his friend Rufus King, the American minister to Great Britain, for an expedition to invade the empire of France's ally, Spain. The British were to supply the naval force, Hamilton informed King, but

> I should be glad that the principal agency was in the United States—they to furnish the whole land force necessary. The command in this case would very naturally fall upon me. . . . The independency of the separated territory under a moderate government, with the joint guarantee of the cooperating powers, stipulating equal privileges in commerce, would be the sum of the results to be accomplished.[89]

Subsequent letters to King and others expressed Hamilton's mounting excitement—an excitement so great that Hamilton neglected even to ask how President Adams (unsympathetic to imperial adventure and deeply mistrustful of Hamilton) could possibly be brought to sanction such an expedition. Even as Adams was beginning his moves to seek peace with France and to dash any imperial schemes, Hamilton was caught up in the rhetoric of destiny and desire. He assured King that "the country will ere long assume an attitude correspondent with its great destinies, majestic, efficient, and operative of great things." He requested Senator James Gunn to secure appropriations for mortars for "offensive operations," since once war with France began, "tempting objects will be within our grasp." The empire that Hamilton proposed to carve out with the aid of Britain would be an enormous boon to American commercial interests, but it would be an even greater boon to his own desire for fame and glory. The aristocratic statesman whose classical desires had become bound up with the creation of a modern capitalist economy found their ultimate fusion in imperialism.[90]

Conclusion

The most vehement critics of Hamiltonian statesmanship were his great adversaries, John Adams and Thomas Jefferson. During his presidency, Adams came to believe that Hamilton's successes stemmed from systematic deception and cunning. Firing Secretary of War James McHenry for being Hamilton's tool, Adams angrily told him that "Hamilton is an intriguant—the greatest intriguant in the world—a man devoid of every moral principle—a bastard, and as much a foreigner as [Albert] Gallatin." Jefferson, too, insisted that Hamilton's methods and objectives had no legitimate place in the American polity. He viewed Hamilton as the leader of "an Anglican, monarchical, aristocratic party." Hamilton's system, he charged, "flowed from principles adverse to liberty, and was calculated to undermine and demolish the republic."[91]

Both Adams and Jefferson exaggerated their foe's malign intentions. Neither could grasp the sources of Hamilton's power and success. Hamilton was indeed given to intrigue, but he was too frank and indiscreet to be a very effective "intriguant." Adams was blind to the actual bases of Hamilton's ascendancy: his vision, drive, and polemical brilliance. Jefferson's accusation of concealed monarchism was also off the mark. While Hamilton had no deep love for republicanism, his code of practical statesmanship led him to adapt his plans to the sentiments and prejudices of a people whose republicanism was unshakable. Hamilton's centralized and capitalist regime may have seemed to Jefferson to doom the Republic, but American historical development would prove Jefferson wrong.

Yet if they were wrong about the essential nature of Hamiltonian statesmanship, both Adams and Jefferson did correctly grasp some of its more disturbing features. Adams saw that Hamilton's desire to stand above the people and channel their behavior, while manipulating all the instruments of government to contribute to his plans, did not promote aristocratic wisdom. Rather, it weakened honest and accountable government by destroying political balance and fostering the power of a small and unrepresentative elite. Jefferson saw that Hamiltonian statesmanship was hostile to the classical spirit of republicanism and would, if not defeated, supplant it with a different kind of spirit—one that was acquisitive and militaristic. Hamilton wanted the American people to identify with the power of government and to admire the potency of wealth. Jefferson feared that would undermine the people's passion for their own liberty.[92]

What disturbed Adams and Jefferson has also made many historians and political theorists uneasy about Alexander Hamilton. Still, Hamilton has never been rendered a "foreigner" to American thinking about political leadership. Hamiltonian images—the energetic and practical statesman, the masterful executive who shapes and commands an efficient administrative machine, the armed statesman who is a "Hercules" to America's enemies, the sponsor of industrial growth who seeks economic rather than civic virtue from the people—have possessed considerable power in American history. Refurbished versions of these images can be found in the careers of disparate American leaders: Andrew Jackson, Theodore Roosevelt, John Kennedy, even Ronald Reagan.

In the bitter years between Jefferson's election to the presidency and his own violent death, Hamilton bemoaned the resistance of Americans to his aristocratic leadership. Recounting to Gouverneur Morris his "odd destiny," he wrote: "Every day proves to me more and more that this American world was not made for me." Hamilton's destiny was to be "odd" in ways that he could never have envisioned. His images of leadership would be resisted by most Americans so long as they were overtly aristocratic, the property of a professed elite with a condescending view of the people. But once these images were given a democratic cast and wrapped in democratic symbols, they would find an appreciative audience.[93]

Indeed, they would often be mistaken for desirable images of democratic leadership. Many Americans would be impressed by leaders who staked their claims to authority on the superiority of their talents and the strength of their will. Many would come to accept the claim that they were politically weak and inadequate in themselves and thus required surrogates—energetic and masterful leaders who would act in their name and champion their cause. Many would be enticed by leaders who offered a Hamiltonian vision of capitalist abundance and expansionist glory. Hamiltonian statesmanship would live on in new guises—even if some of these guises required doses of demagoguery that Hamilton himself would have abhorred. If we wish to understand what have been the most powerful, alluring, and dangerous images of leadership in American political life, the exemplary figure thus remains Alexander Hamilton.

John Adams

Merit, Fame, and
Political Leadership

W HEN JOHN ADAMS ARRIVED IN FRANCE IN 1778 AS THE DIPLO-
matic representative of the new American republic, he was
feted as a renowned champion of liberty. Delighted by the
effusive reception, his subsequent mortification was all the greater:
the French had, he learned, mistaken him for his kinsman Samuel
Adams. He depicted the incident in his diary with a mixture of comic
self-deprecation and deep hurt: "It being settled that he was not the
famous Adams, the consequence was plain: he was some man that nobody had ever heard of before—and therefore a man of no consequence—a cipher."[1]

This story can easily be related to Adams's most notorious weakness: vanity. But it also introduces the theme that lay at the heart of
his political thought. John Adams believed that the health of a republican political order depended upon a just distribution of fame. His
ideal was an American republic in which the recognition and reward
of merit in political actors would be of the highest importance. His
deepest discouragement came when merit was defeated in practice by
intrigue, artifice, or incomprehension. For Adams, forging the link between fame and merit involved more than ensuring just treatment to
worthy individuals. The underlying issue was how the republic could
attract its best citizens to be its political leaders and how, in a society
where the temptations of wealth and the urgings of self-interest were
so prevalent, civic rewards could be sufficiently alluring to keep leaders faithful to the public good.

In this preoccupation with merit, fame, and the public good,
Adams was a self-conscious inheritor of "classical republicanism," an

intellectual tradition whose significance for the founding generation in America has been described by Bernard Bailyn, Gordon Wood, and J. G. A. Pocock. Rooted in ancient Greece and Rome, Renaissance Florence, and English critics of the Crown and court, classical republican thought defined human beings as political animals and set public action above any private activity. In Pocock's words, classical republicans adhered to a demanding conception of politics as "the erection of conditions under which men might freely exercise active virtue." The classical republican was expected to express his personal integrity and to find his chance for honor in public action. His "civic virtue," Wood observed, prepared him for "the sacrifice of individual interests to the greater good of the whole."[2]

As we have seen in the case of the young Hamilton, classical republicanism was a theory of political disease as well as political health. What jeopardized republics was the decline of "virtue" and the spread of "corruption." Political institutions could be corrupted—the executive might, for example, come to exercise improper influence over the legislature—but the greatest danger of corruption lay in the moral degradation of the citizenry. Classical republican writers thus feared the effects of commerce, which, by introducing wealth and luxury into the republic, threatened to sap the foundations of civic virtue. As new forms of wealth proliferated, British writers in the republican mold proclaimed an even more insidious form of corruption: a volatile economy based upon credit and public debt which would seduce men from the solid independence of land ownership into "a shifting mobility of objects that were desired and fictions that were fantasized about."[3]

As a classical republican, John Adams insisted on the primacy of politics over economics. When his opponents blasted him as a believer in aristocracy, their charge was half-true: Adams wanted a political aristocracy but feared an American aristocracy based upon wealth. While Alexander Hamilton, his rival as a proponent of aristocratic leadership, centered his efforts on the construction of a new political economy, John Adams placed a higher value on the promotion of political virtue. Hamilton's economic program was designed to draw the "monied men" to the support of the national government. Adams was more concerned with attracting "the men of merit." Hamilton believed that avarice could be transmuted by a statesman into a bountiful entrepreneurial energy. Adams believed that "commerce, luxury, and avarice have destroyed every republican government."[4]

That Adams wanted to place politics above economics may seem quaint to a modern observer. I want to suggest, however, that Adams is worth our attention precisely because of his classical re-

publican preoccupation with politics. An American tradition largely
dominated by fear of the state and faith in the market offers few intellectual resources for thinking about political action and public
men or women. Adams can thus serve as a guide to the lineaments
of an American leadership grounded in genuinely political passions
and commitments. He can reveal to us some of the impediments to,
and counterfeits of, such leadership. Through Adams, we can re-
cover and reexamine a lost "classical" dimension of American political leadership.

Of the principal figures of the American founding, none explored
as deeply or as passionately as Adams the question of how the new
American republic could use—or misuse—its public men. Focusing,
then, on his lifelong preoccupation with political leadership, I highlight moments in his thought where he looked to a classical, Roman
politics in America, in which great "talents, virtues, and services"
would be evoked and lauded by a luminous political order. And I examine those more frequent moments in which political and personal
frustrations led him to analyze the derangements of the republican
order, characterized above all by the celebration of the unworthy and
the neglect of the most meritorious public men. The writings and actions of John Adams provide an intriguing commentary on the possibilities and ultimate failures of aristocratic political leadership in the
American republic. They also raise critical questions for any conception of democratic political leadership in America.[5]

The Psychology of Political Leadership

John Adams was an inveterate political psychologist. The practice of
uncovering and dissecting the underlying motives for both his own
and others' actions was one of the earliest and most enduring characteristics of his intellect. Adams's preoccupation with motives and passions was in part an obsessive trait, rooted in anguished introspection
wedded to Puritan self-doubt. But there was another, deliberate side
to this preoccupation. As a practitioner and theorist of political leadership, Adams wanted to inquire into the range of motivations to be
found among public men. He sought to know public men from the inside. Plumbing what he termed "the great spring of human actions,"
Adams came up with four types of motivation: disinterestedness, the
love of fame, ambition, and avarice, which constituted, in descending
order, the politically pertinent motives. Adams's psychology of political leadership is couched in terms that today sound archaic—but it

contains some of the most fecund insights into political motivation to be found in all of American thought.[6]

Disinterestedness, a familiar theme in classical republican thought, always intrigued Adams. It required the service of public ends without the intrusion of personal interests. Its command of selflessness further entailed sacrifice whenever personal goals clashed with public needs. In 1776 Adams equated this demanding psychology with "public virtue," and made it the defining characteristic of republican citizens. He wrote to Mercy Otis Warren: "There must be a positive passion for the public good, the public interest, honor, power, and glory, established in the minds of the people, or there can be no republican government. . . . Men must be ready, they must pride themselves, and be happy to sacrifice their private pleasures, passions and interests, nay their private friendships and dearest connections, when they stand in competition with the rights of society."[7]

The heroic self-denial of disinterestedness powerfully appealed to Adams, and he often asserted that his own political deeds had been rooted in this austere virtue. He took greatest pride in those moments—such as his defense of the British soldiers in the Boston Massacre trial of 1770 or his dispatch of a peace mission to France in 1799—in which he had acted on behalf of the public good despite an anticipated loss of popular favor or elite support. Indeed, he seemed to exaggerate the criticism or decline in popularity that his actions had produced, regarding these as proofs of his disinterestedness. But if Adams clung to a conviction of his own disinterestedness, he was increasingly disinclined to attribute that virtue to others. Although he had tied American republican hopes to public virtue in 1776 (while retaining a nagging doubt of Americans' capacity for such virtue), by the time he produced his major theoretical works in the late 1780s he was in search of other foundations for republicanism. Disinterestedness remained a glorious virtue for Adams, but he had concluded that it was too rare to sustain a republican order. "There are in history examples of characters wholly disinterested. . . . But how few have they been! . . . Societies should not depend upon a succession of such men for the preservation of their liberties."[8]

Political psychology could not, then, ignore the primacy of self-interest. "Though we allow benevolence and generous affections to exist in the human breast, yet every moral theorist will admit the selfish passions in the generality of men to be the strongest." Having accepted the ubiquity of selfishness, Adams was sometimes carried away by visions of its terrible propensities and insisted that "all men are ferocious monsters when their passions are unrestrained." Nevertheless, what is most characteristic and interesting about his political psychology is not these periodic shudders at human depravity but the careful, analytical distinctions Adams drew between different forms of self-interest and their political ramifications.[9]

In his most sustained psychological analysis, the *Discourses on Davila*, Adams argued that the key to human motivation was "the passion for distinction," which he defined as the individual's "desire to be observed, considered, esteemed, praised, beloved, and admired by his fellows." The desires for riches, family prestige, scholarly achievement, military or political rank could all be traced back to this root passion. Most people, Adams suggested, were inclined to pursue distinction "by riches, by family records, by play, and by other frivolous personal accomplishments." But a few choice spirits aimed higher. "They aim at approbation as well as attention; at esteem as well as consideration; and at admiration and gratitude, as well as congratulation. . . . This last description of persons is the tribe out of which proceed your patriots and heroes, and most of the great benefactors to mankind." The desire for fame was the passion that moved this elite—and it was in this desire that Adams, having abandoned the expectation of widespread public virtue, placed his highest political hopes.[10]

In some of his earliest diary entries, Adams recorded his own struggles with the desire for fame. He could not escape a profound uneasiness about this desire. Not only was it contrary to the "habits of piety and virtue" that his Puritan heritage imposed upon him, but in pursuing fame, a man might lose self-control and debase himself: "Men of the most exalted genius and active minds are generally perfect slaves to the love of fame. They sometimes descend to as mean tricks and artifices, in pursuit of honor or reputation, as the miser descends to, in pursuit of gold." There was also, Adams noted in a comment all too prophetic of his own subsequent career, a pretentiousness about this desire that exposed its devotee to ridicule: "The love of fame naturally betrays a man into several weaknesses and fopperies that tend very much to diminish his reputation, and so defeats itself."[11]

The disordering of the self that was potential in the love of fame might also result in the disordering of the commonwealth. Frustrated by the lack of opportunities to shine, men hungry for fame might stir up popular discontents and unsettle existing governments. Writing in his diary, a young John Adams envisioned the same kind of destructive political genius that would fascinate the young Abraham Lincoln: "All the tumults, insurrections, and revolutions that have disturbed the peace of society and spilled oceans of blood have arisen from the giddy rashness and extravagance of the sublimest minds. . . . That unquenchable thirst of superiority and power . . . often precipitates persons of [the] character I describe into the wildest projects and adventures, to set the world aware of their parts and persons, without attending to the calamities that must ensue."[12]

It might seem surprising that Adams could discover any political value in such an explosive passion. Yet these early anxieties about the love of fame, while never disappearing from his thought, were gradually outweighed by a more favorable perspective. As hard as he struggled, Adams could not suppress his own awareness: "I have a dread of contempt, a quick sense of neglect, a strong desire of distinction." Experiencing the force of this desire in himself, he began, somewhat pompously, to treat it as the sign of a certain grandness of character and to look askance at those with more mundane aspirations. Observing the "desire of money" in his neighbor, Dr. Savel, he wrote in his diary: "These driveling souls, oh! He aims not at fame, only at a living and a fortune!"[13]

While the attractiveness of fame to the young Adams was in good part a reflection of narcissistic self-absorption, in the mature thought of the *Discourses on Davila* one finds a well-reasoned case for the love of fame. Squarely confronting the power and danger of this passion, Adams nonetheless hoped to tame and employ it for public purposes. "To regulate and not to eradicate [the passions] is the province of policy. It is of the highest importance to education, to life, and to society, not only that they should not be destroyed, but that they should be gratified, encouraged, and arranged on the side of virtue."[14]

Adams's republican vision came to depend upon finding political means to encourage the love of fame, to provide it with ample gratifications, and to enlist it on behalf of the public good. If a political order could be constituted in which only actions genuinely productive of public advantages brought the desired honors and applause, the passion accompanying the love of fame might energize the republic. Boundaries would always be required to contain this energy; balanced institutions would always be necessary to hold it in check. Yet Adams hoped for more than passions simply neutralizing one another. He wanted this particular passion to prevail, for the benefit of its possessors, but even more for the sake of the republic.

Unfortunately, while the desire for fame might uphold a republican edifice, other, more prevalent desires threatened to undermine its foundations. Chief among these were ambition and avarice, two passions that Adams, in the fashion of eighteenth-century political thought, often paired. He had no illusions that ambition or avarice might be arranged on the side of virtue; their unifying characteristic was self-gratification at the expense of the public good. As he wrote to James Warren in 1778, "Ambition and avarice . . . have been the bane of liberty, and the great curse of humankind in all ages and countries."[15]

Ambition involved "a love of power or a desire of public offices" without regard for the public welfare. That Adams generally considered "ambition" a dark motive was evidenced by his application of the term to his political rivals or opponents. He could be quite generous in his estimations of his contemporaries, but once they incurred his anger by threatening his own political position or stature, he tended to demote them to the class of ambitious men. While his lifelong practice of imputing ambition to his rivals—to Hutchinson, Hancock, Franklin, Jefferson, and Hamilton—was obviously self-serving (although not always inaccurate), his sensitivity to this motive brought him to some penetrating insights. Because ambition had to be shielded from the light of public awareness, Adams observed, it compelled a public man to become circumspect and artful (qualities Adams knew he himself lacked). Observing John Hancock's unacknowledged hunger for political power in Massachusetts, Adams wrote in his diary: "How subtle, sagacious and judicious this passion is! How clearly it sees its object, how constantly it pursues it, and what wise plans it devises for obtaining it!" By its nature, this passion was so entangled in deception that it might come to fool not only its external audience but even its possessor. "Ambition is the subtlest beast of the intellectual and moral field. It is wonderfully adroit in concealing itself from its owner, I almost said from itself."[16]

Ambition was a particularly dangerous passion in republican politics. Imbued with this passion, designing and artful men schemed for power and self-aggrandizement and imperiled public liberty. Yet as much as Adams feared ambition, when he contrasted it to avarice he could not deny it a measure of grandeur. The metaphors he sometimes adopted to dramatize ambition and avarice signaled his relative evaluation of the two. Thus, he interrupted the translation of Enrico Davila's narrative of the French barons' wars during the sixteenth century to comment: "Eagle-eyed, high-souled ambition seldom misses its opportunity." Avarice reminded Adams of a different breed of bird. Referring to the profits being made from the American Revolution in the Paris of 1778, he wrote to James Warren that "where the carcass is, there the crows will assemble."[17]

Avarice posed a different threat to a republic than did ambition. Greed drew many capable individuals away from public concerns. It propelled others toward corruption in their conduct of public business. Adams rejected as illusory the hope of yoking avarice to the public good—the vision that excited Alexander Hamilton:

The wisdom of nations has remarked the universal consideration paid to wealth; and that the passion of avarice excited by it, pro-

duced treachery, cowardice, and a selfish, unsocial meanness, but
had no tendency to produce those virtues of patience, courage, fortitude, honor, or patriotism, which the service of the public required
in their citizens in peace and war.

Once wealth and luxury became the principal marks of distinction,
avarice would corrode even the strongest of republican structures.[18]

Perpetually threatened by ambition and avarice, the most prevalent
modes of self-interest, a republic would require complex balancing
mechanisms to temper their effects. Adams's psychology thus led him
to seek political rationality and stability from institutional arrangements. Yet his theory of republicanism did not end with institutional
mechanisms. Beyond these lay a dimension of political symbolism designed not to convince the intellect but to lure the senses and the
imagination. Igniting the love of fame in the souls of its best citizens
and drawing them into positions of leadership, the republic could
both contain and exploit the passions that John Adams regarded as
the "great spring of human actions."

Meritorious Leadership and Symbolic Rewards

How might a republic channel a passionate desire for fame in the direction of public service? If the citizen under a properly balanced government, Adams wrote in *A Defence of the Constitutions of Government of the United States of America,* "sees honors, offices, rewards,
distributed to valiant, virtuous, or learned men, he esteems them his
own, as long as the door is left open to succeed in the same dignities
and enjoyment, if he can attain to the same measure of desert. Men
aspire to great actions when rewards depend on merit."[19]

The idea of a political order in which rank and honor would depend upon merit rather than upon birth or wealth was central to the
revolutionary vision of the "old Whigs" of 1776. Gordon Wood has
suggested that John Adams abandoned this idea in the 1780s, having
come to believe "the republican hope that only real merit should govern the world was laudable but hollow." But there is abundant evidence, both in Adams's writings and in his political actions, that he
was too passionately committed to the ideal of merit ever to abandon
it. The search for a republic in which merit and fame were inextricably linked continued to attract—and torment—him throughout his
life.[20]

His concern for passion, fame, merit, and the public good all came together in a remarkable passage on Roman politics in *Discourses on Davila*. Nowhere else did John Adams disclose so fully the classical vision that excited his theoretical imagination:

> Has there ever been a nation who understood the human heart better than the Romans, or made a better use of the passion for consideration, congratulation, and distinction? They considered that, as reason is the guide of life, the senses, the imagination and the affections are the springs of activity. Reason holds the helm, but passions are the gales. And as the direct road to these is through the senses, the language of signs was employed by Roman wisdom to excite the emulation and active virtue of the citizens. Distinctions of conditions, as well as of ages, were made by difference of clothing. . . . The chairs of ivory; the lictors; the rods; the axes; the crowns of gold; . . . their ovations; and their triumphs; everything in religion, government, and common life, among the Romans, was parade, representation, and ceremony. Everything was addressed to the emulation of the citizens, and everything was calculated to attract the attention, to allure the consideration and excite the congratulations of the people; to attach their hearts to individual citizens according to their merit; and to their lawgivers, magistrates, and judges, according to their rank, station, and importance in the state. And this was in the true spirit of republics, in which form of government there is no other consistent method of preserving order, or procuring submission to the laws.[21]

Radical republicans, such as Thomas Paine, associated political symbolism with the old regime and denounced it as a bag of tricks calculated to keep the people in ignorance and awe. But for John Adams, a republican "language of signs" was needed to evoke the virtues of both leaders and citizens. If the symbols of honor and reputation that men craved were politicized and made luminous, then the most energetic and talented would be inspired to public-spirited actions. The force of emulation would drive political leaders to outdo one another in public services that brought fame and greatness. Since symbolic rewards were to be distributed only on the basis of genuine services, the people would "attach their hearts to individual citizens according to their merit." They would be fascinated by and respectful of a realm of political action in which meritorious men competed not for wealth or power but for their applause.

It was critical to the workings of this symbol-rich republic that the distribution of fame be just. Virtuous actions had to be acknowledged and rewarded; false pretensions to merit had to be unmasked and rebuffed. Adams thus wanted a public space in which actions would be visible and transparent. When a public man's character and activity were open to maximum scrutiny, the people had a fair opportunity to assess his real desert.

Ironically, Adams's concern for the transparency of public action led him to adopt one of his opponents' most cherished positions. The radical Pennsylvania Constitution of 1776, which Adams generally detested, had stipulated that the doors of the legislature be open so that "all persons who behave decently" might observe their representatives. Adams also wanted legislators to operate in full view, not out of the radicals' concern for accountability but so that the public could know upon whom to bestow its plaudits. In his *Autobiography*, he recalled his unsuccessful efforts in 1776 to open up the proceedings of the Continental Congress:

> Mr. Wilson of Pennsylvania . . . moved that the debates should [be] public. . . . Mr. John Adams seconded the motion and supported it with zeal. But no: neither party were willing: some were afraid of divisions among the people: but more were afraid to let the people see the insignificant figures they made in that assembly. Nothing indeed was less understood, abroad among the people, than the real constitution of Congress and the characters of those who conducted the business of it.

In a visible public space, "insignificant figures" could not hide. Significant figures would stand out and be sure of gaining their proper rewards.[22]

Given a visible public space, Adams hoped to witness the rebirth in America of classical political talents. In one of his more visionary moments Adams, writing to the president of Congress from Amsterdam in 1780, proposed the establishment of an "American Academy for refining, improving, and ascertaining the English language." Thinking perhaps of one of his Roman heroes, Cicero, he argued that such an academy would stimulate the cultivation of public eloquence in America. Brilliant oratory would raise the tone of republican society: "It is not to be disputed that the form of government has an influence upon language, and language in its turn influences not only the form of government, but the temper, the sentiments, and manners of the people." It would also be required as a sign of merit in a public man: "The constitutions of all the States in the Union are so democratical that eloquence will become the instrument for recommending men to their fellow-citizens, and the principal means of advancement through the various ranks and offices of society."[23]

Adams wanted to see generous and impressive political acts played out before a generous and understanding public. But the audience, he warned, must not become too uncritical or grateful toward its leaders. Adams never ceased to complain of the people's tendency to excessive adulation of its favorites. In 1771, for example, he castigated the citizens of Massachusetts in his diary for their "mad idolatry" toward Governor Hutchinson; in 1813, in a letter to Jefferson he denounced "the impious idolatry to Washington." It is easy to ascribe these complaints to envy, but he had a valid point to make. The public must recognize that esteem for its leaders necessarily had to have limits in a republic; it must comprehend the distinction between rewarding merit and exalting a leader so high that it diminished itself. If citizens did not ultimately respect themselves more than any single leader, they would fall into dangerous habits of subservience. Voicing this caution, Adams managed to sound like the kind of radical democrat he ordinarily pilloried. The people, he wrote to John Jebb in 1785, "must be taught to reverence themselves, instead of adoring their servants."[24]

Adams devoted considerable attention to the symbolic rewards that the American republic should provide its worthy public men. This concern of his, however, drew down upon his head incomprehension and ridicule. In a manner that inevitably excited the suspicions of most "old Whigs," he began at the end of the 1780s to insist that the American republic could not flourish without titles. In *Discourses on Davila*, he described them as valuable on several counts: they appealed to "the passion for distinction," and they channeled that passion toward virtuous action. "As virtue is the only rational source and eternal foundation of honor, the wisdom of nations, in the titles they have established as the marks of order and subordination, has generally given an intimation, not of personal qualities, nor of the qualities of fortune; but of some particular virtues, more specially becoming men in the high stations they possess." Titles lured the imagination, calling their possessors to live up to the demands of high-minded action that they symbolized.[25]

Acting upon this view, Adams as vice president proposed to the Senate a lofty title for the president, such as "His most benign highness." Without such a title, Adams contended, the president (and, by extension, other top national officers) would lack dignity in the eyes of foreign governments. Nor would he command respect from his own people—Adams saw titles as marking out lines of deference and thus as important instruments of social order. With its poor pay and uncertain stature, the new federal government badly needed titles to entice able public men into service. Adams won backing for his campaign for titles in the Senate (working in alliance with Richard Henry Lee), but the House balked. The whole affair only enhanced Adams's reputation as a political apostate given to monarchist or aristocratic sentiments, as well as a pretentious little man who deserved the mocking title of "His Rotundity." Yet his public advocacy of titles was in keeping with his vision of a classical republican politics in America. As he reminded Mercy Warren years later: "Titles of office are very different from titles of nobility. Titles of office are not hereditary."[26]

For Adams, perhaps the saddest aspect of the American rejection of luminous political titles was the self-deception it involved. He proclaimed to Mercy Warren: "After all, there is not a country under heaven in which titles and precedency are more eagerly coveted than in this country." If the political order was to be barren of attractive symbols, if Americans demanded a plain and functional republic, "the passion for distinction" would only be channeled elsewhere. With considerable insight, Adams foresaw the predominance in America of economic over political symbols. And he recognized that once popular applause and congratulations flowed to rich men rather than to public men, the spirit of the republic would be altered. As he explained in a letter to Elbridge Gerry in 1785, once men come to pride themselves on "show," on magnificent houses, carriages, and the like, "this species of vanity commonly changes the whole moral and political character of a people, by turning their attention, esteem, admiration, and even their confidence and affection, from talents and virtues, to these external appearances."[27]

The problem with this transformed republic was not only that the pursuit of self-interest would drive out concern for public matters. More important to Adams was the irrelevance of merit in such a society. Republican political symbols were designed to honor virtuous and talented public acts. Economic symbols lent their aura to individuals who were not necessarily virtuous or talented. Political symbols focused a people on who public actors really were and what merits they could claim; economic symbols shifted the people's gaze to the impressive possessions that private persons owned and displayed.

Adams was never sanguine that political merit would find ready acknowledgment in America. A problem that haunted him and drew his thought into dangerous perplexities was how to shape institutional mechanisms that would select meritorious men and place them in prominent public posts. He struggled with this issue at length in *Discourses on Davila*:

> There is a voice within us, which seems to intimate that real merit should govern the world; and that men ought to be respected only in

proportion to their talents, virtues, and services. But the question always has been, how can this arrangement be accomplished? How
shall the men of merit be discovered? How shall the proportions of
merit be ascertained and graduated? Who shall be the judge?[28]

National elections, Adams contended, were a dubious mechanism
for judging public men. "There is no individual personally known to
an hundredth part of the nation. The voters, then, must be exposed to
deception, from intrigues and maneuvers without number, . . . with
scarce a possibility of preferring real merit." He suggested that hereditary institutions were superior for raising men with education and integrity to positions of political authority. But a dominant aristocracy
produced results as pernicious as a corrupted electoral system. The
people were rendered politically helpless, while aristocratic pride en-
gendered "a thousand years of barons' wars."[29]

The best hope for the selection of real merit, Adams ultimately concluded, lay with an independent executive. If the people or the legislature were given the responsibility of distributing honors, factional rivalries would devastate the republic. In contrast, "when the emulation
of all the citizens looks up to one point, like the rays of the circle from
all parts of the circumference, meeting and uniting in the center, you
may hope for uniformity, consistency, and subordination." By granting to what he indifferently termed the executive or the "monarchical"
power the dispensation of political honors, Adams opened himself to
attack as a proponent of a royal court in America. Not only was his reliance on the executive as the fount of honor damaging to his own political stature, it was also inconsistent with his desire for a transparent
order in which public judgment would operate freely and intelligently.
But his aim was not, as his accusers claimed, to inflate the executive's
social sway or to extend his political influence. Rather, Adams wanted
to draw upon an executive's personal knowledge and judgment of
men's character to promote the most deserving to offices of public
trust.[30]

The arduous problem of providing for "justice in the distribution of
fame" always remained at the heart of his political thought. In the
next section, I shall examine Adams's repeated disappointments when
merit (especially his own) was misunderstood or neglected. Even with
these disappointments, he could not forget those moments in which
recognition of "talents, virtues, and services" brought a pleasure that
was "exquisite and inexpressible." If Adams was to be driven in old
age to his most obnoxious self-justification by what he took to be the
slighting treatment of him in Mercy Warren's history of the American
Revolution, perhaps it was because he remembered the kind of praise

she had once lavished on him. Congratulating the American diplomat in 1783 for his successful peace negotiations, she had characterized his actions in words that spoke directly to both his personal passion for distinction and his vision of a republic in which merit prevailed.

> A people destitute of public or private virtue cannot be long happy by the exertions of a few of the best or wisest of her citizens. Yet I believe the example of one good man, unawed by threats, uncorrupted by gold, and unmoved by the machinations, refinements, and duplicity of systematical villainy, has a greater tendency to keep alive the respect due to real merit than either judiciary restraints or the best digested code of moral injunction.[31]

Injustices in the Distribution of Fame

The classical republican visionary in John Adams directed his theoretical and practical efforts to establishing a symbol-rich republic in which political merit would receive its due. But the Puritan pessimist, the more familiar Adams, recognized with impressive insight the obstacles to the success of merit. He wrote in the *Defence* that "the real merit of public men is rarely fully known and impartially considered." It was not that the citizens of republics were resentful or ungrateful toward those who served them well. The problem lay in the difficulty they faced sorting out the false from the deserving claimants. Writing to Mercy Warren in 1786, Adams predicted that Americans would have a hard time seeing through the dissemblers: "Our country will do like all others—play their affairs into the hands of a few cunning fellows. . . . Human nature is not ungrateful. But while many rate their merits higher than the truth, it is almost impossible that the public mind should be exactly informed to whom they are really obliged." As Adams became increasingly convinced of Americans' inability to distinguish the authentic from the counterfeit in the character and action of their public men, his expressions of frustration became more vehement. Distress at his own political reversals was merged with a deeper disappointment: the realization that the assumptions of classical republican politics would not hold in America.[32]

Since most of Adams's complaints about the distortions of merit stemmed from his feelings that his rivals were harvesting undeserved applause while his own services were neglected or misunderstood, those who write about him have typically treated these complaints mainly as signs of his irascible and envious temperament. Adams would not have been surprised; he once predicted to Jefferson that some of his musings would be dismissed twenty-five years later as "the effusions of a splenetic mind." But it is not necessary to ignore the personal hurt that undeniably fueled his comments to see that in this sour mood Adams could also be a perceptive critic and a wonderfully comic satirist. In elaborating upon the methods and modes by which real merit would be obscured and illusory merit fabricated, he diagnosed some of the most enduring disorders of political leadership in America.[33]

For John Adams, integrity was an inherent component of merit. A public man had to be honest and straightforward in all his dealings. His character and actions ought to be transparent to the people, with flaws unconcealed and strengths unexaggerated. When Adams or his old Whig colleagues spoke of "real merit," they referred to a quality that was not fabricated by a political actor or his partisans to impress the people; it was, rather, a quality that wanted nothing more than the opportunity to shine forth in its true light. Adams's ideal of a transparent republican order—one of his most attractive conceptions to modern democrats concerned with restoring openness and vitality to American public life—stemmed directly from his recognition that the validity of the citizens' judgments depended upon their exposure to the truth about political actions and actors.

Adams came increasingly to believe, however, that what appeared in public was less important than what went on behind the scene. The road to political success most often opened to the silent and the secretive, rather than to those who exposed themselves to public scrutiny. Adams's early hopes for a republican America in which eloquence would be critical to political advancement had been misplaced—so he ruefully concluded in his *Autobiography*. "The examples of Washington, Franklin, and Jefferson are enough to show that silence and reserve in public are more efficacious than argumentation or oratory. A public speaker who inserts himself, or is urged by others into the conduct of affairs . . . makes himself too familiar with the public, and unavoidably makes himself enemies." Ignoring a problem observed by theorists as far back as Plato—that the tricks of the rhetorician could inflate the stature of a "public speaker"—Adams believed that a public man's reputation was easiest to maintain when it was least open to public inspection.[34]

While "silence and reserve" in public did not necessarily betoken a lack of integrity, Adams was invariably suspicious of what lay behind them. In the case of those he took to be his adversaries, the geography of secret affairs was equated with "the foul regions of Machiavellian politics." In a particularly bitter moment, Adams insisted to Benjamin

Rush that the meaning of merit had been reversed in these "foul regions." "Eternal silence! Impenetrable secrecy! Deep cunning! These are the talents and virtues which are triumphant in these days. And in ancient days was it much otherwise? Demosthenes and Cicero, the two consummate masters, died martyrs to their excellence." A politics whose mainsprings were secret and whose masters were practitioners of intrigue and dissimulation would present nearly insuperable obstacles to men of merit. Depicting to Mercy Warren in 1807 how his own career had been terminated through the machinations of Alexander Hamilton, Adams expressed metaphorically the power of secret over public action:

> [In a] dark and insidious manner did this intriguer lay schemes against me; and, like the worm at the root of the peach, did he labor for twelve years, underground and in darkness, to girdle the root, while all the axes of the Anti-federalists, Democrats, Jacobins, Virginia debtors to English merchants, and French hirelings, chopping as they were for the whole time at the trunk, could not fell the tree.[35]

Adams had indeed been sabotaged during his presidency by Hamilton and his adherents in the cabinet. Although his comments on the power of secrecy were overdramatized, he had touched on a genuine problem in the distribution of fame. A republic was supposed to make political action visible to the people; but how much would the people really see? "I have sometimes thought," Adams wrote to Rush, "that the public opinion is never right concerning present measures or future events. The secret of affairs is never known to the public till after the event, and often not then. Even in the freest and most popular governments, events are preparing by causes that are at work in secret." If the public so often judged men's characters and actions unfairly, it was because political realities had been rendered opaque by those who worked best in secrecy.[36]

Not only did "real merit" have to grapple with Machiavellian cunning and intrigue; it also had to contend with artful impostures. The space of visible public action was crowded with claimants—some offering genuine talents and virtues, but many more promoting themselves far above their deserts. In this competition, integrity was placed at a disadvantage by self-promotion. Writing to James Warren from France in 1778, Adams bemoaned the triumphs of publicity:

> Modest merit! Is there such a thing remaining in public life? It is now become a maxim with some, who are even men of merit, that the world esteems a man in proportion as he esteems himself. . . . I

am often astonished at the boldness with which persons make their
pretensions. A man must be his own trumpeter, he must write or
dictate paragraphs of praise in the newspapers, . . . he must get his
picture drawn, his statue made, and must hire all the artists in his
turn, to set about works to spread his name, make the mob stare
and gape, and perpetuate his fame.[37]

To Adams, a just distribution of fame could occur only when there
were no intermediaries between meritorious action and the public's
recognition of it. The "trumpeters" of publicity used money and media
to intervene between act and recognition so as to manipulate the latter. As the arts of publicity became prevalent, even some who possessed genuine merit took them up. But publicity corrupted merit, fueling egotism while diminishing the sense of service and sacrifice to
the republic. And it confounded public judgment, by allowing medioc-
rity to appear as greatness.

The specific stimulus for Adams's remarks to Warren had been the
public relations coup scored by Benjamin Franklin in Europe. For
over forty years, whenever Adams thought about the phenomenon of
fame through publicity, his memories of Franklin continued to rankle.
Franklin's diplomatic career in Paris was an outrage to Adams's republican sensibilities. While Adams as diplomat followed the path of
republican simplicity and industry, Franklin lived luxuriously and in-
dolently, subordinating public duties, Adams charged, to personal
gratification. Adams adhered to a strict code of honesty: "A sacred regard to truth is among the first and most essential virtues of a public
man." But Franklin's word was unreliable: "I never know when he
speaks the truth, and when not." Adams prided himself upon a personal independence that was the right and the duty of republicans;
but Franklin made himself "so convenient a minister" to the French
that he enjoyed all the rewards of a court favorite.[38]

Adams was willing to concede that Franklin was intellectually brilliant as well as politically astute, but he denied to Franklin the attributes of political greatness. "That he was a great genius, a great wit, . . .
and a great politician is certain. That he was a great philosopher, a
great moralist, and a great statesman is more questionable." How,
then, had this indolent, evasive, and servile character acquired his
image as the giant of Revolutionary diplomacy? To Adams, Franklin's
reputation as a diplomat was "one of the grossest impostures that has
ever been practiced upon mankind since the days of Mahomet."
Thanks to repeated demonstrations of his usefulness to the French
foreign minister, Count de Vergennes, Franklin had added to his own
talents at self-promotion the extensive publicity resources of the

French court. Adams described to James Warren how Vergennes and "his office of interpreters have filled all the gazettes of Europe with the most senseless flattery of him, and by means of the police set every spectacle, society, and even private club and circle to clapping him with such applause as they give to opera girls."[39]

Whatever truth there was in these condemnations (historians are divided on this score), Adams's view of Franklin clearly was tinctured by his sense of his own obscurity as an American diplomat. This wound inflamed his judgments—but it also left him with a lifelong sensitivity to the power of publicity. More than any other figure in the founding generation, he understood the impact of image making by aspiring politicians and their trumpeters. Adams believed that republican integrity required a public man to stand alone before the people, without pretenses, but he came to be convinced that American politics would be dominated by a different kind of political figure, one whose reputation would be an artifact of "puffers" and "scribblers."[40]

Just as the faults of public men could be concealed by the power of secrecy, so their talents could be inflated by the power of publicity. In addition to these obstacles to the recognition of "real merit" and the just "distribution of fame," Adams recognized a more subtle difficulty. Superficial signs of greatness might impress the public more than genuinely virtuous—but less obvious—qualities and accomplishments. That the appearances of leadership would count for more in America than its substance was the lesson Adams derived from the extraordinary fame of George Washington.

Toward Washington, Adams harbored a respectful attitude quite different from his views of Franklin, Jefferson, or Hamilton. Nevertheless, he thought Washington's greatness was exaggerated, and he was intrigued by the task of trying to understand how Washington had come to be so idolized. In an exchange with Benjamin Rush in 1807, Adams elaborated what he termed Washington's "ten talents." His analysis of Washington would delight a modern semiologist, for it was a masterful, satirical demystification of the signs of greatness. Washington's talents, Adams suggested, were:

> 1. An handsome face. That this is a talent, I can prove by the authority of a thousand instances in all ages. . . . 2. A tall stature, like the Hebrew sovereign chosen because he was taller by the head than the other Jews. 3. An elegant form. 4. Graceful attitudes and movements. 5. A large, imposing fortune. . . . There is nothing, except bloody battles and splendid victories, to which mankind bow down with more reverence than to great fortune. . . . 6. Washington was a Virginian. This is equivalent to five talents. Virginian geese are all

swans. . . . 7. Washington was preceded by favorable anecdotes. . . .
8. He possessed the gift of silence. This I esteem as one of the most
precious talents. 9. He had great self-command. . . . 10. Whenever
he lost his temper as he did sometimes, either love or fear in those
about him induced them to conceal his weakness from the world.[41]

Adams was keenly attuned to these "talents" in Washington because he himself possessed none of them. (He once portrayed himself
in his diary as "this assemblage of sloth, sleep, and littleness.") What
both amused and disturbed him in Washington's case was how much
the external signs of a great political character were preferred over its
inner core: learning, wise judgment, commitment to principle. Adams
agreed with Rush that Washington had not been distinguished by his
intellect. "Here you see I have made out ten talents without saying a
word about reading, thinking, or writing." While not as deep or as
farseeing as many of his contemporaries, Washington's "talents"
nonetheless had carried him to a far greater fame.[42]

A fame based on externalities could, however, be manipulated.
Washington's reputation, Adams perceived, was not simply a product
of the people's propensity to revere imposing appearances. It had also
been given a boost by those who understood its uses. The Hamiltonian Federalists had deliberately made Washington into an icon as a
cover for their schemes. "They puffed Washington like an air balloon
to raise Hamilton into the air." Adams knew that Washington himself
had been a man of "integrity and public virtue," but his fame, Adams
believed (a belief shared by some contemporary historians), had been
an instrument for self-seeking and dishonest men.[43]

Always fascinated by "the language of signs," Adams was quick to
scent its corruption in American political life. As he became increasingly alienated from the Federalists in his old age, he began to indict
them for manipulating symbols not only to mask dubious political
ends but also to cover up even more unworthy pecuniary objectives.
Thus, he wrote to Rush in 1809: "The feasts and funerals in honor of
Washington, Hamilton, and Ames are mere hypocritical pageantry to
keep in credit, banks, funding systems, and other aristocratical speculation."[44]

The Romans had employed "the language of signs" to excite emulation and virtuous action and to direct the citizens' feelings towards
men of political merit. But in America, as Adams lamented in his old
age, much of political symbolism had been concocted to further greed
and to bury merit. Writing to Jefferson in 1816 about the exploitation
of the deaths of Washington and Hamilton, Adams cried out: "All this
by people who have buried Otis, Sam Adams, Hancock, and Gerry in

comparative obscurity. And why? Merely to disgrace the old Whigs, and keep the funds and banks in countenance."[45]

Having observed so much distortion of merit and mystification of fame in contemporary American politics, Adams had little hope that greater justice would be done by history. Nonetheless, he battled to prevent what he believed were the erroneous evaluations of the present from assuming the sanctified status of historical truths. Adams always held to a classical perspective on the meaning and uses of history. For him, history was political education. It was the medium through which the young were instructed about and encouraged to model themselves after virtuous public men. Thus, he advised his ten-year-old son, John Quincy: "It will become you to make yourself master of all the considerable characters which have figured upon the stage of civil, political, or military life."[46]

But where classical history had inspired American patriots to heroic acts of virtue and courage, American history, Adams feared, would lack such a salutary effect. Legendary figures with mythicized reputations would tower over a historical landscape in which men of real, imitable merit were relegated to the background. With mordant humor, Adams wrote to Rush in 1790:

> The history of our revolution will be one continued lie from one end to the other. The essence of the whole will be that Dr. Franklin's electrical rod smote the earth, and out sprung General Washington. That Franklin electrised him with his rod and thenceforward the two conducted all the policy, negotiation, legislation, and war.[47]

Driven by a love of fame, but with too much integrity to seek it through imposture or puffery, John Adams was destined for repeated disappointment. Understanding his plight, one can sympathetically consider Adams's most notorious trait: vanity. Adams struggled against excessive self-regard from his youth, writing in his diary that "vanity, I am sensible, is my cardinal vice and cardinal folly." In spite of all his efforts, the lustrous estimation he sometimes placed upon his own virtues and services brought him frequent political criticism, climaxing in Hamilton's charge during the 1800 election that Adams's vanity rendered him unfit for the presidency. In his old age, Adams seemed to acknowledge this weakness with weary resignation: "It seems to be generally agreed and settled among men, that John Adams is a weak and vain man."[48]

Yet he had, on occasion, probed more deeply into the subject of vanity. In a remarkable letter written (but not mailed) to Elbridge Gerry in 1785, he distinguished "various kinds of vanity." When a person's vanity centered around "show" and "external appearances," it indeed merited reproach. But Adams proceeded in this discourse on vanity to describe a different species, which was, "although a weakness and, if you will, a vice, a real proof of a valuable character." With his own pride, so often wounded, in mind, he wrote:

> When a man is conscious of services and exertions, from the purest principles of virtue and benevolence, and looks back on a course of years, spent in the service of other men, without attention to himself, when he recollects sacrifices, sufferings, and dangers, which have fallen in his way, and sees himself preserved through all and his labors crowned with transcendent success, there arises a satisfaction, and sometimes a transport, which he must be very wise, indeed, if he can at all times conceal.

Adams recognized that in a political world where "real merit" was so often undermined by secret intrigue, outshined by imposture, mystified by publicity, and neglected by history, vanity might be its last refuge. Where the popular audience had so little opportunity to know the merits of a public man, the one remaining audience able to grant him the respect that was his due was the self.[49]

Aristocrats and Democrats

Suspecting that "real merit" would not generally govern the Republic, Adams devoted himself to managing the lower political passions through constitutional contrivances. For him, the centerpiece of constitutional wisdom was the idea of balance. A republic could survive only if it established an equilibrium between the three great social orders—the body of the people, the aristocracy, and the monarchical element. The first volume of his *Defence* laboriously tracked down the guises under which balanced governments had functioned.

> In every republic—in the smallest and most popular, in the larger and more aristocratical, as well as in the largest and most monarchical—we have observed a multitude of curious and ingenious inventions to balance, in their turn, all those powers, to check the passions peculiar to them, and to control them from rushing into those exorbitancies to which they are most addicted.

Balanced government appeared to Adams to deserve the status of a classical republican theorem, yet it was to be roundly rejected in

America. For Adams was proposing not only an equilibrium between three different institutions but also one between three different categories of public men. To understand his prescriptions for the American republic, it is essential to understand how he conceived of both the dangers and the potential merits of aristocrats, democrats, and "monarchical" executives.[50]

Aristocracy was a subject that always fascinated Adams—and always got him into trouble. As he wrote to Jefferson in 1813:

> I recollect, near 30 years ago, to have said carelessly to you, that I wished I could find time and means to write something upon aristocracy. You seized upon the idea, and encouraged me to do it. . . . I soon began, and have been writing upon that subject ever since. I have been so unfortunate as never to be able to make myself understood. Your "aristoi" are the most difficult animals to manage, of anything in the whole theory and practice of government.[51]

When, after many misunderstandings, Adams sought finally to pin down the meaning of aristocracy, he emphasized its sources and its political implications. To Jefferson, he wrote: "The five pillars of aristocracy are beauty, wealth, birth, genius, and virtues. Any one of the three first can at any time overbear any one or both of the two last." To John Taylor, he explained: "By aristocracy, I understand all those men who can command, influence, or procure more than an average of votes; by an aristocrat, every man who can and will influence one man to vote besides himself." Adams never restricted the idea of aristocracy to a hereditary order. Hereditary titles in leading families were only one form of a phenomenon he believed to be pervasive in all societies (a phenomenon modern analysts would call the dominant position of elites).[52]

His critics thought that Adams—the son of a farmer, shoemaker, and town selectman who was a quintessential New Englander and hardly a member of gentry society—had abandoned his original Revolutionary faith and turned into a devotee of aristocracy. Yet he could assail aristocrats with a ferocity that rivaled that of Thomas Paine:

> When I consider the weakness, the folly, the pride, the vanity, the selfishness, the artifice, the low craft and mean cunning, the want of principle, the avarice, the unbounded ambition, the unfeeling cruelty of a majority of those (in all nations) who are allowed an aristocratical influence; and on the other hand, the stupidity with which the more numerous multitude not only become their dupes, but even love to be taken in by their tricks: I feel a stronger disposition to weep at their destiny, than to laugh at their folly.[53]

Adams's purpose, however, was neither to condemn nor to praise the aristocracy but rather to insist upon its inevitable presence in every society. Human equality, he contended, extended only to the question of rights; the distribution of ability, knowledge, and social influence was always marked by profound inequalities. Countering the criticisms of John Taylor, Adams asked:

> From these inequalities, physical, intellectual, and moral, does there or does there not arise a natural aristocracy among mankind, or, in other words, some men who have greater capacities and advantages to acquire the love, esteem, and respect of their fellow men, more wealth, fame, consideration, honor, influence, and power in society than other men?

Political arrangements that attempted to suppress the influence of this elite were exercises in self-deception. Commenting on Machiavelli's *History of Florence* in the second volume of the *Defence*, Adams wrote: "Exclude the aristocratical part of the community by laws as tyrannical as you will, they will still govern the state underhand; the persons elected into office will be their tools, and, in constant fear of them, will behave like mere puppets danced upon their wires."[54]

Adams most irritated his democratic adversaries in his suggestion that this irrepressible elite be guaranteed a major political role in the American republic: the institutional home for aristocratic passion ought to be a senate. Whereas during the ratification debates the Federalists were intent for polemical purposes upon removing the aristocratic aura from the upper house of the legislature and portraying it mainly as a second representation of popular power, Adams adhered to the classical conception of an aristocratic senate. He wanted an American upper house that would both confine and tap the energies of the elite. In a senate the aristocrats could no longer overawe or manipulate the common people.

> The rich, the well-born, and the able acquire an influence among the people that will soon be too much for simple honesty and plain sense, in a house of representatives. The most illustrious of them must, therefore, be separated from the mass, and placed by themselves in a senate; this is, to all honest and useful intents, an ostracism.[55]

Ostracized into a senate, the aristocracy would offer valuable services to the republic. It would be the bulwark of property against unjust leveling schemes among the people, which might win a favorable reception in a single representative assembly. It would be a potent check against executive despotism, as aristocratic pride responded vigorously to an executive's grasp for dominion. Hedged in by the popular assembly and the executive, aristocratic passions in a senate would be able to promote only desirable public ends.

Ironically, while Adams's theoretical defense of an aristocratic senate clashed so dramatically with American egalitarian values that it severely undermined his reputation as a republican, he believed that the Constitution had granted the new United States Senate too much power. Complaining about the Senate's role in approving executive nominations, he wrote to Jefferson in December 1787: "You are afraid of the one—I, of the few. . . . You are apprehensive of monarchy; I, of aristocracy. I would therefore have given more power to the president and less to the Senate." During his campaign for a luminous title for the president, he explained to William Tudor that the symbolic enhancement of the executive represented a necessary rebuff to aristocratic arrogance and presumption:

> It is aristocratical pride alone that feels itself hurt by a distinction of the president. . . . But the common people, if they understood their own cause and interest, will take effectual care to mortify that pride, by making the executive magistrate a balance against it, which can only be done by distinguishing him clearly and decidedly, far above others.[56]

In Adams's old age, his hopes for a meritorious political aristocracy in America faded. He came to believe that America's elite would be based upon only one criterion: wealth. "Talents, birth, virtues, services, sacrifices, are of little consideration with us. The greatest talents, the highest virtues, the most important services are thrown aside as useless, unless they are supported by riches or parties, and the object of both parties is chiefly wealth." He sadly concluded that the United States would follow the example of Rome, not in its period of glory, but in its days of corruption. "An aristocracy of wealth, without any check but a democracy of licentiousness, is our curse."[57]

While Adams's institutional prescriptions for the elite were at odds with the emerging American understanding of a constitutional order, his insights into the role that elites would play in American life remain impressive. The same cannot be said for his view of the American people. His voracious reading in classical and European history and his erudition in political theory proved to be a handicap in his attempts to gauge the political impulses of the masses. Steeped in European categories, he was unable to grasp the character of the American people. When Jefferson pointed out to him that American legislatures had never displayed any tendencies toward "an equalisation of property," and that in America "every one, by his property, or by his satisfactory situation, is interested in the support of law and order," Adams dismissed these arguments as one more American self-deception.[58]

Adams held to a distorted, fearful view of the American people—though never from a hostile standpoint. Unlike Alexander Hamilton, Adams expressed sympathy for ordinary Americans. As he explained to Benjamin Rush: "I love the people of America and believe them to be incapable of ingratitude. They have been, they may be, and they are deceived. It is the duty of somebody to undeceive them." Presenting what he took to be unwelcome truths, no matter how unpopular they might make him, was John Adams's self-ordained duty toward the American people.[59]

If Adams could on occasion praise the people, he was resolutely determined not to romanticize them. Like the aristocracy, the common people were prone to their own particular set of political vices. It was envy that most terrified Adams. In a balanced constitution, where passions could flow only in demarcated channels, the people would learn to respect talent, virtue, birth, and wealth. If they were thrown together with the aristocrats in a singular and unbounded political arena, however, popular envy would flourish. The aristocracy might still succeed in overawing or tricking the multitude, but if they failed they were sure to be despoiled. "In every society where property exists," Adams wrote, "there will ever be a struggle between rich and poor. Mixed in one assembly, equal laws can never be expected. They will either be made by numbers, to plunder the few who are rich, or by influence, to fleece the many who are poor."[60]

Adams's most savage comments on the people always referred to an unbalanced institutional order—termed by him "simple democracy"—in which popular power knew no counterpoises. From his historical reading he drew the stark lesson that simple democracy was a tale of horror. "Remember," he told John Taylor, "democracy never lasts long. It soon wastes, exhausts, and murders itself. There never was a democracy yet that did not commit suicide." But democracy as one element of a mixed polity found in Adams a fervent advocate. For him, genuine democracy meant a popular assembly sharing power with an aristocratic senate and a monarchical executive. Just as a senate both delimited and fructified aristocratic passions, so a popular assembly in a balanced government would bring out the best qualities of the people, as the home for their political interests and activities.[61]

Adams did not devote as much attention to popular leadership as to aristocratic leadership. But he did suggest in scattered comments that the same passion for distinction that motivated the senatorial elite would be found, and could be utilized, among the people's representatives. Reading Turgot's criticism of the American constitutions for piling so much business upon the state legislatures as to invite abuses by legislators, Adams responded that the French philosophe had failed to comprehend the attraction of assembly life. "The legislative assemblies in free governments will always be sought as a school, or as a theater, to learn or to display accomplishments, to acquire the public confidence and a reputation." For those who lacked the lustrous credentials of the aristocracy, the assembly remained open as the field for their honorable political aspirations.[62]

Rarely was Adams to be found on the democratic side in the great political debates of his era. But neither was he—by family background, economic status, or personal instincts—a member of the aristocracy. Poised uncomfortably outside the two camps and committed to an independent stance, he labored to avert the excesses and foster the virtues of both aristocrats and democrats. As skeptical as other antidemocratic theorists about the beauties of democracy, Adams nonetheless refused to echo their traditional disdain for the common people. Criticizing Aristotle in the final volume of the *Defence*, he wrote: "The understandings . . . of husbandmen, merchants, and mechanics are not always the meanest; there arise, in the course of human life, many among them of the most splendid geniuses, the most active and benevolent dispositions, and most undaunted bravery." In the balanced government that he propounded, Adams believed that democratic merit would thrive and would be accorded the respect due to all talents, virtues, and services that aimed at the public good.[63]

The Meritorious Executive

In his attempts to show the American people the kind of executive they required, Adams met with the same incomprehension that greeted his view of aristocracy. His difficulties stemmed in part from his impolitic language, for he refused to cast aside the classical usages and to adapt his words to the new fashion. More seriously, he also deviated from both sides of the prevailing debate in the new United States about the character of a republican executive. If his proposed executive was far too powerful and regal to please the Anti-federalists or their successors, it was also too nonpartisan and passive to impress those whose model of the executive derived from James Wilson and

Alexander Hamilton. The executive figure so dear to John Adams—
and so anachronistic to most other Americans—was the purest exemplar of his classical politics of meritorious leadership.

Adams was impatient with the animus of the radical Whigs against
executive power. To deny the need for this power was to ignore the
propensities of human nature and the patterns of human history.
"There is a strong and continual effort in every society of men, arising
from the constitution of their minds, towards a kingly power." He was
furthermore impatient with the prevailing obsession about shunning
the vocabulary of monarchy, believing that it sidetracked political theorizing from the essence of the phenomenon that monarchy named:

> Everybody knows that the word monarchy has its etymology in the
> Greek . . . and signifies single rule or authority in one. This author-
> ity may be limited or unlimited, of temporary or perpetual duration.
> . . . Nevertheless, as far as it extends, and as long as it lasts, it may
> be called a monarchical authority with great propriety, by any man
> who is not afraid of a popular clamor and a scurrilous abuse of
> words.[64]

Although Adams strongly opposed unlimited executive authority,
he believed that the executive would play an indispensable part in a
balanced government, for it was ultimately he who would uphold the
balance. Detached from the contending classes and parties, Adams's
executive would prevent anyone from obtaining a dominant position.
"Neither the poor nor the rich should ever be suffered to be masters.
They should have equal power to defend themselves; and that their
power may be always equal, there should be an independent mediator
between them, always ready, always able, and always interested to as-
sist the weakest."[65]

Edward Handler has suggested that Adams set out two inconsistent
descriptions of the executive; in one, the executive served as mediator
between the aristocracy and the people, while in the other, the executive championed the people's cause against the aristocracy. It is true
that both conceptions of the executive can be found in Adams, but
their apparent inconsistency is resolved once his view of the political
struggle between aristocrats and democrats is recalled. Because conflict between the few and the many threatened political equilibrium,
the executive sometimes had to assume the role of "a third party,
whose interest and duty it [is] to do justice to the other two." Because
the aristocracy ordinarily brought to this conflict superior resources
and wiles, the executive sometimes had to act as "the natural friend of
the people, and the only defense which they or their representatives

can have against the avarice and ambition of the rich and distinguished citizens."[66]

What was most striking about Adams's conception of the executive was not the shifting roles this figure would have to assume in order to maintain the political balance but the peculiar blend of power and passivity that would typify his actions. Adams wanted to vest in an American executive all the essential prerogatives of the British monarch. His chief magistrate would possess unencumbered power to make appointments, treaties, and wars, and he would be armed with an absolute veto over the products of legislative action. Yet Adams believed that this panoply of powers would be used sparingly and defensively, for the executive, unlike the democratic assembly or aristocratic senate, was not given to aggression.[67]

The defensiveness and passivity that characterized his conception become clearer when Adams's executive figure is contrasted with the chief magistrates advocated by James Wilson and Alexander Hamilton. Wilson was the principal architect of a strong and unitary executive at the Constitutional Convention, where he highlighted the "energy, dispatch, and responsibility" such an executive would provide. Hamilton, in his famous *Federalist* 70, further developed this notion by his demonstration that "all men of sense will agree in the necessity of an energetic executive." Adams agreed with much of the traditional case for a unitary executive; he wrote in the first volume of the *Defence* that "the unity, the secrecy, the dispatch of one man has no equal." Further, he endorsed the idea, shared by Wilson and Hamilton, that unity brought responsibility and that "the attention of the whole nation should be fixed upon one point." What was lacking in Adams was the idea of executive energy: the driving, dominating, committed executive envisioned by Hamilton was the opposite of what Adams wanted.[68]

When Adams spoke of the executive's motives, he adopted a different tone from that he employed to describe aristocratic or democratic motives. Ambition and avarice typically drove the few and the many; in the best of institutional contexts, their desire for fame might come to play a significant role. About the executive, however, Adams seemed to assume that either disinterestedness or the love of fame would be uppermost. Standing apart from the passions of the aristocratic and democratic parties, the executive as mediator was supposed to "calm and restrain the ardor of both." Favoring neither the interests of the few nor the interests of the many but seeking instead to do "justice to all sides," the executive would become a rallying point for "the honest and virtuous of all sides." He was to be a figure marked not by energy but by impartiality and integrity.[69]

Serving as the balancing force between social classes, political parties, and legislative branches, the executive might have to move with decisiveness and firmness. Yet since he lacked any interest or program of his own, save the preservation of his own independence, his characteristic stance was to wait. His power would be held in abeyance until he had to defend the weaker party against the stronger or until a line of action opened up that was independent of either party and conducive to the national welfare. This executive therefore did not search out opportunities for action or grasp at instruments for aggression.

For a commentary on Adams's conception of the executive, one can turn to his own presidency. Assuming the presidency of a young republic caught between two warring giants abroad, with increasingly antagonistic domestic parties accusing each other of allegiance to one of those foreign giants, Adams stepped into a situation straight out of his earlier theoretical writings:

> The parties of rich and poor, of gentlemen and simplemen, unbalanced by some third power, will always look out for foreign aid, and never be at a loss for names, pretexts, and distinctions. . . . The great desideratum in a government is a distinct executive power, of sufficient strength and weight to compel both these parties, in turn, to submit to the laws.[70]

Adams attempted to act the part of the independent executive throughout his presidency, an effort that proved an ordeal for him. The chief stigma on his presidential record was the Alien and Sedition Acts during America's "quasi war" with France. While this repressive legislation was the handiwork of Federalists in Congress, Adams was culpable both in creating the bellicose political climate that made the acts possible and in authorizing prosecutions under their aegis. He held back, however, from a policy of sweeping repression, restraining the zealotry of the leading Hamiltonian Federalist in his cabinet, Secretary of State Timothy Pickering. And he rejected the most blatantly partisan uses of the Alien and Sedition Acts. From Adams's perspective, these laws were instruments of self-preservation for a republic threatened by a foreign power and its domestic adherents. They aimed not at legitimate public discourse but at the licentious and false rhetoric with which democratic extremists stirred up popular passions. The independent executive could, in Adams's conception, become a repressive—though not a partisan—figure, employing his "strength and weight to compel" the democratic party "to submit to the laws."[71]

In turn, the aristocratic party, too, would be compelled "to submit to the laws." Mounting tensions between the United States and France had allowed the Hamiltonian Federalists to expand the army as well as to enact repressive legislation. President Adams wanted to impress the French with American naval preparedness and was troubled by the buildup of the army, especially after Hamilton's partisans successfully intrigued to make their champion its effective commander (Washington was appointed head of the "new army" but stipulated that he would not begin active duty until hostilities impended). Adams appears to have intentionally dallied with military appointments to impede Hamilton's plans. But he was aware that so long as war with France remained a distinct possibility, events might still play into Hamilton's hands. Hence, he decided to make the most dramatic move of his presidency. On February 18, 1799, he nominated William Vans Murray as a peace envoy to France. Adams had arrived at this decision on his own, without consulting his cabinet, which he recognized by now to be dominated by Hamilton's partisans.

His decision stunned and outraged the Hamiltonian Federalists. When they pressured him to withdraw the Vans Murray nomination, he bridled against their "oligarchic influence." He was willing to add two additional envoys to the mission, but, after a considerable delay, it was dispatched in the face of a last, desperate effort by the Hamiltonian Federalists to forestall it. Public opinion embraced this turn toward peace. The "new army" was disbanded, and Hamilton was returned to civilian life. As Richard H. Kohn observes, "To save himself and the nation from . . . a dangerous course, Adams had exploded Hamilton's dreams." But the political cost was high. As the Federalist party split, Adams went down to defeat in the election of 1800 with the bitter satisfaction of having rendered yet another great but unrewarded service to his country.[72]

True to his theoretical prescriptions, Adams employed his presidential power as an instrument of balance. In the first half of his term he directed most of his efforts against what he took to be the excesses of the democratic or "French" party. Facing what he considered familiar democratic vices—demagoguery, licentiousness, turbulence—he was ready to utilize the heavy hand of repression. Halfway through the term, having become persuaded of the dangers attendant on a war with France (upon which all of the Hamiltonians' plans hinged), he carried out a dramatic reversal which thwarted the aristocratic or "British" party. Facing what he considered familiar aristocratic vices—intrigue, manipulation, grandiose ambition—he was ready to circumvent the intriguers, to overcome their manipulations, and to puncture their imperious visions. Adams hardly conducted these shifts in policy flawlessly. Yet their character was not an indication of his indecision or weakness but a reflection of his commitment to fulfill the responsibilities of the independent executive.

Adams's refusal to adapt to the emerging realities of party politics doomed his presidency to a short life and a dim historical reputation. One may sympathize with his search for a position above parties—particularly given the intemperance of partisan conflict in the late 1790s—but it was nonetheless a futile quest. Judged by the Hamiltonian desideratum of energy, and by that standard of mastery that has dominated twentieth-century American thinking about leadership, his presidency does not appear impressive. But Adams also deserves to be judged by his own standards. In the fashion of the Roman leadership that he revered, he understood his role as president as preserving the republic from the internal and external dangers that threatened to corrupt or destroy it. In his finest moment as president—the French peace mission—he adhered admirably to the demanding code of that role. Anachronistic as it may have been, his presidency did at times exemplify the meritorious leadership that, despite his frustration and pessimism, he continued to hope would find a place in American politics.

Conclusion

When John Adams defended his own achievements, he would claim extraordinary influence for his political ideas. Feeling himself snubbed in Mercy Warren's history of the American Revolution, he informed her that his *Defence* had been responsible for uniting the delegates at the Constitutional Convention and that "the general principles and system of that book were adopted by the writers of Publius or the Federalist." But it was more typical—and realistic—of Adams to complain about the unhappy fate of his writings. "Of the few who have taken the pains to read them," he observed to Jefferson in 1791, "some have misunderstood them and others have willfully misrepresented them, and these misunderstandings and misrepresentations have been made the pretence for overwhelming me with floods and whirlwinds of tempestuous abuse, unexampled in the history of this country." Even allowing for Adams's characteristic exaggeration when his wounded self-esteem was at stake, his belief that there was hardly any audience for his political theory was largely justified. The furor over his supposed apostasy from republicanism had ensured not only that his simplest ideas would be distorted but also that the deeper issues with which he struggled would be almost totally obscured.[73]

Adams's insights into the "passion for distinction" and his proposals for a republican symbolism that would link fame to meritorious political leadership were not, therefore, to have a significant impact on subsequent political thought in America. Neither the obscurity of his ideas nor the aristocratic conceits that sit so badly with a modern reader should, however, preclude a recognition that Adams raised questions about leadership that still need to be addressed. Contemporary American thinking about political leaders is particularly shallow when it comes to the issues that preoccupied John Adams. Little attention is paid (apart from the primers on manipulation and power) to the kind of "talents, virtues, and services" that are to be sought from public actors. Few intellectual resources are employed to distinguish authentic political merit from puffery. Cultivation of political virtue and provision for its reward are mired between a stale patriotic rhetoric and a depoliticizing cynicism.

The ideas and the career of John Adams provide rich material for reflection on the character of political leadership in America. Adams proposed—and embodied—a distinctly political conception of a leader's proper motivation and rewards. He grappled with the difficult issues of how to transmute self-seeking passions into political virtue and how to encourage leaders to prefer public to economic rewards. He explored the need for signs of political honor and a vocabulary of public esteem—ideas that are essential to a conception of democratic leadership if it is not to demand self-sacrifice from prospective leaders. Adams was also prescient (sometimes in sour observations that made him perhaps the funniest of the Founding Fathers) in diagnosing the ways in which political appearances could be falsified and political virtue corrupted in the American republic.

Because Adams's classical conception of leadership was pitted against an emerging capitalist order that would swiftly overwhelm it, his frustrations are as instructive as his hopes. Adams teaches us about the effects on political leadership when the trappings of wealth outshine the symbols of political merit. His pessimistic reflections point out how difficult it is for American leaders either to transcend their roots in a capitalist economy or to avoid serving—even if unintentionally—its imperatives. Yet his own example of independence and probity testifies to the occasional power of political impulses to resist economic seduction.

John Adams may seem like an unlikely preceptor to democratic theorists of political leadership. Convinced that inequalities would make a democratic society infeasible and that mass passions would make it unjust, he allowed only a limited space for popular action and leadership. But for those who seek to broaden and vivify that space,

Adams's vision of a transparent political order, in which public-spirited actions are recognized and honored and in which self-seeking impostures are exposed and rejected, remains intriguing. Democratic leadership requires a respect for and dialogue with followers to which Adams's conception of leadership did not speak. It also requires a grounding in that political passion and "real merit" of which Adams was the founding generation's most compelling spokesman.

3

Abraham Lincoln

Democratic Leadership and the Tribe of the Eagle

I N AN EXPLORATION OF THE AMERICAN POLITICAL TRADITION FOR CLUES
to the possibilities of democratic leadership, no other figure looms
as large as Abraham Lincoln. It is daunting to write about Lincoln.
Amid the mountains of trivia and sentimentality devoted to his life
and legacy are a formidable body of distinguished scholarship and a
bewildering array of imaginative interpretations. Even after a would-
be commentator on Lincoln has confronted these, he or she must
come up against Lincoln's own irreducible elusiveness and mysteri-
ousness. Nevertheless, for anyone who seeks to study American images of political leadership, Lincoln remains an absolutely essential
figure. It matters that since his assassination he has been the most
revered of all American leaders. It matters even more that, unlike some
other prominent American heroes, Lincoln's leadership had democratic
depths that still have much to teach.

Lincoln's brand of democratic leadership stands in sharp contrast
to the aristocratic leadership we have examined in previous chapters.
Where the aristocratic leader sought a commanding eminence far
above the people, the democratic leader attempted to remain close to
his followers. The aristocratic leader claimed preeminent ability and
wisdom and insisted on channeling popular behavior; the democratic
leader hoped to share his insights and his experiences with followers
through a process of political education. In demeanor, language, and
vision, the aristocratic leader operated from an assumption of superiority, while the democratic leader began with the premise of mutuality. Democratic leadership in this sense would not have been conceiv-

able in the hierarchical and deferential political culture of the founding era. It became a possibility as a result of the gradual democratization of American political culture—what Robert Wiebe has called "the
opening of American society"—in the first half of the nineteenth century. If Abraham Lincoln fits his own time, even as he transcends it,
one cannot imagine him in the world of Washington, Adams, Jefferson, and Hamilton.[1]

Democratic leadership must be recognized not only as a special
kind of historical possibility but also as a difficult accomplishment.
Americans have often seen Lincoln as a born democrat. This chapter
suggests that he was a democrat by dint of hard effort: he disciplined
himself to be democratic. Driven by a fierce ambition, he struggled to
give that ambition democratic meaning. Angered by apologists for
slavery and inequality, he struggled (though not always successfully)
to resist the temptation to condemn others from a plane of moral superiority. Vexed by combative rivals and (later) by feuding and complaining subordinates, he reined in his "crossness" and sought to respect the democratic dignity of everyone with whom he had to deal.
Some who knew him well perceived in him, in the words of John Hay,
his Civil War secretary, an "unconscious assumption of superiority."
But he did not act out that superiority. Lincoln provides a compelling
image of democratic leadership because his choice to be a democratic
leader was neither easy nor without cost.[2]

If Lincoln exemplifies democratic leadership, he also gives it unexpected dimensions. He subverts some of the most familiar and conventional American categories—especially those that link leadership
to masculinity. The most haunting images of Lincoln are often unmistakably feminine.

"Lincoln is a man of heart—aye, as gentle as a woman's and as tender." William Herndon thus described his law partner, then president-
elect, to an Eastern politician in December 1860. If Herndon saw in
Abraham Lincoln's emotional makeup those qualities that American
culture defined as predominantly feminine, the poet William Carlos
Williams went much further and imagined Lincoln *as* a woman: "The
least private would find a woman to caress him, a woman in an old
shawl—with a great bearded face and a towering black hat above it, to
give unearthly reality." Not all observers were touched by Lincoln's
feminine qualities. George Forgie observes that the historian Francis
Parkman ranked Lincoln well below Washington as a president, because Lincoln "failed to meet his standard that men should be masculine and women feminine." But the more typical view was expressed
by Robert Ingersoll, Republican politician and celebrated agnostic, in
a line that evokes nineteenth-century sentimentality toward mother-

hood yet still manages to be poignant: "He is the gentlest memory of our world."[3]

There was more to Lincoln than his "heart." After citing Lincoln's tender feelings, Herndon immediately emphasized that "he has a will strong as iron." Charles Dana, Lincoln's assistant secretary of war, recalled that "even in his freest moments one always felt the presence of a will and an intellectual power which maintained the ascendancy of the President." In his inflexible determination to carry the Civil War through to a successful conclusion, in his sarcastic complaint about those who would fight the war with "elder-stalk squirts, charged with rose water," in his willingness to endorse such brutal methods of warfare as Sherman's scorched-earth campaigns, Lincoln displayed qualities that should have satisfied the most strident advocates of manliness. That conventional definitions of masculinity were not foreign to his own thought was apparent in his response to those who appealed to him to let the South go in peace: "There is no Washington in that—no Jackson in that—no manhood nor honor in that."[4]

Lincoln can thus be considered as a masculine/feminine figure, so long as this is understood to be a metaphorical statement about his character rather than a psychological statement about his sexual identity. As a blend of qualities that American culture has normally sorted out as masculine and feminine, he had little in common with more exclusively masculine political leaders, especially such nineteenth-century types as Andrew Jackson and Theodore Roosevelt. Lincoln's masculine/feminine character was central to his practice of democratic leadership. Machiavelli argued that the successful prince must be both lion and fox. Lincoln's example suggests that a genuinely democratic leader should be both masculine and feminine. Such a leader should have the strength of purpose and tenacity of will that American culture has generally designated as masculine, but also the sensitivity, openness, and willingness to nurture others that American culture has typically disparaged as women's ways. Ideally, this combination of qualities could be described in terms that transcend conventions of gender. But so long as most American leaders deny the feminine side, it remains important to validate this side and to show, with Lincoln, how relevant it is to a democratic polity.[5]

The Lyceum Myth and Lincoln's Ambition

That Abraham Lincoln was a democratic leader seems an uncontroversial assertion. Yet several of the most imaginative modern students of Lincoln have, in effect, denied it, portraying Lincoln instead as a man of boundless ambition who sought and ultimately found a political role far above the ranks of his fellow citizens. Differing as to whether Lincoln projected himself as destroyer or savior of the political order established by the Founding Fathers, they have agreed that he must be understood in terms that transcend democratic politics. The seminal text for all of these scholars is "The Perpetuation of Our Political Institutions," a speech that Lincoln delivered at the Young Men's Lyceum of Springfield, Illinois, on January 27, 1838. This speech (hereafter referred to as the Lyceum speech), written by a then-obscure politician shortly before his twenty-ninth birthday, has been treated not merely as a fascinating foreshadowing of central themes in Lincoln's later career but as the essential key to everything that Lincoln was to become. If we wish to claim Lincoln as a democratic leader, we need to confront the current fixation on this one speech.

The principal threat to "the perpetuation of our political institutions" that Lincoln identified in the Lyceum speech was an "increasing disregard for law" and an upsurge in mob violence. Toward the end of the speech, however, he focused on a different danger that arose with the passing of the Revolutionary generation and the coming to political maturity of Lincoln's own generation. In the generation that founded the American republic, "all that sought celebrity and fame" staked their ambition upon "a practical demonstration of the truth of a proposition, which had hitherto been considered, at best no better than, problematical; namely, *the capability of a people to govern themselves*." While their gamble for fame had succeeded, while they had "won their deathless names in making it so," they had also cast a large shadow over their political heirs.

> This field of glory is harvested, and the crop is already appropriated. But new reapers will arise, and *they*, too, will seek a field. It is to deny, what the history of the world tells us is true, to suppose that men of ambition and talents will not continue to spring up amongst us. And, when they do, they will as naturally seek the gratification of their ruling passion, as others have *so* done before them. The question then, is, can that gratification be found in supporting and maintaining an edifice that has been erected by others? Most certainly it cannot. Many great and good men sufficiently qualified for any task they should undertake, may ever be found, whose ambition would aspire to nothing beyond a seat in Congress, a gubernatorial or a presidential chair; *but such belong not to the family of the lion, or the tribe of the eagle*[.] What! think you these places would satisfy

an Alexander, a Caesar, or a Napoleon? Never! Towering genius disdains a beaten path. It seeks regions hitherto unexplored. It sees *no distinction* in adding story to story, upon the monuments of fame, erected to the memory of others. It *denies* that it is glory enough to serve under any chief. It *scorns* to tread in the footsteps of *any* predecessor, however illustrious. It thirsts and burns for distinction; and, if possible, it will have it, whether at the expense of emancipating slaves, or enslaving freemen. Is it unreasonable then to expect, that some man possessed of the loftiest genius, coupled with ambition sufficient to push it to its utmost stretch, will at some time, spring up among us? And when such a one does, it will require the people to be united with each other, attached to the government and laws, and generally intelligent, to successfully frustrate his designs.[6]

Despite the florid rhetoric (which Lincoln was to prune in his later prose), this is a stunning passage. It seems to cry out not only for analysis but also for speculation; and some ingenious edifices of speculation have indeed been built upon its foundation.

Edmund Wilson was the first author to find autobiographical resonance in this passage. As Wilson reads it, Lincoln's Lyceum speech contained an "equivocal warning against the ambitious leader, describing this figure with a fire that seemed to derive as much from admiration as from apprehension." Wilson claims that Lincoln's "admiration" was a clue to his own fantasies, for he had "projected himself into the role against which he is warning [the people]." Extending Wilson's speculation, Dwight Anderson portrays a Lincoln who found in the condemnation of slavery an outlet for "his personal vengefulness against Washington and the founders of the Constitution, for denying that he was their equal." Finally fulfilling the prophecy of the Lyceum speech with his presidency, Lincoln, according to Anderson, became "a tyrant who would preside over the destruction of the Constitution in order to gratify his own ambition." Other interpreters have rejected the claim that Lincoln was projecting himself into the role of incipient tyrant and have found in his Lyceum speech a prophecy of a different kind: the emergence of a towering genius (of course, Lincoln himself) who will save the fathers' republic. In Harry Jaffa's reading, the young Lincoln was consciously preparing himself to become not the dreaded destroyer of the republic but the leader who defeats the destroyer. "Lincoln's conception of the highest political role," Jaffa says, "fits the Aristotelian conception of the man of godlike virtue." Where Jaffa advances philosophical arguments to present the Lincoln of the Lyceum speech as the self-conscious future savior of the Republic, George Forgie arrives at a similar conclusion on psychological grounds. According to Forgie, Lincoln's speech implies that "the only way that both ambition and filiopiety could be satisfied in a post-heroic age was if a good (rational, renunciatory, obedient) son were to rescue the fathers' institutions from some *other* ambitious person." Having projected this formula for heroic action as a young politician, Lincoln then applied it in the 1850s by treating his chief rival, Stephen A. Douglas, as the "bad son" and aspiring despot.[7]

Edmund Wilson's original thesis of a Lincoln projecting himself into the role of the "towering genius" was an intriguing literary speculation. But as subsequent writers have tried to develop this thesis with argument and evidence, its flaws have become glaring. The idea that Lincoln cast himself as the destructive genius requires us to believe that he was prepared to trample on everything he ever professed to believe about free institutions and equal rights. It makes him one of the supreme hypocrites in history—and, especially in Anderson's telling, a man of such bitter and violent passions that he felt no compunctions about sacrificing the lives and liberties of his countrymen for his own immortality. This monomaniacal figure, bent upon revenge against the godlike creatures who have frustrated him, resembles Melville's Ahab far more than it does the Abraham Lincoln described by his contemporaries or by his major biographers.[8]

It seems more plausible and more in keeping with his personality and subsequent career to interpret the Lincoln of the Lyceum speech as Jaffa and Forgie do, in the role of savior of the fathers' republic from the destructive genius. Yet there is no textual evidence in the Lyceum speech to support this interpretation. Lincoln makes no reference to any savior figure. He places responsibility for the defense of the Republic upon the people, not upon a heroic leader. Portraits of the young Lincoln as prophetic savior also jar with biographical facts. Jaffa requires us to believe that a twenty-eight-year-old politician and lawyer, undistinguished in achievement and insecure in personal and social relationships, confidently glimpses a future in which he will exercise "godlike virtue." Forgie slights the fact that Lincoln depicted Douglas as an instrument of the slave-power conspiracy rather than as the principal in a despotic conspiracy of his own.[9]

Lincoln's Lyceum speech has been made to carry far more interpretive weight than it can legitimately bear. The language of the "towering genius" passage suggests a young man both attracted and troubled, as had been the young John Adams, by the "ruling passion" for glory. The Lyceum speech is an important window into the mind and emotions of the young Lincoln, but it should not be made into the master clue to unlocking the mystery of everything that came later. Reading back Lincoln's eventual greatness into his youthful rhetoric,

Wilson and his successors have fashioned variants of a new Lincoln myth. They have also diverted our attention from what Lincoln himself had to say in later years about his own ambition: it was largely in his later struggles with the problem of ambition that Lincoln defined himself as a public man and made himself into an exemplary democratic leader.[10]

A good starting place for a discussion of the mature Lincoln's ambitions is a letter that he wrote to General Joseph Hooker in January 1863. In making Hooker the head of the Army of the Potomac, Lincoln informed him, he was signaling his appreciation of the general's military abilities. He went on: "You are ambitious, which, within reasonable bounds, does good rather than harm." But Lincoln was not happy about the signs of egotism Hooker had displayed. He chastised Hooker for thwarting his previous commander, General Burnside, in order to further his own ambition and noted that he had heard convincing reports that Hooker was calling for a dictator. Despite this, Lincoln was willing to take a chance on Hooker: "What I now ask is military success, and I will risk the dictatorship."[11]

Lincoln was not much worried about potential dictators by this point; he knew that Hooker was no "towering genius." But he did encourage a more moderate form of ambition. Such ambition would have to remain within "reasonable bounds," to be productive of "good rather than harm." Lincoln spoke about ambition in these terms because he had long struggled to define his own ambition and to give it a meaning compatible with democratic purposes and values.

Prior to his emergence as an antislavery politician, Lincoln's ambition had seemed to center on the conventional goals of high office and public esteem. But the Lincoln of the 1850s was constructing himself as more than a conventional American politician. His chief reference points at the time were Henry Clay and Stephen A. Douglas. Lincoln cited Clay in 1858 as "my beau ideal of a statesman." His eulogy upon the Kentuckian's death in 1852 spelled out the abilities of a statesman that Lincoln sought: eloquence, excellent judgment, indomitable will. Lincoln admired Clay equally for his "deep devotion to the cause of human liberty—a strong sympathy with the oppressed everywhere, and an ardent wish for their elevation." Douglas was also a crucial figure for Lincoln in the 1850s—though hardly as a model. Rather, Douglas represented egotistical and "unreasonable" ambition, devoid of moral justification or democratic responsibility. The "Little Giant" was not only Lincoln's political rival; he was the foil against which Lincoln shaped his own understanding of legitimate democratic ambition.[12]

In both private musings and public statements, Lincoln put forward several different versions of legitimate democratic ambition. Three of these will be considered here: greatness as liberator of the oppressed, posthumous fame through service in a noble cause, and martyrdom to liberty. The first is evident in a fragment that the editors of Lincoln's *Collected Works* have dated to 1856:

> Twenty-two years ago Judge Douglas and I first became acquainted. We were both young then; he a trifle younger than I. Even then, we were both ambitious; I, perhaps, quite as much so as he. With *me*, the race of ambition has been a failure—a flat failure; with *him* it has been one of splendid success. His name fills the nation; and is not unknown, even, in foreign lands. I affect no contempt for the high eminence he has reached. So reached, that the oppressed of my species, might have shared with me in the elevation, I would rather stand on that eminence, than wear the richest crown that ever pressed a monarch's brow.[13]

Lincoln apparently meant this passage for his own contemplation. In it he faced up honestly to his ambition and desire for fame, and was clear about his profound sense of disappointment. Yet he also made it plain in the final sentence that he did not want fame on Douglas's terms. Douglas had expressed indifference to the plight of the slaves and the extension of slavery; his elevation came at the expense of the oppressed. But Lincoln's path to fame would only be justified if—to recall the words he had spoken about Clay—it stemmed from "an ardent wish" to elevate the oppressed and contributed powerfully to their liberation. Lincoln wanted no monarch's crown; he wanted the fame of a true republican.

A second rendering of Lincoln's ambition came in another fragment, ascribed to 1858:

> I have never professed an indifference to the honors of official station; and were I to do so now, I should only make myself ridiculous. Yet I have never failed—do not now fail—to remember that in the republican cause there is a higher aim than that of mere office. I have not allowed myself to forget that the abolition of the Slave-trade by Great Britain, was agitated a hundred years before it was a final success; that the measure had its open fire-eating opponents; its stealthy "don't care" opponents, its dollar and cents opponents; its inferior race opponents; its negro equality opponents; and its religion and good order opponents; that all these opponents got offices, and their adversaries got none. But I have also remembered that though they blazed, like tallow-candles for a century, at last

they flickered in the socket, died out, stank in the dark for a brief season, and were remembered no more, even by the smell. School-boys know that Wilberforce, and Granville Sharpe, helped that cause forward; but who can now name a single man who labored to retard it? Remembering these things I can not but regard it as possible that the higher object of this contest may not be completely attained within the term of my natural life. But I can not doubt either that it will come in due time. Even in this view, I am proud, in my passing speck of time, to contribute an humble mite to that glorious consummation, which my own poor eyes may not last to see.[14]

This passage contains an unusual expression of scorn and bitterness—perhaps the reason Lincoln did not include it in the speech for which it appeared to be intended. He compared Douglas (with his "don't care," dollar and cents, and inferior race arguments), as well as more candid slavery apologists, with British opponents of abolition whose transient power was followed by the "smell" of their true rankness before they faded into complete obscurity. The pursuit of fame through the advocacy of immoral principles was, he implied, a self-defeating enterprise. Lincoln's characteristic modesty in the closing sentence should not obscure his own identification with the most famous of the British abolitionists. The fame he sought was, like theirs, inextricable from "a higher aim." It might prove to be posthumous—but it would endure.

If Lincoln could imagine himself as elevating the oppressed or as achieving posthumous fame in a cause that triumphed "in due time," he could also project himself into the role of martyr to liberty. During his contest with Douglas, he made several "martyr" statements. The most melodramatic came in a speech at Lewistown, Illinois, just before the first debate with Douglas:

> Think nothing of me—take no thought for the political fate of any man whomsoever—but come back to the truths that are in the Declaration of Independence. You may do anything with me you choose, if you will but heed these sacred principles. You may not only defeat me for the Senate, but you may take me and put me to death. . . . I am nothing; Judge Douglas is nothing. *But do not destroy that immortal emblem of Humanity—the Declaration of American Independence.*[15]

The role of martyr seemed to strike some deep chord in Lincoln. Even as a young man, he had portrayed himself playing this part. Concluding a speech in December 1839 attacking the subtreasury scheme of the Democrats, he had depicted the Van Buren administration as a "great volcano" spewing corruption over the land and promised that he would never bow to this tyranny, even if his defiance left him "in disaster, in chains, in torture, in death." Lincoln's images of martyrdom testify to the powerful ambivalence of his ambition. They are grandiose, the fantasies of a man whose ambitions demanded heroic fulfillment. They are also self-sacrificing, checking egotism by throwing away life itself in the name of liberty.[16]

Once "the glittering prize of the presidency" came within Lincoln's own reach after 1858, he went after it with all of his political skill. But his surprising triumph did not end the struggle to keep his ambition within "reasonable bounds." Although he had always emphasized his own humility, his expressions of humbleness became even more frequent as he approached the power of the presidency. Leaving Springfield for Washington, D.C., in the tense days of the "secession winter," Lincoln observed that he was faced "with a task before me greater than that which rested upon Washington." As he spoke to the crowds that greeted him in his numerous stops along the way, he repeatedly stressed that he was "a mere instrument, an accidental instrument, I should say, of a great cause," dependent upon the American people and upon God for any success he might achieve. "It is true," he told the New York legislature, "that while I hold myself without mock modesty, the humblest of all individuals that have ever been elevated to the Presidency, I have a more difficult task to perform than any one of them."[17]

Skeptical observers might suspect that Lincoln's humility was something of a pose. Lincoln certainly felt in himself what John Adams had called "the passion for distinction." But his expressions of humility seemed to be less a disguise for this passion than a way of countering its effects upon the ego. It is revealing that the more public acclaim Lincoln received (as on the trip from Springfield to Washington), the more he felt compelled to profess his humbleness. Adams's notorious vanity was, I have suggested, the refuge of a man whose "virtues, talents, and services" had not received the acclaim that he felt was due to them. Lincoln's humility was the defense of a man who feared that he was receiving too much acclaim and who wished to ward off that tempting food for passions that he struggled so hard to control.[18]

In the presidency, Lincoln's ambition took on its final shape. Convinced that his course would save the Union and its precious cargo of liberty and that his critics' demands would destroy the Union and wreck the American experiment in self-government, Lincoln merged his fate with that of the nation. During the 1864 campaign, he wrote:

"In taking the various steps which have led to my present position in relation to the war, the public interest and my private interest, have been perfectly parallel, because in no other way could I serve myself so well, as by truly serving the Union." Lincoln's success, indeed his reelection, were defined as inseparable from the nation's welfare. But there could be no sense of exultation in this merger. Responding to a serenade that followed his electoral victory, Lincoln said, "I am thankful to God for this approval of the people. But while deeply grateful for this mark of their confidence in me, if I know my heart, my gratitude is free from any taint of personal triumph."[19]

Perhaps despite his disavowals Lincoln did feel a sense of fulfilled ambition in the White House. In a letter to William Herndon, Joshua Speed, Lincoln's closest friend as a young man, recalled that during a visit with Lincoln in Washington, the president had reminded Speed of his youthful ambition to link his name with great events and with "something that would redound to the interest of his fellow man," and had proclaimed that the Emancipation Proclamation marked the realization of his "fondest hope." But Lincoln's anguish at the suffering and death to which his own political choices had contributed made impossible any lasting sense of gratification. As Richard Hofstadter has written, "He had had his ambitions and fulfilled them, and met heartache in his triumph."[20]

Lincoln in the White House was too racked by questions of great magnitude to provide unambiguous testimony about his final understanding of the place of ambition in a democratic polity. What remains instructive, however, is his long struggle to discipline his own ambition in a democratic fashion. The young Lincoln had warned at the Lyceum of the inflamed ambitions of destructive geniuses who belonged to "the tribe of the eagle." The later Lincoln would find democratic meanings for powerful ambition and genius and would recast "the tribe of the eagle" as a more benign image of American political leadership.

Leader and People

The portrait of Lincoln as the "towering genius" of the Lyceum speech has served not only to distort his ambition but to obscure his relationship with the people he sought to lead. The Lincoln of the Lyceum myth is a figure of overwhelming will and power, whose relationship to the public can be understood only in terms of dominance and submission. By contrast, Lincoln's actual dealings with the people called into play all the complex elements of his masculine/feminine character. In working out how a democratic leader must relate to a democratic people, Lincoln sought a balance between openness to others and commitment to a principled vision. In attempting to educate followers to his own understanding of the tenets of liberty, he also tried to stay as close to those followers as was politically feasible. At least in his own mind, leader and follower would eventually symbolically merge—Lincoln would humble himself before a people who were himself writ large.

Lincoln was not what modern commentators would call a "charismatic leader." Comparing Douglas and Lincoln in 1858, William Herndon noted that it was Douglas who "had that unique trait, magnetism, . . . that attracted a host of friends and readily made him a popular idol." This trait was lacking in Lincoln: "In physical make-up he was cold—at least not magnetic—and made no effort to dazzle people by his bearing. . . . He never acted for stage effect. . . . He despised glitter, show, set forms, and shams." While Lincoln's unwillingness to dramatize his political personality (a sentiment not shared by Republican campaign strategists in 1860) may seem admirable, it left him vulnerable to insult and caricature. J. G. Randall has written, in "The Unpopular Mr. Lincoln," that the incoming president was "dubbed a 'Simple Susan,' a 'baboon,' and a 'gorilla.' In Washington chatter and in news sheets he was labeled an 'ape,' a 'demon,' an 'Illinois beast'. . . . Inadequacy, weakness, vacillation, even 'imbecility' (a favorite word) were attributed to the new leader."[21]

Lacking charisma, Lincoln was nonetheless successful in his campaigns for popular support. Several of the most distinguished Lincoln scholars have, however, gone to considerable lengths to demonstrate that his achievements rested less on public support than upon the skilled employment of the politician's arts. In "A. Lincoln, Politician," David Donald writes that the "secret of Lincoln's success is simple: he was an astute and dexterous operator of the political machine." Donald cites such politically effective traits as "secrecy, passivity, and pragmatism" and highlights the brilliant handling of patronage and deployment of the soldier vote in the 1864 election. A similar view is expressed by Richard Current: "Direct, popular appeal does not appear to have been one of the strong points of Lincoln the political master. Rather, his strengths seem to have been those of a politician's politician, a manager of the party machine, a wire puller."[22]

The work of Donald and Current is valuable in debunking images of a saintly Lincoln who would never stoop to the politician's ways. Both have shown convincingly how much Lincoln relied on his long training in politics to achieve his objectives in the presidency. Yet in characterizing Lincoln as an "operator of the political machine" or a "wire puller," they come close to making him indistinguishable from a Thurlow Weed, the most notorious political manager in the Republican party of the day. While we always need to keep in mind that Lincoln was, as he himself readily acknowledged, "more of a politician than anything else," we also need to explore what made him more than a conventional American politician.[23]

As a young Illinois legislator, Lincoln announced both his membership in the politician's club and his divergence from his colleagues on a fundamental point. Defending the Illinois State Bank against the attacks of Democratic legislators, Lincoln proclaimed that the controversy "is exclusively the work of politicians; a set of men who have interests aside from the interests of the people, and who, to say the most of them, are, taken as a mass, at least one long step removed from honest men. I say this with the greater freedom because, being a politician myself, none can regard it as personal." If Lincoln was a politician, he would not be one of that "mass" who employed dishonest methods to pursue interests at odds with the public welfare. Especially as he matured, he would approach politics with a moral and intellectual seriousness that distinguished him from mere "operators" and "wire pullers." He would grapple self-consciously with fundamental issues of democratic politics in his effort to become a politician who was also a democratic leader.[24]

An essential maxim of democratic leadership for Lincoln was closeness to the people. (The "people" was not, for Lincoln, an all-inclusive category; the most obvious and unfortunate exclusion from his vision was blacks.) Lincoln took to heart the convention of nineteenth-century American democratic thought that a leader should represent his constituents' wishes. The young legislative candidate from Sangamon County promised the voters that "while acting as their representative, I shall be governed by their will, on all subjects upon which I have the means of knowing what their will is." The Whig congressman from Illinois, slightly more than a decade later, lambasted the Democrats because they had "violated the primary, the cardinal, the one great living principle of all democratic representative government— the principle, that the representative is bound to carry out the known will [wishes] of his constituents." The young Lincoln rejected any notion that a representative must, in the mode prescribed by James Madison, filter out the people's passions and narrow interests in order to arrive at a rational judgment of the public good; he believed that a leader must respect, and thus mirror, the wishes of the people.[25]

If closeness to the people was a point of democratic doctrine, it was also a lesson inculcated by political sagacity. In the open and rela-

tively egalitarian political climate in which Lincoln grew up, an aspiring politician who conveyed to his followers a sense of distance or superiority would breed dangerous resentments. Lincoln indirectly testified to his awareness of this point in an 1842 lecture on temperance,
in which he attributed previous problems encountered by the temperance movement to the character of its advocates.

> These champions for the most part, have been preachers, lawyers,
> and hired agents. Between these and the mass of mankind, there is a
> want of *approachability*, if the term be admissible, partially at least,
> fatal to their success. They are supposed to have no sympathy of
> feeling or interest, with those very persons whom it is their object to
> convince and persuade.[26]

Both principle and politics, then, impelled Lincoln to establish
close relationships with his public. So, too, did emotional need. As a
man who spoke with reticence and apparent embarrassment of his
unprepossessing origins, popular support and public office were more
important sources of self-esteem than money or bourgeois comfort. In
the flat and awkward autobiographical statement that he wrote for
John L. Scripps to use in preparing a campaign biography in 1860,
the passages describing his first political successes are suggestive of
what popular favor meant to Lincoln. When the Black Hawk war
began in 1832, he wrote,

> A joined a volunteer company, and to his own surprise, was elected
> captain of it. He says he has not since had any success in life which
> gave him so much satisfaction. . . . Returning from the campaign,
> and encouraged by his great popularity among his immediate neigh-
> bors, he, the same year, ran for the Legislature and was beaten—his
> own precinct, however, casting its votes 277 for and 7, against
> him. . . . This was the only time A was ever beaten on a direct vote of
> the people.

Lincoln could find many reasons for the political frustrations that he
had experienced prior to 1860, but he would cling with uncharacteristic pride to the claim that the people always supported him once they,
like his New Salem neighbors, came to know him.[27]

Although closeness to the people was essential to democratic leadership, Lincoln came to recognize that it was not an unproblematic
relationship. That the public will might conflict with fundamental
principle and press a faithful representative of the people to violate
his own conscience was a possibility brought home to Lincoln by the

Mexican War. Lincoln had joined his Whig colleagues in Congress in voting to condemn President Polk for unnecessarily and unconstitutionally provoking the war; he had delivered a lengthy speech excoriating the president for justifying his war policy with flimsy and deceptive arguments that resembled "the half insane mumbling of a fever-dream." When William Herndon sent Lincoln a letter criticizing his vote of censure, Lincoln responded: "I will stake my life, that if you had been in my place, you would have voted just as I did. Would you have voted what you felt you knew to be a lie?" But if Lincoln's stance was a matter of principle (as well as partisanship), it was not clear that his Illinois constituents approved of his actions. Debating Murray McConnel, a Democrat, during the 1848 presidential canvass, Lincoln (according to a hostile newspaper report) "pronounced the conduct of Mr. Polk, and the democratic party, anti-democratic and wrong, and said it was the duty of every representative truly to represent his constituents." McConnel retorted by citing Lincoln's vote to censure Polk and asking "if Mr. Lincoln did not know when he gave that vote that he was *misrepresenting* the wishes of the patriotic people of this district."[28]

A leader holding firm to principle might then find himself at odds with his followers. He might be scorned (Democratic opponents never ceased reminding voters of Lincoln's "unpatriotic" opposition to Polk's policies), and he might fail. As Lincoln came to define it in the 1850s, the question was how a leader could educate people to understand and adhere to the higher demands of the principles of liberty without forfeiting his own closeness to the public. As he thought through this question, he seemed to arrive at a view in which the leader shaped the public's thinking more than he reflected it. On a number of occasions in the late 1850s, Lincoln set forward a bold view of the leader's potential power over public opinion. During the first debate with Douglas, he put it this way:

> In this and like communities, public sentiment is everything. With public sentiment, nothing can fail; without it nothing can succeed. Consequently he who moulds public sentiment, goes deeper than he who enacts statutes or pronounces decisions. He makes statutes and decisions possible or impossible to be executed.[29]

These words are often cited as expressive of Lincoln's own self-conception as a molder of public opinion. What is seldom noted, however, is that Lincoln was talking not about himself but about Stephen A. Douglas. Public sentiment in America, Lincoln suggested, had long revolved around a "central idea": the standard of equality set down in the Declaration of Independence. Douglas and the Democrats were, he charged, attempting to undermine that "central idea" and replace it with an acceptance of inequality. In molding a public opinion that had rested on the fundamental principle of liberty to become indifferent to the spread of slavery, Douglas was corrupting it. Lincoln thus warned his audiences of "this gradual and steady debauching of public opinion, this course of preparation for the revival of the slave trade, for the territorial slave code, and the new Dred Scott decision that is to carry slavery into the free States." His mission in the 1850s, then, was not to "mould public sentiment" in a new way but to combat Douglas's efforts and to revitalize the "central idea" upon which American freedom had always depended.[30]

Lincoln often emphasized the limits that confronted a democratic leader as he attempted to influence public opinion. A leader, he believed, could not change public sentiments that were too widely and deeply shared. Echoing Henry Clay, Lincoln argued that racial equality was not possible in America because it conflicted too profoundly with the feelings of "the great mass of white people. . . . Whether this feeling accords with justice and sound judgment, is not the sole question, if indeed, it is any part of it. A universal feeling, whether well or ill-founded, can not be safely disregarded." But slavery, too, clashed with the feelings—in this case, the "sense of justice"—of most people; this sentiment was so powerful that "no statesman can safely disregard it."[31]

That Lincoln approached public opinion with caution, that he sought to contest dangerous innovations in public sentiment rather than to innovate himself, does not mean that his approach to the education of the public was shallow or timid. What he did—with greater eloquence and intellectual force than any other leader in the American "mainstream"—was to take the conventional ideas of the American political faith and clarify them, develop their implications, cut to the core of their meaning. Lincoln was educating the public to conserve what he regarded as the liberating set of principles forged by the Revolutionary creativity of 1776.

During his running debates with Douglas in the 1850s, Lincoln had held out the ominous possibility that the American people might be won over to Douglas's position of indifference toward slavery—a first step, he warned, toward indifference to their own freedom. But the enthusiastic response of ordinary Northerners in 1861 to the cause of the Union reassured him. In his first major discussion of the Civil War—his message to Congress in special session of July 4, 1861—Lincoln asserted that the contest for public opinion had been won by the right side. He repeatedly lavished praise on a people who both understood and exemplified the principles of liberty:

> It may be affirmed, without extravagance, that the free institutions
> we enjoy, have developed the powers, and improved the condition,
> of our whole people, beyond any example in the world. Of this we
> now have a striking, and an impressive illustration. So large an
> army as the government has now on foot, was never before known,
> without a soldier in it, but who had taken his place there, of his own
> free choice. But more than this: there are many single regiments
> whose members, one and another, possess full practical knowledge
> of all the arts, sciences, professions, and whatever else, whether use-
> ful or elegant, is known in the world; and there is scarcely one, from
> which there could not be selected, a President, a Cabinet, a Con-
> gress, and perhaps a Court, abundantly competent to administer the
> government itself.[32]

The war, then, was

> essentially a people's contest. On the side of the Union, it is a strug-
> gle for maintaining in the world, that form, and substance of gov-
> ernment, whose leading object is, to elevate the condition of men—
> to lift artificial weights from all shoulders—to clear the paths of
> laudable pursuit for all—to afford all, an unfettered start, and a fair
> chance, in the race of life.

According to Lincoln, the differing responses of military elites and
"the plain people" underscored the democratic character of the Union
cause. He found it "worthy of note, that while in this, the government's hour of trial, large numbers of those in the Army and Navy,
who have been favored with the offices, have resigned, and proved
false to the hand which had pampered them, not one common soldier,
or common sailor is known to have deserted his flag."[33]

At this moment—before the harrowing casualties, draft riots, war
weariness—Lincoln seemed to have resolved the tension between
closeness to the people and education of the people to observe the demanding principles of liberty. His resolution was to portray the people as already carrying out those principles in heroic fashion. The
"people" in this message, with their commitment to equality of opportunity, their multiplicity of talents, their unswerving loyalty, were the
people of Lincoln's vision, worthy inheritors of the fathers, reenacting
their original struggle for liberty. The images through which he depicted them—their "practical knowledge," striving in the "race of life,"
unpampered devotion to Union and liberty—were the same images

through which he understood his own life. Lincoln was projecting himself onto the American people.

As the masterful politician depicted by Donald and Current, Lincoln conducted his presidency through the maneuvers and tactics of party and patronage. As the democratic leader that I have sought to depict, Lincoln relied above all on language. The remarkable prose of the presidential years must be considered not only as rhetoric or political theory but also as the instrument of democratic leadership.

The Language of Democratic Leadership

The seriousness with which Lincoln regarded words during the Civil War is attested to by a statement in his 1862 message to Congress: "In times like the present, men should utter nothing for which they would not willingly be responsible through time and in eternity." His wartime words were spare and painstakingly chosen, but they amply expressed his purposes and vision. And they were couched in a style that was appropriate for democratic leadership. In public letters, messages to Congress, and especially in the few major addresses he chose to deliver, Lincoln's language was grave, sonorous, richly figurative. It was aimed at the many rather than the few, for as Herndon observed, Lincoln "wanted to be distinctly understood by the common people." Several examples of this democratic language might be considered. For the sake of brevity, I shall concentrate on the two most justly famous of Lincoln's speeches: the Gettysburg Address and the second inaugural address.[34]

James Hurt has suggested that the power of the Gettysburg Address does not lie in the political ideas it espouses, which were commonplaces to Lincoln's audience, but in the emotional resonance of its images. The nature of these images has been the subject of varied readings. In one interpretation, Lincoln's images are potent because they link the personal and familial (birth/death/rebirth, fathers/sons) with the public and the collective. In another view, the Gettysburg Address infuses the secular system of democracy with sacred, Christian imagery of sacrifice and redemption. Domestic and Christian images are to be found in the speech, but they are subordinated to images that are distinctly political and democratic. The devotion and sacrifice that the Gettysburg Address honors are not directed to the service of God. Neither do they link men to primordial experiences of soil and hearth. On the contrary, their meaning is found on an abstract political plane, where men will die for "the proposition that all men are created equal" and in order that "government of the people, by the people, for the people, shall not perish from the earth."[35]

Lincoln established the framework of meaning for his speech in the opening statement: "Four score and seven years ago our fathers brought forth on this continent, a new nation, conceived in Liberty, and dedicated to the proposition that all men are created equal." He took his own interpretation of the Declaration of Independence, expounded so frequently in his speeches during the 1850s, and crystallized it in a single sentence: the Declaration's maxim of equality was the defining characteristic of the American nation. Cloaking himself in the mantle of the fathers, Lincoln asserted his final ideological triumph over both Douglas and the South—his view came to be the definitive meaning of America.[36]

The bulk of the brief speech was a funeral oration (reminiscent more of a classical occasion, such as Pericles' funeral oration, than of any Christian ceremony) that took the sacrifice of young soldiers' lives as a commentary on the meaning of the polity they served. In Lincoln's vision, the dead who lay buried at Gettysburg became exemplary American citizens. Like the fathers, their lives could be summed up in terms of dedication and devotion (words Lincoln repeated over and over) to the ideals of democracy. Their heroism was commemorated not only because of its contribution to winning the war but because it made palpable why what they loved—"that cause for which they gave the last full measure of devotion"—was worthy of their sacrifice. The survivors had to make good their love through "a new birth of freedom." To be, like the dead, worthy sons of those fathers who "conceived in Liberty" (a masculine/feminine image), they would have to become fathers/mothers themselves and give freedom an even greater birth than before.[37]

Lincoln cast himself in this speech merely as among "us the living." In a rhetorical voice that turned democracy into timeless poetry, he placed himself along with the rest of the living in the shadow of the heroic dead. Earlier, he had merged himself with the great body of the Northern "plain people" in depicting the Civil War as a "people's contest." Now, in the face of masses of Union dead, his democratic imagery became deeper and more tragic. Understanding what those masses had done, he said, should make the living more committed democrats. For among these dead, distinctions were rendered irrelevant; there could be no mention of generals, officers, even individual heroes in the presence of this egalitarianism of sacrifice. The sacrificial community, linking the living, through their dedication, to both the fathers of the Revolution and the martyred sons of the Civil War, was Lincoln's image of a democracy personified, purified, and meant to last forever.[38]

Lincoln painted the American nation in its ideal guise at Gettysburg. But the mounting carnage and horror of the Civil War ultimately called into question this ideal guise and forced Lincoln to reconsider his vision of America. In the second inaugural address, he confronted the darker side of the American experience—the sins rather than the greatness of the nation.

The second inaugural attempted to shift the public's focus from heroism to guilt. The sacrificial community hymned at Gettysburg now became a sinful community undergoing the chastisement of God. As Lincoln unfolded his final, tragic vision of the meaning of the Civil War, his language took on a haunted beauty:

> The Almighty has His own purposes. "Woe unto the world because of offences! for it must needs be that offences come; but woe to that man by whom the offence cometh!" If we shall suppose that American Slavery is one of those offences which, in the providence of God, must needs come, but which, having continued through His appointed time, He now wills to remove, and that He gives to both North and South, this terrible war, as the woe due to those by whom the offence came, shall we discern therein any departure from those divine attributes which the believers in a Living God always ascribe to Him? Fondly do we hope—fervently do we pray—that this mighty scourge of war may speedily pass away. Yet, if God wills that it continue, until all the wealth piled by the bond-man's two hundred and fifty years of unrequited toil shall be sunk, and until every drop of blood drawn with the lash, shall be paid by another drawn with the sword, as was said three thousand years ago, so still it must be said "the judgments of the Lord, are true and righteous altogether."
>
> With malice toward none; with charity for all; with firmness in the right, as God gives us to see the right, let us strive on to finish the work we are in; to bind up the nation's wounds; to care for him who shall have borne the battle, and for his widow, and his orphan—to do all which may achieve and cherish a just, and a lasting peace, among ourselves, and with all nations.[39]

Here was Lincoln—the first president to win reelection since Andrew Jackson, the commander in chief of a mighty war effort on the eve of victory—in what could have been a triumphant moment. Yet he claimed no credit for himself, extolled no achievement of the Union. He resisted the temptation of righteousness, of interpreting the South's military failure as a sign of its moral failure. (And the temptation was felt—less than two weeks later he told an Indiana regiment that "whenever I hear anyone, arguing for slavery I feel a strong impulse to see it tried on him personally.") Lincoln no longer described the Civil War as a successful trial of free government. He rejected any note of triumph and self-satisfaction in favor of the language of the jeremiad—the president, as secular prophet, calling his people to admit their sins.[40]

The second inaugural was, of course, a jeremiad not only about guilt but also about redemption. Its final passage prescribed for the nation a new assumption of moral responsibility. Lincoln's call for charity has usually been viewed as Christian in character. The "Christian principle of forgiveness" was, indeed, much on his mind in this period. Yet the imagery of the passage was also feminine. "To care for him who shall have borne the battle, and for his widow, and his orphan" recalled the Union's sanitary fairs, organized largely by women, in which funds were raised for the relief of suffering soldiers and their families. Lincoln had earlier praised "our noble women for their angel-ministering to the suffering soldiers." Now he was suggesting that the entire nation turn from the spirit of violence, symbolized by slavery and magnified by war, to the Christian spirit of forgiveness and the spirit of caring that was epitomized by women. A nation that learned from its "woe" would, like Lincoln himself, become feminine as well as masculine; it would seek to be not only strong and prosperous but also gentle and giving.[41]

The second inaugural address represented a departure for a democratic leader who had always approached public opinion with caution. Lincoln himself provided a commentary on his motives in a letter to Thurlow Weed:

> I expect [the second inaugural address] to wear as well as—perhaps better than—any thing I have produced; but I believe it is not immediately popular. Men are not flattered by being shown that there has been a difference of purpose between the Almighty and them. . . . It is a truth which I thought needed to be told; and as whatever of humiliation there is in it, falls most directly on myself, I thought others might afford for me to tell it.

Lincoln allowed a bit of the pride and ambition that he otherwise so strongly reined in to peek out in his expectation that posterity would admire this speech. But he had few illusions about the contemporary reaction. Americans would not be flattered by the idea that God and history were not necessarily on their side. They would find it easier to believe in "a new birth of freedom" for the former slave than to act upon the sense of collective responsibility that would redeem this freedom.[42]

Perhaps it was the circumstances of the moment that permitted Lincoln to depart from his habitual caution. With the war all but won, with his reelection secured and his place in history already taking form, Lincoln was ready to ask more of the American people than he had ever done before. The second inaugural address called for a painful self-examination, so that the American people could come to terms with their historic failings. Lincoln himself had undergone this self-examination and had accepted the "humiliation" it necessitated. Remaining close to the people as a democratic leader, he asked them to share his experience and to face the deepest truths about themselves. The democratic leader would not speak to the people from on high or proclaim the superiority of his own political burdens; he would educate the people about a legacy of guilt and a possibility of redemption that leader and followers shared. In the second inaugural address, Lincoln left a remarkable example of what democratic leadership in America might attempt to be.

Yet one must wonder whether Lincoln's greatest speech had much of an impact. It was not merely that his vision of the Civil War was hard on the North and magnanimous to the South. Lincoln's message in the second inaugural address ran counter to the most powerful side of the American spirit—the optimistic, assertive, expansionist assumptions of a people who believed themselves "chosen." The character of the Gilded Age that followed rapidly upon Lincoln's death suggests that he became more an icon than a teacher of democracy.

Democratic Relationships

In order to understand Lincoln as a democratic leader, it is necessary to look not only at his ambitions, relationship with the people, and language, but also at his dealings with individuals. Democratic concepts, such as majority rule and public good, have often been applied in ways that prove indifferent or injurious to individuals. It is easy, too, for a leader to think of the people he seeks to lead as an abstraction and to ignore the consequences of his actions in the lives of specific people. Lincoln did not fall victim to these tendencies. He treated democratic leadership as a relationship involving individuals as well as large groups. In his compassionate and nurturing practices as president, in his resistance to quarreling and freedom from malice, he most fully disclosed his masculine/feminine quality of democratic leadership.

The work of Carol Gilligan can help to clarify how Lincoln's character combined qualities that are usually separated as masculine or feminine. Gilligan suggests that the moral development of males usually entails the learning of an "ethic of rights," geared to "arriving at an objectively fair or just resolution to moral dilemmas upon which all rational persons could agree." In contrast, females develop what Gilligan calls an "ethic of care" or an "ethic of responsibility," whose focus is not the application of abstract justice to autonomous persons. In the female ethic, "sensitivity to the needs of others and the assumption of responsibility for taking care lead women to attend to voices other than their own and to include in their judgment other points of view." Lincoln has long been understood as one of America's greatest proponents of an "ethic of rights"; he is often quoted for his rigorously logical refutations of the inegalitarian position of the advocates of slavery. He can also be understood as epitomizing an "ethic of care" typically associated with a feminine perspective.[43]

With all the burdens of the Civil War presidency—military strategy, recruitment of hundreds of thousands of troops, conflicts with Congress over emancipation and reconstruction—Lincoln insisted upon remaining accessible to individuals who wanted to see him personally. His assistant attorney general, Titian J. Coffey, recalled that in wartime Washington "it was a common saying that he was far more accessible than many a chief of bureau or clerk." Initially, he made himself available to all callers; his secretaries, Nicolay and Hay, had to prevail upon him to restrict the hours open to the public on the prudent grounds that otherwise he could get nothing else done. Even with these restrictions, it was not hard for petitioners to reach him.[44]

Although the time spent with all these visitors added measurably to Lincoln's exhaustion, he could not shut them out. He felt empathy with many of them, as he told Henry Wilson. "They don't want much; they get but little, and I must see them." He also felt that he learned from them. He described his hours spent with ordinary people in the White House as "public opinion baths," in which he immersed himself in the thinking of the people.[45]

Accessibility to ordinary individuals gave Lincoln another kind of knowledge as well. He tended to think about the war in the framework of grand abstractions, such as the fate of free government. While his reasoning was powerful, it needed to be tempered by an understanding of the war as the lived experience of millions of Americans. The myriad White House visitors kept Lincoln in touch with such lived experience. They helped him to respond compassionately to it and thereby to deepen his vision. Lincoln's own experience became intertwined with that of the people he led; closeness to the people grew into the mutuality of shared commitment and shared suffering.

Of all the requests that he received, Lincoln was most concerned with pleas for pardons. He did not always agree to grant pardons; executions were ordered to be carried out in what he considered to be "very flagrant cases." Yet he granted so many pardons that stories of his clemency toward the condemned became a major part of his contemporary reputation and his subsequent legend. The stories are largely true and genuinely moving; they reveal not only a kind man but a leader who knows the political uses of kindness.[46]

The ability to spare men's lives was therapeutic for Lincoln. Granting a pardon request from Congressman Schuyler Colfax, the president told him: "Some of my generals complain that I impair discipline by my frequent pardons and reprieves; but it rests me, after a day's hard work, that I can find some excuse for saving some poor fellow's life, and I shall go to bed happy tonight as I think how joyous the signing of this name will make himself, his family and friends." As a wartime president, Lincoln had to make large decisions, the consequences of which were often suffering and death for many people. His pardons were small decisions, but their saving of life was a valuable compensation of his office. Pardons represented, for him, the gentle side of power. If Lincoln's unyielding determination to fight the war to a successful conclusion expressed an admirable self-assertiveness conventionally labeled as masculine, his yielding to the dictates of the heart in pardon cases expressed the necessary counterbalance of the feminine spirit of care.[47]

Lincoln's numerous pardons seemed impolitic to many contemporaries because of their negative effect upon military discipline. Yet a few observers have suspected a prudential motive behind his pardoning policy. As Richard Current has put the argument, Lincoln

> had to deal with an army consisting mainly of citizen soldiers. . . . With such men as these, frequent pardons may have been bad for discipline, but the regimen of the regular army, if unrelieved, might have been even worse for morale. The service needed to be made as popular and attractive as it could be, and Lincoln's clemency made it less unattractive than it otherwise would have been.[48]

We do not, however, have to choose between an interpretation of Lincoln's pardons as saintly forgiveness and an interpretation of the same pardons as canny politics. For Lincoln knew that what was kind was often politic as well. In a different context, he complained to Secretary of War Stanton about "the dismissal of officers when neither incompetency, nor intentional wrong, nor real injury to the service, is imputed" because "it is both cruel and impolitic, to crush the man, and make him and his friends permanent enemies to the administration, if not to the government itself." Kindness was part of Lincoln's political as well as personal makeup. Cruelty, however, was not; he could not be cruel even when that might be politic. Although he signed an order pledging that Confederate executions of captured black soldiers would be met with the retaliatory executions of captured Confederates, he shied away from killing innocent men for what others on their side had done. Despite reports of Confederate atrocities toward captured blacks, the retaliatory order was never implemented.[49]

Lincoln's mode of dealing with individual citizens and condemned soldiers combined democratic openness and kindness with political advantage. A similar approach governed his dealings with fellow politicians, generals, and subordinates in the executive branch. That approach was revealed in the counsel that Lincoln offered James M. Cutts, Jr., a young officer who had been court-martialed for quarreling with fellow officers:

> The advice of a father to his son "Beware of entrance to a quarrel, but being in, bear it that the opposed may beware of thee," is good, and yet not the best. Quarrel not at all. No man resolved to make the most of himself, can spare time for personal contention. Still less can he afford to take all the consequences, including the vitiating of his temper, and the loss of self-control. Yield larger things to which you can show no more than equal right; and yield lesser ones, though clearly your own.[50]

The man who would avoid quarrels would also avoid resentments and grudges. Lincoln taught himself to resist antagonistic feelings toward those who had caused him grief. The final passage of his second inaugural address amplified a personal code of conduct expressed earlier in the war: "I shall do nothing in malice. What I deal with is too vast for malicious dealing." Lincoln was outraged by the South's arguments for slavery and assaults on free government, but he reminded himself to "judge not that we be not judged," and planned to treat the miscreant section with magnanimity. On a more personal plane, he was harassed by Secretary of the Treasury Chase's scheming to take the 1864 Republican nomination away from him, but he nominated Chase, when the opportunity arose after the election, to become chief justice of the Supreme Court.[51]

Lincoln's philosophy of "quarrel not" demanded considerable self-discipline. As a young man active in partisan politics, Lincoln had become embroiled in a number of personal contentions. In 1842 he almost found himself in a duel with James Shields, Illinois state auditor, who was furious over a satirical attack that Lincoln had published under a pseudonym. The young Lincoln could be a combative character. Responding indignantly to a political handbill that distorted his legislative record, he wrote in his own handbill to the voters of Sangamon County: "All I have to say is that the author is a *liar* and a *scoundrel*, and that if he will avow the authorship to me, I promise to give his proboscis a good wringing."[52]

Lincoln was, however, quick to patch up quarrels. And as his personal and political maturation proceeded, he began to construct the more gentle self with which we are familiar. In his eulogy for President Zachary Taylor in 1850, there are several passages that reveal Lincoln seeking to learn from Taylor's example a democratic leadership style free from contentiousness. Lincoln wrote of Taylor: "He was alike averse to *sudden*, and to *startling* quarrels; and he pursued no man with *revenge*." After a long description of "a notable, and a noble instance of this," stemming from the Mexican War, Lincoln went on to praise Taylor's relations with his troops: "Of the many who served with him through the long course of forty years, all testify to the uniform kindness, and his constant care for, and hearty sympathy with, their every want and every suffering; while none can be found to declare, that he was ever a tyrant anywhere, in anything." With a few changes in particulars, these words could be used to describe Lincoln as president.[53]

Lincoln did not eschew quarrels and resentments from a stance of Olympian superiority and indifference to his subordinates. On the contrary, he displayed a concern for the feelings of others that was rare in an American political leader. His papers contain numerous letters of exceptional sensitivity. For example, he wrote to General Nathaniel Banks: "In superseding you, by returning General Butler to command the Department of the Gulf, I have trusted that you will not understand me as being even indifferent to your feelings and your honor. I would be as careful of yours as of my own." The same day, he wrote to Secretary of War Stanton that the change of command at New Orleans "must be so managed as to not wrong, or wound the feelings of General Banks." Lincoln did not treat subordinates as instruments of his masterful will; he followed the dictates of an ethic of care and paid heed to their individual needs.[54]

Such sensitivity was rooted in empathy. Lincoln knew what it felt like to have wounded feelings. As he wrote to James Hackett, "I have endured a great deal of ridicule without much malice; and have received a great deal of kindness, not quite free from ridicule." But sensitivity was also an obligation for the kind of democratic leader that Lincoln sought to be. By avoiding quarrels, by shunning resentments, by paying attention to feelings, Lincoln could approach others with respect for their talents, their services, and, above all, their dignity. In emphasizing mutual dignity, he could lessen the inherent distance between leader and subordinate. This egalitarian manner saved him from guarded counsels and sycophantic praise and made possible a dialogue between leader and subordinates.[55]

Sensitivity to others' feelings and respect for their dignity was, Lincoln recognized, a potential source of political advantage. His manner was well designed to make friends of former opponents. After the Republican convention of 1860, he wooed the important German American politician Carl Schurz: "I beg you to be assured that your having supported Governor Seward in preference to myself in the convention, is not even remembered by me for any practical purpose, or the slightest unpleasant feeling. I go not back of the convention, to make distinctions among its members." Similarly, he was adept at mediating between conflicting factions both in the Republican party and in the Union cause. Kindness, forgiveness, and sensitivity did not detract from Lincoln's effectiveness as president. While their feminine quality led some contemporaries to underrate his political skill, they were central to his political prowess as well as to his democratic convictions.[56]

The democratic manner that Lincoln cultivated was not, however, always appropriate. When he attempted to instruct others to adopt this manner, he sometimes lost touch with the context in which such conduct was feasible. An interesting case in point was his advice to Governor Thomas Fletcher of Missouri in February 1865, about how to halt continued violence by Missourians still bitterly suspicious of one another after their earlier border warfare.

> Let neighborhood meetings be everywhere called and held, of all entertaining a sincere purpose for mutual security in the future. . . . Let all such meet and waiving all else pledge each to cease harassing others and to make common cause against whomever persists in making, aiding, or encouraging further disturbance. . . . At such meetings old friendships will cross the memory; and honor and Christian Charity will come in to help.[57]

In extending his "quarrel not" philosophy as practical advice to feuding Missourians, Lincoln asserted that mutual promises, friendship, and charity could bring an end to violence without the need for military repression of malefactors. Governor Fletcher agreed to try the president's plan, but he was rightly skeptical. He told Lincoln that

> the destruction of life and property in every part of Missouri which has been going on for nearly four years and which is yet going on, is not the result of the immediate action of men who can be reached by any amicable propositions. The State being infested with thousands of outlaws who are naturally and practically "robbers" and "cut-throats," no good man desires to reach any understanding with them.

The brutal passions and deeds of a border war did not create a political climate in which Lincoln's kind of democratic relationships could work. Lincoln did not face up to the limits of forgiveness and kindness in a situation that foreshadowed the terrors that the Ku Klux Klan would propagate in the postwar South.[58]

If Lincoln misjudged this particular situation, his personal code of democratic behavior was still applicable in many other instances. One of the more important of these instances was his relationship with the most militant faction in his own party, the "radical Republicans." An older historical view depicted this relationship as fiercely antagonistic, with a vindictive coterie of "Jacobins" in Congress battering away at a beleaguered president. The newer view emphasizes a fruitful if often tense collaboration between Lincoln and the radicals. Although this view sometimes exaggerates the coincidence of their aims, the case for a collaborative relationship between Lincoln and the radicals appears basically sound. Given the vehemence with which many of the radicals attacked Lincoln, the way he conducted his side of the relationship is all the more striking. It was, above all, his "quarrel not" philosophy, his ability to look beyond contention and resentment to more important ends, that made collaboration possible. Lincoln's attitude toward radical attacks was vividly expressed in a remark he made to John Hay about the radical faction in Missouri: "They are nearer to me than the other side, in thought and sentiment, though bitterly hostile personally. They are utterly lawless—the unhandiest devils in the world to deal with—but after all their faces are set Zionwards."[59]

Considerations of principle, along with calculations of politics, impelled Lincoln to work with the radicals; his masculine/feminine temperament allowed that work to continue amid storms of abuse. Lincoln opened himself fully to the radicals' arguments, meeting frequently with radical delegations, even attending antislavery lectures at the Smithsonian Institution. He cultivated a valuable friendship with one of the leading radicals, Senator Charles Sumner. And he was careful not to speak ill of them in public, no matter what they said about him.

While Lincoln worked with the radical Republicans and respected their quest for Zion, they remained, in his eyes, a faction. He viewed himself as standing apart from all factions. Thus, he wrote to a radical correspondent who had asked him to dismiss the conservative general in chief, Henry Halleck: "I am compelled to take a more impartial and unprejudiced view of things." Blunting the demands of a visiting delegation of Missouri and Kansas radicals, he told them: "It is my duty to hear all; but at last, I must, within my sphere, judge what to do, and what to forbear." Lincoln skillfully used radical pressure to win conservative acquiescence for forceful moves; but he also used conservative pressure to temper radical zeal and justify his cautious approach. Influenced though he was by radical arguments and pressures—traveling, like them, in the direction of Zion—he nonetheless moved in his own distinctive fashion to achieve ends that he hoped would be "impartial and unprejudiced."[60]

Lincoln's gentleness and kindness were not the marks of an effusive character. He could be aloof, brooding, mysterious. But out of the depths of his personality and response to experience he developed a masculine/feminine temperament that governed his personal relationships. His fusion of an ethic of rights and an ethic of care was a matter of political conviction as well as temperament. As a democratic leader, Lincoln believed that he must not only represent and educate the people as a collectivity but also care for the dignity and needs of the individual.

The Power of the Presidency

A democratic leader in high office must do more than represent, educate, and care for the people. He/she must come to terms with the exercise of power—and its fascination. The logic of power can easily become a substitute for the understanding of democratic leadership. Lincoln faced these issues under extraordinary circumstances: his presidency was marked by unprecedented assertions of executive power, yet he resisted the personal—and undemocratic—intoxication of power.[61]

The Lincoln who stretched presidential powers during the Civil War had once been a young Whig who vigorously denounced the practices of the strong Jacksonian executive. In his attacks on Polk's Mexican policy, Lincoln condemned presidential deception and war making in language that well served critics of the Vietnam War. He was equally severe on presidential assertions in the domestic sphere. In 1848 he wrote: "Were I president, I should desire the legislation of the country to rest with Congress, uninfluenced by the executive in its origin or progress, and undisturbed by the veto unless in very special and clear cases."[62]

Although Lincoln shared the Whig mistrust of executive power, he was an astute student of public opinion and could perceive the appeal of executive strength. When President Taylor turned over patronage appointments to his cabinet secretaries, Lincoln recognized that Whig doctrine here was inconsistent with public expectations. He was willing, therefore, to modify the doctrine, even if it meant borrowing from an old adversary:

> The appointments need be no better than they have been, but the public must be brought to understand, that they are the *President's* appointments. He must occasionally say, or seem to say, "by the Eternal," "I take the responsibility." These phrases were the "Samson's locks" of General Jackson, and we dare not disregard the lessons of experience.[63]

Thus, Lincoln saw value in the image of executive strength. But these words barely hint at the extent to which he would be willing to claim power for the presidency during a crisis that threatened the existence of the nation. In his first inaugural address, he warned the secessionists: "*You* have no oath registered in Heaven to destroy the government, while *I* shall have the most solemn one to 'preserve, protect, and defend' it." Lincoln repeatedly cited his oath as the basis for his position that the executive had a special duty and role to save the Union. In pursuance of that duty, Lincoln would venture into territory that no previous president had entered. "It became necessary for me," he told Congress in 1862, "to choose whether, using only the existing means, agencies, and processes which Congress had provided, I should let the government fall at once into ruin, or whether, availing myself of the broader powers conferred by the Constitution in cases of insurrection, I would make an effort to save it with all its blessings for the present age and for posterity."[64]

Employing his own interpretation of the Constitution's "broader powers," Lincoln sought unilateral control over civil liberties, military conscription, emancipation of the slaves, and the terms of reconstruction in the South. Perhaps the most sweeping—and disturbing—assertion of presidential power came in the area of individual rights. The president suspended the writ of habeas corpus, first in specific locales and then generally. His agents rounded up thousands of civilians and held them without sworn charges or, in most cases, trials. Critics hurled epithets of "dictator" and "tyrant" at Lincoln—yet the arrests were not usually political. As Mark E. Neely, Jr., has demonstrated, the majority of those seized were citizens of Confederate and border states, draft evaders, traders in contraband, and other civilians caught in the swirl of military events. To justify his constitutionally question-able acts, Lincoln put forth a doctrine of emergency power: "Are all the laws, *but one*, to go unexecuted, and the government itself go to pieces, lest that one be violated? Even in such a case, would not the official oath be broken, if the government should be overthrown, when it was believed that disregarding the single law, would tend to preserve it?"[65]

Much can be said in defense of Lincoln's abridgment of civil liber-ties. The internal threat was more severe than the threats invoked by later wartime presidents to justify their policies of repression. No pop-ulation group was singled out for repressive treatment, unlike Woodrow Wilson's prosecutions of radicals in World War I and Franklin Roosevelt's internment of Japanese Americans in World War II. Conscientious efforts were made to distinguish dissent from dis-loyal action; as a consequence, Clinton Rossiter has observed, "free-dom of speech and press flourished almost unchecked, and no leader of a country at war ever received such shocking and vituperative treat-ment from prominent citizens and journals alike as did Abraham Lin-coln."[66]

Lincoln's policy of suspension of the writ of habeas corpus and martial law did not aim at political advantage or permanent aggran-dizement of the executive. Still, it remains, in the words of a sympa-thetic J. G. Randall, "unfortunate" and "too expansive." It was a policy whose limits were murky and whose depredations of due process of law were extensive. It was, too, a precedent for later presidents, all the more dangerous because it was sanctioned by the example of the revered Lincoln.[67]

The young Whig critic of the presidency became the most powerful president in the first century of American constitutional government. Yet, as David Donald has established in a seminal essay, Lincoln re-mained in important respects a "Whig in the White House." Donald shows convincingly that Lincoln had little influence over Congress, paid scant attention to major domestic legislation not directly tied to the war effort, and gave free rein to most of his cabinet members over the business of their own departments. Lincoln's assertions of un-precedented "war powers" were, Donald suggests, based upon the im-perative demands of "necessity"; his relative passivity in other facets of the presidency reflected the continuing hold of Whig doctrine over his thinking.[68]

As a "Whig in the White House," Lincoln rejected the Jacksonian equation of presidential power with democratic action. He did not view the president as the rightfully dominant actor in the normal political process or as a steward of the people, uniquely situated to know and carry out the people's needs. Lincoln seized enormous power to cope with an enormous threat to the Union he had promised to preserve; but he regarded that power as abnormal and transient. "The Executive Power itself," he said in his 1864 annual message to Congress, "would be greatly diminished by the cessation of actual war."[69]

The clearest expression of Lincoln's understanding of his own presidency came in a conversation with three visiting leaders from Kentucky in the spring of 1864. In his infrequent public addresses during the Civil War, Lincoln generally adopted an impersonal tone. Meeting with the three Kentuckians, however, he seemed to want to speak about himself. He asked them, he later told Orville Browning, if "he could make a little speech to them" about his course of conduct in the presidency. Subsequently, at the request of one of them, he wrote his remarks down.[70]

Lincoln's "little speech" went through the history of his steps toward the Emancipation Proclamation and justified its legality. More important for present purposes, he elaborated upon the distinction between presidential duty and presidential will. "I am naturally antislavery. If slavery is not wrong, nothing is wrong. I can not remember when I did not so think and feel. And yet I have never understood that the Presidency conferred upon me an unrestricted right to act officially upon this judgment and feeling." The argument that Lincoln had to act upon the basis of official duty rather than antislavery feelings was a defense against radical Republican criticisms prior to the promulgation of the Emancipation Proclamation and against conservative criticisms afterward. Yet its political expedience did not mean that the argument was insincere. To Lincoln, the presidency was not a field for the exercise of personal power but a repository of binding national responsibilities.[71]

It was not merely duty that constrained Lincoln's actions as president; events, too, resisted the fulfillment of personal will. From three years of painful experience in the White House, Lincoln added a postscript to his "little speech" to emphasize the limits of presidential power and the pathos of human action:

> I add a word which was not in the verbal conversation. In telling this tale I attempt no compliment to my own sagacity. I claim not to

have controlled events, but confess plainly that events have controlled me. Now, at the end of three years' struggle the nation's condition is not what either party, or any man devised, or expected.
God alone can claim it.[72]

Lincoln escaped the illusion that has haunted the modern presidency—that the president is an incarnation of American democracy,
with a mandate from the people to control events at home and abroad
in its sacred name. His view of presidential leadership was more modest, more in keeping with a dialogic conception of democracy. He assumed vast presidential powers as emergency instruments, but their
justification, in his eyes, derived from necessity and disappeared with
the termination of war. Lincoln was a powerful president but not a
willful one. He opened up dangerous terrain for his successors, but he
also demonstrated that the arrogance of power in the presidency was
not inevitable.

"The Just and Generous and Prosperous System"

Lincoln's conception of democracy was, of course, economic and social as well as political. His vision in these areas, however, was more
limited than his political understanding. A brief consideration of three
issues—economic opportunity, racial equality, and expansionism—
underscores some of the tensions between Lincoln's democratic leadership and his vision of American society.

As a young, aspiring politician, Lincoln sought to build his career
largely around economic issues. He was an ardent Whig in economic
matters, favoring a vigorous government role in stimulating economic
development. His advocacy of banks, tariffs, and internal improvements seemed to link him to the political economy of Alexander
Hamilton. But this appearance was deceptive. Lincoln's version of
economic development placed its hopes on the energies of small entrepreneurs rather than the ambitions and interests of large capitalists. He could be a sharp critic of economic power. "These capitalists,"
he told the Illinois legislature in a speech defending the state bank,
"generally act harmoniously, and in concert, to fleece the people."[73]

Lincoln's allegiances were to Jefferson and not to Hamilton. But
his economic vision departed as much from Jefferson as from Hamilton. He was interested less in the sturdy virtues of the husbandman
than in the potential for a more scientific farming, and in agriculture
itself less than in the development of a commercial and industrial

economy. Lincoln's Illinois was not a prairie version of Jefferson's agrarian Virginia. As Don Fehrenbacher has observed, "By 1860 almost half of those gainfully employed [in Illinois] were engaged in pursuits other than farming." A long association, as an attorney, with the railroads in Illinois symbolized Lincoln's own involvement in this process of economic transformation.[74]

At the core of Lincoln's political economy was a commitment to democratic mobility, to what G. S. Boritt has aptly called "the right to rise." His most distinctive image of American society, repeated on numerous occasions, focused on economic mobility both as present reality and future promise:

> Many independent men everywhere in these States, a few years back in their lives, were hired laborers. The prudent, penniless beginner in the world, labors for wages awhile, saves a surplus with which to buy tools or land for himself; then labors on his own account another while, and at length hires another new beginner to help him. This is the just, and generous, and prosperous system, which opens the way to all—gives hope to all, and consequent energy, and progress, and improvement of condition to all.[75]

As these words indicate, Lincoln considered labor the key to economic advancement. Insisting that labor was both prior and superior to capital, he wanted government to champion and protect free labor. "To secure to each laborer the whole product of his labor, or as nearly as possible, is a most worthy object of any good government." His conception of labor—like that of most of the men who formed the new Republican party—was broad, encompassing middle-class entrepreneurs as well as mechanics and farmers. It rejected any notion of a permanent working class and paid little attention to an emerging industrial work force. Nevertheless, Lincoln was sympathetic to the problems of this work force; for example, he defended the right of workers to strike.[76]

Later generations of American radicals liked to quote lines from Lincoln advocating the rights of working people, but they had a difficult time making him into a prophet of class conflict. If Lincoln saw capital as derivative from labor, he nonetheless blessed the product. He told a delegation of New York workers in 1864: "Property is the fruit of labor—property is desirable—is a positive good in the world. That some should be rich, shows that others may become rich, and hence is just encouragement to industry and enterprise." In Lincoln's vision, there was a fundamental harmony of interests between economic actors, regardless of wealth or status. The "American dream" of rising in life could honestly be dreamed by all.[77]

Lincoln's conception of the American political economy, though egalitarian and humane, was also limited in vision and doomed by history. A number of observers have remarked upon his failure to recognize the emerging contours of industrialization or to grasp how a system of corporate capitalism would undercut "the right to rise." As Richard Hofstadter puts it: "Had he lived to seventy, he would have seen the generation brought up on self-help come into its own, build oppressive business corporations, and begin to close off those treasured opportunities for the little man."[78]

There was a second and more subtle flaw in Lincoln's political economy—he did not realize that the passionate affirmation of liberty as economic opportunity might gradually erode the passion for liberty as political freedom. Lincoln himself successfully combined the political and economic meanings of liberty. His own life exemplified commitment to the principles of democracy even more than to economic mobility and success. But his society was moving away from the political view of the Revolutionary age. Not only in its public discourse, but even in its favorite icons, Michael Kammen has suggested, nineteenth-century America was moving to substitute prosperity for liberty. Lincoln unwittingly endorsed this substitution through his fervent depictions of economic mobility.[79]

Turning from economics to race, we immediately find ourselves in the midst of a notorious controversy. Highlighted by iconoclastic historians, paraded by white bigots, denounced by black militants, Lincoln's racial statements from the 1850s have become some of his best-known words. Perhaps the most famous came during his fourth debate with Stephen Douglas:

> I will say then that I am not, nor ever have been in favor of bringing about in any way the social and political equality of the white and black races—that I am not nor ever have been in favor of making voters or jurors of negroes, nor of qualifying them to hold office, nor to intermarry with white people; and I will say in addition to this that there is a physical difference between the white and black races which I believe will for ever forbid the two races living together on terms of social and political equality. And inasmuch as they cannot so live, while they do remain together there must be the position of superior and inferior, and I as much as any other man am in favor of having the superior position assigned to the white race.[80]

Placed in historical context, however, these words lose their shock value. Numerous scholars have fleshed out that context by way of defending Lincoln. They have emphasized that Lincoln was harried by incessant and sometimes vulgar race-baiting from Douglas and the Democrats, before an audience whose racist sentiments he could safely assume (these sentiments were reflected in Illinois laws that denied blacks access to the ballot, the legal system, and education). In such a climate, support for full equality between the races would have been political suicide. Lincoln's statements were not designed to stir up racial antipathies; they were disclaimers whose aim was to neutralize a charged, but essentially irrelevant electoral issue. Lincoln emerges from this historical scholarship as a cautious politician rather than a callous racist. Still, he hardly appears at his most appealing.[81]

Nor does one see him at his best as a democratic leader in his advocacy of colonization schemes for freed blacks. It has been cogently argued by Don Fehrenbacher and Stephen Oates that Lincoln stressed the emigration of blacks from the United States during the months preceding the Emancipation Proclamation as a political tactic, hoping thereby to assuage white fears. Nevertheless, when he invited a delegation of free blacks to the White House and urged them to serve as pioneers for a Central American colony, he was not prepared to hear potential black objections to colonization. The meeting was, Benjamin Quarles writes, essentially a presidential "monologue," since what the president wanted "was not to find out what the Negro was thinking, but to let the Negro know what he had in mind." Again speaking the language of the cautious politician, Lincoln warned his black auditors that they could not hope to find equality with whites on American soil and that there was nothing he could do to help them overcome white prejudice. "Go where you are treated the best," he said, "and the ban is still upon you. I do not propose to discuss this, but to present it as a fact with which we have to deal. I cannot alter it if I would." On this occasion the limits of Lincoln's democratic vision in the area of race undercut his normal democratic practice; he produced a stern lecture rather than a sensitive dialogue.[82]

Those authors who have tried to absolve Lincoln completely from the inegalitarian statements of the 1850s and the colonization schemes of the early war years have a stronger case for his growth on the subject of race during the Civil War. Even as Lincoln was proposing a constitutional amendment in December 1862 to allow Congress to appropriate money for colonization, he was also arguing that if freed blacks remained in America they would not pose a threat to the interests of white labor. And as the number of freed blacks swelled, he accepted the fact that the problem of race would have to be faced by American society. He offered his support to those who welcomed the freedmen in the North, writing to the governor of Massachusetts in February 1864 that if "it really be true that Massachusetts wishes to afford a permanent home within her borders, for all, or even a large number of colored persons who will come to her, I shall be only too glad to know it." He expressed optimism for the programs under way to promote the "moral and physical elevation" of freedmen in the South, writing to Thomas Conway in March 1865: "The blessing of God and the efforts of good and faithful men will bring us to an earlier and happier consummation than the most sanguine friends of the freedmen could reasonably expect."[83]

Defending the humanity of the slave in the 1850s against the assaults of proslavery apologists, Lincoln had considered blacks as passive victims of injustice. But during the Civil War he came to recognize blacks as active and vital participants in the cause of democracy. He was particularly impressed by the contributions of black soldiers. To detractors of the Emancipation Proclamation, he pointed out that when peace came and the Union was restored,

> there will be some black men who can remember that, with silent tongue, and clenched teeth, and steady eye, and well-poised bayonet, they have helped mankind on to this great consummation; while, I fear, there will be some white ones, unable to forget that, with malignant heart, and deceitful speech, they have strove to hinder it.

Lincoln expected blacks to continue playing an important role in defending democracy after the war. In a letter to Louisiana's first free-state governor, Michael Hahn, the president suggested extending the suffrage to those blacks who were "very intelligent" or who "have fought gallantly in our ranks." "They would probably help," he prophesied, "in some trying time to come, to keep the jewel of liberty within the family of freedom." Lincoln can be credited with a growing recognition of black agency. But he never approached blacks in the same spirit of democratic mutuality that marked his relationships with whites.[84]

After all of the controversy over Lincoln's racial attitudes and actions in recent years, perhaps the best assessment remains that of Frederick Douglass, speaking at the unveiling of a freedmen's monument to Lincoln in Washington, D.C., in 1876. Douglass and Lincoln developed a warm personal relationship during the Civil War, and Douglass later remarked that "in all my interviews with Mr. Lincoln I was impressed with his entire freedom from popular prejudice against the colored race." Yet in summing up Lincoln's relationship with blacks in his 1876 oration, he looked beyond personal warmth to political commitment and reached a more complex judgment:

> Abraham Lincoln was not, in the fullest sense of the word, either our man or our model. In his interests, in his associations, in his habits of thought, and in his prejudices, he was a white man. He was preeminently the white man's President, entirely devoted to the welfare of white men. He was ready and willing at any time during the first years of his administration to deny, postpone, and sacrifice the rights of humanity in the colored people to promote the welfare of the white people of this country.[85]

This "white man's President" had nonetheless become, Douglass recognized, "the man of our redemption." Indeed, the black leader found a powerful historical irony in Lincoln's racial stance: had Lincoln been a more passionate friend of blacks, he would have been a less effective emancipator. Douglass thus praised Lincoln's statesmanship:

> Had he put the abolition of slavery before the salvation of the Union, he would have inevitably driven from him a powerful class of the American people and rendered resistance to rebellion impossible. Viewed from the genuine abolition ground, Mr. Lincoln seemed tardy, cold, dull, and indifferent; but measuring him by the sentiment of his country, a sentiment he was bound as a statesman to consult, he was swift, zealous, radical, and determined.[86]

Douglass's assessment captures not only the ambivalent nature of Lincoln's racial progress but also the central tension in his democratic leadership. Closeness to the people, sensitivity to the conventional sentiments of the majority, circumspection in political innovations— all these made Lincoln an effective leader who could bring off the most fundamental reform in American history. The same qualities, however, often left him unwilling to push very far in the direction of the democratic ends he professed. The colonization advocate who would not challenge the "fact" of a "ban" upon black people was, in that moment at least, elevating popular prejudice over democratic responsibility. In his second inaugural address, Lincoln expressed his final—and finest—understanding of democratic responsibility. Whether he would have fulfilled that understanding in dealing with the postwar problems of the newly freed blacks is a question that history cannot answer.

In at least one earlier case, Lincoln had shown himself up to the requirements of his democratic faith. During the 1840s and 1850s he was an articulate critic of American expansionism. His stance, while reflective of Whig doctrine, was not without political cost; a decade after his attack on Polk's Mexican adventure, Stephen Douglas was still blasting Lincoln for "taking the side of the common enemy against his own country." Yet Lincoln would not acquiesce to imperialist passions as he did to racist sentiments; in this area, far more than in the area of race, he respected the logic of democracy too much to accept its inversion.[87]

Lincoln's version of American development stressed internal growth over territorial expansion. In the 1848 presidential campaign, he defined "all real Whigs" as "those who wished to keep up the character of the Union; who did not believe in enlarging our field, but in keeping our fences where they are and cultivating our present possession, making it a garden, improving the morals and education of the people; devoting the administration to this purpose." Lincoln saw the lure of Manifest Destiny as a diversion from the important economic, political, and moral issues that ought to concern the American people.[88]

He also recognized the moral corruption that threatened an American democracy bent upon expansion. When Lincoln read John M. Peck's defense of Polk's conduct, based purportedly upon the facts concerning the beginning of the Mexican War, he wrote to the Illinois journalist that some facts had been omitted from his argument. "It is a fact," Lincoln noted, "that the United States Army, in marching to the Rio Grande, marched into a peaceful Mexican settlement, and frightened the inhabitants away from their homes and their growing crops. It is a fact, that Fort Brown, opposite Matamoras, was built by that army, within a Mexican cotton-field." Lincoln understood the kind of expansionist mentality that conveniently ignored such facts, and he lamented it in a comment that speaks to much of subsequent American history:

> Possibly you consider those acts too small for notice. Would you venture to so consider them, had they been committed by any nation on earth, against the humblest of our people? I know you would not. Then I ask, is the precept "Whatsoever ye would that men should do to you, do ye even so to them" obsolete?—of no force?—of no application?[89]

The moral hypocrisy of an American expansionism pursued under the banner of democracy was exacerbated by the self-aggrandizing motives that Lincoln detected in its champions. He perceived that behind all the talk about supporting liberty abroad lay calculations of economic advantage. Lincoln rose to sarcastic heights in 1859 to characterize the expansionist figure of the Young America movement (with which Stephen Douglas was associated):

> He is a great friend of humanity; and his desire for land is not selfish, but merely an impulse to extend the area of freedom. He is very anxious to fight for the liberation of enslaved nations and colonies, provided, always, they *have* land, and have *not* any liking for his interference. As to those who have no land, and would be glad of help from any quarter, he considers *they* can afford to wait a few hundred years longer.

If Lincoln's paeans to individual mobility inadvertently shifted democratic understanding too far in the direction of an economic definition, if his response to the American racial dilemma was too constrained by the politician's natural caution, his penetrating assaults on the doctrines of expansion and empire nevertheless brought democratic vision and democratic leadership into an admirable unity.[90]

Conclusion

Abraham Lincoln demonstrated how powerful ambition could be reconciled with—and serve—democratic purposes. Lincoln was the most striking confirmation in American history of John Adams's assertions about the political importance of the "passion for distinction." But where Adams saw that passion as an aristocratic attribute, Lincoln democratized it. He embodied the potential for great political action and enduring fame that a democracy offered to the most "common" of individuals. He also embodied the democratic disciplining of ambition, as he channeled his passion into the service of democratic causes and deliberately humbled himself to ward off the temptations of public acclaim. Lincoln did not equate democracy with altruism or self-sacrifice (although he could project himself into a martyr's role); rather, he conceived of democracy as a vehicle for fusing personal and public good.

Lincoln showed, too, how a powerful, even superior person could nonetheless open himself to others, could learn as well as teach, could nurture as well as direct. If his hard-won understanding provided him with a more profound perspective than his fellow citizens had, he was ready to share that understanding in language that aimed to be accessible without violating the integrity of its message. In his relationship with the public, his dealings with individuals, his comprehension and uses of power, Lincoln turned democratic theory into personal practice.

Eschewing the masculine view of leadership as will and mastery, Lincoln achieved a masculine/feminine fusion that has been too little understood. He recognized that the democratic dignity of citizens requires nurturance and that the democratic perspective of leaders requires an openness to citizens' views and a sensitivity to their needs. His approach avoided paternalism—except in the case of blacks—because he began from the premise of mutuality, always regarding ordinary citizens as capable of everything that he himself had achieved. Lincoln's self-assertion was balanced by his regard for others; he overcame much of the inherent distance between leaders and followers by identifying himself with those followers. Especially in his final years, he demonstrated how democratic leadership could combine an abstract set of principles—an ethic of rights—with a concrete and empathic ethic of care.

Lincoln also demonstrated how an ethic of care could be a practical politics. The side of him that I have characterized as feminine did not undercut his masculine political skills, did not weaken him as a political leader. Lincoln's career reveals the inadequacy of hard-boiled, or realist, perspectives that equate leadership with power, dominance, and manipulation. For he gained political support through his kindness and political insight through the mutuality of democratic relationships. He was strong as a democratic leader because he was both masculine and feminine.

Yet Lincoln could not escape some of the characteristic tensions of democratic leadership. The vision of society that he articulated sometimes fell short of the democratic practices to which he adhered; this was most painfully apparent in the area of race. Conventional ideas and electoral caution limited his democratic reach even as they enhanced his short-term political effectiveness. Lincoln has often been dubbed a pragmatist, and in his flexibility toward policy and his penchant for practical political maneuvering he merits the label. But he was also a man who professed a deep democratic faith. His pragmatism proved to be as much a limitation upon the fulfillment of that faith as an instrument for its realization.[91]

Americans' reverence for Lincoln has made him into a favorite source of authority for subsequent political leaders. Yet he has seldom been imitated for his most democratic qualities. Recent presidents have turned to him not to find an exemplar of gentleness or nurturance but in search of precedents for unilateral assertions of presidential power and repressive attacks on civil liberties. The White House staffs of Richard Nixon and Ronald Reagan tracked down Lincoln quotations as part of an effort to justify antidemocratic programs.[92]

Lincoln deserves much of the reverence that he has received from Americans. But reverence has too often led to mythologizing. We do better not to revere Lincoln but to understand him and to consider his relevance as an image and as a model. He does not answer all the questions that need to be raised about democratic leadership in America. But of all those figures who have labored and risen to positions of power within the American political mainstream, Lincoln remains the best model Americans have of democratic leadership.

4

Elizabeth Cady Stanton

Dissenting Leadership and Feminist Vision

ABRAHAM LINCOLN'S MODEL OF DEMOCRATIC LEADERSHIP WAS NOT AN option for all American citizens during his lifetime. For a group that was denied the fundamental rights of citizenship and was excluded from participation in public life, a different model was required: dissenting leadership. The suffering, the passion, and the vision that fuel democratic dissent are all readily apparent in the feminist leadership of Elizabeth Cady Stanton.

Stanton, the boldest and most brilliant leader of the feminist movement in nineteenth-century America, knew firsthand the cost of women's restricted place in the Republic. Particularly at moments of national crisis, she experienced her own domestic confinement, in what American culture proclaimed was "woman's sphere," as a mark of shame. One such moment came late in 1859, when she was driven to the edge of despair by the execution of John Brown and the consequent mental breakdown of Gerrit Smith, Brown's backer and Stanton's cousin, coupled with the death of Stanton's beloved father. In a letter to her closest friend and coworker, Susan B. Anthony, Stanton poignantly evoked the powerlessness that was women's common lot in the American republic:

> The death of my father, the worse than death of my dear Cousin Gerrit, the martyrdom of that grand and glorious John Brown—all this conspires to make me regret more than ever my dwarfed womanhood. In times like these, everyone should do the work of a full-grown man. When I pass the gate of the celestial city and good Peter

asks me where I would sit, I shall say, "Anywhere, so that I am neither a negro nor a woman. Confer on me, good angel, the glory of
white manhood so that henceforth, sitting or standing, rising up or
lying down, I may enjoy the most unlimited freedom."[1]

But Stanton overcame this "regret" and rose far above "dwarfed
womanhood." Making herself the voice of a group excluded from public life, she became the founding mother of feminist politics in America. At the first women's rights convention in the United States, in her
hometown of Seneca Falls, New York, she turned her own experience
of domestic confinement into a metaphor for women's lack of freedom and adopted a republican idiom that simultaneously subverted
and fulfilled traditional American values. Stanton went on to become
a militant spokeswoman for a broadening vision of equality for her
sex. Her commitment to women sometimes led her to devalue other
excluded groups, as was evidenced in the bitter debates of the Reconstruction years over the respective claims of freed black males and
white females. But her devotion to the maximum freedom for women
(and men), expressed in her richly complex public persona as much as
in her speeches and writings, unified an extraordinarily long and creative career as a dissenting leader.

Elizabeth Cady Stanton is the first exemplar of dissenting leadership presented in this book: later chapters will treat Eugene V. Debs
and Martin Luther King, Jr. The brand of dissenting leadership that
these three shared has been committed to the furtherance of American democratic values but has acted on that commitment with a style
and vision very much at odds with the kind of democratic leadership
exemplified by an Abraham Lincoln. Where leaders such as Lincoln
accept and defend the main features of the existing regime, dissenting
leaders pose fundamental challenges to the status quo. They may
ground their dissent in ancestral American values, but their vision of
the political good requires transformation more than preservation.
Dissenting leaders can also be differentiated from mainstream democratic leaders on the basis of their attitude toward office and power.
Their goal is not to win a high place for themselves within the existing
regime but to alter their followers' understanding, so that those followers will demand a higher conception of equality and democracy
for themselves.

Both Richard Hofstadter and Garry Wills have suggested that progressive change in America often rests upon a division of labor between dissenting leaders and democratic politicians. The dissenting
leaders ("agitators" for Hofstadter, "prophets" to Wills) scorn the
favor of the majority and the prospect of immediate success and in-

stead pursue daunting transformations of popular understanding. If their efforts bear fruit and unsettle the existing regime, the prudent politicians will eventually respond and craft moderate statutory versions of the dissenters' objectives. Hofstadter and Wills see the two kinds of leadership as antithetical in nature, yet—to the good fortune of the American republic—symbiotic on a higher plane. In the words of Wills: "The politicians maintain our country. Keep it running, make fine adjustments, conserve and react—'save' it in that sense. The prophets make it worth saving."[2]

Although the antithesis drawn by Hofstadter and Wills between dissenting leaders and politicians is illuminating, the division of labor they propound may be too neat. It locks dissenting leaders and politicians into rigid and narrow roles. Dissenting leaders are absolved from developing a concern for political effectiveness and a sense of responsibility for the consequences of their actions. Politicians are absolved from the need to hold any principles whatsoever or to care about the impact of their own acts and words on public consciousness. The dissenting leader and the politician are indeed different types, but each can draw insights from the other. The dissenting leader can learn from the politician about political motives and skills. The politician can learn from the dissenting leader about the responsibilities of democratic education and the power of democratic vision. In the latter case, one of the most neglected sources of insight has been the feminist leadership of Elizabeth Cady Stanton.[3]

The Founding Mother

The women's rights convention at Seneca Falls in 1848 founded a women's movement in America. It also launched the public career of the driving force behind this event: Elizabeth Cady Stanton. Like the more familiar foundings at Philadelphia in 1776 and 1787, the one at Seneca Falls in 1848 shaped a new form of public discourse in America. Most of the essential themes of American feminism were expressed there: the outrage of women's subjugation, the connection between personal discontent and political issues, the development of a distinctive women's voice, the creation of a powerful sense of sisterhood. In the articulation—and agitation—of these themes, Elizabeth Cady Stanton forged a new identity for herself and came to exemplify the possibility of a new identity for women in America.

The Seneca Falls Convention proclaimed a rebellion against a dominant cultural convention of the early nineteenth century in America:

separate spheres for men and women. Under the doctrine of separate spheres, the world of business and politics was the domain of men, while women's place was in the home. Contemporary students of women's history have found that nineteenth-century domesticity had numerous and sometimes surprising ramifications for women. Domesticity provided a platform upon which some women launched movements for moral reform and temperance. It generated a female subculture marked by friendships of an intensity seldom found in the sphere of male activities. But domesticity could also be experienced as confinement, as a denial of larger freedoms. Nancy Cott observes that in the parlance of the early nineteenth century, "'home' became synonymous with 'retirement' or 'retreat' from the world at large." It was this conception of domesticity that provoked Elizabeth Cady Stanton to become a dissenting leader.[4]

Stanton's life prior to the convention at Seneca Falls was marked by a dialectic between domesticity and rebellion. She was born in 1815 in Johnstown, New York. Her mother was a strong woman, but it was Elizabeth's father, a judge and wealthy landowner, who exercised the decisive influence on her childhood. When her father became distraught over the death of his only son, Elizabeth, then aged ten, resolved to take her brother's place and fulfill her father's shattered ambitions. She learned to ride on horseback, studied Greek, and became a star student at the local academy. But as much as her father loved her and took pride in her accomplishments, he set strict limits to how far she could breach the proprieties of a "woman's sphere." When the male classmates that she had bested in school competitions went off to college, he forbade her to go. Many years later, in one of her most popular lectures, "Our Young Girls," Elizabeth Cady Stanton would tell a sad tale of the "proud girl" who, rejecting "these invidious distinctions" between the sexes and feeling herself to be "the peer of any boy she knows," would find everything conspiring to defeat her aspirations. Perhaps remembering her own defeat, she would conclude the tale by asking: "But what can one brave girl do against the world?"[5]

If Elizabeth's father insisted that her life follow a conventional path of marriage and domesticity, he could not prevent her from following that path into unconventional circles. Making frequent visits to the Peterboro home of her older cousin, Gerrit Smith, a prominent antislavery leader, she came into contact with numerous abolitionists and other reformers who congregated under the hospitable Smith's roof. Among these was Henry Stanton, a romantic young abolitionist agitator, whom she married in 1840. Elizabeth Cady Stanton was thus drawn into the most radical and egalitarian network in antebellum

America. Like a number of other women in this network, she responded passionately to its language of equality, finding in the arguments directed toward emancipating the slave a potent vocabulary for women as well. Still, her husband was the public actor, and she was his domestic counterpart. On their honeymoon trip to England, to attend the World Anti-Slavery Convention, he chided her for bridling in public at offensive male remarks. The agitator who stirred up public opinion expected his wife to be demure.[6]

In 1844 the Stantons settled in Boston, the capital of political and intellectual reform. For Elizabeth, domestic life in Boston was pleasurable, balanced as it was by intellectual and social stimulation. She threw her enormous energies and talents into housekeeping and motherhood (she had two small children at the time) and imagined the home as an arena for female power. But when the family moved a few years later to the small town of Seneca Falls in the Finger Lakes region of New York, domesticity lost its savor. In her autobiography, *Eighty Years and More,* Stanton recalled the impact of Seneca Falls: "Up to this time life had glided by with comparative ease, but now the real struggle was upon me. My duties were too numerous and varied, and none sufficiently exhilarating or intellectual to bring into play my higher faculties. I suffered with mental hunger, which, like an empty stomach, is very depressing." In a letter written during these years to her cousin, Elizabeth Smith Miller, she focused less on her "mental hunger" than on the grueling tasks that comprised the reality of "woman's sphere": "I am desperate sick of working and attending to the fleshly needs."[7]

The dialectic between domesticity and rebellion in Stanton's life was about to move to a higher plane. With her rebellious temperament and her grounding in reform movements, Stanton was not the type to succumb to isolation and depression or to accept domesticity as defeat. Instead, she began to see her own confinement in the home as representative, her own hunger for a larger life as a metaphor for women's unfulfilled needs:

The general discontent I felt with woman's portion as wife, mother, housekeeper, physician, and spiritual guide, the chaotic conditions into which everything fell without her constant supervision, and the wearied, anxious look of the majority of women impressed me with a strong feeling that some active measures should be taken to remedy the wrongs of society in general, and of women in particular.

The slogan of the modern women's movement—"the personal is political"—would have come as no surprise to Elizabeth Cady Stanton.

From her personal discontent with domesticity, she derived a fundamental insight into the oppression confronting all women, oppression that needed to be combated through political action. Stanton had ample amounts of the frustration, passion, and vision necessary for the founding of a feminist politics in America. All she lacked was a catalyst.[8]

That catalyst was Lucretia Mott. Stanton had become friendly with Mott, a pioneer woman abolitionist and feminist, at the international antislavery gathering in 1840. The two had been outraged by the overwhelming majority vote at this gathering to exclude women as delegates and had talked of convening a meeting to discuss women's rights as soon as they returned to America. Although this plan was not carried out, Stanton remained in touch with Mott, whom she came to look upon as her mentor and role model. In the summer of 1848 Mott visited Waterloo, a town near Seneca Falls. Meeting there with her and three other women on July 13, 1848, Stanton knew that at last she had a sympathetic audience: "I poured out, that day, the torrent of my long-accumulating discontent, with such vehemence and indignation that I stirred myself, as well as the rest of the party, to do and dare anything. . . . [W]e decided, then and there, to call a 'Woman's Rights Convention.'"[9]

Lacking a model of feminist political discourse for their call to action, the five women were driven to peruse "various masculine productions." But their choice of a male discourse to adapt to their purposes was brilliant. The Declaration of Sentiments that Stanton drafted for the convention transformed the American Declaration of Independence into a women's declaration of independence. Retaining most of the language of the Declaration's opening paragraphs, Stanton altered several of the most powerful phrases to make the women's case. "All men and women," she wrote, "are created equal." But men had long trampled on women's equality: "The history of mankind is a history of repeated injuries and usurpations on the part of man toward woman, having in direct object the establishment of an absolute tyranny over her." Following this preamble with eighteen grievances, the same number as the colonists had advanced, Stanton compiled a revolutionary indictment of men's oppression of women.[10]

Although the Declaration of Sentiments was Stanton's first venture into political theory and rhetoric, it already contained the marks of her distinctive feminist style. Stanton took a sanctified American idiom and infused it with a radical message not contemplated by its authors. She took the most democratic and liberating American values and turned them against a dominant culture that claimed to uphold them. The Declaration of Independence was genuinely sacred to

Stanton, who remained throughout her life a passionate believer in republicanism. At Seneca Falls she discovered the subversive possibilities of republicanism.

On July 19, 1848, only six days after Stanton had poured out her personal discontents, the first women's rights convention began. Despite the five women's fears, the hastily organized convention was well attended. Several hundred women and several dozen men came from a radius of fifty miles to the small Wesleyan chapel at Seneca Falls to hear Stanton and her coadjutors proclaim a new struggle for female equality. The response of the audience was favorable; at the conclusion of the convention, sixty-eight women and thirty-two men signed the Declaration of Principles that Stanton had prepared.[11]

Stanton's speech at the convention refuted every ground—physical, intellectual, moral—for men's self-proclaimed superiority over women. This speech was more than a brief for women's equality, however; it was also a declaration of vocation. Propelling herself from domesticity to public action in a single leap, Stanton made herself into a political voice for her sex. In the opening lines of her speech, she set out the fundamental task of the dissenting leader in the cause of women:

> I should feel exceedingly diffident to appear before you at this time, having never before spoken in public, were I not nerved by a sense of right and duty, did I not feel the time had fully come for the question of woman's wrongs to be laid before the public, did I not believe that woman herself must do this work; for woman alone can understand the height, the depth, the length, and the breadth of her own degradation. Man cannot speak for her.[12]

That women must speak for themselves, that they must find their own public voice, was for Stanton the key to their struggle. Men had monopolized public speech up to now and had used their monopoly to define women into subservience. The Declaration of Sentiments that Stanton wrote for the convention spelled out the consequences of man's power over public discourse:

> He has created a false public sentiment by giving to the world a different code of morals for men and women, by which moral delinquencies which exclude women from society, are not only tolerated, but deemed of little account in men.
>
> He has usurped the prerogative of Jehovah himself, claiming it as his right to assign for her a sphere of action, when that belongs to her conscience and to her God.

He has endeavored, in every way that he could, to destroy her
confidence in her own powers, to lessen her self-respect, and to
make her willing to lead a dependent and abject life.[13]

Relating the aftermath of the Seneca Falls Convention in *History of
Woman Suffrage*, written in the 1880s, Stanton employed a striking
trope to dramatize women's experience of finding their public voice.
"Those who took part in the Convention at Seneca Falls," she wrote,
discovered that "the gift of tongues had been vouchsafed to them." In
finding their voice, these women found their self-esteem, their political talent, their life's mission. Decades later, the experience still
seemed miraculous.[14]

But the miracle did not strike every woman at once. In her description of the Rochester convention that carried on the work begun at
Seneca Falls, Stanton noted the difficulties presented by women's
"feeble voices and timid manners." Helping—or prodding—other
women to find their voices became one of Stanton's central tasks as a
feminist leader. As she wrote to an Ohio women's rights convention in
1850: "It needs no argument to teach woman that she is interested in
the laws which govern her. Suffering has taught her this already. It is
important now that a change is proposed, that she speak, and loudly
too."[15]

Stanton insisted that the voice of a woman also be the voice of a republican citizen. It was through her efforts that suffrage for women
became a demand of the Seneca Falls Convention. Lucretia Mott did
not want to include the enfranchisement of women among the proposed resolutions, fearing that it would make the convention "look
ridiculous." Henry Stanton cautioned his wife in similar language.
But Elizabeth Cady Stanton swept aside these cautions and fought for
a suffrage plank: "*Resolved,* That it is the duty of the women of this
country to secure to themselves their sacred right to the elective franchise." With the support of Frederick Douglass, she carried this
plank—the only one not to receive unanimous approval—by a small
majority.[16]

Because few of the hopes that Stanton and other pioneer feminists
entertained for women's suffrage as an instrument for political transformation were to be realized in the twentieth century, it has been
common for later observers to criticize their focus on suffrage as misguided or naïve. Ellen Dubois has countered this criticism by pointing
to the radical meaning of women's suffrage in the context of a culture
divided into separate spheres. She argues: "By demanding a permanent, public role for all women, suffragists began to demolish the absolute, sexually defined barrier marking the public world of men off

from the private world of women." Further, she writes, women's demand for a public role "allowed them to project a vision of female experience and action that went beyond the family and the subordination of women which the family upheld." For Elizabeth Cady Stanton in particular, suffrage was always more than a liberal or legal reform aimed at giving equal protection to women's interests. It was the prerequisite to women's freedom and dignity, the basis upon which woman could "stand on an even pedestal with man [and] look him in the face as an equal."[17]

With the Seneca Falls founding of 1848, Elizabeth Cady Stanton began a public career that would span more than half a century. But before she could fully come into her own as a dissenting feminist leader, she would have to surmount a series of formidable obstacles. The first of these was the ridicule of men. In her speech at the convention, Stanton had predicted that the women's protest would raise a storm. But she and her colleagues were unprepared for the contemptuous sarcasm that would greet their handiwork. Newspapers throughout the nation vied in lampooning the Seneca Falls declaration and resolutions. A Lowell, Massachusetts, paper complained that if the women wished to be consistent, they should have adopted a resolution obliging men

> to wash dishes, scour up, be put to the tub, handle the broom, darn stockings, patch breeches, scold the servants, dress in the latest fashion, wear trinkets, look beautiful, and be as fascinating as those blessed morsels of humanity whom God gave to preserve that rough animal man, in something like a reasonable civilization.

A Philadelphia newspaper was less fanciful and more blunt: "A woman is a nobody. A wife is everything. A pretty girl is equal to ten thousand men, and a mother is, next to God, all powerful."[18]

Stanton soon learned to counter or ignore male ridicule. A more disturbing obstacle than the sarcasm of men was the silence of women. The initial constituency for a women's rights movement was largely confined to the ranks of abolitionists. Pioneer feminists were almost all Anglo-Saxon and middle class. The great majority of American women, whatever their class, did not flock to the banners that had been unfurled at Seneca Falls in 1848. Some agreed with the new feminist arguments but held back from public support out of a fear of male disapproval. A larger number clung to the dominant conventions of separate spheres. The imperviousness of the latter group to a discourse of equality sometimes stung Stanton into vehement exclamations of frustration. In 1857, when Susan B. Anthony reported her failure to stir a meeting of female teachers to demand equal pay with male teachers, Stanton wrote back:

> What an infernal set of fools these schoolmarms must be!! Well, if in order to please men they wish to live on air, let them. The sooner the present generation of women die out the better. We have jack-asses enough in the world now without such women propagating any more.[19]

The obstacles to Stanton's feminist leadership were also closer to home. She was a founding mother in a literal as well as figurative sense; by 1859, she had seven children to bind her to the domestic sphere. Her husband, frequently absent on legal and political business, expected her to stay at home and place maternal and household cares above feminist endeavors. Her father, the person whose approval she always most desired, warned her that she would pay an emotional and financial price for her public voice, threatening to disinherit her if she became a feminist lecturer. (He carried through with the threat but later relented.) Even as a feminist founder, then, Elizabeth Cady Stanton remained locked in the dialectic of domesticity and rebellion that had always defined her life. Loving her children intensely, glorying in her experiences as a mother, Stanton still repeatedly lamented the restricted public role that seemed to be the concomitant of her motherhood. Writing to Susan B. Anthony in 1852, she cried out: "I am at the boiling point! If I do not find some day the use of my tongue on this question, I shall die of an intellectual repression, a woman's rights convulsion!"[20]

Throughout these years of domestic confinement, however, Stanton was honing her feminist consciousness. Anthony visited her often, bringing news of the movement and temporarily relieving her of household duties so that she could write the speeches and tracts that made her the unquestioned theoretician of the women's cause. The laments about how domestic cares hobbled the public career for which she yearned were balanced by a recognition that those cares strengthened her identification with other women and deepened her perception of the obstacles before a women's movement. "It may be well for me to understand all the trials of woman's lot, that I may more eloquently proclaim them when the time comes." Stanton had to bide her time, waiting for the demands of domesticity to recede so that her rebellious feminist spirit could have full play. In 1857 she laid out her future in a prescient prediction to Anthony: "You and I have a prospect of a good long life. We shall not be in our prime before fifty, and after that we shall be good for twenty years at least."[21]

The public career that Elizabeth Cady Stanton had launched at Seneca Falls in 1848 would not come into its full flowering until the 1860s. But the founding moment at Seneca Falls would always remain in her eyes the benchmark against which women's emancipation was measured. In 1876, frustrated by recent judicial decisions antagonistic to women's rights, and galled by centennial celebrations for a republic that excluded women as full citizens, Stanton looked upon the years since the feminist founding as a progress in disillusionment. "As I sum up the indignities toward women, . . . I feel the degradation of sex more bitterly than I did on that July 19, 1848." Two years later, however, she gave a much more positive account of developments since 1848. Her remarks on the occasion of the thirtieth anniversary of the Seneca Falls Convention testified to the political and personal achievements of the movement of which she was a founding mother:

> Looking back over the past thirty years, how long ago seems that July morning when we gathered round the altar in the old Wesleyan church in Seneca Falls! It taxes and wearies the memory to think of all the conventions we have held, the legislatures we have besieged, the petitions and tracts we have circulated, the speeches, the calls, the resolutions we have penned. . . . [O]ur work has not been in vain. True, we have not yet secured the suffrage, but we have aroused public thought to the many disabilities of our sex, and our countrywomen to higher self-respect and worthier ambition, and in this struggle for justice we have deepened and broadened our own lives and extended the horizon of our vision.[22]

The Politics of the Excluded

When Elizabeth Cady Stanton finally shed the remaining hobbles of domesticity and began a full-time public career, it was in the heated political atmosphere of the Civil War and Reconstruction. As the dominant political agenda of Reconstruction came to promote the rights of black men while ignoring the rights of women, Stanton threw herself into what was to be the most painful episode in her public career. In the name of a passionate and outraged defense of women's rights, she broke with her former abolitionist and radical Republican allies and opposed passage of the Fourteenth and Fifteenth amendments because they excluded women. Stanton went beyond principled opposition to black manhood suffrage to articulate a racist and nativist position that violated her own republican convictions. Fighting for the cause of women regardless of the damage she might inflict on other excluded groups, she helped to shape a more autonomous women's movement—but at a heavy cost to her own democratic vision.

During the Civil War, Stanton had been an enthusiastic proponent of black emancipation. Impatient with the conservative view of a war merely to restore the Union, she set aside women's issues and helped to form the National Woman's Loyal League, which conducted a mammoth petition campaign on behalf of a Thirteenth Amendment giving permanent freedom to the slaves. As the president of the Loyal League, Stanton took advanced positions not only on black emancipation but on black dignity and agency as well. Writing to Elizabeth Smith Miller, Stanton observed that the membership badge of the league "represents a negro, half risen, breaking his own chains. We have had the negro in every variety of posture—hopeless, imploring, crouching at the feet of the Goddess of Liberty. But now, in harmony with our day, *our* negro is striking the blow himself with his own right hand."[23]

To Stanton, the Civil War represented a second—and more radical—American revolution. She considered the Union's cause to be the struggle of the pure principles of republicanism and democracy against their eternal enemies. The Stanton of the Civil War years was a militant republican egalitarian, prepared for a war to the death against "the hateful principle of caste and class." She condemned Northern women who refused to back the cause of the slaves as "traitor snobs," infected with the aristocratic germs of Europe and the South. In contrast, the Northern women who mobilized on behalf of emancipation were dedicated to "the divine idea of equality."[24]

The abolitionists and radical Republicans with whom Stanton associated herself emerged as an influential bloc in the postwar politics of Reconstruction. But as they began to press for black legal equality and then for black manhood suffrage, they also made it plain that any advances for women would have to wait. In order to avert any potential controversy over female enfranchisement, the authors of the Fourteenth Amendment interjected the word "male," which had not previously appeared in the United States Constitution, into their statement of the rights of citizens and voters. Most abolitionists and radical Republicans argued that coupling suffrage for women with suffrage for the freedmen would ensure the defeat of both. Therefore, women should stand aside and let black rights take precedence. Their turn would come later, at some unspecified future date.

The most powerful argument for giving black rights precedence over equal rights for women in the era of Reconstruction was not one of political practicability but one of moral urgency. Nobody made this argument more forcefully than Frederick Douglass:

> With us, the matter is a question of life and death, at least, in fifteen States of the Union. When women, because they are women, are hunted down through the cities of New York and New Orleans; when they are dragged from their houses and hung upon lamp-posts; when their children are torn from their arms, and their brains dashed out upon the pavement; when they are objects of insult and outrage at every turn; when they are in danger of having their homes burnt down over their heads; when their children are not allowed to enter schools; then they will have an urgency to obtain the ballot equal to our own.[25]

If there was a strong case to be made for the priority of black rights, there was also a strong one to be made for placing women on a par with blacks. Elizabeth Cady Stanton would argue that case with a force equal to that of Frederick Douglass. But she would never view the debate over black rights versus women's rights as one involving conflicting moral claims. For Stanton was too outraged over the betrayal of women's rights by former male supporters to give much credence to their arguments. The abolitionist stalwarts, such as Douglass, Wendell Phillips, and William Lloyd Garrison, who asked women to grant that this was "the negro's hour," had been her patrons and her heroes. Speaking before the American Anti-Slavery Society in 1860, she had proclaimed: "All time would not be long enough to pay the debt of gratitude we owe these noble men, who spoke for us when we were dumb, who roused us to a sense of our own rights, to the dignity of our high calling." But now "these noble men" were ignoring all of their earlier arguments about universal human rights. They were closing their newspapers to feminist arguments and standing by in silence when women asked for their aid. That "our best men stood silent" in the face of women's campaign for equality meant, for Stanton, that the real meaning of Reconstruction was one of male privilege. Reflecting on this period in *History of Woman Suffrage*, she concluded that women would have to fight for and win their rights mainly on their own: "Standing alone we learned our power; we repudiated man's counsels forevermore; and solemnly vowed that there should never be another season of silence until woman had the same rights everywhere on this green earth, as man."[26]

Stanton insisted that Reconstruction must be "the woman's hour also." Once the most progressive political forces appeared to be in the driver's seat, they should seize the moment to fulfill the revolutionary pledge of the Civil War. With considerable acumen, Stanton recognized that the time for reform was brief:

> The few who had the prescience to see the long years of apathy that always follow a great conflict, strained every nerve to settle the broad question of suffrage on its true basis while the people were awake to its importance, but the blindness of reformers themselves in playing into the hands of the opposition, made all efforts unavailing.[27]

Since the Fourteenth and Fifteenth amendments excluded women from their new declaration of American rights, Stanton was quick to oppose both. She attacked them as antirepublican, contending that universal manhood suffrage represented "the last stronghold of aristocracy in the country." She attacked them because there was already too much male aggressiveness and violence in the governance of the nation. She attacked them in the name of black women, arguing that they were being transferred from bondage to the slavemaster to bondage to the black male. Battling for the inclusion of women with black males in the Reconstruction amendments, Stanton mustered the rhetoric of universal rights that the abolitionists and radical Republicans had largely abandoned. She seized the republican high ground and challenged her opponents to justify their exclusion of women. "We demand in the reconstruction," she wrote, "suffrage for all the citizens of the Republic. I would not talk of negroes or women, but of citizens."[28]

Stanton's initial impulse in the Reconstruction era was to win back erstwhile male allies to the support of universal rights. Along with Susan B. Anthony, who shared her perspective, she worked to reunite feminists and abolitionists in the American Equal Rights Association. But the strains of the conflict between precedence for the black cause and equal rights for women were too great for this organization to surmount. The two sides split over the disastrous Kansas campaign of 1867 for both black and women's suffrage. Belated and lukewarm support from abolitionists and active opposition from Kansas Republicans to women's suffrage alienated the feminists, while the defeat of black suffrage along with women's suffrage was taken by abolitionists and Republicans as confirmation of their fears about the imprudence of pushing for both reforms at once. The Kansas campaign proved to be a watershed for Elizabeth Cady Stanton. It led her to abandon any hope of a continuing coalition with her longtime allies and to seek new friends in some unexpected places.[29]

Stanton's response to Republican rebuffs in the Kansas campaign was to turn to the Democrats—a party that included the proslavery,

Copperhead elements she had excoriated during the Civil War. Her abolitionist friends were especially appalled by the association of Stanton and Anthony with George Francis Train. A strong supporter of women's rights, Train was also a self-promoting crank whose Copperhead past was reflected in flagrant racist rhetoric. Train campaigned with Stanton and Anthony in Kansas, helped to organize a lecture tour for their return to the East, and promised them a feminist newspaper of their own, which they dubbed the *Revolution*. Stanton defended Train against the furious criticisms of abolitionists, insisting that he was a man of "spotless moral character," of "genius and rare gifts." But she also insisted that it would not have mattered if Train was as evil a character as his critics had alleged: "It seems to me it would be right and wise to accept aid from the devil himself, provided he did not tempt us to lower our standard."[30]

Train's influence furthered—but did not initiate—Elizabeth Cady Stanton's own turn to the "devil" of racism. Even before Kansas, she began to denigrate and devalue blacks and immigrants as a way of boosting the claims of women. Confronted by the argument that black men must take precedence and that women must subordinate their own demand for equality, she responded with an appeal to racist and nativist sentiments. Just as any admirer of Abraham Lincoln must confront his statements about white supremacy in the 1850s, so must any admirer of Elizabeth Cady Stanton confront her statements about the superiority of Anglo-Saxon and middle-class females in the 1860s. Stanton's racism during the Reconstruction period is more than an unfortunate blot on her public career. It reflects a dangerous temptation often found in the situation of dissenting leaders: to advance the cause of one excluded group by making a scapegoat of another.

One of Stanton's most frequent rhetorical devices during the Reconstruction era was to project middle-class white women as the only possible saviors of the American republic from the dangerous hordes empowered by universal manhood suffrage:

> In view of the fact that the Freedmen of the South and the millions of foreigners now crowding our shores, most of whom represent neither property, education, nor civilization, are all in the progress of events to be enfranchised, the best interests of the nation demand that we outweigh this incoming pauperism, ignorance, and degradation, with the wealth, education, and refinement of the women of the republic.

This language of class superiority sometimes became more overtly racist. "If woman finds it hard," she wrote, "to bear the oppressive laws of a few Saxon fathers, of the best orders of manhood, what may she not be called to endure when all the lower orders, natives and foreigners, Dutch, Irish, Chinese, and African, legislate for her and her daughters?" Stanton's racist rhetoric becomes most painful to read when it transformed the freedmen of the South from victims of oppression to potential oppressors. In 1869, while accurately pointing out how the exclusion of women from the Fifteenth Amendment pitted blacks and women against one another, she predicted mounting hostility between the two groups. On the side of women, this hostility would foster prejudice. On the side of blacks, much worse was to be feared: "Antagonism between black men and all women . . . will culminate in fearful outrages, especially in the southern states." In Stanton's most lurid prophecy, the freed slave became the black rapist.[31]

Stanton's harsh rhetoric toward the freedmen was accompanied by scornful comments about their political patrons. Responding to abolitionist criticisms of her collaboration with Train and of her racist language, she accused her former allies of political enervation and cowardice. A sign of just how hurt and angry Stanton felt toward friends that she believed had betrayed her was her cruel retort to William Lloyd Garrison, who had written to assail her collaboration with Train. Discussing a man who had been a lifelong inspiration and hero to her, she wrote in the *Revolution:* "In respect to the *debris* of negro agitation, Mr. Garrison is as dead as the 'royal Dane.' We suspect he thinks so himself; for we have not heard from him for years at any of those anti-slavery convocations where he used to forge thunderbolts and gather laurels. He should be content to remain in his sepulchre."[32]

Elizabeth Cady Stanton could hardly have been comfortable in deploying racist and nativist rhetoric. Her republican faith, expressed vividly during the Civil War years, showed her to be a passionate advocate of equality and a sworn enemy of caste and class distinctions. On one level, Stanton's stand during Reconstruction was consistent with these convictions. As a proponent of universal suffrage, she could still claim that her goal was to build "a true republic." But when she urged that middle-class white women be enfranchised so that they could "outweigh" the suffrage of uneducated and impoverished blacks and immigrants, she fell into a language of caste and class of her own. Why, then, did Stanton choose to adopt a rhetoric so at odds with her political faith?[33]

Her turn to racism appears in the most pardonable light when it is considered as an expression of frustrated hopes for equality. To Stanton, the proclamation of a "negro's hour" that excluded women was one more outrageous demonstration of the gendered nature of political justice in America. Less pardonable as a source of Stanton's racist rhetoric was her class bias. Coming from a background of privilege, and living the life of a bourgeois matron as well as a feminist agitator, Stanton's vision was obstructed by the blinders of her class. Her genuine sympathies for workers, the poor, and minorities were generally tinged with an element of class condescension. During Reconstruction, concern for middle-class women drove out those sympathies. Believing that the emancipation of the freedmen placed them on a par with middle-class white women—both groups lacking only the suffrage to attain full equality—she failed to comprehend the very different situations of the two groups in the structure of postwar American capitalism. If Stanton overlooked the crucial economic difference between freedmen and middle-class white women, she also neglected the most important commonalities between the two groups. Contrasting ignorant, debased freedmen and immigrants to educated, propertied, and virtuous white women, she failed to comprehend their shared bonds of subordination in the existing social order. Her racism was thus an intellectual as well as a moral failure, an inability to understand the complexities as well as the inequities of power in America.[34]

Stanton's racism was an expression of outrage and a projection of class. It was also a political choice. Stanton deliberately employed racist rhetoric to persuade middle-class white males that they needed their female counterparts as allies if they hoped to control the rising political power of immigrants and blacks. In so doing, she pitted the political aspirations of one excluded group against those of another.

That Stanton's racist rhetoric during Reconstruction was more a product of the era's politics and emotions than of a deep-seated personal prejudice is suggested by her later statements about blacks. Her most common stance in later years was to defend the rights and dignity of blacks and to link the causes of women, who were still deprived of the suffrage, and blacks, whose use of the franchise was threatened by the rise of Jim Crow. Perhaps the most revealing comment about race in Stanton's later years—both in its denunciation of white chauvinism and its underlying hint of persisting guilt—came in a diary entry from 1893:

> We had a pleasant entertainment at Mrs. Villard's today. The African and Indian students from Hampton Institute were there and sung for us. What cause for reflection! Representatives of these two subordinated races standing side by side to amuse the arrogant dominant race. Well, my conscience was clear, for my very first efforts in reform were for the negro.[35]

Stanton's appeal to racism and collaboration with the Democrats
cannot be said to have furthered women's immediate political
prospects during the Reconstruction years. As Elisabeth Griffith has
observed, when Stanton and Anthony turned away in fury from the
politically dominant Republicans, they "undercut any chance they
might have had for success." In her retrospective accounts of this period, Stanton refused to concede that she had made any political errors. But she did confess to the anguish of her break with her old allies: "With all their long-time friends against them, . . . the position of
the women seemed so untenable to the majority that at times a sense
of utter loneliness and desertion made the bravest of them doubt the
possibility of maintaining the struggle or making themselves fairly understood." For Stanton, Reconstruction was, understandably, "one of
the most trying periods in the woman suffrage movement."[36]

She emerged from the era shaken but undaunted. Women's immediate political prospects may have been bleak, but Elizabeth Cady
Stanton and Susan B. Anthony were committed to continue the fight
for equal rights, underscored by the formation of the National
Woman Suffrage Association in 1869. The Reconstruction era produced a more autonomous women's movement, interested in alliances
with other progressive forces but insistent on avoiding the subordination of women's cause to any other. The fashioning of this independent movement has been hailed by Ellen Dubois as "the greatest
achievement of feminists in the postwar period."[37]

The conflicts of the Reconstruction era inspired Stanton to become
an even more militant and penetrating critic of women's oppression.
But she purchased her new insights about women at the cost of dis-
paraging the dignity of blacks and immigrants. Speaking in the name
of inclusion for women, she fell prey during the Reconstruction years
to a dangerous brand of the politics of the excluded.

The Persona of an Agitator

The three decades remaining to Stanton after Reconstruction, up to
her death in 1902, were filled with the vigorous public activities of a
dissenting leader. In the 1870s her principal role was as a traveling
lecturer, disseminating her feminist views across the nation. In the
1880s she joined with Susan B. Anthony and Matilda Joslyn Gage to
compile the multivolume *History of Woman Suffrage*, preserving the
words and deeds of early feminists for later generations. During the
final years of her life, she became convinced that religious teachings

about the inferiority of women stood in the way of equality between the sexes and produced *The Woman's Bible,* a critical commentary on the biblical depiction of women.

Throughout Stanton's long and creative public career, stretching from 1848 to 1902, she reveled in the twin roles of agitator and theorist. Both her persona as an agitator and her vision as a feminist theorist revolved around a complex set of seeming opposites. Yet the tensions in her public identity and political thought seemed only to make her stronger as a dissenting leader.

As a celebrated suffrage leader and feminist orator, Elizabeth Cady Stanton gave voice to a radical vision. She went beyond the demand for equality for women in every sphere of life, to insist upon profound transformations of both the public and the private spheres. Stanton was a critic of marriage and a proponent of greater sexual freedom. She was a biting detractor of organized religion, which she increasingly came to regard as the chief intellectual and moral culprit behind women's degradation. Yet this voice that threatened the political and social proprieties of nineteenth-century America came from a woman whose appearance in public was unthreatening, indeed reassuring. On the public platform, Elizabeth Cady Stanton was matronly, gracious, affable. As the description of biographer Alma Lutz suggests, Stanton lived up fully to the expectations set for the bourgeois lady: "She was very fastidious about her platform appearance. Her dress was of black silk, with the inevitable lacy white collar and cuffs. Her white hair, beautifully arranged, always impressed everyone who saw her."[38]

How can one reconcile this peculiar combination of militant feminist and bourgeois matron? An imaginative attempt at explanation has come from Stanton's most recent biographer, Elisabeth Griffith. According to Griffith, Stanton's radical message was her real public personality; the feminine garb and style were her mask. In Griffith's words: "At the same time that she was moving out of her domestic sphere, Stanton began to use her maternal role to legitimize her public activities. She shrewdly chose to appear matronly, respectable, charming, and genial." Griffith further suggests that Stanton "exploited her maternal identification to legitimize her revolutionary vocation."[39]

Evidence can be adduced to support Griffith's hypothesis that Stanton attempted to make her radical message more palatable. Entries in Stanton's diary demonstrate her concern to promote her perspective without offending the sensibilities of more conservative women (and men). In one such entry from 1889, she wrote: "I often spoke in the churches, when I would sow as much good seed as possible, though I was careful never to try and set out full-grown plants, especially if they were of a prickly nature, which was more often than not the species taken from my nursery." Stanton was willing to mask her radicalism before certain kinds of audiences. She was also willing to conceal the rage she sometimes felt toward men as oppressors, a rage vividly expressed in an 1871 letter to Martha C. Wright: "When I think of all the wrongs that have been heaped upon womankind, I am ashamed that I am not forever in a condition of chronic wrath, stark mad, skin and bone, my eyes a fountain of tears, my lips overflowing with curses, and my hand against every man and brother!" The genial public Stanton knew private moments when she imagined herself as a feminist Captain Ahab.[40]

There is, however, a fundamental problem with Griffith's view that Stanton adopted femininity and a maternal posture as public masks. These "masks" were, in fact, essential facets of Elizabeth Cady Stanton's character. Stanton was not only the mother of seven children but a woman who prided herself on her mothering skills; she was genuinely eager to present herself as a sort of supermother. She loved beautiful clothes and graceful appearances; even when joining the pioneer dress reformers and donning bloomers (a short skirt over Turkish trousers that offered women greater freedom of movement than conventional attire) in the early 1850s, she insisted that "in introducing a new dress, we ought to use the richest materials, not gaudy, but everything as tasteful as possible." While Stanton knew many moments of private feminist rage, she was generally a happy and humorous person both in private and in public. Humor softened her public persona—but it also served her as a sharp rhetorical weapon, especially when directed at oafish men.[41]

Elizabeth Cady Stanton was just what she appeared to be—feminist militant *and* bourgeois matron. The bourgeois matron in her was evident in a column she wrote for a local newspaper in 1884. Railing against American propensities to litter in public places, Stanton wrote: "It rests with our women to train the present generation of boys and girls into more refined tastes and habits." A striking illustration of the mix of feminist and matron was a public letter Stanton addressed "To Miss Cleveland" in 1886. The president's sister had endorsed low-cut gowns for young women attending White House social functions; Stanton objected on solid feminist grounds. Why should young women have to make themselves into sexual objects; why should they have to "unveil their charms while men so carefully conceal all theirs. . . ?" Her objection was also based on the hygienic principles common to nineteenth-century reformers: it was unhealthy for young women to expose their upper torsos to the chill of drafty ballrooms. But Stanton's remonstrance to Miss Cleveland also spoke the language of the offended bourgeois lady, as it pronounced "the disgust with which all persons of refinement regard such women."[42]

The antipodes within Stanton's public persona made her a more effective agitator. As her persona embodied the experiences of the majority of women, it made it easier for her audiences to identify with her. That persona spoke to the ambivalence that many women, torn between prevailing codes of femininity and feminist visions of changed womanhood, seemed to be feeling in nineteenth-century America. What appears in one light as inconsistency can even be seen, in a different light, as an essential attribute of Stanton's feminism. Through her persona, as much as through her public arguments, Stanton was asserting that women did not have to give up valued experiences *as* women—such as motherhood or the expression of a special moral sensitivity—in order to stake their claim to a share in all the domains previously monopolized by men. What she wrote in 1885—"surely maternity is an added power and development of some of the most tender sentiments of the human heart and not a 'limitation'" upon women in politics—she lived out on the public stage.[43]

Stanton drew strength from her complex public persona. But she did not want her particular fusion of feminism and femininity to be the only model available to female activists. She often praised the unstinting efforts that unmarried women, such as Susan B. Anthony, were able to provide to the feminist movement. She defended the "women who are called masculine," arguing that men hurled this epithet at the women who were most "brave, courageous, self-reliant, and independent." If Stanton remained addicted to beautiful clothing and gloried in the trappings of motherhood, she was not unaware of the price women paid for these feminine pleasures. She knew that woman "is a slave to her rags." And she knew the ambiguous joy of feminist motherhood. Upon returning home from a brief political trip in 1855, she wrote to her cousin, Elizabeth Smith Miller: "The joy a mother feels on seeing her baby after a short absence is a bliss that no man's soul can ever know. There we have something that they have not! But we have purchased the ecstasy in deep sorrow and suffering."[44]

The rich complexity of her persona infused the role of feminist agitator that Stanton had adopted at Seneca Falls in 1848 and elaborated in later years. Initiated into politics by the abolitionist movement, she had powerful role models in William Lloyd Garrison and Wendell Phillips. While Stanton was more willing to work within the framework of political parties than Garrison or Phillips, she shared their disdain for the politician and their pride in the stance of the agitator. "Politic" was a pejorative word in her vocabulary, the antonym of principle. If agitators were the public voices of sacred causes, the generality of politicians were "earth-born souls."[45]

As Stanton saw it, an agitator was one guided by the truth of a principle rather than by the numbers who adhered to it. She should anticipate an initial hostility and scorn from the majority rather than understanding and applause: "The history of the world shows that the vast majority in every generation passively accept the conditions into which they are born, while those who demand larger liberties are ever a small, ostracised minority whose claims are ridiculed and ignored." The paramount task of the agitator was both to defy and to transform public opinion. Confronting a majority steeped in outmoded customs and unjust values, the agitator sought to open its eyes to political rights and moral responsibilities.[46]

Apart from occasional moments of doubt, Stanton was optimistic about the potential for educating the public. The essential simplicity of her nineteenth-century democratic faith is apparent in her conviction that true principles, if effectively conveyed, will ultimately be accepted by the majority. In a diary entry from 1888, she observed: "If I were to draw up a set of rules for the guidance of reformers, . . . I should put at the head of the list: 'Do all you can, *no matter what*, to get people to think on your reform, and then, if the reform is good, it will come about in due season.'" Stanton's faith in this passage is both touching and naïve. Her own reform, women's rights, was opposed not only out of misguided sentiments but by various economic interests (such as the liquor industry) and by men fearful of losing their bastions of privilege. Although Stanton recognized with great clarity the democratic potential of political education, she failed to acknowledge the realities of power that leaders in a democracy also need to understand. She was an agitator, not a politician—but the politician's insight would sometimes have made her stronger as a dissenting leader.[47]

Agitation fit Stanton's personal proclivities as well as her principles. Her pleasure in agitation was matched by her dislike for organizational politics. Stanton viewed organizational responsibilities as cribbing her independent and militant voice. In this vein, she wrote to Anthony in 1869: "I do hate conventions, for I dislike to be in a position where any set of people have the right to say, 'For the sake of the cause, don't do this or that.'" In her dislike for the political conflicts as well as the mundane work of a reform organization, Stanton was similar to Eugene V. Debs. In Debs's case, as we shall see, the flight from organizational affairs was a major political weakness. Stanton was saved from similar problems by her long-standing partnership with Susan B. Anthony: where Stanton delighted in being free from organizational constraints, Anthony was most happy in the organizational milieu that suited her special talents. With Anthony to tend to the organizational work, Stanton could enjoy the freedom of the lone-wolf agitator and not suffer the loss of political influence that often comes with eschewing organizational affairs.[48]

Independent, militant, impassioned, and dramatic, Elizabeth Cady Stanton was a superb feminist agitator. Nowhere was her brilliance more evident than in her grasp of the subversive uses of dominant discourses. The feminist transformation of the Declaration of Independence that she produced at Seneca Falls was only the first in a line of similar ventures. By reconceptualizing dominant discourses as platforms for feminism, Stanton unlocked their subversive potential.

Republicanism especially became, in Stanton's hands, a powerful vehicle for the emancipation of women. Speaking authentically as a committed republican, Stanton articulated a feminist republicanism subversive of the existing order of male dominance. She demonstrated repeatedly that the basic principles of republican government logically entailed the enfranchisement of women. "This is declared to be a government 'of the people.' . . . When we say people, do we not mean women as well as men? . . . When we place in the hands of one class of citizens the right to make, interpret, and execute the law for another class wholly unrepresented in the government, we have made an order of nobility." Stanton also claimed a direct republican lineage for women. Addressing the New York legislature in 1854, she said: "Yes, gentlemen, in republican America in the nineteenth century, we, the daughters of the revolutionary heroes of '76, demand at your hands the redress of our grievances." Indeed, the daughters were more faithful heirs than the sons. In their haste to acquire property and gratify private passions, the majority of nineteenth-century men had abandoned the Revolutionary code of civic virtue. But women, "the repository of all that is noble and virtuous in national character," kept alive the republican spirit of 1776.[49]

The nineteenth-century cult of motherhood was another dominant discourse that Stanton turned to subversive ends. She fused maternal feelings and republican passions into a sentimental claim for women's civic participation. According to the prevailing doctrine of "republican motherhood," women had a responsibility in the domestic province to raise virtuous sons—but this responsibility ceased once the sons left the home. According to Stanton, the public sphere would debase and corrupt those sons unless their mothers first purged it of its evils. Responding to rowdy crowds that disrupted the speaking tour which Stanton and other abolitionists undertook in the tense "secession winter" of 1861, she used the phenomenon of mob action to demonstrate the need for "republican mothers" in politics. "When I look around and see brave, strong, full grown men swamped in the whirlpool of numbers, I feel that a mother's duty is not all at home. Love prompts us to clear up the rubbish in the outer world, and pluck the thorns from the paths our sons so soon must tread."[50]

Dominant discourses were refashioned by Stanton into warrants for women's full entry into public life. In seeking to undermine the definition of republican political power as exclusively male, she also aimed to subvert the male monopoly of public distinction. We saw earlier how John Adams sought to make the "passion for distinction" into the guiding motive for political actors in the American republic, and how Abraham Lincoln struggled to give democratic meaning to this passion. Elizabeth Cady Stanton went a step further, insisting that this passion was just as legitimate and worthy among the excluded as among white males. In the republic for which she battled, meritorious women would receive equal gratification of their "passion for distinction."

In her popular lecture, "Our Young Girls," Stanton detailed how the prevailing canon of separate spheres repressed "ambition and love of distinction" in the most high-spirited females. Her own repressed aspirations had initially found vicarious satisfaction through marriage to a romantic abolitionist agitator. Once she emerged as an active feminist, however, her husband's reflected fame was no longer satisfying. As Henry Stanton entered partisan politics (and became something of an opportunist), his wife supplanted him as the romantic agitator. She became the famous Stanton.[51]

Like many deeply principled dissenting leaders, Stanton wanted to believe that her actions were disinterested and that she was affected by neither praise nor blame. But as she grew older, she increasingly came to acknowledge the pleasures that her distinction brought her. When a young girl told Stanton at a Paris reception in 1887 that her father had instructed her to "look well at this woman, for she is one of the most famous of America," her response could have come from the diary of John Adams. In her diary, she wrote: "This is the kind of compliment that touches the heart and makes amends for so many rebuffs." The following year, her diary echoed the hope Lincoln had expressed in the 1850s for posthumous fame from service to a great cause. When the suffrage movement finally achieves complete success, she wrote,

> those of us who have kept "pegging away" for these many years, in
> season and out of season, will come into our just rewards, though
> we will probably be under the sod. I do hope the departed can see

what is going on on this earth, for I admit that such tardy recognition will give me pleasure even though I be enjoying the bliss of paradise.[52]

If fame was gratifying to Stanton's ego, it was also a fulfillment of her feminist principles. She recognized clearly that the public obscurity of women reinforced their political subservience. In 1892, joining a million spectators thronging the Columbus Day parade in New York City, she observed that no women had been invited to march in the procession and concluded that "neither in the government nor in the religion of the nation is woman anywhere honored as an equal." The experience was still fresh in her mind two months later, when she joined with other feminists in the first celebration of "Foremothers' Day." Speaking at the Foremothers dinner, she expressed her delight that "the daughters of the Pilgrim Mothers are learning the a, b, c of self-respect and self-assertion. If we had been apt pupils, we should have learned the lesson of self-glorification from our forefathers long ago."[53]

Becoming more comfortable with her own pleasure in distinction was, for Stanton, an experience representative of the feminist triumph over male denigration and female self-abasement. In her "passion for distinction"—as well as in her complex persona, her militant agitation, and her subversive discourse—Stanton made herself into an emblematic figure. The significations of equality and personal freedom in her public career, as much as in her words, advanced the strongest possible claims both for herself and for all women.

A Feminist Vision

Elizabeth Cady Stanton's feminist vision was as complex as her public persona. Conflicting strains and impulses pulled her thought in different directions. She emphasized that women resembled men in their capacities and life needs—but also argued that they were fundamentally different by virtue of their special qualities of morality and mercy. She demanded equal access for women to all the spheres of life that men currently monopolized—but also demanded a revolution in male/female relations. She reshaped the liberal ideal of self-reliance into a doctrine of female individualism—but also bound women together through a vision of sisterhood.

These conflicting strains were less marks of inconsistency than signs of a legitimate tension at the heart of Stanton's vision. Recognizing the sharp dichotomies in prevailing codes of male domination and female subordination, she constantly struggled to transcend them. She wanted to deny that women had to choose between their identity as women and their complete freedom and equality. She wanted to affirm that women could value their distinctive experiences, ethics, and solidarity while still overcoming any limits placed on them by men.

Nancy Cott has pointed out that the women's movement of the nineteenth and early twentieth centuries staked a claim to equal rights on grounds of both "sameness" and "difference" between men and women. Elizabeth Cady Stanton is a prime specimen of this tendency to hold to what Cott calls "two logically opposing poles" of argument. Sometimes, Stanton stressed "the identity of the race in capabilities and responsibilities." At other times, she depicted women as uniquely able to bring to public affairs a "purifying power" and a "spirit of mercy and love." Arguments from sameness and arguments from difference were even mixed together in the same letter or speech. Writing to an Ohio women's rights convention in 1850, she complained that "it is impossible for us to convince man that we think and feel exactly as he does; that we have the same sense of right and justice, the same love of freedom and independence." But in the very next paragraph, she made it plain that women did not "think and feel exactly" like men:

> Had the women of this country had a voice in the Government, think you our national escutcheon would have been stained with the guilt of aggressive warfare upon such weak, defenseless nations as the Seminoles and Mexicans? Think you we should cherish and defend, in the heart of our nation, such a wholesale system of piracy, cruelty, licentiousness, and ignorance as is our slavery? . . . Verily, no, or I mistake woman's heart, her instinctive love of justice, and mercy, and truth![54]

After the Civil War the argument from difference came to preponderate in Stanton's rhetoric. Opposing black manhood suffrage during Reconstruction, she insisted that in an increasingly corrupted republic it was more important to enfranchise women. "To woman it is given to save the Republic." In a more modest statement from the same period, she wrote: "The ballot in the hand of woman will bring neither the millennium nor pandemonium the next day; but it will surely right many wrongs." The argument from difference may have appealed to Stanton during the Reconstruction years because she was intensely alienated from most of her former male friends. There was also, however, a tactical choice in her rhetoric of women's "difference." Writing in the *Revolution,* she spoke candidly of how she and her coadjutors had asserted similarities of mind between the sexes "until we saw that stronger arguments could be drawn from a difference in sex, in mind as well as body." Still, she was quick to add, "while admitting a difference, we claim that that difference gives man no superiority, no rights over women that she has not over him."[55]

Tactically, Stanton pushed women's distinctive kind of public participation as a necessary balance to the dangerous tendencies that men brought to politics. Philosophically, she pushed beyond the dichotomy between male and female. At the core of her vision was a masculine/feminine synthesis, in which individuals developed the best qualities of both genders. She once described herself and Susan B. Anthony as being as tough as "pine knots." In contrast, her beloved father was recalled after his death as "truly great and good—an ideal judge; and to his sober, taciturn and majestic bearing he added the tenderness, purity and refinement of a true woman." Her God, whom she heretically trumpeted as an alternative to the Christian version that degraded women, was described as the "Heavenly Mother and Father."[56]

At her most visionary, Stanton proclaimed that "in the education and elevation of woman we are yet to learn the true manhood and womanhood, the true masculine and feminine elements." She recognized that male oppression and female degradation had distorted the qualities of both genders. What women and men would truly be like was a question that only the future could answer. That future was not predestined; it was the task of the feminist movement to create it.[57]

Whether she argued from "sameness" or from "difference," Stanton's point was always equality for women. But her understanding of equality was complex. In contemporary terms, her thought encompassed both liberal and radical feminism. The liberal side of Stanton's thought fixed on winning equal rights for women, principally in the area of the suffrage, but also in such fields as ownership of property and access to the professions. The disfranchisement of women was, in her view, a basic "disability" that lay at the core of women's grievances. Deprived of political power, women could not gain equal opportunity in any sphere of life. Deprived of citizen responsibilities, they could not gain equal respect either. Through what Stanton called "the degradation of disfranchisement," women "feel the humiliation of . . . petty distinctions of sex precisely as the black man feels those of color."[58]

Obtaining the suffrage was, in Stanton's liberal arguments, the key to the protection of women's interests. Despite all of the male claims of protective sentiments toward women, a perusal of constitutions and laws demonstrated that men as an enfranchised class exploited

women as a disenfranchised class. Speaking before the New York legislature in 1860, Stanton asked: "You who have read the history of nations, from Moses down to our last election, where have you ever seen
one class looking after the interests of another?" Suffrage was
women's natural right. Stanton thus argued before a congressional
committee in 1884 that "the right of suffrage is simply the right to
govern one's self. Every human being is born into the world with this
right." The liberal language of right and self-interest was a powerful
instrument for Stanton, as she constructed a case for women's political and legal equality that was unanswerable by men in terms of their
own principles.[59]

If much of Stanton's case for women's equality stressed equal access to existing social structures, her conception of equality could not
be satisfied merely by inclusion of women into the status quo. Her liberal feminism shaded over into a more radical brand in her diagnosis
of male resistance to granting the ballot: "Here is the secret of the opposition to woman's equality in the state and the church—men are not
ready to recognize it in the home." Stanton came increasingly to see
the home, rather than the state, as the locus of oppression. In the
home "the woman is uniformly sacrificed to the wife and mother."
Law reinforced custom in making the marital bond into "the man
marriage," in which "the woman is regarded and spoken of simply as
the toy of man—made for his special use—to meet his most gross and
sensuous desires."[60]

Stanton courageously ventured into the domain of sexuality, arguing that men's power over women was anchored in an autocratic assertion of sexual prerogative. To win equality with men, women
would have to fight for their sexual self-determination: "Man in his
lust has regulated long enough this whole question of sexual intercourse." Stanton wanted women not only to be able to say no to their
husbands but also to have the personal and economic freedom to dispense with marriage if they found it too oppressive. She thus championed liberalized divorce laws. And she advocated greater freedom of
sexual choice, calling it "freedom of love," sometimes even admitting
that what she envisioned could be construed as "the obnoxious doctrine of Free Love." Stanton's radical feminism refused to accept the
liberal separation of public and private. Bringing the political back to
the personal, it demanded a radical transformation of relations between the sexes.[61]

There were times in Stanton's public career when the issue of marriage seemed far more pressing than the demand for the suffrage.
Writing to Susan B. Anthony in 1860, she emphasized the priority of
changing the core of male-female relations: "How this marriage ques-

tion grows on me. It lies at the very foundation of all progress." Knowing how explosive the question was, Stanton began, after the Civil War, to speak about it mostly in meetings restricted to women. She discovered that it was even harder to make progress in the domain of sexual relations than in the domain of the suffrage, where victories were few and defeats painfully frequent. As Ellen Dubois points out, Stanton's female audiences often responded to her insights, but they could not follow her leadership beyond the sexual status quo. Economic and social conditions in nineteenth-century America, Dubois writes, ensured that most women "had no alternative to marriage. They could not support themselves through wage labor." Stanton's liberal-feminist language of rights and interests provided a basis for a suffrage movement that reached its goal, albeit after an extraordinarily protracted struggle. Her radical-feminist call for a transformation in relations between the sexes had to function mainly as a prophetic rhetoric.[62]

Just as Stanton was pulled by the opposing poles of sameness and difference, of equal opportunity and radical transformation of gendered relationships, she was also tugged by the opposing poles of individualism and sisterhood. The language of individual freedom and self-development for women was one of the enduring themes in her rhetoric after 1848. Stanton's individualism only reached its apogee, however, with her 1892 speech, "The Solitude of Self." This speech, which she described in her diary as "the best thing I have ever written, at least in my declining years," is an eloquent manifesto for a feminist individualism. It is perhaps the closest feminist counterpart in nineteenth-century America to the romantic individualism of Emerson and Thoreau—save that Stanton's vision of the individual, rooted in women's experiences of suffering, is less self-exalting and more somber.[63]

"The Solitude of Self" declared that women's campaign for equal rights had its ultimate justification in the solitariness of each human life. No person, group, or class could fully understand or take responsibility for any other. "The strongest reason," Stanton wrote,

> why we ask for woman a voice in the government under which she lives; in the religion she is asked to believe; equality in social life, where she is the chief factor; a place in the trades and professions, where she may earn her bread, is because of her birthright to self-sovereignty; because as an individual, she must rely on herself. No matter how much women prefer to lean, to be protected and supported, no matter how much men desire to have them do so, they must make the voyage of life alone.

At times in the speech, Stanton spoke a hopeful language reminiscent of Emerson, whom she admired: "Nothing strengthens the judgment and quickens the conscience like individual responsibility." Yet in her closing passages, she underscored with bleak images the distances separating each individual from all others: "There is a solitude which each and every one of us has always carried with him, more inaccessible than the ice-cold mountains, more profound than the midnight sea; the solitude of self."[64]

As a sermon on the need for women to take responsibility for their own lives, "The Solitude of Self" was powerful and moving. But when Stanton posited freedom as the condition of a solitary self—making reference even to "an imaginary Robinson Crusoe, with her woman, Friday, on a solitary island"—she verged on the atomized individualism of the classical liberal philosophers. Such an individualism did away with the rigid spheres and hierarchies that oppressed women. But it also did away with the rich social networks and bonds of sisterhood that sustained women in their struggles to overcome oppression.[65]

What ultimately drew Stanton away from the pole of an atomized individualism was her commitment to sisterhood. Her broad sympathies for women of all kinds were especially evident during the same period in which she produced "The Solitude of Self." In the final decades of the nineteenth century, the women's movement grew increasingly narrow. Shedding more radical demands and concentrating only on the suffrage, the movement was now dominated by white, middle-class Christian women who sought respectability in the eyes of the powers that be. Because it no longer spoke for all of women's needs or for all classes of women, Elizabeth Cady Stanton found herself at odds with such a movement—and with her closest friend, Susan B. Anthony, who accommodated herself to the new conservatism. Against the new tendency to work only for the suffrage, she insisted on a struggle in every arena in which women were oppressed: "To emancipate woman from the fourfold bondage she has so long suffered in the State, the church, the home and the world of work, harder battles than we have yet fought are still before us." Against the new tendency to push only the claims of the most respectable women, she called upon feminists to recapture their broader vision of sisterhood. Speaking before the founding convention of the National American Woman Suffrage Association in 1890, she inveighed against the new conservatism:

> Wherever and whatever any class of women suffer whether in the home, the church, the courts, in the world of work, in the statute

books, a voice in their behalf should be heard in our conventions. We must manifest a broad catholic spirit for all shades of opinion in which we may differ and recognize the equal right of all parties, sects and races, tribes and colors. Colored women, Indian women, Mormon women and women from every quarter of the globe have been heard in these Washington conventions and I trust they always will be.[66]

Elizabeth Cady Stanton could be prickly in her feminist individualism. Her proud self-assertion sometimes conveyed an air of superiority. But the primary force in her public life was always a sense of outrage at the degradation of women and an empathy for all women confronting that degradation. The individualist who plumbed her own "solitude of self" never forgot her bond to the multitudes of women whose redemption she once described as her "whole-souled, all-absorbing, agonizing interest."[67]

Conclusion

In her old age Elizabeth Cady Stanton's thoughts often turned to religion. It was not the appeal of faith in the face of impending death that sparked her interest, but a growing conviction that "the arch enemy to woman's freedom skulks behind the altar." Stanton scandalized more conservative feminists by organizing and heading a team of writers that produced *The Woman's Bible*, a critical commentary on the depictions of women in the Scriptures.[68]

When Stanton arrived in her Biblical commentary at the incident in Genesis where the serpent tempts Eve, her subversive imagination took flight:

> In this prolonged interview, the unprejudiced reader must be impressed with the courage, the dignity, and the lofty ambition of the woman. The tempter evidently had a profound knowledge of human nature, and saw at a glance the high character of the person he met by chance in his walks in the garden. He did not try to tempt her from the path of duty by brilliant jewels, rich dresses, worldly luxuries or pleasures, but with the promise of knowledge, with the wisdom of the Gods. . . . Compared with Adam she appears to great advantage through the entire drama.

Stanton reinterpreted the Fall as a feminist parable, with Eve cast as the primal heroine. Blamed by men as the source of the curses that plagued them, Eve was reclaimed for women as a representative of the highest strivings of the human spirit. In the character of this feminist Eve, it is not hard to discern the self-projection of Elizabeth Cady Stanton.[69]

Like her Eve, Stanton was a woman of "lofty ambition." She was the driving force behind the creation of a women's rights movement in America in 1848 and became its most distinctive and powerful voice. From her own experience of stifled aspirations and domestic frustrations, she made an empathic leap to the disabilities and discontents of other women, proclaiming a rebellion against everything that degraded and oppressed her sex. In her passionate identification with her sisters, and in her protracted campaign to transform their condition and to raise their self-respect, Stanton was an exemplary dissenting leader. Unfortunately, she sometimes fell prey to one of the more dangerous temptations of dissenting leadership as well. Understandably aggrieved when her former abolitionist and radical Republican allies subordinated women's rights to the cause of black manhood suffrage during Reconstruction, she struck back through a racist denigration of blacks and immigrants. Turning her fire against other oppressed groups, rather than against the dominant powers in American society, Stanton undercut her own vision of republican equality in a futile quest for support from the middle-class white males she ordinarily challenged.

Once she overcame the restrictions of her domesticity, Stanton enjoyed a long career as a feminist agitator and theoretician. In her public persona, she embodied the ambivalent impulses of many nineteenth-century women. Her refined femininity clashed with her radical feminist message, but the combination of the two also affirmed women's right to have different experiences and values than men had and yet be fully equal. In her role as agitator, Stanton brilliantly subverted the dominant discourses of nineteenth-century America, turning republicanism and motherhood into vehicles for the political emancipation of women. A visionary as well as a subversive, she constructed a feminist theory that held in tension the conflicting aspects of women's lives. Her feminism spoke of sameness and difference between women and men, of equal opportunity under the status quo and radical transformation in the status quo, of self-reliant female individualism and supportive sisterhood. She spoke to the complexities of women's needs and dreams and imagined a fuller array of possibilities for both women and men.

Stanton's public career holds important lessons for both dissenting leaders and mainstream democratic politicians. Her descent into racist and nativist rhetoric during Reconstruction suggests how both frustration and calculations of political expedience can lead even committed democrats to abandon the search for common ground among the excluded and to promote the interests of their own group at the expense of those equally oppressed. But for this painful episode, however, Stanton has much to teach advocates of democratic political leadership. She stands as an example of how excluded groups can find a voice that turns what has been repressed or ignored into an insistent public presence. She demonstrates a commitment to political education, to a struggle against conventional opinion animated by the conviction that the majority can be successfully challenged to acknowledge the rights of others and their own responsibilities as American citizens. In her commitment to the republican tradition, and the subversive uses she made of that tradition, she indicates how America's classical political idiom contains a continuing potential for radical democratic change.

Paying tribute to Stanton upon her death in 1902, feminist Helen Gardener wrote, "What she sought for herself, she sought, also, for others." From the moment she made the link between the personal and the political at Seneca Falls, Stanton understood that her own struggle for freedom and dignity was inextricably bound to a larger struggle on behalf of women. Neither her talent nor her desire for distinction ever led her to forget the sense of mutuality between leaders and followers that was a hallmark of the women's movement. Political leadership in America has most often been discussed as an exclusively male competition for power and dominance. The example of Elizabeth Cady Stanton suggests how truncated that dominant discourse has been.[70]

5

Theodore Roosevelt

Heroic Leadership and Masculine Spectacle

In 1894 and early 1895, during one of the few slack-water periods in his frenetic career, Theodore Roosevelt collaborated with his closest friend, Henry Cabot Lodge, on *Hero Tales from American History*. Roosevelt was usually more active at constructing his own life as a hero tale. Through a succession of remarkable dramatis personae—the cowboy of the Dakotas, the police commissioner patrolling New York's mean streets, the Rough Rider charging up San Juan Hill, the progressive president scourging predatory capitalists, the African big game hunter, and more—Roosevelt made himself the first great American hero of a new age of mass media. Endlessly entertaining, he left generation after generation of admirers to marvel at "the fun of him."[1]

Democrats since the time of ancient Athens, however, have regarded heroes like Theodore Roosevelt as problematic figures, potential threats to the power and self-confidence of the people. To introduce some of the fundamental problems with Roosevelt's brand of heroic leadership, let us turn to an updated Athenian chorus, drawn from his contemporaries. For commentary about Roosevelt as vivid—and as fiercely opinionated—as the man himself, we have the trio of Henry Adams, Mark Twain, and Eugene V. Debs.

Of the three, Henry Adams had the most extensive personal contact with Roosevelt. The patrician Adams scorned Roosevelt's adaptation to a political world he considered crass and corrupt. But it was Roosevelt's egotism that most appalled Adams, who had inherited his great-grandfather's disdain for the man who trumpeted his own pretensions to greatness. In an often-quoted passage from his memoirs, Henry Adams described Roosevelt as "pure act." In his private letters, he was more pungent; writing to his friend Elizabeth Cameron after attending a dinner party at the White House in 1904, he depicted Roosevelt as pure ego:

> Never have I had an hour of worse social *malaise*. We were overwhelmed in a torrent of oratory, and at last I heard only the repetition of I-I-I attached to indiscretions greater one than another. . . . The wild talk about everything . . . belonged not to the bar-room but to the asylum.[2]

Mark Twain considered the idolization of Theodore Roosevelt by the American people to be prime evidence for his thesis about the folly of the human species. He viewed the president as an overgrown adolescent who resembled one of his most famous fictional characters. Roosevelt reminded him not of the morally complex Huckleberry Finn but of his more self-centered and shallow friend:

> Mr. Roosevelt is the Tom Sawyer of the political world of the twentieth century; always showing off; always hunting for a chance to show off; in his frenzied imagination the Great Republic is a vast Barnum circus with him for a clown and the whole world for audience; he would go to Halifax for half a chance to show off, and he would go to hell for a whole one.[3]

Writing about Theodore Roosevelt in January 1918, Socialist leader Eugene V. Debs, much loved by his followers for the gentleness of his soul, erupted in a paroxysm of loathing. The two men were old antagonists: Roosevelt had, as president, classified Debs as an "undesirable citizen," and Debs had frequently assailed the president as an infuriating example of the capitalist politician who deludes and defrauds the American masses. Now Debs had fresh reasons to attack Roosevelt. Preaching that opposition to World War I was treason to the nation, and calling for a host of repressive measures, Roosevelt had branded Debs and the Socialists (along with many others) as disloyal. Debs, who believed that his claim to the American democratic tradition was more authentic than Roosevelt's, fired back with every contemptuous metaphor he could muster:

> This political pet of the plutocrats, this bogus reformer, this shrieking charlatan, this raving mountebank, this crazy-horse of Oyster Bay ranch, this blood and thunder prophet, this opera bouffe ghost-

dancer, this blatant quack hero, this freak of froth and foam and buncombe, this nauseating moralizer, this dysenteric scold, this chattering midwife and meddler and all-around nuisance has buncoed the people long enough and they at last know him for what he is, at least those of them who have mentality above a shell-fish, and who can tell a jibbering fraud after he has exhibited himself to them daily for a score of years.[4]

Even after discounting for the personal animus of this trio, we are left forewarned about the dangers of taking Theodore Roosevelt as an exemplary leader for a democratic polity. Roosevelt rose to prominence as American democracy was experiencing the strains of industrial development, overseas expansion, and heightened political conflict, all dramatized by the new mass media of large-circulation newspapers. It was still possible in this democracy to pursue a form of leadership modeled after Lincoln's and committed to the goals of equality and universal dignity. But another choice was available: to use the new media to play to subtle currents of democratic self-doubt and to find a new guise for aristocratic superiority, in the character of the popular hero. An energetic, masterful leader could stake his claim to popular support as a heroic surrogate for a people too scattered, divided, or passive to act on their own.

Although Theodore Roosevelt loved to uncover parallels between himself and America's greatest democratic figure, Abraham Lincoln, his leadership had far more in common with the aristocratic statesmanship of his other political hero, Alexander Hamilton. Roosevelt's leadership was Hamiltonianism adapted to an age of democratic ideology. By constructing images of himself as an overwhelmingly masculine and masterful figure, and inviting his mass audience to consume these images as a form of vicarious political participation, Roosevelt solved the symbolic problem that had defeated Hamilton: how aristocratic leadership could thrive under the conditions of mass democracy.

This chapter tracks Theodore Roosevelt in his heroic guises and democratic disguises. I begin with Roosevelt's political identity, a mix of masculinity and moralism that produced perhaps the most remarkable ego in the history of American politics. Having established Roosevelt's political identity, I turn to his dramatization of it, his genius at dominating public attention through what Mark Twain had derided as "showing off." Given to spinning captivating tales of his own heroics, Roosevelt was nevertheless a shrewd politician; his neo-Hamiltonianism was sharply marked in his dread of demagogues, creed of practical politics, and fascination with the potential of executive power and an administrative state. Following the heroic executive into action, I find his natural field for mastery in imperialism and his thorniest governing dilemma in the encounter with corporate capitalism. I also follow the hero out of power, as his colorful countenance turned frightful: the chapter closes with Roosevelt at the end of his life, in the cauldron of World War I, where he demonstrated how heroic leadership in America could indulge in what it professed most to abhor.

The Man in the Arena

The starting point for an examination of Theodore Roosevelt's heroic leadership should be his obsession with masculinity—indeed, masculine imagery pervaded his descriptions of politics. He portrayed a world divided between the timid men of words, sitting in the stands and carping at their betters, and the heroic men of action, gladiators in the political arena. Speaking at the Sorbonne in Paris during his 1910 European tour, Roosevelt expatiated on one of his favorite metaphors:

> It is not the critic who counts; not the man who points out how the strong man stumbles, or where the doer of deeds could have done them better. The credit belongs to the man who is actually in the arena, whose face is marred by dust and sweat and blood; who strives valiantly; who errs, and comes short again and again, because there is no effort without error and shortcoming; but who does actually strive to do the deeds.[5]

Roosevelt despised the corrupt machine politician, or boss, but he reserved his greatest contempt for "emasculated sentimentalists," who were, in his eyes, too soft and squeamish for practical politics. Such men had no business in the man's world of political competition. Explaining his code of masculinity in an 1894 essay, "The Manly Virtues and Practical Politics," Roosevelt drew on his self-image to create the model of the muscular reformer. "If we wish to do good work for our country," he wrote,

> we must be unselfish, disinterested, sincerely desirous of the well-being of the commonwealth, and capable of devoted adherence to a lofty ideal; but in addition we must be vigorous in mind and body, able to hold our own in rough conflict with our fellows, able to suf-

fer punishment without flinching, and, at need, to repay it in kind with full interest.[6]

To Roosevelt, the unmanly were a threat not only to political reform at home but also to political greatness abroad. When he preached his famous cult of "the strenuous life" in 1899, before the upper-class Hamilton Club of Chicago, it was as much to chastise an ease-loving bourgeoisie as to inspire it. America's newly acquired empire was endangered less by foreign rivals than by a paucity of masculine virtue:

> The timid man, the lazy man, the man who distrusts his country, the over-civilized man, who has lost the great fighting, masterful virtues, the ignorant man, and the man of dull mind, whose soul is incapable of feeling the mighty lift that thrills "stern men with empires in their brains"—all these, of course, shrink from seeing the nation undertake its new duties. . . . These are the men who fear the strenuous life, who fear the only national life which is really worth leading.[7]

Roosevelt did have a softer side. His considerable capacity for love and tenderness emerged in his private life, which he largely exempted from his aggressive masculine philosophy of politics and warfare. Particularly in his role as a father, as any reader of his letters or autobiography finds, Roosevelt was an endearing figure, nurturing, playful, only occasionally (and with effort) stern and punitive. Yet even after separating private life from public life and making it a haven where gentleness was permissible, Roosevelt could not completely free it from unrelenting masculine demands. An affectionate father to his four sons, he nonetheless drove them hard and allowed them no leeway: "'I would rather one of them should die,'" he said, "'than have them grow up weaklings.'"[8]

Some biographers have suggested that in his preoccupation with masculinity, Roosevelt was compensating for a childhood of ill health and physical weakness. But we do not possess a fully convincing analysis along these lines; Roosevelt's personality still awaits the excavations of a skilled psychobiographer. In the absence of such a study, we can find clues to Roosevelt's masculinity in his culture as much as in his character. For Roosevelt's martial ideal was, as Jackson Lears has demonstrated, an obsession among many of the upper bourgeoisie in turn-of-the-century America. Roosevelt was a scion of a traditional upper class that increasingly felt itself atavistic and enfeebled, easily shouldered aside by the more aggressive and effective bourgeois parvenus and political bosses. He was hardly alone among his class in his almost desperate efforts to prove himself fully the equal of the new American rulers in manliness, while remaining their superior in the purity of his morals and the elevation of his cultural ideals.[9]

Perhaps the most revealing statement Roosevelt ever made about the roots of his own strident masculinity spoke of this cultural unease. When his oldest son, Ted, became embroiled in fights at school, Roosevelt wrote to Edward Sanford Martin, the father of one of Ted's schoolmates, in explanation of "the real underlying feeling which has made me fight myself and want Ted to fight." Fighting, he suggested, was the sign of manliness that shielded the son of the gentry from the scorn of the lower classes. Recalling his own days at Harvard, Roosevelt recounted: "I went in for boxing and wrestling a great deal, and I really think that while this was partly because I liked them as sports, it was even more because I intended to be a middling decent fellow, and I did not intend that anyone should laugh at me with impunity because I was decent." The father's experience was passed on to the son; Ted was taught that "he could be just as virtuous as he wished *if only he was prepared to fight.*"[10]

Roosevelt, who felt the need to fight so as not to be taunted as a sissy, hurled the same kind of taunts at others to distance himself from the members of his class who did not adopt the same approach. If one can sympathize with his desire to overcome the pressures placed on male identity, it is difficult to feel anything but repugnance for the accusations of effeminacy that he hurled against anti-imperialists and pacifists. To Roosevelt, the critics of his Panama policy were "a small body of shrill eunuchs." Pacifists who placed high hopes on arbitration treaties between nations were, he said in 1911, a "male shrieking sisterhood." Thus, Roosevelt fought in order to silence the bullies who would otherwise have laughed at his decency but joined them to jeer at men just as decent as he was.[11]

Masculine assertiveness allowed Roosevelt to hold on to his decency. His moral convictions were sincere, although capacious enough to coincide with his political ambitions. They were also highly combative. Not only did fighting protect decency; it also transformed it in the process into an aggressive moralism. Roosevelt was happiest when he could present himself as the moral battler in politics, engaged in holy combat against the perverse alliance of the effete and the corrupt. As governor of New York, for example, he characterized the opponents of his reelection as "the lunatic Goo-Goo, the wealthy corporation corruptionist, and the basest variety of machine politician."[12]

The mix of masculinity and moralism did not make for a tolerant man. Sure of his rectitude whatever position he adopted, Roosevelt generally ascribed to his adversaries either base motives or low intelligence. Assessing the Democrats during the presidential campaign of 1900, he envisioned a coalition of "all the lunatics, all the idiots, all the knaves, all the cowards, and all the honest people who are hopelessly slow-witted . . . backed by the solid South." Insanity was, according to Roosevelt, a common disorder among those who opposed him. He wrote to a British friend that the man who attempted to assassinate him during the 1912 campaign reminded him of his rivals on the left during his Progressive period: "I very gravely question if he has a more unsound brain than Senator La Follette or Eugene Debs."[13]

Masculine will clothed in moral righteousness appeared as an ego of heroic proportions. Numerous of his contemporaries attested— some in amusement, some out of frustration—to Roosevelt's outsized egotism. His tendency to monopolize conversations, for example, was legendary. Secretary of State John Hay told Henry Adams of a White House dinner at which the president "'began talking at the oysters, and the *pousse-café* found him still at it.'" The experience of Louis Van Norman, a member of a women's suffrage delegation that met with the president, was less comic. Roosevelt, he recalled, "talked every moment we were there. Apparently he did not listen at all." Roosevelt's need to dominate every scene was so palpable that even his children sometimes rebelled against it. His English friend, Arthur Lee, remembered that on Roosevelt's 1910 visit to London, "Ethel and Kermit complained to Mrs. Roosevelt that their father talked too much about himself" and asked Lee to "'persuade Father not to write his name so large' in the visitor book." As another one of his children put it, Theodore Roosevelt wanted to be "'the bride at every wedding, and the corpse at every funeral.'"[14]

Evident as his egotism was to those around him, Roosevelt was largely blind to it himself. Denials figured frequently in his voluminous correspondence. Thus, his hunger for power appeared to him as an eagerness for duty. As John Morton Blum has observed, Roosevelt became a master politician because he loved power, yet he was never candid about this love. He was equally adept at concealing from himself his passion for distinction and could admit to it only in reference to others. When John Hay died in 1905, for instance, Roosevelt expressed a wish that he too could die "in the harness at the zenith of his fame." But when the subject of his own immortality came up, he was resolutely modest. In 1906, at the height of his presidential success, he wrote to William Allen White: "I am not in the least concerned as to whether I will have any place in history, and, indeed, I do not remember ever thinking about it."[15]

Roosevelt's need both to exalt and to deny his ego was strikingly displayed in his fascination with Abraham Lincoln. During his first summer as president, he read the ten-volume biography of Lincoln by John Hay and John Nicolay, secretaries to the president during the Civil War. The more he read, the more he identified with Lincoln. Every important problem Roosevelt faced was now compared with the trials faced by Lincoln. In dealing with the Philippines and Panama, Roosevelt saw himself as following Lincoln's example of high idealism tempered by political prudence. In mediating the anthracite coal strike of 1902, he again sought Lincoln's wise middle path: "Just as Lincoln got contradictory advice from the extremists on both sides at every phase of the struggle for unity and freedom, so I now have carefully to guard myself against the extremists on both sides." But it was not enough to act like Lincoln; Roosevelt wanted to be like Lincoln. He wrote to Hay that his Lincoln biography "has made me of set purpose to try to be good-natured and forbearing and to free myself from vindictiveness."[16]

The mask of Abraham Lincoln could not, however, fit Theodore Roosevelt. Within a few months of his pledge of gentleness, he had resumed his old habits, lashing out at his adversaries in the coal strike as "the two vicious extremes" and castigating their arguments as "the ravings of the demagogues." Lincoln's masculine/feminine synthesis, the key to his democratic character, was thoroughly alien to Roosevelt. In Roosevelt's exclusively masculine political arena, to be forbearing was to be effeminate. His martial ideal identified war as a path to personal and national renewal, not a haunting tragedy calling out for providential explanation. There was little place for charity in the rough, manly politics of Theodore Roosevelt.[17]

Ironically, John Hay, who had taught Roosevelt about Lincoln (and who had given him as an inauguration gift a ring containing hair from Lincoln's head), ultimately became a target of Roosevelt's vindictiveness. Hay's letters, posthumously published in 1909, contained unflattering anecdotes about Roosevelt's egotism, and, more importantly, they claimed credit for foreign policy achievements that Roosevelt thought were rightly his. The highly vexed Roosevelt struck back in a lengthy letter to Henry Cabot Lodge. Hay, he wrote, had been a delightful conversationalist and a charming correspondent, but "he was not a great Secretary of State." A man of words, Hay had not been a genuine man of action. "He had," Roosevelt told Lodge, "a very ease-loving nature and a moral timidity which made him shrink from all that was rough in life, and therefore from practical affairs. . . . He was always afraid of Senators and Congressmen who possessed any power or robustness." In defending his ego and fame, Roosevelt was incapable of forbearance. It was not enough for him to deny Hay a measure of greatness; he had to deny Hay's manhood as well.[18]

Roosevelt's heroic ego chafed at the democratic disciplining to which Lincoln had subjected his own instinct for superiority. That ego could, at its most impressive, be the source of a sublime courage. Roosevelt was remarkably brave, even to the point of foolhardiness. When one of his former Rough Riders offered to serve him as a bodyguard for the 1912 campaign, Roosevelt responded that he did not want one. "Though I do not carry a gun, I am rather quick in my movements, and I would stand a reasonably good chance of getting anyone who tried to get me." Roosevelt was not quick enough; a would-be assassin shot him on a dark Milwaukee street as he headed for a campaign appearance. But the same benevolent fortune that had brought him through numerous narrow escapes at San Juan Hill was still at his side; the bullet struck the manuscript of his speech and his iron spectacles case, and barely penetrated his chest. The bleeding campaigner insisted on delivering his speech, waving off pleas that he go to a hospital with the pronouncement, "I do not care a rap about being shot."[19]

The heroic ego's defiance of limits could be awe-inspiring or it could be terrifying. When eight anarchist leaders were accused of a deadly bombing at Haymarket Square in Chicago in 1886, Roosevelt was on his Dakota ranch. The Haymarket affair stirred up his concern for property and order, but it also aroused his desire to demonstrate his manhood in battle with the largely immigrant ranks of radicalism. As he wrote to his sister, Anna:

> My men here are hardworking, labouring men, who work longer hours for no greater wages than many of the strikers; but they are Americans through and through; I believe nothing would give them greater pleasure than a chance with their rifles at one of the mobs. . . . I wish I had them with me, and a fair show at ten times our number of rioters; my men shoot well and fear very little.

This fantasy of vigilantism cannot, unfortunately, be written off as youthful bravado. It presaged the repressive and violent spirit with which the aged Theodore Roosevelt went after other "mobs" that he had decided were not "Americans through and through."[20]

Images of the Hero

In March 1906 Sereno Pratt, editor of the *Wall Street Journal,* warned President Roosevelt, mistakenly, that his stance on railroad rate legislation would cost him dearly in popularity. Replying to Pratt, Roosevelt sniffed at the notion that he should worry about something as evanescent as public favor. "I have felt a slightly contemptuous amusement," he claimed, "over the discussion that has been going on for several months about my popularity or waning popularity or absence of popularity. I am not a college freshman, . . . and therefore I am not concerned about my 'popularity' save in exactly so far as it is an instrument which will help me to achieve my purposes." Roosevelt abhorred imputations that he was a popularity seeker. Like one of his principal heroes, Alexander Hamilton, his conception of the cheap politician who lusts after popularity for its own sake was Thomas Jefferson, "that slippery demagogue."[21]

In Roosevelt's eyes, Jefferson "was infinitely below Hamilton." Roosevelt admired Hamilton as a "wonderful genius" and shared his passion for centralized power, aggressive nationalism, and the heroic presidency. But he dissociated himself from those of Hamilton's qualities that were impractical or offensive in a more democratic age. In 1906, in his enthusiastic response to British writer Frederick Scott Oliver's new biography of Hamilton, Roosevelt emphasized two major flaws in the aristocratic statesman. First, Hamilton had not been a politician; he had refused to practice the art of political management, which was indispensable to winning the backing of a free people. Second, he had nurtured a fundamental distrust of democracy itself. Roosevelt, by contrast, was a master of practical politics and an ardent proponent of a democracy that adored him. Superior to Hamilton in these two essential qualities, Roosevelt could be a Hamilton for a democratic age.[22]

For all his genius, Hamilton had been clumsy at symbolic politics. Roosevelt was brilliant at it. In constructing colorful images of a heroic personality, he had found the key to transporting aristocratic superiority into a democratic political culture. The aristocrat's sense of superior talent and need for mastery could no longer be revealed through a condescending attitude toward the people; on the contrary, prowess and mastery would now be showcased in spectacles designed to impress the public. Roosevelt was distinctively modern in courting popular adulation through the politics of personality.

His genius at this consisted, in part, of recognizing the potential of the mass media, which had not been available to previous generations of American leaders. As John Milton Cooper, Jr., has noted, Roosevelt enjoyed "the first major career in American politics to be conducted wholly within the era and under the influence of modern journalistic media." American newspapers had been dramatically transformed between the era of the Civil War and the end of the century, the very years of Roosevelt's own maturation. New technologies, such as the linotype machine and photoengraving, and new business methods, fueled by growing advertising revenues, produced mass-circulation giants unknown to the previous era. A burgeoning corps of more professionalized journalists raced after news that would interest and entertain their rapidly increasing readership. In this media environment, a public man did not need to represent an important constituency and to articulate its problems in order to attain prominence. As Roosevelt instinctively grasped, he could instead offer himself as a colorful news maker.[23]

Roosevelt's image making was extraordinarily entertaining. At the same time it involved nothing less than a redefinition of democratic politics. He ascended to national prominence as tensions over industrialization were coming to a head. After the polarizing election of 1896, industrial and urban elites enacted electoral reforms that more tightly controlled immigrant and working-class voters, producing a notable decline in political participation over the ensuing decades. In what Walter Dean Burnham labels "the movement toward depoliticization," the heroic leader played a complementary role, presenting himself through the new journalistic media as an object of mass fascination and identification. Mass-circulation newspapers expanded the audience he could reach, while simultaneously conveying a greater sense of intimacy between leader and followers through the new fixation on personality. As the heroic leader came to expand his role in public life, ordinary citizens, who had enjoyed high rates of political participation during the late nineteenth century, increasingly retreated to a passive role as spectators. The modern aristocrat wore his democratic disguise with flair; no longer seeking to rise above the masses, he offered them instead his persona.[24]

Roosevelt's talent for heroic spectacle was first honed in his frontier days in the Dakotas. The young rancher and hunter not only hardened his body and democratized his patrician image on the frontier; he also began to craft his own hero tale in magazine articles and books. Perhaps the most marvelous of Roosevelt's western yarns told of his capture of three fugitive desperadoes. Fearful of a lynching because of their horse-stealing exploits, the three had stolen a boat belonging to the Roosevelt ranch and headed down the Little Missouri River. The dangerous trio was led by a brawny redhead named Finnegan, who had, Roosevelt noted, "been chief actor in a number of shooting scrapes." Building a second boat, Roosevelt and two of his men pursued the thieves down the perilously icy river and ultimately took them by surprise. In the tale's dramatic climax, Roosevelt got the drop on two of the fugitives and ordered them to put up their hands.

"Finnegan hesitated for a second," he wrote, "his eyes fairly wolfish; then, as I walked up within a few paces, covering the center of his chest so as to avoid overshooting, and repeating the command, he saw that he had no show, and, with an oath, let his rifle drop and held his hands up beside his head." This exciting, hard-boiled prose, worthy of the best western dime novel, marked Roosevelt as a budding master at image making. More remarkable than his storytelling, however, was a photograph that accompanied the story when it first appeared in *Century* magazine in 1888. It showed Roosevelt training his rifle on the three subdued desperadoes. Knowing that he would turn this adventure into spectacle, Roosevelt, the media-conscious cowboy, had brought along a camera.[25]

The climactic spectacle in Roosevelt's rise—and the one that became the centerpiece of his legend—was San Juan Hill. A complex set of motives propelled Roosevelt, against the advice of all his friends, to resign his position as assistant secretary of the navy once war was declared with Spain in April 1898 and to obtain a commission as a lieutenant colonel of the First U.S. Volunteer Cavalry, soon to be dubbed the Rough Riders by the press. There is no reason to question his own stated motive for going to Cuba: he had been one of the most vociferous advocates of war with Spain, and he had to practice what he had preached or be scorned as one of the "armchair and parlor jingoes." Some biographers have also suggested a deeper familial source: Roosevelt's father had stayed out of the military during the Civil War in deference to his Southern-born wife, and the son's ego demanded that he make up for his father's lack of heroic service by taking part in the first war that came to hand. Patriotism, pride, the desire once more to prove his masculinity all played a part as well. But to the list of motives that can be compiled to explain Roosevelt's eagerness to see combat in Cuba, self-dramatization must be added. From the Rough Riders' training camp outside San Antonio, Texas, Roosevelt arranged with Robert Bridges, assistant editor at *Scribner's Magazine*, for publication of a war memoir that would "appear in magazine form, that is, in popular form, first, yet when it comes out as a book to be in shape as a permanent historical work." His adventure as a Rough Rider was lived with the awareness that he would transform it into a dramatic prose work, first for a popular audience and then for posterity.[26]

Already deft at publicity, Lieutenant Colonel Roosevelt arranged for reporters and photographers to accompany him in Cuba; he even found space aboard his overcrowded troop ship for two motion-picture cameramen from the Vitagraph Company. His truly daring and courageous leadership at Kettle and San Juan hills thus received abundant coverage in the press, and he became an instant national hero. Others would begin, even before the chief of the Rough Riders could, to re-count Roosevelt's blazing exploits in Cuba. Yet the most important version of what became the legend of San Juan Hill was composed by the hero himself. Published in 1899—first as six magazine articles and then as a book—Roosevelt's *Rough Riders* deserves special attention. In both its self-conscious strategies and its unconscious self-revela-tions, the work was the epic of a master self-dramatizer.[27]

Although Colonel Leonard Wood was the ostensible commander of the First U.S. Volunteer Cavalry, the press had been right to depict the regiment as Roosevelt's Rough Riders. In its composition, the regi-ment recapitulated Roosevelt's career. The bulk of the men were the kind of frontiersmen among whom Roosevelt had proved his tough-ness in his Dakota days: "tall and sinewy, with resolute, weather-beaten faces, and eyes that looked a man straight in the face without flinching." But there were also four policemen who had served under Roosevelt in New York and an impressive assortment of Knicker-bocker and Ivy League athletes, such as Dudley Dean, "perhaps the best quarterback who ever played on a Harvard eleven," and Bob Wrenn, "the champion tennis player of America." The ranks of the Rough Riders thus reminded Roosevelt's audience of his prior ex-ploits. By combining rough men with gentlemen, the regiment also burnished his image as the aristocrat turned democrat, the descen-dant of a patrician family who was at home with, and loved by, the hardest specimens of the working class.[28]

Recounting the background of his troops, Roosevelt relished their prowess as athletes, cowboys, hunters, and Indian fighters. His Rough Riders "were to a man born adventurers in the old sense of the word." They were chivalric heroes, knights-errant who had put their individ-ual skills at the service of their commander and their country. "We knew not," Roosevelt wrote, "whither we were bound, nor what we were to do; but we believed that the nearing future held for us many chances of death and hardship, of honor and renown." Roosevelt, a military amateur, was the ideal chieftain for this brave band of volun-teer warriors:

> Such a regiment, in spite of, or indeed I might almost say because of, the characteristics which made the individual men so exception-ally formidable as soldiers, could very readily have been spoiled. Any weakness in the commander would have ruined it. On the other hand, to treat it from the standpoint of the martinet and military pedant would have been almost equally fatal.[29]

Fearful that the war might end before the Rough Riders could go into battle, Roosevelt and Wood managed to move their cavalry to

Cuba quickly, sans most of the horses, and pressed to the front of the fighting. Although they were there to liberate the Cuban people from the oppressive yoke of the Spanish, the Cuban people were largely absent from the pages of *The Rough Riders*. Roosevelt's brief description of Cuban revolutionaries was contemptuous and dismissive: upon landing "we found hundreds of Cuban insurgents, a crew of as utter tatterdemalions as human eyes ever looked on. . . . It was evident, at a glance, that they would be no use in serious fighting." The Cuban landscape was beautiful, but it harbored hellish threats. The vultures waiting to devour the dead had to compete with "big, hideous land-crabs," who surrounded American casualties in a "gruesome ring." The balmy tropical air carried malaria and yellow fever. Roosevelt's Cuba was a dreamland, where the native inhabitants had disappeared, clearing the field for American valor.[30]

The thrilling high point of Roosevelt's epic was the charge up Kettle and San Juan hills in the face of withering Spanish fire. Steeped in the literature of hero tales, he told his own brilliantly. The reader could almost feel Roosevelt's adrenaline pumping as he reenacted the breathless excitement of the headlong rush to capture the Spanish positions. Urging his men forward, Roosevelt fearlessly surged to the front of the line charging the heights. At the top of Kettle Hill, he shot a Spaniard with a revolver taken from the sunken battleship *Maine*. Roosevelt expressed unconcealed pride in this killing; while most of the American troops had picked off the Spaniards with rifle fire, he had shot at close range and taken symbolic American revenge for the *Maine*.[31]

What made Roosevelt's derring-do even more amazing were the dangers that he had survived, seemingly miraculously. His "crowded hour" at Kettle and San Juan hills was a succession of narrow escapes. Shrapnel struck his wrist, leaving "a bump about as big as a hickory-nut." A soldier whom Roosevelt ordered to carry a message stood up to salute him "and then pitched forward across my knees, a bullet having gone through his throat." Another soldier whom the mounted Roosevelt had ordered to stand did not respond initially to his command:

> I again bade him rise, jeering him and saying: "Are you afraid to stand up when I am on horseback?" As I spoke, he suddenly fell forward on his face, a bullet having struck him and gone through him lengthwise. I suppose the bullet had been aimed at me; at any rate, I, who was on horseback in the open, was unhurt, and the man lying flat on the ground in the cover beside me was killed.

These near misses provided Roosevelt's tale with an ancient resonance. They recall Joseph Campbell's description of the timeless myths of "the road of trials," in which the hero undergoes "miraculous tests and ordeals" and "discovers for the first time that there is a benign power everywhere supporting him in his superhuman passage." That the deadly Spanish bullets cut down so many of his troops yet could not touch Theodore Roosevelt marked him as a man of destiny.[32]

After the tension of the battles, during the long waiting for the negotiators to terminate hostilities, Roosevelt provided a moment of comic relief. When a fierce storm struck his encampment, his tent was blown over. Roosevelt described his predicament: "I had for the first time in a fortnight undressed myself completely, and I felt fully punished for my love of luxury when I jumped out into the driving downpour of tropic rain, and groped blindly in the darkness for my clothes as they lay in the liquid mud." Unable to find them, "I basely made my way to the kitchen tent, where good Holderman, the Cherokee, wrapped me in dry blankets, and put me to sleep on a table which he had just procured from an abandoned Spanish house." Roosevelt consciously enlivened his saga with a bit of comic self-deprecation, but his unconscious was richer still. Here, at the dawn of American overseas empire, was the naked white man as infant, cuddled and put to bed by the red man he had previously conquered. Asleep on his captured Spanish table, Roosevelt was an American innocent, reborn in imperial glory.[33]

The Rough Riders concluded with Roosevelt's leave-taking from his men. He mentioned with pride that while "there were a few weaklings among them," the great majority of the men, self-reliant to the last, refused all offers of financial assistance upon their demobilization. With these comrades of combat, these fellow warriors who were not "weaklings," Roosevelt could accept and express tender emotions. After incorporating into his text a poignant letter from an Oklahoma woman telling of the death of Holderman, the Cherokee, who "'loved you so,'" Roosevelt appended the final sentence of his tale: "Is it any wonder that I loved my regiment?"[34]

Within three years the hero of San Juan Hill was in the White House. Roosevelt now enjoyed opportunities to monopolize the media of which the politician on the rise could only have dreamed. The dramatic feats and controversies of his administration—from the symbolic antitrust prosecution of the rail barons' Northern Securities Company at the beginning to the globe-circling voyage of the big-stick Great White Fleet at the end—created a larger-than-life figure, as depicted in words, photographs, and cartoons. Throughout his two terms in the presidency, his flamboyant persona was *the* central story in American politics.

To ensure that news about him was not only constant but favorable as well, Roosevelt cultivated the press as no president before him had. Finding quarters for journalists in the White House, he established the institution of the White House press corps. George Juergens, the most penetrating chronicler of Roosevelt's press relations, has observed that "as long as he intended to dominate the headlines, it made sense to arrange that reporters be conveniently on hand; in a way almost extensions of his own staff." Meeting daily with reporters, Roosevelt was open and voluble, providing the press with a flood of material. He was also calculating and cagey, a pioneer of such news-management techniques as the backgrounder, the trial balloon, and the deliberate leak.[35]

White House reporters had never before enjoyed such access to or appreciation from a president. But in return, Juergens notes, they had "to agree to print only what he wanted printed" and to "color their reporting to get his point of view across." Reporters who deviated from this standard, or who aroused Roosevelt's ire for some other dereliction, were frozen out: he divided the press into insiders and outsiders, friendly scribes and exiles who were to be cut off from the vital sources of their trade. Still immature and uncertain of its rights, the White House press corps accepted from Roosevelt what, in later generations, it would never have tolerated. In Juergens's words, Roosevelt "upgraded the press corps at the price of corrupting it."[36]

In protecting his heroic reputation, President Roosevelt was sensitive about even the smallest chinks in his armor. When he failed to bag any of his prey on a Mississippi bear hunt in 1902, the press engaged in good-humored ribbing of the famed big game hunter. Planning a hunting trip in the Rockies after his reelection in 1904, Roosevelt wanted no repetition of the earlier incident. To John Goff, his hunting companion, Roosevelt confided that "we must be dead sure that there is no slip-up and that I get the game. I think the thing to do is to say we are after mountain lions, and we could make sure of killing one or two of them; but I should most want to get a bear. Have you a thoroughly good pack, and do you know the ground so that we could be sure of getting the bear?" Setting low and misleading expectations with the press for this hunt, Roosevelt provided a comic illustration of a phenomenon that would grow progressively more dangerous: presidential publicity as deception.[37]

His talents at self-dramatization often served Roosevelt well, but they were not suitable for conveying a larger message. John Milton Cooper, Jr., has argued that in his later years as president and in his postpresidential career as a Progressive, Roosevelt, usually thought of as the political realist in contradistinction to Woodrow Wilson, was in fact struggling to get across to the American people his own brand of transcendent idealism. Dreading both the softening impact of spreading material comforts and the hardening lines of class hostility, Roosevelt called on Americans to take up his creed of national service and international duty. But to a people steeped in the pursuit of self-interest, his was a doomed crusade. Sadly, Cooper writes, Roosevelt's "greatest failure as president lay in his attempt to get the people to avoid class politics and rise above material concerns."[38]

Cooper is right to credit Roosevelt with the impulse to elevate the American people. Still, Roosevelt as educator was far less impressive than Roosevelt as dramatic hero. There were problems with both the style and the substance of his educational message. When Roosevelt lectured the American people, his speeches were rife with what he once conceded were "platitudes"—he lacked Lincoln's belief in the capacity of democratic language to be both accessible and profound. The public, he told Henry Cabot Lodge in 1916, "cannot take in an etching. They want something along the lines of a circus poster." In words that were often very banal, Roosevelt preached a creed that was often not very credible. Summoning Americans to forget the divisions of class, he surrounded himself with colleagues drawn preponderantly from the gentry. Trumpeting the fatuity of materialism, he spent his presidential summers in a bourgeois idyll at his Sagamore Hill estate. More importantly, as Cooper acknowledges, Roosevelt "never seemed to recognize either that the dominant groups in society would continue to fare better than others under his programs or that it was unjust to ask the disadvantaged to forgo their interests."[39]

Nor were language and thematics the sum of Roosevelt's limitations as an educator. He was too much the flamboyant political personality to be the effective democratic teacher. His personal drama overshadowed whatever it was he had to say about his society. As Willard Gatewood, Jr., has remarked, "In political campaigns, Roosevelt himself rather than his accomplishments or the Square Deal was likely to be the principal issue." When Roosevelt called Americans to transcend self-seeking and to serve in the cause of a "new nationalism," he offered up himself as exemplar. What he could not comprehend was the incongruity between his persona and his message: the most publicized ego in America was preaching the subordination of self.[40]

That mastery of publicity of which John Adams had complained in his mordant commentary on Benjamin Franklin in Paris was advanced by Theodore Roosevelt to heights that would have driven Adams to despair. A pioneer of the modern politics of personality, Roosevelt was a spectacular case of the possibilities for heroic leadership in a democratic age. Unlike a number of those who have followed his lead, however, there were some substantial talents and real accomplishments in the shows he staged. Surrounded by hosts of public-relations experts, Roosevelt's political descendants have not had to emulate his "strenuous life" or to share his genius for self-dramatization. The manufacture of images of the hero is now routine.[41]

Demagogues and Stewards

One of the ways that Theodore Roosevelt resembled Alexander Hamilton was in the gallery of political characters that he sketched. Like Hamilton, Roosevelt placed the conflict between the statesman and the demagogue at the center of the political scene. A neo-Hamiltonian in his institutional thinking, he once more looked for statesmanship to flourish through presidential power and administrative expertise. But Roosevelt criticized Hamilton for failing to understand that in a democratic polity "it is only in very exceptional circumstances that a statesman can be efficient, can be of use to the country, unless he is also (not as a substitute, but in addition) a politician." The statesman who had learned the arts of the practical politician was, for Roosevelt, the antitype not only of the demagogue, but of the spoilsman and the doctrinaire reformer as well. Recognizing the inadequacy of Hamiltonian statesmanship for an age of mass democracy, Roosevelt replaced Hamilton's self-portrait with his own.[42]

Roosevelt's political rise took place during a period of growing conflict over the terms of industrialization. As the American economy rapidly expanded to become the foremost in the world, the inequalities and injustices of this economy produced a series of dramatic clashes between opponents and defenders of the existing order: the Haymarket bombing, the Homestead strike, the Populist crusade, the Pullman strike. These seeming portents of radical change deeply disturbed Roosevelt, who was, William Harbaugh observes, "obsessive . . . [in] his fear of upheaval from below." Any manifestations of collective militancy—from Populist farmers, Socialist workers, blacks, even suffragists—drew fire from an anxious Roosevelt. What most frightened him, however, was the prospect that this upheaval could be organized and turned to the conquest of state power by the figure of the demagogue.[43]

Hamilton's fear of the demagogue reached its apex when Aaron Burr tied Thomas Jefferson in electoral votes in the 1800 presidential contest. The election campaign of 1896 was Roosevelt's 1800. Speaking for William McKinley against William Jennings Bryan, Roosevelt gave vivid voice to his anxieties in a remarkable campaign address, "The Menace of the Demagogue." In his overheated imagination, the American republic now trembled on the brink of catastrophe. "Hysteria" was loose in the land, fostered by demagogues "strikingly like the leaders of the Terror of France in mental and moral attitude." One hundred years after Hamilton, the specter of Jacobinism still caused a shudder.[44]

Where Hamilton had depicted one master demagogue, however, Roosevelt portrayed a more diffuse threat. He could not take William Jennings Bryan altogether seriously. "For Mr. Bryan," he said, "we can feel the contemptuous pity always felt for the small man unexpectedly thrust into a big place." Behind Bryan, however, stood a figure far more sinister in Roosevelt's eyes: John Peter Altgeld, the former governor of Illinois. Because Altgeld had pardoned the three anarchist leaders who had not been hanged for their alleged part in the Haymarket bombing and had opposed the actions of the Cleveland administration in crushing the Pullman strike of 1894 with federal troops, Roosevelt regarded him as a conniver in murder and a preacher of lawlessness. He detected in the former governor who had dared to take the side of labor "the jaws and the hide of the wolf through the fleecy covering. Mr. Altgeld is a far more dangerous man than Mr. Bryan. He is much slyer, much more intelligent, much less silly, much more free from all the restraints of public morality."[45]

Bryan, Altgeld, and their ilk were, according to Roosevelt, serving up the same stale fodder of resentment that demagogues had offered for centuries. They represented the class of the embittered, not the working class: "The forces which they have rallied behind them and which give them their only real power are the dark and mean hostility and envy felt for all men of ability by those unworthy men who care more to see their brethren fail than themselves to win success by earning and deserving it." The goal of the Democrats in 1896, Roosevelt insisted, was to invert and mock Lincoln's democracy: "Instead of a government of the people, for the people, and by the people, which we now have, Mr. Bryan would substitute a government of a mob, by the demagogue, for the shiftless and disorderly and the criminal and the semicriminal."[46]

Roosevelt warned his audience that if the Democrats won the election, America would face a nightmare. Demons would emerge from the subterranean depths of American life and wreak their worst impulses in a fiery but futile apocalypse:

Mr. Bryan and the men who stand at his right and his left hands . . . are fit representatives of those forces which simmer beneath the surface of every civilized community, and which, if they could break out, would destroy not only property and civilization but finally even themselves, leaving after them a mere burnt-out waste, as a cooled lava overflow becomes mere slag and cinders.

Lacking an Aaron Burr to epitomize the danger, Roosevelt envisioned a legion of demagogues, a corps of destroyers. In an age of industrial crisis and looming radicalism, he was battling something larger than the dark ambitions of a single demagogic figure. He took his stand against a spirit of discontent with the new industrial capitalist order that would, if not properly handled, explode as soon as successful demagogues could strike the match.[47]

The skills of the practical politician were required to combat the demagogic specter. In a democratic polity, the man who lacked these skills could do nothing. Theodore Roosevelt thus saw himself as a model of the practical political reformer, the foe of political corruptionists and business standpatters on his right as well as demagogic radicals to his left.

For a scion of a genteel upper class that had largely been displaced in politics by the rougher and less scrupulous politicos of the Gilded Age, Roosevelt's self-education in the political arts was impressive. Unlike most of his peers, he was able to perceive that the upper-class distaste for the political machine and preoccupation with the purification of the government through civil-service reform (although attitudes that he shared) were rooted in a chilly and self-defeating disdain for the masses. He pointed out in his *Autobiography* that silk-stocking reformers "had not the slightest understanding of the needs, interests, ways of thought, and convictions of the average small man; and the small man felt this, although he could not express it, and sensed that they were really not concerned with his welfare, and that they did not offer him anything materially better from his point of view than the machine." Becoming a shrewd student of the psychology and interests of average voters, Roosevelt demonstrated how a "gentleman" could win a wide public following.[48]

Roosevelt not only followed a credo of practical politics but preached it at every opportunity. He had two political gospels: "the gospel of morality" and "the gospel of efficiency." According to these gospels,

a man must not only be disinterested, but he must be efficient. If he goes into politics he must go into practical politics, in order to make his influence felt. . . . He must be prepared to meet men of far lower ideals than his own. . . . He must stand firmly for what he believes,

and yet he must realize that political action, to be effective, must be
the joint action of many men, and that he must sacrifice somewhat
of his own opinions to those of his associates if he ever hopes to see
his desires take practical shape.[49]

Useful as a personal defense against attacks from moralistic gentry
of the mugwump type, Roosevelt's exhortations to practical politics
were, nonetheless, genuinely high-minded. They gave only a faint
hint, however, of the tensions between morality and efficiency that he
himself had to sustain in his political career. A case in point was his
relationship with New York's Republican boss, Thomas C. Platt. Roosevelt wrote to Lodge in 1895 that "Platt succeeds in identifying himself with the worst men and the worst forces in every struggle, so that
a decent man *must* oppose him." Three years later, the still decent
Roosevelt worked out a modus vivendi with Platt and accepted his
offer of the Republican nomination for the governorship.[50]

"The gospel of efficiency" prescribed rules that Roosevelt never put
into print. He was adept, as a master politician, at sending antithetical
messages to opposing constituencies. Pursuing railroad rate legislation in his second presidential term, he assured conservatives that his
moderate reform program was the only way to stave off government
ownership of the railroads and other anticorporate measures, while
instructing impatient reformers that his brand of moderation was
preferable to the quest for "the perfect cure" that "often results in securing no betterment whatever."[51]

Ego and ambition, his morality's silent partners, propelled Roosevelt to be just as "efficient" a politician as the Boss Platts with
whom he had to deal. But he was never an ordinary politician. Keenly
attuned to how his own dramatic persona could mask the politician's
less seemly arts and offer answers to the social discontent of his era,
Roosevelt sought the one political stage that was too lofty and exposed for any boss. Naturally, and with a seeming inevitability, he
headed for the White House.

Although Roosevelt got his start in politics as a New York assem-
blyman, he soon gravitated to executive positions. He was a fervent
champion of the strong, unitary executive, whose twin pillars of energy and responsibility perfectly matched his driving ego and aggressive rectitude. Fuming as New York police commissioner when one of
his fellow commissioners, Andrew Parker, began to obstruct his plans,
he confided to his sister, Anna: "If I were . . . a single-headed Commissioner, with absolute power, . . . I could in a couple of years have accomplished almost all I could desire." Roosevelt was thus in his glory

when he reached the pinnacle of "single-headed" executive posts. In November 1908, contemplating the imminent end of his presidency, he wrote to his son, Ted: "I have had the best time of any man of my age in all the world . . . [and] have enjoyed myself in the White House more than I have ever known any other President to enjoy himself."[52]

In a famous passage in his *Autobiography*, Roosevelt set forth the theory that had guided his presidential behavior:

> My view was that every executive officer, and above all every execu-
> tive officer in high position, was a steward of the people bound ac-
> tively and affirmatively to do all he could for the people, and not to
> content himself with the negative merit of keeping his talents un-
> damaged in a napkin. I declined to adopt the view that what was
> imperatively necessary for the Nation could not be done by the
> President unless he could find some specific authorization to do it.
> My belief was that it was not only his right but his duty to do any-
> thing that the needs of the Nation demanded unless such action was
> forbidden by the Constitution or by the laws.

Roosevelt claimed that he belonged to the "Lincoln-Jackson" rather than the "Buchanan-Taft" school of presidential power. But we also hear echoes of Alexander Hamilton's sweeping assertion of executive authority in the Pacificus papers. The uniquely Rooseveltian note in this passage was its masculine combativeness: there would be no ef-fete "napkins" concealing his talents in the presidency.[53]

Roosevelt in fact faced major constraints during his presidency, es-pecially from the Republican Old Guard in domestic policy and an iso-lationist public in foreign policy. But he pushed his role as steward as far as he could, and he could be an appealing figure in this role. In 1907, when lumber interests secured an amendment to an agricultural bill that would have blocked the president from setting aside any addi-tional forest lands in the northwestern states, Roosevelt rushed out an executive proclamation, creating or expanding thirty-two forest re-serves, before the bill became law. As he explained in triumph, "When the friends of the special interests in the Senate got their amendment through and woke up, they discovered that sixteen million acres of timberland had been saved for the people by putting them in the Na-tional Forests before the land grabbers could get at them."[54]

He could also be an ominous figure as steward, aggressive and ar-bitrary in committing the essential interests of the nation. Having dis-patched the Navy's Great White Fleet on an unprecedented voyage around the globe, Roosevelt boasted, "I determined on the move with-

out consulting the Cabinet, precisely as I took Panama without consulting the Cabinet. A council of war never fights, and in a crisis the
duty of a leader is to lead and not to take refuge behind the generally
timid wisdom of a multitude of councillors." From this standpoint,
Roosevelt took it as one more sign that his choice of William Howard
Taft as his successor was a mistake when Taft turned to Congress for
advice at the outbreak of the Mexican Revolution in 1911. In his
hastily written 1899 biography of Oliver Cromwell, Roosevelt had said
of his subject that "all his qualities, both good and bad, tended to render the forms and the narrowly limited powers of constitutional government irksome to him." The same words might be applied, albeit on
a lesser scale, to Roosevelt. What later generations would praise as the
"strong" presidency and condemn as the "imperial" presidency were
both readily apparent in his presidency.[55]

Roosevelt's importance for the emergence of the modern presidency extended beyond his theory of presidential prerogative. He was
a pioneer as well in establishing a personal connection between the
president and the public. Of the crowds of farmers that flocked into
towns to see him on his tour of the West in 1903, he wrote:

> Most of these people habitually led rather gray lives, and they came
> in to see the President much as they would have come in to see a
> circus. It was something to talk over and remember and tell their
> children about. But I think that besides the mere curiosity there was
> a good feeling behind it all, a feeling that the President was their
> man and symbolized their government, and that they had a propri-
> etary interest in him and wished to see him, and that they hoped he
> embodied their aspirations and their best thought.[56]

By turning the executive branch into a personal presidency, Roosevelt enhanced his popularity and influence. More subtly, he found a
powerful antidote to the mass militancy and radical leadership that he
so feared. He was not hesitant to employ the executive's instrument of
repressive force to stave off working-class upheaval. Applauding President Cleveland for forcibly crushing the Pullman strike, Roosevelt
was equally quick to order federal troops to scenes of class conflict.
Unlike Cleveland, however, Roosevelt offered the disadvantaged and
the discontented something more attractive than repression. He offered them the promise of reform, in the exciting framework of his
personal drama. Proclaiming himself the champion of Lincoln's
"plain people," Roosevelt discovered in the personal presidency a sta-
bilizing focus for mass emotions.[57]

This personal presidency was also an increasingly bureaucratic presidency. If the president was personally to champion the public interest against the special interests ensconced in Congress, he would need his visible stewardship on the grand issues of politics to be implemented in fine detail by a corps of professional assistants. Roosevelt thus was sympathetic to the elite reformers who wanted to strengthen the administrative capacities of government. He was eager to employ the expertise of the new class of professionals emerging in fields as disparate as economics, social welfare, and forestry and as president was a strong force for bureaucratic expansion. "In his neo-Hamiltonian scheme," Stephen Skowronek observes, "the position of the President as a nationally elected officer was to be coupled with the professional discipline of the bureaucrat. . . . If the power of the President and his top administrators could only be freed from past restraints, nationalism, imperialism, and industrialism could be properly joined, controlled, and legitimized in a strong bureaucratic state."[58]

Roosevelt's aims in building this bureaucratic state were reflected in the work of the Keep Commission. This commission, appointed in 1905, included two of Roosevelt's most ardent administrative helpers, James Garfield and Gifford Pinchot. Its mandate from the president was "to investigate and find out what changes are needed to place the conduct of the executive business of the Government in all its branches on the most economical and effective basis in the light of the best modern business practice." Linking himself to the emerging professional class, Roosevelt was, in the guise of a search for businesslike efficiency, mounting a challenge to the traditional patronage and pork-barrel powers of Congress. But Congress fought off the challenge, not only rejecting the recommendations of the Keep Commission but also refusing even to fund a public printing of its final reports.[59]

Having tasted the sweetness of presidential power, Roosevelt's life after yielding the executive office was a long tale of frustration. As he prepared to leave the White House, he insisted that "I emphatically do not desire to clutch at the fringe of departing greatness." Yet each succeeding presidential election found him, despite protestations to the contrary, seeking a way back to that former greatness. Roosevelt could not really be happy with lesser men (in his eyes) in the White House. As we shall see, he became one of those former chief executives described by Alexander Hamilton, "wandering among the people like discontented ghosts and sighing for a place which they were destined never more to possess."[60]

"A Bit of a Jingo"

Before he was carried away by his desire for imperial glory, Alexander Hamilton had recognized that the new nation he sought to shape was "a Hercules in the cradle." Exulting in the industrial muscle and bursting energies of the nation as the nineteenth century closed, a new generation of imperial dreamers believed that the American Hercules was at last on the threshold of maturity. The most prominent of these dreamers was Theodore Roosevelt. A quintessential Hamiltonian statesman in the skill, energy, and forcefulness that he brought to the conduct of American foreign policy, Roosevelt was equally the Hamiltonian in responding to the dangerous lure of empire. Subsequent commentators on Roosevelt's foreign policy have not improved on the judgment of Howard Beale at the close of his classic study: "One comes away . . . with admiration for Roosevelt's ability, his energy, and his devotion to his country's interests as he saw them, but with a sense of tragedy that his abilities were turned toward imperialism and an urge for power, which were to have consequences so serious for the future."[61]

Roosevelt added a racial dimension to Hamilton's vision of empire. "During the past three centuries," he proclaimed in the opening sentence of his historical epic, *The Winning of the West*, "the spread of the English-speaking peoples over the world's waste spaces has been not only the most striking feature in the world's history, but also the event of all others most far-reaching in its effects and its importance." His history of the American West was full of savage deeds by whites as well as Indians, but he castigated those who lamented the dispossession of the native inhabitants as adherents of "a warped, perverse, and silly morality." In the Indians' hands, the West had been a "waste space"; only their conquest by English-speaking white men had watered it with the blessings of civilization. As America's continental growth through removal of the Indians reached its natural limits, Roosevelt looked overseas. Defending American expansion in the Philippines in 1900, he stressed its continuity with the conquest of the West: "The history of the nation is in large part the history of the nation's expansion."[62]

As a self-proclaimed "expansionist" (he insisted that America was not "imperialist"), Roosevelt was well aware of the commercial benefits to be obtained from the projection of American power abroad. But he preferred to highlight the psychological benefits to Americans: the testing of manhood, the discipline of mastery, the fulfillment of racial destiny. At bottom, Roosevelt was a romantic imperialist, bidding for the glory of the ages. In 1899 he wrote to his British friend, Cecil Arthur Spring Rice:

> I believe in the expansion of great nations. India has done an incalculable amount for the English character. If we do our work well in the Philippines and the West Indies, it will do a great deal for our character. In the long run I suppose all nations pass away, and then the great thing is to have left the record of the nation that counts—the record left by the Romans—the record that will be left by the English-speaking peoples.[63]

The American people could rise to their heroic destiny, Roosevelt believed, only through the summons of their leaders. Depicting empire as the testing ground of the people, the subtext of his imperial sermons was heroic leadership. Empire was a field in which heroic leaders could operate openly, dividing the world into superiors and inferiors and pursuing unqualified mastery. It offered a stage for conquest that would never be permitted the heroic leader in domestic politics.

Cuba first brought Roosevelt imperial glory, but it was another trophy of the war with Spain—the Philippines—that most fully elicited his imperial vision. When Filipino nationalists under the leadership of Emilio Aguinaldo proclaimed the independence of their country, the United States, having recently condemned the Spanish for a brutal colonial war in Cuba, reenacted (albeit more successfully) the Spanish part on the distant Pacific islands. Arguing that imperial war undermined the fundamental values of a constitutional republic, anti-imperialists urged that the Filipinos be allowed to form their own government without American tutoring. But any renunciation of imperial duty was unthinkable for Roosevelt: "To refuse to attempt to secure good government in the new territories ... would simply mean that we were weaklings, not worthy to stand among the great races of the world." Eager to be on the front line of the imperial struggle, Roosevelt, then governor of New York, unsuccessfully sought the position of governor-general for the Philippines.[64]

Aware of the likely cruelties of imperial war, Roosevelt nevertheless had no qualms about undertaking one. "The most ultimately righteous of all wars," he had proclaimed in *The Winning of the West*, "is a war with savages, though it is apt to be also the most terrible and inhuman." Convinced that the American war against the Filipino nationalists would be as "righteous" as the heroic frontiersmen's conquest of the Indians, Roosevelt called for an aggressive military approach. "In the Philippines," he wrote to his former comrade in Cuba, Leonard Wood, "we still seem to be having ugly work, but if only our people stand firm and take a little punishment and send if necessary a few tens of thousands of reinforcements there, we will have the islands absolutely pacified once and for all in a short time." He urged Secretary of State John Hay that American forces not only defend Manila but also "assume aggressive operations and . . . harass and smash the insurgents in every way until they are literally beaten into peace."[65]

In Roosevelt's thinking, the Philippines provided a valuable learning experience for a nation new to the challenge of overseas empire. The American army was one of the pupils. To his friend Hermann Speck Von Sternberg, a German diplomat well schooled in imperialism, Roosevelt wrote in 1900: "The Philippines are an excellent training ground for our younger officers. In Cuba on the contrary where our army is engaged mainly in the work of civil administration, I believe there has been a considerable falling off in our military work, notably in marksmanship." Roosevelt was even more enthused about the Philippines as a "training ground" for American character. "In this world," he thundered in his "strenuous life" speech in 1899,

> the nation that has trained itself to a career of unwarlike and isolated ease is bound, in the end, to go down before other nations which have not lost the manly and adventurous qualities. If we are to be a really great people, we must strive in good faith to play a great part in the world. We cannot avoid meeting great issues.[66]

Although Roosevelt characterized the American war in the Philippines as "rough work," he was adamant in his insistence that the core of the American imperial project was benevolence. Left to their own devices, he claimed, the barbarous Filipinos would descend into a morass of misery, ignorance, and bloody lawlessness. The guns of the American forces, by contrast, paved the way for schools, roads, and the other prerequisites of civilization. Americans were not interested in a permanent colonial possession; once having imposed order, they would tutor the Filipinos in the lessons of self-government. Roosevelt insisted that the Filipinos receive justice at the hands of the United States—so long as they were also "made to realize that justice does not proceed from a sense of weakness on our part, that we are the masters."[67]

Whatever arguments can be advanced for later American benevolence in the Philippines, the war that began in 1899 and wound down during Roosevelt's presidency was one of the most shameful events in

American history. Driven by racial prejudices, frustrated by harsh physical conditions, maddened by the atrocities sometimes inflicted by the Filipino guerrillas, American troops did not, as Roosevelt hoped, have their character strengthened through imperial war. They pacified the islands by burning villages, massacring the peasants' indispensable water buffalo, and slaughtering large numbers of civilians who were assumed to be just as hostile as Aguinaldo's soldiers. Filipino villagers who refused to supply Americans with information were often tortured. The recipients of "imperial benevolence" paid a high price. As Stanley Karnow sums it up: "The U.S. forces, by their own count, killed some twenty thousand native soldiers. As many as two hundred thousand civilians may also have died from famine and various other causes, including atrocities committed by both sides."[68]

Newspaper accounts and congressional hearings eventually brought this horror home to Americans, and the excitement of imperial war gave way to a growing revulsion. In charge of the war as the new president, Roosevelt first denied that Americans were guilty of any atrocities in the Philippines, then had to concede that some acts of brutality had taken place. But he was never shaken from the view of America's role that he expressed in his first annual message as president: "History may safely be challenged to show a single instance in which a masterful race such as ours, having been forced by the exigencies of war to take possession of an alien land, has behaved to its inhabitants with the disinterested zeal for their progress that our people have shown in the Philippines."[69]

As president, Roosevelt's attention shifted from the Philippines to Latin America, where once more he would deal with nations he regarded as inferior. His high-handed treatment of Colombia over the Isthmus of Panama is too oft told to require review here. The same is true for the Roosevelt corollary to the Monroe Doctrine, which announced that the United States would police the hemisphere to ensure political stability and financial propriety in its more wayward neighbors. Roosevelt was, however, more cautious in his Latin American policy than one would have predicted from his earlier imperial posture. Breathlessly eager to get to Cuba in 1898, he intervened in the Cuban revolution of 1906 with considerable reluctance. Enthused by acquisition of Puerto Rico and the Philippines in 1898, he did not, apart from the Panama Canal Zone, seek further American territorial expansion during his presidency. Emphasizing this caution, recent defenders of Roosevelt's diplomacy have claimed that, in the words of Frederick Marks III, "he cannot be styled an ardent imperialist."[70]

It was not the absence of ardor, however, but the presence of practical political considerations that explains the somewhat subdued

imperial politics of Roosevelt's presidency. The Senate, regarding
Roosevelt as a usurper prone to trampling on its traditional prerogatives in foreign policy, was a continual thorn in his side on Latin
American matters. But Roosevelt's larger problem in diplomacy was
public opinion. Citing his interventions in Cuba, Santo Domingo, and
Panama in a letter to William Bayard Hale in December 1908, Roosevelt continued: "I would have interfered in some similar fashion in
Venezuela, in at least one Central American State, and in Haiti already, simply in the interest of civilization, if I could have waked up
our people so that they would back a reasonable and intelligent foreign policy. . . . Our prime necessity is that public opinion should be
properly educated." The American public, still predominantly isolationist (and perhaps still chary of armed interventions abroad after
its exposure to the appalling revelations about the war in the Philippines), was not enthusiastic about Roosevelt's creed of international
duty—it apparently was in need of further imperial education. Roosevelt, like Hamilton before him, found that the American people
provided recalcitrant material for the greatness he planned for
them.[71]

Surveying the world at the end of his presidency, Roosevelt was
distressed to see that doubts about empire were not only widespread
in the United States but were mounting as well in his model imperial
power, Great Britain. Upon leaving the presidency, he immediately
proceeded to Africa for a big game hunt. Delighted by what he saw of
the British colonies in sub-Saharan Africa, he exclaimed to Arthur
Lee: "I am, as I expected I would be, a pretty good Imperialist!" But
the threat to empire from the nascent nationalism of colonized peoples was ominously evident to Roosevelt when he reached the Sudan
and Egypt. Dismayed by what he took to be "an uncomfortable flabbiness" in the British stance toward Egyptian unrest, he sought,
through speeches in both Cairo and London, to firm up his erstwhile
mentors.[72]

Roosevelt always remained what he called himself in 1897: "a bit of
a jingo." His considerable diplomatic talents could be placed in the
service of better objectives than empire. The skillful mediation that
brought an end to the Russo-Japanese War and won for Roosevelt the
Nobel Peace Prize still deserves admiration. But Roosevelt the peace-
maker and Roosevelt the ardent imperialist were not, ultimately, inconsistent figures. He dreaded—and sought to avert—wars between
the nations he considered in the forefront of the global movement for
civilization, yet he favored wars through which those same nations
could bring civilization to the barbarous regions of the globe. Roo-

sevelt has often been praised as the first great American leader to preach the realities of international responsibility to an isolationist and self-absorbed people. He also needs to be seen as preaching the dangerous illusion that would enthrall many American leaders who followed him: that the United States would be the best of all empires, the most progressive and the most moral.[73]

The Hero and the Capitalist

While the romantic imperialism of Theodore Roosevelt changed little during his life, there was a striking progression in his views of political economy. Beginning as a conventional Hamiltonian of the right, Roosevelt wound up as a new kind of Hamiltonian on the left, an advocate of controls over corporations and redistributive measures that still sound radical today. Roosevelt's evolution from right to left on matters of political economy reflected both the moralist's unease with a predatory economic order and the politician's insight into popular discontent. It also reflected the dilemmas of Hamiltonian leadership in the era of industrial capitalism.

Roosevelt's stance with respect to the political economy evolved through three relatively distinct phases: the traditional conservative (up to 1898); the conservative reformer as safety valve for mass discontent (1899–1906); and the radical conservative seeking the subordination of property to the public welfare (1907–19). The young Theodore Roosevelt, although rejecting dogmatic laissez-faire doctrines, subscribed to orthodox conservative assumptions about American economic life. As late as 1897 Roosevelt could respond to Populist leader Tom Watson that the evils of which Watson complained existed "not because of the shortcomings of society, but because of the existence of human nature itself." The only classes that Roosevelt would recognize were those of the thrifty and the improvident. Admitting that "good laws" and "honest administration" could bring about improvements, Roosevelt maintained that more could be achieved "by frowning resolutely upon the preachers of vague discontent; and by upholding the true doctrine of self-reliance, self-help, and self-mastery."[74]

Much like Alexander Hamilton, the young Roosevelt proposed differential treatment for the errant capitalist and the unruly proletariat. But where Hamilton sought to cow a protesting mass with a massive show of force, Roosevelt was more sanguinary. Writing to James

Brander Matthews a few months after the Pullman strike of 1894, led by Eugene V. Debs, had been broken by federal troops, Roosevelt proclaimed: "I know the populists and the laboring-men well, and their faults; I like to see a mob handled by the regulars, or by good State guards, not over-scrupulous about bloodshed; but I know the banker, merchant, and railroad king well too, and *they* also need education and sound chastisement."[75]

First as governor of New York and then as the successor to President McKinley, Roosevelt shed his traditional conservatism and emerged as a conservative reformer. His moral instincts and political senses were attuned to the unsettling transformation of American capitalism at the turn of the century. The shift from a competitive economy of small producers to a corporate economy of giant trusts accelerated dramatically in the years between 1898 and 1904 through what Martin Sklar has called an "avalanche of corporate reorganization in industrial enterprise." Already troubled by the moral laxity of the corporate elite, Roosevelt now became more alarmed by their growing power—and by the radical specter that they were raising. His response however, was cautious and moderate, consistent with his own conservative proclivities and, even more important, acceptable to the Republican Old Guard—those powerful representatives of corporate property who dominated Congress.[76]

The fundamental premise of Roosevelt's viewpoint in this second phase was mild government regulation of an economy characterized by large corporations and large labor unions. Never enthusiastic about breaking up large corporations (despite some shrewdly symbolic antitrust prosecutions during his administration), he argued that "these big aggregations are an inevitable development of modern industrialism." He regarded labor unions, the workers' response to the rise of the giant corporation, as equally inevitable. As a conservative reformer, Roosevelt at first hoped that big business abuses could be checked by his new Bureau of Corporations, which collected and publicized information about the activities of industrial corporations. His reform agenda during this period, although hardly threatening to business, was not a sham designed merely to shield the new corporate order. Roosevelt wanted the national government to assert its superiority to both business and labor and to become, in the words of Richard Hofstadter, "a neutral state which would realize as fully as possible the preference of the middle class for moderation, impartiality, and 'law.'" The executive, as the steward of the public welfare, was Roosevelt's personal answer to the menace of plutocracy and its even more frightening twin, "red radicalism."[77]

The muffled response to corporate power that Roosevelt presented during his first term as president was acceptable to many business leaders, who contributed almost three-quarters of the funds collected for his reelection campaign in 1904. Nonetheless, Roosevelt was beginning to distance himself, emotionally as well as politically, from the capitalist class. In 1901 he told Cecil Arthur Spring Rice: "I do not see very much of the big-moneyed men in New York, simply because very few of them possess the traits which would make them companionable to me. . . . To spend the day with them at Newport, or on one of their yachts, or even to dine with them save under exceptional circumstances, fills me with frank horror." Feeling that he had to bully profit-seeking businessmen into a patriotic war with Spain, Roosevelt regarded bourgeois calculation as an enemy of a "strenuous life" of national service. Increasingly, he came to rank the capitalist as the inferior of the statesman and the warrior. "It is a debasing thing," he said in 1911, "for a nation to choose as its heroes the men of mere wealth."[78]

Roosevelt was even more distant from the working class. His pledge to all Americans was the "square deal": "I am President of the United States, and my business is to see fair play among all men, capitalists or wageworkers." This promise of evenhanded treatment was seldom fulfilled. Since corporate capital towered over organized labor in resources and power, a neutral stance in the competition between capital and labor was bound to favor the status quo. But Roosevelt could not even be neutral. For example, when mine workers in the Arizona territory began a strike that turned violent in 1903, Roosevelt responded promptly to the request of local authorities for help and had federal troops on the scene within twenty-four hours. The following year, when mine workers in Colorado, attacked by thugs hired by the company and unable to obtain protection from local authorities, requested federal intervention, Roosevelt protested that his hands were tied. To send troops in this instance, he said, would set a precedent for endless interventions in labor disputes. Even worse, he told Ray Stannard Baker, the "contention raised by the miners that I should interfere, if true, would require my interference in every State where a negro is lynched."[79]

Roosevelt's underlying concern during this period was labor radicalism rather than corporate misconduct. Indeed, he was most furious at wealthy capitalists when their shortsighted greed stimulated militant class consciousness among their foes. To William Howard Taft, Roosevelt complained in 1906 that the "dull, purblind folly of the very rich men . . . and the corruption in business and politics, have tended to produce a very unhealthy condition of excitement and irritation in the popular mind, which shows itself in part in the enormous increase in the socialistic propaganda." The threat to the established order was even more menacing than it had been in 1896: "I have felt," Roosevelt wrote in 1905, "that the growth of the socialist party in this country was far more ominous than any populist or similar movement in time past." If the traditional conservatism of William McKinley had staved off the apocalypse in 1896, this time it would take a shrewder and more supple brand of conservatism.[80]

The moderate reforms that President Roosevelt sponsored between 1901 and 1906, culminating in the Hepburn Act, which regulated railroad rates, cut into the power of business in order to make American capitalism both more politically secure and more economically efficient. In strengthening the Interstate Commerce Commission's regulatory powers, the Hepburn Act was, in Roosevelt's thinking, a politically prudent response to the growing public clamor against the railroads. Federal regulation was also a more efficient approach than a patchwork of state controls. The ICC's new mandate to set "reasonable rates" signified for Roosevelt substantial progress toward the goal of a more rational, equitable, and harmonious political economy.

Over and over, Roosevelt tried to teach businessmen that a reform like the Hepburn Act was "not the precursor but the preventive of Socialism." He wanted them to understand that rather than fostering hostility to the corporations through his reform efforts, "I have furnished a safety-valve for the popular unrest and indignation." A minority of sophisticated business leaders did understand and appreciate Roosevelt's approach. But when the Hepburn Act was followed by a financial panic in 1907, Roosevelt became the target of a torrent of corporate criticism. The majority of the corporate class, feeling the flush of their enormous economic power, would not stand for a Hamiltonian statesman who presumed to dominate them in their supposed best interests. Roosevelt would either have to back down in the face of corporate opposition or else become a novel kind of Hamiltonian, pitting the power of the state directly against the power of capital. The stage was set for the conservative Roosevelt to make a dramatic move to the left.[81]

His combative temperament and shrewd political instincts impelled Roosevelt to resist the corporate clamor. As the financial panic spread, he was deluged with demands to reassure the business community by easing up on the pursuit of corporate malefactors. But the president was determined—good Hamiltonian that he was—to see to it that the federal government maintained the upper hand: "I shall enforce the laws; I shall enforce them against men of vast wealth just exactly as I enforce them against ordinary criminals; and I shall not flinch from this course, come weal or come woe." The more the businessmen howled, the more Roosevelt came to think that the mild reforms he had sponsored heretofore were insufficient. The captains of finance, he believed, were exploiting the unstable economic situation "to try to escape from all government control." In response, Roosevelt's judgment was "more firmly than ever that they must be brought under control."[82]

No previous president had come close to the fiery rhetoric that Roosevelt now turned against his corporate adversaries. In a special message to Congress on January 31, 1908, Roosevelt announced a new reform agenda: an employers' liability law, relief for organized labor from the abuse of court injunctions, measures to control stock watering and overcapitalization by corporations, and more. But his specific proposals paled before the militancy of his rhetoric. He drew a battle line between himself, as the steward of the people, and his critics, who were, he argued,

> representatives of predatory wealth—of the wealth accumulated on a giant scale by all forms of iniquity, ranging from the oppression of wageworkers to unfair and unwholesome methods of crushing out competition, and to defrauding the public by stock jobbing and the manipulation of securities. Certain wealthy men of this stamp, whose conduct should be abhorrent to every man of ordinarily decent conscience, . . . have during the last few months made it apparent that they have banded together to work for a reaction.

Although the ultimate danger, for Roosevelt, remained a "vindictive and dreadful radicalism," he trained his immediate fire on "law-defying wealth."[83]

Roosevelt's new stance was more than a matter of rhetoric. Martin Sklar has reconstructed Roosevelt's behind-the-scenes efforts to write a tough corporate control law in 1908. The bill he sought provided for corporate registration with the Bureau of Corporations, with the requirements for registration subject to change at the discretion of the president. Once registered, corporations were to file their contracts or combinations with the bureau, which could disallow them as unreasonable restraints of trade. Roosevelt concealed his role in fashioning this bill, knowing that it went well beyond what Congress would accept. Yet it represented, Sklar notes, what the lame-duck president really wanted: "a stringent license system with extraordinary executive powers." To guide a corporate sector that had grown too powerful for mild controls, the presidency, the bastion of Hamiltonian statesmanship, would have to regain some of the power over the economy that Hamilton had once wielded.[84]

Stymied in his final year as president by the mounting hostility of business and the Republican Old Guard, Roosevelt became an even more fervent reformer when he returned to the United States in 1910 after his postpresidential African safari and triumphal European tour. Disappointed with his hand-picked heir, Taft, and responsive to the surge of progressivism that Taft's alliance with the Old Guard was fueling, Roosevelt broadened his reform agenda once more. To his proposals for stringent administrative controls over business conduct he added a fresh focus on the question of economic equity. The Progressive Roosevelt called for a more equitable distribution of material well-being. He favored "the effort to secure a better and a higher standard of living, of remuneration, of safety, for wage-workers." The watchword of this emerging prophet of welfare-state capitalism was "social and industrial justice" through more direct popular rule. Even in his Progressive period, Roosevelt still counted himself as a conservative—but he was a conservative with a radical point: "The true friend of property, the true conservative, is he who insists that property shall be the servant and not the master of the commonwealth."[85]

Perhaps the most remarkable aspect of Roosevelt's evolution into a radical conservative was his growing sympathy for those he had written off in his youth as failures of human nature. Once he came to denounce "predatory wealth," he was more inclined to attribute poverty and suffering to exploitation than to improvidence. Hence, he championed the cause of young women striking in the garment trades and that of unemployed, destitute men during the recession of 1913–14. In his new recognition that economic inequality inflicted deeper wounds than those to the body, Roosevelt could even sound like a man he still viewed as an archenemy, Eugene V. Debs. He wanted labor to regain the dignity it had lost under the sway of industrial capitalism. And he insisted that greater economic justice was a prerequisite for a democratic society: "We keep countless men from being good citizens by the conditions of life with which we surround them." There was, in the Progressive Roosevelt, a strong streak of personal ambition and a persisting fear of "overradicalism." There was also a commitment to the disadvantaged that had not previously graced his character.[86]

By 1912 Roosevelt had become the hero of many Progressives. Denied the 1912 Republican presidential nomination by the machinations of the party's Old Guard, he bolted and formed his own Progressive party. His Progressive candidacy crystallized the reform enthusiasms of the previous decade. Observers noted that the delegates who came to Chicago to nominate him for the presidency were largely political amateurs fired with the zeal of a religious crusade. Roosevelt's acceptance speech, "A Confession of Faith," brought this crowd to a frenzy with its closing line: "We stand at Armageddon, and we battle for the Lord." Yet he was too much the politician to be fully comfortable with the role of political evangelist. Behind the scenes at the convention, he sided with the party's chief financial backer, George Perkins, against the majority of party enthusiasts and excised an antitrust plank from the Progressive platform.[87]

The Progressive years revealed an admirably humane dimension to the otherwise bellicose figure of Theodore Roosevelt. In his proposals for "social and industrial justice," he transcended his customary Hamiltonianism and accepted one of the central responsibilities of democratic leadership—for the first time in his career. Still, the radical conservative of 1907–19, if not the "bogus reformer" assailed by Debs, was nonetheless limited in his approach to the problems of capital and labor. Roosevelt remained a paternalist as Progressive, anchored in the middle class and holding the labor movement at arm's length. His neo-Hamiltonian plan for guiding capital, through the heroic efforts of an executive soaring above the clash of classes, was not a viable approach in an age of mature capitalist power. In his prescription for taming corporate capital through noblesse oblige, the realist sounded oddly utopian: "The Progressive plan would give the people full control of, and in masterful fashion prevent all wrongdoing by, the trusts, while utilizing for the public welfare every industrial energy and ability that operates to swell abundance, while obeying strictly the moral law and the law of the land." The executive and bureaucracy upon which Roosevelt counted would need far more help than he realized to contain the power of corporate capital in twentieth-century America.[88]

The Hero as Demagogue

The heroic impulse in Theodore Roosevelt could not be sated by the glory of San Juan Hill or the White House. As an ex-president, Roosevelt was restless, even desperate, in his search for new arenas of heroic leadership. On three occasions—in March 1911, May 1914, and

July 1916—he volunteered for a war in Mexico. He was dubious that policing revolution-torn Mexico was a large enough task for a figure of his stature. "But if by any remote chance," he wrote to President Taft in 1911, "there should be a serious war, a war in which Mexico was backed by Japan or some other big power, then I would wish immediately to apply for permission to raise a division of cavalry, such as the regiment I commanded in Cuba."[89]

When the "serious war" broke out in Europe in 1914, Roosevelt pronounced himself "inexpressibly saddened." Any precognition he may have had of the impending European tragedy, however, was undermined by his attraction to a romantic view of the war. In one of his earliest newspaper articles on the war, he depicted the fate of the European peoples in a vocabulary that reflected his own characteristic obsessions: "At one stroke they were hurled from a life of effortless ease back into elemental disaster; to disaster in which baseness showed naked, and heroism burned like a flame of light." Watching from the sidelines, Roosevelt could not conceal his envy. Writing to Arthur Lee in praise of British heroism during the first month of the war, he lamented: "On this side of the water at the moment there is no opportunity for the display of heroic qualities, and not the slightest indication that there will be a desire to display them if the need arose."[90]

Initially uncertain about whom to blame for the war, Roosevelt soon came to the support of the Allies and to condemn Germany, especially for its brutal invasion of neutral, helpless Belgium. Renouncing Woodrow Wilson's policy of neutrality, he regarded the president as the embodiment of what he most despised in American politics. The president was, Roosevelt charged, "a physically timid man," who pandered to the most callous instincts of Americans and "wrapped the true heart of the nation in a spangled shroud of rhetoric." Roosevelt became Wilson's most vocal critic, as he set out to convince the American public of the need for military preparedness and the duty to punish international miscreants for their crimes against the weak.[91]

The campaign for preparedness and for a patriotic "Americanism" revived Roosevelt's flagging energies. It also launched him on another quest for the presidency. He wanted the Republican nomination in 1916—but only if it meant that the American people were ready to follow him into the war: "It would be a mistake to nominate me unless the country has in its mood something of the heroic." When the Republican Old Guard denied their old enemy the nomination, Roosevelt blamed the professional politicians less than the American people. To his sister, Anna, he sighed, "Well, the country wasn't in heroic mood! We are passing through a thick streak of yellow in our national life." Reluctantly, he supported Charles Evans Hughes, whom he disliked, in order to drive from the White House a president whom he had come to loathe as he had no other political foe before.[92]

Once President Wilson began to move the nation toward war shortly after his reelection, Roosevelt revived his plans for military service. Offering to raise a "Roosevelt Division," he informed Secretary of War Newton Baker that his force "could be sent to the front in the shortest possible time." At the age of fifty-eight, Roosevelt was just as eager to be the first at the front when American forces saw combat in Europe as he had been in Cuba in 1898. But the aged warrior foresaw a different kind of glory than he had won in his prime. "As for myself," he wrote to William Allen White in February 1917, "I think I could do this country most good by dying in a reasonably honorable fashion, at the head of my division in the European War." Roosevelt would not, however, have the chance for a new burst of heroism or a romantic death in battle. The Wilson administration did not, understandably, view the hero of the hell-bent charge up San Juan Hill as a suitable commander for the grim trench warfare of World War I. President Wilson may also have had more personal and political motives in rejecting Roosevelt's offer to raise a volunteer division and rush it to France; desiring to expand his control over American public opinion in wartime, he could hardly have wanted his most celebrated critic to recapture the public's heart at the very outset of the war.[93]

In a eulogy for the legendary British big game hunter, Frederick Courteney Selous, composed at the time he was awaiting word from the Wilson administration on his division, Roosevelt wrote: "Then the Great War came, and for months he ate his heart out while trying in vain to get to the front." Selous, an aged warrior like Roosevelt, was finally accepted into the British military and was killed in battle against the Germans in East Africa. Denied the opportunity ever to get to the front, Roosevelt ate his heart out. His heroic impulse, bottled up by Wilson, soured into rage. In words even more chilling than his youthful fantasy of vigilantism after the Haymarket riot, Roosevelt proclaimed his wartime vocation: "The Hun within our gates masquerades in many disguises; he is our dangerous enemy; and he should be hunted down without mercy." The big game hunter was transforming himself into a witch-hunter. Crusading to step up the war against the Huns abroad and their masked doubles at home, Roosevelt sought to stir up the American people by infusing them with his own rage.[94]

Convinced that the Wilson administration's efforts to ferret out domestic "Huns" were suspiciously derelict, Roosevelt became the most prominent leader and the most important symbolic legitimator of the nongovernmental forces of repression during World War I. He fulminated against any foreign-born American who was not wholeheartedly for the war: "There is no room for the hyphen in our citizenship. There is no place for a fifty-fifty Americanism in the United States. He who is not with us, absolutely and without reserve of any kind, is against us, and should be treated as an alien enemy." Roosevelt called for outlawing the teaching of German in the public schools and insisted that all newspapers be published in English. His demand for absolute loyalty was meant to uncover the native-born as well as the foreign-born Huns. "I heartily approve," he wrote in November 1917, "the effort to secure the dismissal of all teachers who refuse to sign the loyalty pledge or who in any way have shown the slightest symptoms of disloyalty to this nation or of sympathy with Germany." He also heartily approved the hunt of the disloyal launched by "that stirring body of patriots, the Vigilantes"—an organization of writers and artists devoted to his own principles of "one hundred percent Americanism."[95]

The preacher of preparedness strongly defended his right to criticize the timidity of the Wilson administration and the inefficiency of its war effort. But the right of free speech, Roosevelt argued, belonged only to those who supported the war. He exceeded the repressive Wilson administration in his eagerness to punish anyone who spoke out, even indirectly, against the war. German Americans who expressed sympathy for their native land or Irish Americans who denounced England should, Roosevelt wrote, be interned and then sent packing, while the "native American who, during this war, directly or indirectly assails any of our allies, notably England, but also Japan, is a traitor to America and should be promptly imprisoned." Prompt imprisonment was, he believed, an appropriate remedy for any dissent to the war. Apprised that a new book by Thorstein Veblen attacked business and patriotism as threats to a lasting peace, Roosevelt agreed with his informant that "Mr. Thorstein Veblen ought to be in jail" and inquired whether the American Defense Society, of which Roosevelt was honorary president, could do anything to send him there.[96]

Roosevelt still considered himself a radical during World War I and proposed such progressive measures as heavy taxation of excess war profits. The Bolshevik Revolution in Russia, however, led him to war on the American left as the principal arm of the "Hun within our gates." For Roosevelt, "the Bolsheviki of America" was an elastic category, incorporating not only the IWW, the Socialist party, and the anarchists, but also Senator Robert La Follette, William Randolph Hearst, and the *New Republic*. The real, working-class reds, Roosevelt argued, were bomb throwers and murderers. They aroused his loathing but not his contempt, which, as usual, he reserved for those he considered men of words only, the "professional intellectuals" among the Bolsheviki, "who vary from the soft-handed, noisily self-assertive frequenters of frowsy restaurants to the sissy socialists, the pink-tea and parlor Bolshevists." While it was not clear how Roosevelt came to be familiar with the clientele of "frowsy restaurants," it was evident that the Bolsheviks were, for him, a final incarnation of the radical specter he had long dreaded.[97]

Through his campaign to alert the American people to the Bolshevik menace, Roosevelt became one of the fathers of the postwar "red scare" and one of the progenitors of American anticommunism. He was eager to expel from the American republic anyone who dared to associate with the symbols of European radicalism. "Any foreign-born man," he stated in November 1918, "who parades with or backs up a red flag or black flag organization ought to be instantly deported to the country from which he came. Appropriate punishment should be devised for the even more guilty native-born." The last letter that Roosevelt wrote, three days before his death on January 6, 1919, admonished his followers that "there must be no sagging back in the fight for Americanism merely because the war is over." He urged that wartime standards of loyalty be maintained: "There can be no divided allegiance here. Any man who says he is an American but something else also, isn't an American at all. We have room for but one flag, the American flag." Roosevelt's final words were, sadly, a summons to intolerance, a call to the people to mobilize behind a closed-minded, flag-waving, one hundred percent Americanism.[98]

Reconstructing the history of a "countersubversive tradition" in America, Michael Rogin states: "The countersubversive needs monsters to give shape to his anxieties and to permit him to indulge his forbidden desires. Demonization allows the countersubversive, in the name of battling the subversive, to imitate his enemy." Enraged because he was denied a chance for the heroics of the battlefield or the White House in World War I, Theodore Roosevelt projected his fury onto his foes. The Bolsheviki, he warned, were men with "corroded souls," who could only "preach and practice the gospel of hatred and malice. " In the fight against such demonic foes, Roosevelt could vent his own "hatred and malice." Blocked from the channel of heroism, his need for mastery was redirected through the channel of repression, as he assumed his final persona as a demagogue.[99]

Conclusion

Theodore Roosevelt wrote in an 1895 essay, "American Ideals," that a great nation owes its great men most of all for "the immense but indefinable moral influence produced by their deeds and words themselves upon the national character." Citing Washington and Lincoln as his exemplars, he yearned to join their company as an embodiment of high-minded service to the American nation. It has been the argument of this chapter that Roosevelt possessed a different kind of moral influence. Seeking a modern guise for the aristocratic statesmanship of Alexander Hamilton, Roosevelt developed a heroic style of leadership that was unhealthy for the democratic strain in American national character.[100]

It is hard to deny the appeal of Roosevelt's heroic leadership. He was vital, colorful, charismatic; his exploits can still astound anyone who studies his career. But if we look beyond his enduring charm and ask how he affected political life in America, his appeal begins to fade. In a number of ways that matter for a democratic society, Roosevelt's brand of heroic leadership was in conflict with the shared dignity and active citizen participation that characterize a genuinely heroic democracy.

By defining American politics as a domain of masculine competition, Roosevelt excluded those—whether men favoring a less aggressive style, women finding their own public voice, or blacks imbued with the need of the oppressed for solidarity—who did not fit in his "arena." The goal of the competition for him was mastery, so it is not surprising that his favorite metaphors pictured combat and not dialogue as the essence of politics. For those observing the political gladiators from the stands, Roosevelt offered a second set of metaphors—that of politics as drama, show, spectacle. In his spectacular career, Roosevelt became larger than life, grand in his gestures and captivating in the controversies with which he spiced political life in America. Yet if many of Lincoln's "plain people" did thrill to the exploits of Theodore Roosevelt, they did not receive from him that message of democratic competence that Lincoln had brought. Roosevelt's spectacle had only one hero—and many passive spectators.

Roosevelt's followers looked to their champion for rewards more bountiful than mere material prosperity. Their hero promised to lead a crusade to bring economic and social justice and to purify American society. He promised, too, to extend American power and benevolence to the "backward" regions of the globe. But Roosevelt's paternalistic economics and empire building fostered elite power rather than democratic virtue. The bureaucratic state he favored was hardly a training ground for republican citizenship; his militarized empire further corroded democratic morality each time it advanced a new claim of masterful benevolence with its guns.

Driven by the promptings of the swollen ego, heroic leadership, as embodied in the extreme by Roosevelt, could not in the end tolerate opposition or accept failure. When Roosevelt's deepest urges were frustrated, he was prepared to smash through the political and moral limits he had observed in his days of triumph. The heroic leader always contained, as one of his possible personas, the demagogue.

6

Eugene V. Debs

Dissenting Leadership and Democratic Dignity

ON MARCH 12, 1919, EUGENE V. DEBS, THE POPULAR LEADER OF American socialism, delivered his final speech before entering federal prison. The world war was over, but he faced a ten-year prison sentence for violating the wartime Sedition Act in his speech at Canton, Ohio, the previous year. In the face of government repression of radicals and dissenters, Debs was defiant. He held a caustic view of Woodrow Wilson and his allies at the Paris Peace Conference: "They are going to make the world perfectly safe for democracy, and that is why I am going to the penitentiary." But at the age of sixty-three, in poor health, and feeling a sense of depression that he hoped to keep from his supporters, it was a shaken Debs who spoke at Cleveland. The opening words of his speech gave halting expression to his feelings on this painful occasion: "It may seem strange to you, but in my plans, in my dreams, I did not think of going to the penitentiary—and I—I had a thousand times rather go there and spend my remaining days there than betray this great cause."

Debs found respite from his depression by turning to his audience. As a leader who identified profoundly with the rank and file, he drew sustenance from his communion with them:

> It is so perfectly fine to me to look into your faces once more, to draw upon you for the only word I have ever had, the only word that has ever come to me, the only word that I can ever speak for myself. I love mankind, humanity. Can you understand? I am sure you can.

Debs also took sustenance from the company he kept as a leader. He noted that Washington, Jefferson, Sam Adams, and the abolitionists had also been denounced as criminals or traitors by those in power. In going to prison, Debs felt that he was upholding what was best in the American political tradition.[1]

As a young man, Debs held to a conventional conception of leadership as mastery by the heroic few. Through his political evolution into a democratic socialist, he came to articulate a very different conception, in which the leader's most important task was to educate and empower his followers. Debs shared this view with the other dissenting leaders portrayed in this book: Elizabeth Cady Stanton and Martin Luther King, Jr. His task was more daunting than theirs, however. Stanton and King educated Americans to recognize the contradiction between the profession of republican and democratic values, on the one hand, and the denial of freedom to women and blacks, on the other. As a socialist, Debs had to challenge American values more fundamentally, to call into question long-standing American commitments to private property and notions of classlessness. He was proposing to extend the democratic power of the majority into an industrial capitalist sphere that had cloaked itself in the hallowed guise of individual freedom and evoked traditional fears of a meddling, autocratic state. Debs's skills as an educator were as great as those of Stanton and King, and his message was equally rich in democratic instruction, but his more radical vision of the completion of democracy through socialism faced more entrenched opposition and ultimately left a smaller mark on American political life.

In his educational efforts, his oratory, his relations with followers, and his commitment to organizational democracy, Debs adopted a socialist stance that met the most stringent criteria of democratic leadership. There was an important weakness, however, in his understanding and practice of leadership. Though he was strong and inspiring on the public platform, he shied away from political battles within the Socialist party and failed to exert much influence on its direction. Debs justified this political diffidence with a radical-democratic critique of leadership itself as being inherently dangerous to a democratic movement. Claiming a place for himself as a humble member of the rank and file, he concealed from himself his own political failings and refused to acknowledge his own need for public honor. If Debs provides one of the most moving images of education and mutuality in the history of American political leadership, he also serves as a reminder of the price that is paid when committed democrats deny the realities of leadership.

Although Debs was not a learned or brilliant theoretician of socialism, he was something of an American political visionary. In his
hands, the class analysis of Karl Marx became strangely but powerfully blended with the American republican idiom of citizenship and
virtue. A republican tradition that was steadily losing ground to the
economic force of capitalism and the intellectual force of liberalism
had one of its last great metamorphoses in the socialism of Eugene V.
Debs.

Debs's ideal republic required the fullness of democracy not only in
politics and economics but also in the domains of gender and race.
While his democratic hopes were sometimes couched in a language of
Marxist orthodoxy or a rhetoric of Victorian sentimentality, at their
most impressive they had a palpable force. It was these radical American hopes that led him to federal prison. Debs's prison years marked
the greatest suffering of his life, but they also produced his finest testament to democracy. In prison, amid the lowliest and most despised
of Americans, Debs found confirmation of the "democratic dignity"
that was at the heart of his dissenting leadership.

As a socialist and a democrat, Debs stood both outside and inside
the American political tradition. The popularity he attained and the
affection he inspired testified to the potency in his synthesis as well as
to the charismatic appeal of his personality. Yet if he succeeded more
than any other leader in expanding an American audience for socialism, that audience never swelled to match his projections, and it had
already withered away before he died. Raising issues of class and
power that American political culture had historically shunned, his
voice was resisted by a majority of Americans even before it was sup-
pressed by the state. Debs's political career thus encapsulated, in both
its most hopeful and its most tragic forms, the fate of democratic socialism in America.

"The True Leader"

Two texts conveniently measure the democratic evolution of Eugene
V. Debs's thinking about leadership. The first of these is "Masterful
Men," an article written by the twenty-six-year-old Debs in April 1882,
in the *Firemen's Magazine*. Debs was then the editor of this publication of the Brotherhood of Locomotive Firemen and a rising force in
the union. He was already a committed unionist—but also a conservative one, hopeful that there could be harmony between employers and
employees and strongly opposed to strikes as a weapon for the work-

ers. This young man harbored conventional ambitions; he was a promising Democratic politician who in 1882 was serving his second term as the city clerk of Terre Haute, Indiana. It was a time when the icon of Abraham Lincoln pervaded American political culture, and it did not seem unrealistic for the young Debs to entertain grand political aspirations. According to biographer Ray Ginger, Debs at twenty-six "was even said to admit privately that he wanted to be president."[2]

The young Debs was preoccupied with the themes of mastery, heroism, and manliness—his conception of the leader was the exceptional man who towers above the timid mass. "Masterful Men" was the kind of panegyric on heroic leadership that might have come from the pen of Theodore Roosevelt:

> Men confide in leaders. The bold man, the man of action, the man who grasps situations and masters them, he is the man whom his fellows love to honor; he is the man who becomes the standard-bearer in any great moral or political movement; he is the man who brings succor in the hour of danger, and upon him all hearts rely. Few men in moments of personal danger, or in days of national turmoil, act intelligently if left to their own resources. Some leader always springs to the front and assumes a command questioned by none. Such men are self-poised, heroic, calm. The swirl and clash of contending intellects, the mighty shock of arms, the hour fraught with fear and destruction, have no power to disturb that masterful balance of mind possessed by these leaders of men.

Debs presented Alexander the Great and Julius Caesar as examples of such "masterful men." And he related the story of Marshal Mac-Donald, one of Napoleon's commanders at the battle of Austerlitz, who drove his army on to victory despite the slaughter of large numbers of his troops. Debs's choice of models showed how distant he was at that time from a democratic conception of leadership. In his Lyceum speech, the young Lincoln had mentioned Alexander, Caesar, and Napoleon as examples of the destructive political genius who posed a sinister threat to republican institutions. Debs saw the first two of these, and an underling of the third who accepted appalling casualties as the price of conquest, as inspiring models for leadership in America.

Only toward the end of the article did Debs bring his discussion down to the more modest circumstances of his readers. He praised unsung heroes among the locomotive firemen: "The engineman who stands by his engine in the hour of danger, going down with her in order that the lives entrusted to his care may be saved, is no less a hero, is no less a masterful man, than is the hero who dies for his country." These trainmen merited comparison with Marshal Mac-Donald at Austerlitz, a tribute that had a democratic tone to it. Nonetheless, the fascination with masterful conquerors that permeated the article suggested that Debs's own youthful ideal of leadership required more aristocratic imagery.[3]

In 1910 Debs produced a second text on leadership, a series of three letters addressed to Carl Thompson, a Milwaukee Socialist. Debs's words on this occasion could never be mistaken for those of Theodore Roosevelt. The conservative unionist of 1882 had evolved through several stages toward a democratic socialism. Gradually recognizing the weakness of the craft-specific railroad brotherhoods, Debs became the leader of the industry-wide American Railway Union in 1893, only to see it crippled during the Pullman strike the following year by the alliance of corporate and federal power. The Pullman strike played out on the national stage the drama of mounting labor upheaval—and the willingness of the capitalist elite to use any means, from private armies of thugs to the armed forces of the federal government, to crush workers' attempts to organize unions. It became a legendary symbol of the bitterness of class struggle in America. David Montgomery has written that the modern American industrial order "had been created over its workers' protests." Hero and martyr of the doomed Pullman strike, Eugene V. Debs became the most prominent symbol of these protests.[4]

Imprisoned for his role in the strike, Debs emerged from jail to become one of the central figures of the Populist movement, before announcing his conversion to socialism in 1897. Once the Socialist party was formed in 1901, he became its perennial presidential candidate. The Debs of 1910 was the foremost figure in American socialism—and the most popular leader ever of the American left. (Debs's electoral appeal continued to expand after 1910. In the presidential election of 1912, he polled 897,011 votes, 6 percent of the total ballots cast. As a resident of Atlanta penitentiary in 1920, he drew 919,302 votes—although his share of the total ballots dropped to 3.5 percent.)

Although Debs was popular with all kinds of rank-and-file Socialists, he was identified with the left wing of the Socialist party on critical issues of theory and strategy. His three letters to Carl Thompson concerned Victor Berger of Milwaukee, the leader, along with Morris Hillquit, of the right-wing Socialists. Berger had been instrumental in winning Debs to the socialist cause after the failure of the Pullman strike. But Debs rejected his onetime mentor's "step-at-a-time" approach to socialism, scorning its political opportunism and unwillingness to challenge the conservative craft unionism of the American

Federation of Labor. What infuriated Debs even more than Berger's cautious program—and what led him to write to Thompson—was Berger's style of leadership. The imperious Berger was the boss of the Milwaukee Socialists and a would-be boss of the Socialist party at the national level.

Seconding Thompson's judgment of Berger, Debs insisted that the Milwaukee boss's style of leadership had no place in a socialist movement:

> You are absolutely right when you say that at heart Berger is an aristocrat and not a socialist. He holds the common run in as much contempt as did Alexander Hamilton or as does Theodore Roosevelt. . . . Berger really feels that he is made of superior clay and that the tremendous responsibility of making the socialist movement rests upon his shoulders, and his egotism increases and his vanity inflates as he progresses in power.

Debs was quite willing to give credit to Berger for his ability, energy, and intellectual force, but he could not accept the role of political boss. He proposed to Thompson that Berger be called before a national meeting of the Socialist party and "told that henceforth the boss is dead in Milwaukee." If Berger nonetheless refused to relinquish his autocratic power, an all-out struggle would have to be waged to end his reign. This would not be a campaign to unseat a personal and ideological rival; rather, it would be a battle for democracy as the heart of socialism: "If the party has to be disrupted upon the issue of making the socialist party a democratic party in fact as well as in name, then the sooner it comes the better and the sooner the party will be rebuilt on a democratic foundation."

In denouncing Berger, Debs was also defining himself. Much as Stephen A. Douglas had served as a foil against which Abraham Lincoln developed his sense of legitimate democratic ambition, so did Berger become a foil for Debs in his effort to understand the meaning of democratic leadership:

> The power of the boss is the weakness of the movement. This power vanishes with the strength of the movement. The true leader uses all his power, not to rule others, but to impart the power and intelligence to them to rule themselves.[5]

Debs expressed his best democratic understanding of leadership in this passage. Spurning the heroic fantasies of his youth, he now recognized that the paramount role of a leader in a democracy was to educate and empower followers. The truth of leadership was not found in the achievement of mastery over followers but in a mutually vitalizing dialogue with them. Unfortunately, Debs had a hard time holding on to this insight; both his personality and his political creed led him frequently to repudiate the concept of leadership altogether. For now, however, I wish to explore some of the ways in which he successfully functioned as "the true leader."

"The true leader," in Debs's eyes, understood the principal task to be political education. Socialist political education was a formidable undertaking, requiring lessons that would transform not only the political allegiance but also the personal identity of the American working class. As a leader of an oppressed class, the socialist educator had to combat both the false impressions about social reality inculcated by the dominant class and the complacent acceptance by his potential followers of the pittance granted them by that dominant class. Debs complained in 1903 that the average worker was too easily satisfied: "Give him a steady job, enough wages to keep his passive soul within his half-dressed body, and he wants to thank somebody." The dissenting leader had to shock his listeners out of this torpor and meekness and to build upon whatever glimmerings of dissatisfaction he could uncover: "I am doing what little I can to augment the discontent of the working class, to direct that discontent properly and give it intelligence." The first task of political education was to demolish false ideas and deconstruct submissive identities. As Debs wrote to Samuel "Golden Rule" Jones, the reform mayor of Toledo, Ohio, in 1899, "The great work now before us, is to clear the heads of the masses."[6]

"To clear the heads of the masses," Debs sought to break the identification of capitalism with the most sacred American values. Capitalism and not socialism, he charged, was the subversive force in the ancestral American democracy. Capitalism had expropriated the property of independent artisans, had sharpened class divisions, had condemned the great majority to a life of poverty and indignity. In their lurid warnings of the evils that socialism would bring to American life, capitalists were deflecting attention from their own guilt: "They tell you we are going to break up the home. . . . What about the homes of the four million tramps that are looking for work today? How about the thousands and thousands of miserable shacks in New York and every great city where humanity festers?"[7]

Capitalism's deepest hold on the American mind was its allegiance to the creed of individualism. Against this, Debs preached a radical brand of class consciousness that did not so much repudiate individualism as redefine it, stripping away its customary elements of competition and profit seeking and stressing its more noble fulfillment in socialist fraternity:

> We Socialists propose that society in its collective capacity shall produce, not for profit, but in abundance to satisfy human wants. . . . We are not going to destroy private property. We are going to establish private property—all the private property necessary to house man, keep him in comfort and satisfy his wants. Eighty percent of the people of the United States have no property today. A few have got it all. . . . We will reduce the workday and give every man a chance. We will go to the parks, and we will have music, because we will have time to play music and desire to hear it.

Fulfilled in their material needs and awakened to aesthetic pleasures, Americans would also find that socialism freed them from capitalist enmities. "When we are in partnership and have stopped clutching each other's throats, when we have stopped enslaving each other, we will stand together, hands clasped, and be friends."[8]

Debs repeatedly argued that socialism was the true road to the freedom and happiness of the individual. His was a forceful, plausible restatement of American ideals. Still, it faced a huge ideological barrier: the view that socialism was a foreign importation, an alien philosophy whose triumph would rule out the American dream of individual success and realize the American nightmare of losing whatever property the individual had already managed to acquire.

The path to a new consciousness for the working class, according to Debs, was through radical unionism and socialist politics; workers had to overcome long-standing habits of public subservience and shed traditional allegiances to the political parties of their fathers. The Republican party was the party of big business, and the Democratic party was the party of small business; the agendas of both accepted capitalism as a given and sought only to foster its further development. "What the workingmen of the country are profoundly interested in," Debs wrote in 1900,

> is the private ownership of the means of production and distribution, the enslaving and degrading wage-system in which they toil for a pittance at the pleasure of their masters and are bludgeoned, jailed, or shot when they protest—this is the central, controlling, vital issue of the hour, and neither of the old party platforms has a word or even a hint about it.[9]

Thus, when Debs issued what sounded like an innocent call to civic duty, it was in reality a summons to a new kind of politics: "All workingmen and women owe it to themselves, their class, and their country to take an active and intelligent interest in political affairs." As a Marxist, Debs was confident in the historical promise of the socialist republic. As an advocate of political action, he believed that history depended on the political awakening of the working class. "We appeal," he wrote in 1912, "to the workers, the producers, the real supporters of society to dare to think for themselves." The working-class followers envisioned by Debs were not deluded victims of capitalist politicians and self-aggrandizing labor leaders; nor were they rapt admirers of a charismatic radical hero. "My ideal," Debs wrote in 1915, "is a thinker in overalls."[10]

Although Debs sometimes expressed frustration at the resistance of American workers to the socialist message, he never lost faith that they would eventually "clear [their] heads." Signs of emerging radical consciousness thrilled him. Describing the experience of a worker becoming politically conscious, Debs's language unconsciously evoked a sexual awakening: "As he girds himself and touches elbows with his comrades, his own latent resources are developed and his blood thrills with new life as he feels himself rising to the majesty of a man." Through political education, "the true leader" thus helped to liberate the vibrant and intelligent spirit of ordinary men and women that had been buried under capitalism. It was this spirit, Debs believed, that would win the socialist republic. Indeed, without it, the socialist republic would not be worth winning. As Debs put it to journalist Lincoln Steffens in 1908: "There would be no use of getting into power with a people that did not understand. . . . [T]he cooperative commonwealth can come only when the people know enough to want to work together, and when, by working together to win, they have developed a common sense of common service, and a drilled-in capacity for mutual living and cooperative labor."[11]

Debs's greatest tool for political education was his oratory; even his enemies acknowledged him to be one of the great orators of the day. Debs's oratorical skills were not the product of formal training, however; he had left school at the age of fourteen to take a job scraping old paint off railroad cars. Rather, those skills were developed through long practice; this ambitious young man, living in an age of great orators, had worked on his public speaking style at home, even trying out gestures in front of a mirror. Yet it was not his style, Debs claimed, but the substance of what he had to say that accounted for his success. When the Department of Education at the University of Wisconsin queried prominent orators about the key to their art, Debs responded: "The secret of efficient expression in oratory . . . is in having something efficient to express and being so filled with it that it expresses itself."[12]

On the public platform, Debs was riveting. Eyewitness accounts often focused not only on his eloquence but also on the gestures that established an emotional charge between him and his audience. In the words of Elizabeth Gurley Flynn, herself a famed orator for the Industrial Workers of the World (IWW): "Debs paced back and forth on the platform, like a lion ready to spring, then leaned far over the edge, his tall gaunt frame bending like a reed, his long bony finger pointing—his favorite gesture. His deep blue eyes appeared to look searchingly at each one in the audience, he seemed to be speaking directly to each individual." Even amid a vast throng, his listeners felt close to him. Nor was this a mere trick of his stage presence. Debs communicated sincere concern with his body as well as with his words because he genuinely identified with the people he sought to lead.[13]

To Debs, a "true leader" had to recognize that followers and not leaders were the core of the socialist movement. His respect and love for followers were apparent in his comments about "Jimmie Higgins," the fictional, archetypal socialist rank and filer created by Ben Hanford. When Upton Sinclair published a novel about how this character infused strength and fervor into a socialist presidential candidate modeled after Debs, Debs wrote to Sinclair in appreciation:

> JIMMIE HIGGINS is the chap who is always on the job; who does all the needed work that no one else will do; who never grumbles, never finds fault, and is never discouraged. All he asks is the privilege of doing his best for the cause where it is most needed. . . . Almost anyone can be THE CANDIDATE, and almost anyone will do for a speaker, but it takes the rarest of qualities to produce a JIMMIE HIGGINS.[14]

Debs put these sentiments into practice. The bond he felt with the rank and file was particularly evident during the period in which he was awaiting his incarceration in federal prison. In November 1918 he wrote to Cornelius Lehane:

> Among the heaps of unanswered letters on my desk is one from a young woman comrade, a school teacher, tubercular, who has been in a filthy Texas jail for months, . . . with a ten-year sentence on her head, as noble a soul as ever lived in this world, and as heroic, who almost apologetically asks what, if anything, we can do for her. To

these comrades we owe everything, every moment of time and every atom of strength, and God knows there is not enough of either to meet the daily demand.

Depressed by his own impending prison sentence, Debs still did not lose himself in his travails. He recognized that his followers were bravely suffering as much—or more—than he. Debs suffered with them, incorporating their experience into his own.[15]

Identification with followers was one mark of Debs's deep commitment to democracy in his leadership. Another was his concern for openness in socialist politics and fair play for his opponents. As Socialist party factional conflict came to a head in 1912, Debs expressed his conception of a democratic movement in "Sound Socialist Tactics." He advocated the polar opposite of the monolithic vanguard party prescribed by Lenin in *What Is to Be Done?*—the model for revolutionary politics that would haunt the American left for several decades after the Russian Revolution. As Debs saw it, "The matter of tactical differences should be approached with open mind and in the spirit of tolerance. The freest discussion should be allowed." Socialism in the United States, he recognized, must incorporate the spirit of American democracy: "In the matter of tactics we cannot be guided by the precedents of other countries. We have to develop our own and they must be adapted to the American people and to American conditions." Debs saw socialism as the fulfillment of democracy in present practices as well as ultimate objectives.[16]

A democratic socialism had to rise above the ruthless competition of capitalist politics. To Debs, this meant fair play even for the most offensive rivals in the socialist camp. One such rival was the Socialist Labor party, headed by the dogmatic and autocratic Daniel DeLeon. When DeLeon's following declined markedly, Socialist party leader Morris Hillquit proposed to Debs that their party seek additional representation to the International Socialist Bureau at the expense of the Socialist Labor party. But Debs spurned the proposal: "I do not approve that method of extinguishing a rival party. If it is a bona fide national party, no matter how small, it is entitled to representation. . . . I am opposed to striking even the ghost of a dead rival below the belt."[17]

A model American democrat, Debs nonetheless had to battle constantly against charges that he was a subverter of the most fundamental American values. Taking the same pride that Elizabeth Cady Stanton had expressed in the role of an agitator, he located his radical stance squarely within the American political tradition. After the Pullman strike of 1894 made him a symbol of radical disorder to conservatives, Debs pointed out that the same kind of people who were now vilifying him had made the same kind of charges against the most important leaders in American history. "There were tories," he recalled, "who said Washington was a dangerous demagogue, but now the schoolchildren honor his memory. The difference between a demagogue and a demi-god is only about a quarter of a century."

In linking himself to George Washington, Debs revealed some of the pride that he ordinarily kept buried under layer upon layer of humility. But in defiantly accepting the title of "demagogue" and turning its historical associations against his accusers, he was also making an important claim for the democratic value of dissenting leadership:

> I am an agitator. I do not blush when I admit it. I am going to do all that is in my power to change conditions. They do not suit me. I do not see how any man with a heart throbbing in him can be satisfied with the conditions as they are now in this country. There are those who say, "Let well enough alone." If this is well enough, what could be bad enough? Progress is born of agitation.[18]

Theorists of democratic political leadership can find much suggestive material in the image of Eugene V. Debs. His career as a leader was, like Lincoln's, a progression in democratic understanding and practice. From an initial preoccupation with heroic mastery, Debs grew into a profoundly democratic figure who accepted as his central responsibility the task of educating and empowering his followers. He broke down the barriers between leaders and followers not only through his oratorical style but also through an empathy that took the experience of followers as seriously as his own. Tolerant of disagreement, gracious toward weakened rivals, he was not interested in victories that would undermine democratic principles. Debs was right to link himself to the most admired figures in the American political tradition. Without a doubt, he belongs among those American images that foster more democratic forms of leadership.

"A Poor Politician"

In September 1945, nearly two decades after Debs's death, two of his old comrades, Kate Richards O'Hare and Samuel Castleton, reminisced about him in their correspondence. O'Hare had been the most prominent woman in the Socialist party and, like Debs, a victim of government repression during World War I. She remembered him with great fondness and respect, yet her praise was balanced by a revealing criticism: "I think Gene was the soul, the heart, and the spiritual leader of the Socialist movement, but a poor politician."[19]

To understand why Debs was "a poor politician," one needs to look at his position within the Socialist party. Debs wanted the party to follow a left-wing strategy, but he also wanted it to serve as a prefigurative model for a more democratic society. To shape the party in accordance with this vision, he needed to battle "bosses" like Victor Berger. In the letters to Carl Thompson cited earlier, he had pledged that he would "face Berger" and rally the party rank and file against "bossism." The promised confrontation with Berger was not, however, to take place. Debs repeatedly backed away from opportunities for challenging the "boss" of Milwaukee and the right-wing Socialists.[20]

This inability to face Victor Berger was symptomatic of Debs's larger failure to exercise leadership within the party. Although far more popular with the rank and file than his party adversaries were, he did not use his grass-roots support as leverage for moving the party in the direction he thought it should follow. On the contrary, he avoided the conventions and inner councils where party policy was hammered out. When the party programs turned out to be more cautious or the party leadership less democratic than he had wanted, Debs sometimes issued public protests—but he refused to take up the battle within the organization itself. Debs's penchant for floating above the sectarian conflicts of socialist politics as a revered symbol of the protest against American capitalism has drawn criticism from many of those who have written—generally in admiration—about him. Commentators as diverse as H. Wayne Morgan, James Weinstein, and Bert Cochran have all been puzzled by what Cochran calls "the anomaly that socialism's leading spokesman had so little influence inside his own party."[21]

Debs's failure to exert leadership within the party had important consequences for the movement to which he devoted his life. It left the right wing of the party, whose opportunism he scorned, in a position of dominance, while the party's left wing, whose radical spirit he shared, remained bereft of effective leadership. Speaking with sympathy for that left wing, Bert Cochran laments the price paid for Debs's rejection of a leadership role:

> The revolutionary socialists were deprived of the considerable support that Debs could have swung behind their faction. . . . Moreover, by abdicating as a political leader in this matter, he was able to exert little influence in shaping the character of the left wing. And this was a pity, because the revolutionary elements were then sidetracked by [the] syndicalism [of the IWW].

Debs's weakness as a leader thus undercut the radical socialist movement that he hoped to build.[22]

To be sure, stronger leadership from Debs would not have brought final victory to his movement. There were ideological and structural obstacles to socialism in America that even the most extraordinary leadership could not have overcome. Students of socialism have adduced a myriad of explanations for its unhappy fate in America: a hegemonic liberal ideology, relative affluence and social mobility for workers (as compared with the circumstances in Europe), religious, ethnic, and racial divisions in the working class, the political appeal of progressive reformers such as Theodore Roosevelt and Woodrow Wilson, electoral rules favoring a two-party system, and many others. Whatever explanation (or combination of explanations) one prefers, the upshot is that the political reach of Debs and his party was always limited. That Debs was exceptionally popular for an American socialist can be shown by the election results of 1912, in which he received 6 percent of the popular vote total. The limitations of his popularity are also evident in 1912, however, when it is recalled that Theodore Roosevelt, himself running against the two established parties, attracted more than four times as many votes as Debs. Revered by a sizable minority in the working class, Debs and his ideology still were rejected by a majority of American workers.[23]

Although Debs's leadership failures were not ultimately decisive, the "anomaly" of his popularity with the rank and file and his weakness within party councils nonetheless merits analysis. The most persuasive explanation for this anomaly has been offered by Nick Salvatore in his magisterial biography of Debs. According to Salvatore, Debs's weakness as a leader reflected personal insecurities. In eschewing a confrontation with his chief adversaries in the Socialist party, he avoided a conflict that would endanger his public identity:

> Debs was still self-conscious in the presence of such confident theorists as Berger and Hillquit and doubted his ability to carry an argument intellectually. But to enter the battle would also demand that he relinquish the symbolic role of father he had assumed for the whole movement and face as brother and peer the criticism of other Socialists. This possibility jarred abrasively with his own self-image and inner needs. . . . It was to protect his status, so tied to his personality, that Debs ultimately resisted such struggles.[24]

Salvatore supplies ample evidence in support of his analysis. Nevertheless, the psychological explanation of Debs's failure to exercise leadership within the party can be supplemented with a more political explanation—his weakness was conceptual as well as psychological. Indeed, he stands as an instructive example of what happens to radical democrats when they operate upon the basis of a fear of leadership.

Debs argued that power struggles within the party were a distraction from the real content of socialist politics. Writing to C. W. Ervin in 1908, he dismissed these struggles: "Too bad that socialists must waste so much of their time and substance in factional fighting. . . . I can never take a hand in that sort of business and never do unless driven to it. I have no time nor have I the disposition to engage in petty factional quarreling." This sentiment bears some superficial resemblance to Lincoln's philosophy of "quarrel not." Lincoln, to whom Debs was frequently compared by his admirers, had also stressed the waste of time and energy in quarreling. But Lincoln's avoidance of personal conflicts did not extend to political conflicts. He recognized the need to engage his political opponents, using patience, forceful argument, and, when the situation called for it, stratagem and maneuver. By contrast, Debs's equally admirable rejection of personal resentments extended to a flight from the necessity of political conflict. Thus, where Lincoln's "quarrel not" approach actually strengthened him politically, Debs's approach weakened him and diminished his contribution to the socialist cause.[25]

If Debs eschewed intraparty leadership struggles as a drain on energy better spent fighting the capitalist foe, he also feared those struggles as a temptation to corruption. When he surveyed the types of leadership practiced in his society, he saw only multiple forms of self-aggrandizement. The Socialist "boss," exemplified by Victor Berger, represented the corruption of socialist values by leadership ambitions; equally dangerous to the cause of radical change were the majority of the leaders of organized labor. "The labor movement," he wrote in 1917, "has suffered more from false leadership than from any other one cause." He particularly warned workers against those "who have the intelligence and ability to serve but who are lacking in moral stamina and use their influence as leaders to further their own selfish and sordid ends."[26]

Wherever Debs looked, he saw "false leadership." If the American political mainstream had once contained principled leaders, such as Jefferson and Lincoln, now its champions were egotists and charlatans, with Theodore Roosevelt the embodiment of the modern capitalist politician. Roosevelt detested Debs as a radical demagogue, calling him an "undesirable citizen," and Debs returned the loathing:

> Theodore Roosevelt is mainly for Theodore Roosevelt and incidentally for such others as are also for the same distinguished gentle-

man. . . . He is a smooth and slippery politician, swollen purple with self-conceit; he is shrewd enough to gauge the stupidity of the masses and unscrupulous enough to turn it into hero worship. This constitutes the demagogue, and he is that in superlative degree.[27]

When Debs contemplated the tasks of political agitation and education, he recognized the importance of "the true leader" to democratic politics. When he recoiled from the examples of socialist bosses, labor politicians, and capitalist demagogues, however, he turned away from the possibilities for genuinely democratic leadership. Rather than trying to be "the true leader" within the party as well as on the public platform, Debs denied that he was a leader at all.

Contemporary champions of a more participatory democracy sometimes quote Debs on the dangers of leadership. The most famous of his antileadership statements was a staple of his oratory:

> I am no labor leader. I don't want you to follow me, or anyone else. If you are looking for a Moses to lead you out of this capitalist wilderness, you will stay right where you are. I would not lead you into the promised land if I could, because if I could lead you in someone else could lead you out. You must use your heads as well as your hands and get yourselves out of your present condition.

Another noted attack on leadership came from his legendary Canton, Ohio, speech in June 1918—the speech that landed him in federal prison and made him the leading symbol of resistance to America's role in World War I:

> I never had much faith in leaders. I am willing to be charged with anything, rather than to be charged with being a leader. I am suspicious of leaders, and especially of the intellectual variety. Give me the rank and file every day in the week.

Both of these statements are appealing in their modesty, their faith in ordinary people, their concern for the undemocratic potential of leaders who claim the role of political superior. Both are misleading, however, obscuring Debs's own role in the socialist movement and the essential role of leadership in democratic affairs.[28]

Debs adhered to the same radically democratic animus against leadership that Thomas Paine had expressed when he warned Americans against "the slavish custom of following what in other governments are called leaders." But democracy is not a wildflower of spontaneous action by the people. As Debs himself recognized, leadership is needed to educate citizens in democratic ways and to nurture their political self-respect. It is also needed for the struggle against the adherents of economic inequality and hierarchical politics. For that struggle especially, political skill and assertiveness are indispensable to a committed democrat. Like Abraham Lincoln, Eugene V. Debs understood the moral dimensions of democratic leadership; unlike Lincoln, he could not come to terms with its necessarily political dimensions. Kate O'Hare's remark captured both his greatest strength and his greatest weakness: he knew how to touch the souls of his audience, but he did not know how to be the "politician" who could make effective use of the democratic impulses that he had awakened.[29]

Debs's denial of leadership was a complex form of self-denial. His personality and political creed worked together to obscure for him the springs of his own public career. He repeatedly disclaimed that "passion for distinction" in which John Adams had rooted classical republican hopes, Abraham Lincoln had found democratic meaning, and Elizabeth Cady Stanton had recognized women's self-respect. He held instead that socialist principles required the disavowal of any ambition for honor or fame. The coming of socialism, Debs believed, required the overcoming of bourgeois individualism and the establishment of a new psychology premised on social solidarity. The more prominent a comrade was in the socialist cause, the more important it therefore became that he exemplify the new psychology rather than subvert it with shows of egotism. Debs's disavowals of the "passion for distinction," then, were rooted in one of the noblest dreams of virtue that socialism ever advanced. Unfortunately, the demands of that dream were pitched too high for most people; certainly they were too high to square with the desire for mass applause and love that Debs had to deny in himself.

Debs explained his prominence in the socialist cause as a reluctant acquiescence to the demands of his comrades. Accepting the Socialist party nomination for president in 1904, he was a model of humility and socialist virtue. "Personally," he proclaimed, "I could have wished to remain in the ranks, to make my record, humble though it may be, fighting unnamed and unhonored side by side with my comrades. I accept your nomination, not because of any honor it confers. . . . I accept your nomination because of the confidence it implies, because of the duty it imposes."[30]

Although he denied that honor or fame mattered to him personally, Debs was eager to bestow these laurels upon other worthy champions

of labor and socialism. He frequently composed tributes to radical figures who had been slandered or neglected. His homage to Mother
Jones, the elderly labor organizer, was typical of his treatment of
working-class heroes. The working-class hero was selfless, free of any
aspiration for recognition, much less for power or wealth. Of Mother
Jones, he wrote: "With no desire to wear 'distinction's worthless
badge,' utterly forgetful of self and scorning all selfish ambitions, this
brave woman has fought the battles of the oppressed with a heroism
more exalted than ever sustained a soldier upon the field of carnage."
Such selflessness and dutiful service, he suggested, needed to be heralded; the working-class hero deserved lasting honor. Mother Jones,
Debs concluded, "has won her way into the hearts of the nation's toil-
ers, and her name is revered at the altars of their humble firesides and
will be lovingly remembered by their children and their children's
children forever." Selflessness ironically turned out to be a path to distinction in Debs's formula, but committed radicals had to be unmind-
ful of this prospect. It rested with their comrades to grant the honor
that they had to disavow.[31]

Perhaps Debs's portraits of working-class heroes were projections of
a repressed "passion for distinction": only when writing about others
could he acknowledge the legitimate place of honor in a democratic
movement. For himself, denials of personal ambition became something of a ritual; he spoke so often about his lack of desire for fame
that one might easily regard him as a classic case of the man who
protests too much. Debs did reveal personal aspirations on one occasion, but only to show how he had managed to resist them: "When I
first became a Socialist and a member of the party it was with the determination to serve the cause with such zeal and ardor as to consume
all selfish desire." Yet what he had wanted to "consume," he could
only repress. The self-abnegating leader was out of touch with some
of his own deepest impulses.[32]

Selfless dedication, though a noble trait, is not required for democratic leadership or democratic politics. Abraham Lincoln's directness
about the desire for distinction, and the way he linked that desire to a
great democratic cause, seem to me to be preferable to Debs's repression of the same desire. They are preferable not only as a form of self-
understanding but also as an impetus to the development of the political talents and skills required for effective democratic leadership. If
Debs had been more of a "politician," as Kate O'Hare wished, he
might have been somewhat less of the spiritual figure that she
revered. But he also might have done more to advance the cause and
the vision to which both devoted their lives.

The Radical and the Republic

Socialism in the United States has always been handicapped by the charge that it is "un-American." Some socialists have inadvertently reinforced this charge by pitting socialist ideals against America's traditional political values. Eugene V. Debs, however, insisted on a radical synthesis of socialist and American themes. In his conception, socialism was not the negation, but the culmination, of the American political tradition. The radical was the true American republican.

His rivals within the socialist movement often belittled Debs for a lack of theoretical grounding and intellectual power. He was portrayed as the heart, but not the brains, of the Socialist party. On one level, the accusation was valid. An autodidact, like one of his heroes, Thomas Paine, Debs resembled Paine in combining powerful rhetorical skill with a disinclination to engage in prolonged and serious theoretical study. On another level, however, the accusation underestimated Debs's intellectual talent. That he was not as steeped in the leading Marxist texts as his party rivals was, in some respects, advantageous; Debs thought more fluidly than those rivals, with a greater appreciation for American realities.[33]

What remains striking in Debs's thought was his ability to evoke an American tradition of egalitarian democracy and radical dissent as a warrant for his democratic socialism. He constructed a native lineage for his own persona, claiming as his forebears an array of both patriotic heroes and radical firebrands: Thomas Jefferson, Abraham Lincoln, Wendell Phillips, John Brown. His attack on industrial capitalism charged that it was undermining American ideals of personal autonomy, pride of craft, and political dignity. Rooting his socialism in American soil, he imbued it with the ancestral ideal of the virtuous citizen in the free republic. Calling himself a revolutionary, Debs did not look to Europe for inspiration; he preferred to draw parallels between his cause and the "spirit of '76."

The classical republican vision of 1776, with its aspirations to virtue and its fears of corruption, was a declining presence in American political discourse by the late nineteenth century. But that vision could still trouble Americans when it was deployed as social criticism. Dorothy Ross suggests that some of the most prominent social thinkers of the 1880s, Josiah Strong, Henry George, and Edward Bellamy, can be understood as millennialist republicans, individuals who portrayed an America poised at a crossroads between a descent into industrial despotism and an ascent into the ideal republic. Breathing the same air of historic crisis, Eugene V. Debs responded with his own version of millennialist republicanism.[34]

Before his conversion to socialism, Debs's concern had been republican restoration. It was the collusion between the railroad corporations and the federal government to crush the Pullman strike of 1894 that brought home to him the danger to the American republic. Speaking at Fargo, North Dakota, in March 1895, Debs voiced classical republican anxieties. Behind a facade of free markets and government neutrality, a corporate behemoth was transforming the American system: "There is a centralization going forward in this country that is a menace to the republic, by processes that will not bear investigation." Corporate dominance threatened both the economic exploitation and the political enfeeblement of the American people. "The foundations of this republic," Debs argued, "rest in the virtue and intelligence of the people. If multiplied thousands of working men are ground and crushed to an extent that they cannot educate their children, what a change a few generations will produce; and I want to say that the foundations of the republic will rest very insecurely then." Debs echoed Lincoln in depicting the stakes in the current struggle: "When the republic falls, the greatest and brightest light that ever passed through the pathway of progress goes out forever." Also like Lincoln, he committed himself to the proposition that the Republic would not fall: "As a matter of course, I cannot lose faith in the destiny of the republic."[35]

The Republic, Debs argued in 1895, would either be restored to its virtuous prerequisites or else sink beneath a new corruption and oppression brought on by the triumph of industrial capitalism. Once he proclaimed himself a socialist in 1897, he dramatically altered the terms of his millennialist republicanism. Now it was not the old republic that had to be restored but rather "the Socialist republic, the first real republic ever known," that had to be built. The fathers' republic had been a grand step in human freedom, but it had not escaped the fatal taint of all previous social orders. "There has never been a free people, a civilized nation, a real republic on this earth. Human society has always consisted of masters and slaves." Socialism was, Debs insisted, the only antidote to capitalist enslavement, the only means for "changing a republic in name into a republic in fact." Debs's socialist formulation was ambivalent toward the American republic: from its origins, the Republic had been corrupted by class rule, but the ideal of the Republic remained critical to the future that Debs was laboring to create. His version of socialism combined Marx's vision of a classless society with the classical republican vision of a virtuous and self-governing people.[36]

One of the most ominous signs of republican degradation for Debs was America's turn to imperialism. Not surprisingly, the young Debs, who had depicted leadership as mastery by the heroic few, was something of an American jingo. The socialist Debs increasingly perceived American expansionism as a vehicle for class interests. Thus, Woodrow Wilson might talk a democratic game, but his concern for Mexico was, Debs believed, no different from that of the most grasping British capitalists: "The most powerful exploiting interests in the world are fighting for the conquest of Mexico." For the same reasons Debs was a vocal critic of American war fever in 1917; he urged Americans to stay home and instead devote their energies to creating a true republic. As William Appleman Williams has observed, "In Eugene Debs, America produced a man who understood that expansion was a running away, the kind of escape that was destructive of the dignity of men."[37]

Against the capitalist, the imperialist, and the militarist, Debs set the figure of the American citizen. Building on the artisan republicanism of the early nineteenth century, even as he transcended it with a socialist vision for an industrial working class, he protested against the impact of growing economic inequality on republican virtues. Capitalism was obliterating the bases for the independent citizenship that Debs so cherished:

> I love to think of a sovereign citizen. The term appeals to me strongly. But in the present system it is a hollow mockery. Think of a sovereign citizen looking for a boss, going to the factory, quivering at the knees, taking off his hat in the presence of a 2 × 4 boss and announcing himself for sale.[38]

Steeped in the republican tradition of citizenship, Debs maintained his American faith in the ballot. While he located himself on the revolutionary left of the Socialist party, he could not go along with the tactics of sabotage and "direct action" advocated by the syndicalists of the IWW. "Such tactics," he argued in 1912, "appeal to stealth and suspicion, and cannot make for solidarity." A revolutionary movement that rejected republican methods would be ineffectual; worse, it would fail to engage in the open political education needed to nurture socialist citizens. For Debs, the traditional American idiom of citizenship held greater persuasive potential than the syndicalists' "propaganda of the deed," and it was also a genuine idiom for radical, democratic change.[39]

"Lov[ing] to think of a sovereign citizen," Debs put his own sovereignty into practice—and in jeopardy—by speaking out against American involvement in World War I. When he left federal prison in 1921, after President Harding commuted his sentence to the time already served, he assumed that he had lost his own rights as a citizen. Social-ist leader Morris Hillquit, a lawyer, insisted to the contrary that Debs had not been disfranchised by his federal conviction. The ill and feeble Debs devoted a portion of his waning energies to the question of his citizenship during the last few years of his life. In June 1926, four months before his death, he wrote to the federal judge who had sen-tenced him to prison to inquire whether his conviction "resulted in the forfeiture of my citizenship and the revocation of my elective franchise and my civil rights." When the correspondence that resulted proved in-conclusive, Debs decided to bring the matter to a test. The month be-fore his death, he was helped from his sickbed and taken to the city hall in Terre Haute, where he successfully registered to vote in the up-coming election. It is fitting that Debs died a full American citizen.[40]

Contradictions and confusions characterized Debs's amalgam of Marx and the American political tradition. The language of class did not mesh easily with the idiom of citizenship. Still, there was excep-tional resonance in his radical reworking of American political ideals. His turn to Marxism had not turned Debs away from the original American dream of the virtuous republic. There was too much at stake—for his own identity and for the identity of the American peo-ple—to let it go.

Democratic Dignity

To Debs, a principal article of democracy was the dignity of those at the bottom of society. His was the kind of thoroughgoing, militant dem-ocratic faith rarely proclaimed by political leaders in America but memorably voiced by such great writers as Herman Melville, Walt Whitman, and Mark Twain. This faith was given perhaps its classic expression in *Moby Dick:*

> This august dignity I treat of, is not the dignity of kings and robes, but that abounding dignity which has no robed investiture. Thou shalt see it shining in the arm that wields a pick or drives a spike; that democratic dignity which, on all hands, radiates without end from God; Himself! The great God absolute! The centre and circum-ference of all democracy! His omnipresence, our divine equality![41]

Like Elizabeth Cady Stanton, Eugene V. Debs was repulsed by so-cial conditions that degraded large numbers of Americans and thus vi-olated the essential condition of democracy: the equal dignity of every person. Where Stanton principally attacked the degradation of her own sex, Debs's struggle was more inclusive. As a socialist, he placed the economic and political emancipation of the working class at the center of the struggle for democratic dignity. But he was also increasingly sensitive to the social structures and cultural attitudes that degraded blacks and women. He saw the ultimate test of a democratic society in its treatment of its lowliest members. The famous opening words of his statement to the judge who was sentencing him to ten years in prison expressed the core of his democratic faith: "Your Honor, years ago I recognized my kinship with all living beings, and I made up my mind that I was not one bit better than the meanest on earth. I said then, and I say now, that while there is a lower class, I am in it, while there is a criminal element I am of it, and while there is a soul in prison, I am not free."[42]

In the first flush of his introduction to turn-of-the-century orthodox Marxism, Debs's conception of working-class struggle tended to the deterministic. In 1900 he wrote of socialism as "purely an economic question" and depicted its advent as "not a matter of doubt or conjecture, but of scientific calculation." Yet it was more characteristic of Debs, particularly in later years, to emphasize the moral urgency of the socialist cause. During the 1912 presidential campaign he exultantly proclaimed that "for the first time in fifty years, or since the Civil War, a great moral question cleaves the political atmosphere of this nation." Debs's most powerful indictments of capitalism exposed its immoral tendency to degrade a once independent and proud working class.[43]

He held that the degradation of workers under industrial capitalism began with their reduction to a state of poverty and insecurity. "Whatever may be said of the ignorant, barbarous past," he thundered, "there is no excuse for poverty today. And yet it is the scourge of the race. Ten millions, one-eighth of our whole population, are in a state of chronic poverty." Those members of the working class who escaped poverty were nonetheless haunted by its potential recurrence. "Even the most favored wage-worker is left suspended by a single thread. He does not know what hour a machine may be invented to make his trade useless, displace him and throw him into the increasing army of the unemployed." American vainglory about individual freedom and democratic rights, Debs insisted, was mocked by the enslaving poverty and insecurity of the capitalist labor market.[44]

Degradation was apparent not only in the glaring economic inequality between the classes but also in the very language used to address working people. The artisan or craftsman of the past had been turned into the factory "hand"—a word that summed up the indignity at the heart of capitalist society:

> Just a hand! A human factory hand! Think of a hand with a soul in it! In the capitalist system the soul has no business. It cannot produce profit by any process of capitalist calculation. The working hand is what is needed for the capitalist's tool and so the human must be reduced to a hand. No head, no heart, no soul—simply a hand. A thousand hands to one brain—the hands of workingmen, the brain of a capitalist.[45]

Capitalism degraded workers at the point of production and then treated them as debased everywhere else. Polite society, Debs noted, was closed to factory "hands." In a 1904 article facetiously titled "The 'Dignity' of Labor," he observed that "no workingman, though pure as Christ, and wise as Socrates. . . , could be admitted to the exclusive circle of the famed four hundred. He would still be a workingman— plebeian, inferior, vulgar, repulsive." Speaking in the shibboleths of free markets and equal opportunities, capitalists concealed both their exploitation and their scorn.[46]

Equality and dignity, Debs proclaimed, would be restored only with the coming of socialism, which he also called "the cooperative commonwealth"—a term favored by Populists and other late-nineteenth-century radical democrats. His definition of socialism was conventional: "a coming phase of civilization, next in order to the present one, in which the collective people will own and operate the sources and means of wealth production, in which all will have equal right to work and all will cooperate together in producing wealth and all will enjoy all the fruit of their collective labor." Less conventional, however, was his assertion that socialism would be both the product and the fulfillment of American democracy. The working class needed no other weapon than the ballot to win back its dignity. "The united vote of those who toil and have not," Debs wrote in 1904, "will vanquish those who have and toil not, and solve forever the problem of democracy."[47]

In his response to the degradation of blacks and women, Debs was limited both by the cultural conventions with which he had grown up and by the orthodoxies of class analysis that he later embraced. Through the power of his empathy, however, he groped for the terms to accord democratic dignity to blacks and women. In line with the Marxism then prevalent, Debs tended to subsume issues of race and gender under the rubric of class. "The labor question," he wrote in 1904, "has come to be recognized as the foremost of our time. In some form it thrusts itself into every human relation." According to this formulation, the degradation of blacks and women was primarily the product of capitalism; their emancipation waited on the liberation of the working class under socialism.[48]

The young son of Terre Haute, Indiana, knew little of blacks save as the butt of dialect humor. With his turn to socialism, Debs developed more sympathy toward blacks but related their problems only to the dimension of class. Thus, in 1903 he echoed his abolitionist heroes by announcing that "the history of the Negro in the United States is a history of crime without a parallel," yet he promptly ignored the special features of that history, insisting instead that "properly speaking, there is no Negro question outside of the labor question—the working class struggle." Class analysis sensitized Debs to the plight of the black poor. But it clouded his understanding of racism.[49]

Debs eventually came to understand the limits of this class reductionism. He learned about the depths of American racial prejudices from his repeated battles against segregation within the labor and socialist ranks. And he was particularly horrified by the resurgence of racism that followed World War I. In the final years of his life, witnessing a revived Ku Klux Klan and an explosion of lynchings, Debs confronted the racial issue on its own terms. Writing on "Black Persecution" in February 1926, he acknowledged that blacks faced obstacles even greater than those known by white workers. "From first to last," he observed, "the white man has every advantage and the Negro is the victim of the most cruel and wicked discrimination and persecution." Racial discrimination, Debs now insisted, was not a side issue in the struggle for socialism; it was a cancer in the American soul. For its racist sins, American society stood condemned, not by a radical philosopher that it shunned, but by a religious teacher that it worshiped. It was a "hypocritical" civilization "if it dare avow itself Christian in the name of the Galilean Carpenter who would today, were he here, scorn and lash the pharisees who profess to be his followers, while they persecute and brutalize, rob and debase those of their fellow-beings over whom they exercise their despotic and damnable dominion."[50]

As a young man, Debs had broken with the conventional views of his peers on the subject of women's rights. When the literary society of Terre Haute refused to sponsor a lecture by Susan B. Anthony in 1880, he organized the event on his own. Later, as a socialist, he condemned not only women's political disfranchisement but also their economic dependence and social degradation. Debs tended to subsume questions of gender, like questions of race, under the question of class. Still, his vision of women under socialism was staunchly egalitarian: "We want woman to be woman, full statured and independent, man's comrade and equal, and neither a rich man's mistress nor a poor man's slave."[51]

It was not easy, however, for Debs to transcend his upbringing in a culture governed by an ideal of domesticity for women. If his socialist values told him to treat women as "comrades and equals," his nineteenth-century sensibilities led him to a sentimentalization of women that raised doubts about their capacity for equal participation in economic or political life. This sentimental view of women came out during his 1918 trial. Debs used the courtroom in a politically self-conscious fashion, as a platform from which to defend his own conduct and to attack the system that was consigning him to prison. He lost his political composure, though, when the prosecutor made scornful remarks about two female socialists, Rose Pastor Stokes and Kate Richards O'Hare. "Your Honor," Debs protested to the court, "my sainted mother inspired me with a reverence for womanhood that amounts to worship. I can think with disrespect of no woman, and I can think with respect of no man who can. I resent the manner in which the names of two noble women were bandied in this court. The levity and the wantonness in this instance was absolutely inexcusable."[52]

The same cultural order that made women into objects of sentimental veneration enjoined men to be aggressive and courageous. The power of a conventional definition of masculinity was only enhanced for Debs by his sense that industrial capitalism was undermining the manhood of the working class. Compensating for capitalism's assaults on male workers' sense of independence and self-respect, Debs frequently appealed to them to prove their manhood in the war between the classes. Expressive and effective as an instrument for repairing the damaged self-esteem of a subordinated class, his talk of manhood could also take on a disturbing tone of machismo. He liked to contrast the toughness and bravery of the militant worker with the craven softness of the capitalist. "Not one of these blear-eyed capitalist vampires," he sneered, "takes any chance himself. His own precious hide is never perforated. He is never exposed to the flying bullets." The working class would triumph, however, on the basis of its superior masculinity: "We need only to have the manhood to be true, the nerve to do our duty."[53]

Debs embodied the gender conventions of his age yet struggled to transcend them. He was capable not only of mawkish sentimentality and strident masculinity but also of exceptional gentleness and profound courage. At his best, Debs, like Lincoln, stands as an exemplar of the masculine/feminine fusion that sustains genuinely democratic leadership. Indeed, late in his life, Debs explicitly recognized the idea that the antitheses between the sexes, which were a staple of his culture, had to be supplanted by a new synthesis of the masculine and the feminine. The autodidact found that synthesis in the greatest of philosophers and playwrights: "Plato was right in his fancy that man and woman are merely halves of humanity, each requiring the qualities of the other in order to attain the highest character. Shakespeare understood it when he made his noblest women strong as men and his best men tender as women."[54]

Debs's sympathies increasingly extended beyond the working class to include blacks and women. When he was transported to the penitentiary after his wartime conviction in 1918, those sympathies also came to incorporate society's outcasts: the inmates of American prisons. In the midst of writing *Moby Dick*, Herman Melville had informed the more conservative Nathaniel Hawthorne of his commitment to the radical democratic proposition that "a thief in jail is as honorable a personage as Gen. George Washington." During his jail years Debs tested this proposition.[55]

Since his trial had provided a platform for a celebrated defense of his character and his cause, Debs hoped that his incarceration might be of similar political value. The day before he had to report to the federal authorities to begin his sentence, he told a young Socialist reporter: "I stand on the threshold of going to prison with malice toward none, and with perfect faith in the rectitude of my course and an absolute confidence in the justice and ultimate triumph of the cause to which I have gladly given my services." Borrowing from Lincoln's second inaugural, Debs attempted to turn himself into a symbol by giving a historic resonance to his personal drama. As Lincoln had called the nation to come to terms with the guilt of slavery and the need for redemption through charity, so would Debs evoke the guilt of American repression during World War I and the ultimate redemption of a "cooperative commonwealth."[56]

Even as Debs cast himself as a modern-day Lincoln, his trip to prison demonstrated the failure of the parallel he was suggesting. Ray Ginger portrays Debs, the former leader of the American Railway Union, on the train carrying him to Moundsville Prison: "As the prisoner reminisced with his companions, his eye chanced to land on the union button in his conductor's lapel. He slumped back in his seat and commented: 'Were I to engage in satire, I would say how ironical it seems that I, who have been forty years in the service of organized labor, am now being taken to prison by union men.'" That union button, Debs realized, was a more powerful sign than any symbolic gesture he might contrive. It spoke plainly of his failure to win the vast majority of American workers to his vision.[57]

Debs's two years and eight months in prison were to be the most painful period of his life. His advanced age (he was sixty-three when he began his sentence) and poor health contributed to his suffering, especially when he was transferred after two months in the relatively humane Moundsville Prison in West Virginia to the harsh conditions of the federal penitentiary in Atlanta. But there were also deeper sources for the periodic bouts of depression that marked his prison experience. Dependent all his life on the love and admiration of those closest to him, he suffered terribly from his physical isolation, particularly from his brother, Theodore, who had devoted his own life to his sibling's service, and from Mabel Dunlap Curry, the lover who provided Debs with the emotional closeness that he had never found in his marriage. Political isolation reinforced personal isolation. While Debs was locked up, the socialist movement underwent a fateful schism. Facing the brute force of government repression, and carried away by the heady paradigm of the Russian Revolution, a sizable portion of the Socialist party left broke away to form two different Communist parties. The result, James Weinstein notes, was a disaster for the American left: "In the early months of 1919, the Socialist Party had 109,000 members, yet within a year after the split the three parties would have only 36,000 members among them." An imprisoned Debs was helpless to prevent the bitter divisions that would cripple the movement upon which his life's hopes rested.[58]

But Debs mastered his despondency and reaffirmed his political faith. And after leaving the Atlanta penitentiary, he transfigured his prison experience into a testament to democratic dignity. *Walls and Bars,* his memoirs of prison life, was published posthumously in 1927. Valuable in historical terms as an account of prison conditions, *Walls and Bars* rings even more true as a personal document. It remains moving because of the extraordinary spirit that speaks through even its most sentimental passages.[59]

Walls and Bars expressed Debs's sense of responsibility to the unfortunate men he had known in the penitentiary. He wanted to call public attention to their suffering and their debasement. As he had earlier excoriated the capitalist system for degrading workers, now he pointed to the parallels between the worker and the convict. "Persons accused of crime," he observed, "lose their identity as human beings and become 'cases,' just as workingmen are only 'hands' to some employers." Once convicted of a crime and taken to prison, the new inmate "sheds his name and receives a number. He is no longer a man but a thing." Debs insisted that "the inmates of prisons are not the ir-retrievably vicious and depraved element they are commonly believed to be, but upon the average they are like ourselves, and it is more often their misfortune than their crime that is responsible for their plight." Prisons housed the poor, and their brutality and dehumaniza-tion were nothing less than a form of class violence. To expose the re-alities of prison life meant "the impeachment of our smug and self-complacent capitalist society at the bar of civilization."[60]

Typical of his style as a political leader, Debs asserted his identifi-cation with ordinary inmates. In prison, "we were all on a dead level." He did not condescend to the other prisoners, nor did he pity them. Debs was certainly more favored in life and more famous than other convicts, but he too suffered from the harsh conditions and the physi-cal isolation. Watching the socialist movement tear itself apart, he too tasted the bitterness of failure. His account of prison was not the tract of the sympathetic reformer but the narrative of an authentic con-vict.[61]

Walls and Bars is not a tale of unrelieved brutality and sorrow, however. The book achieves its dramatic tension in drawing the con-trast between the degradation of prison life and "the redeeming power of kindness." Debs approached the other convicts with his customary sensitivity and gentleness. In turn, they flocked to him, seeking ad-vice, encouragement, and human warmth. He observed that "by far the most of my fellow prisoners were poor and uneducated men who never had a decent chance in life to cultivate the higher arts of hu-manity." Nonetheless, "every one of those convicts without a single ex-ception responded in kindness to the touch of kindness. I made it my especial duty to seek out those who were regarded as the worst speci-mens, but I never found one who failed to treat me as decently as I treated him."[62]

Against the authoritarian order of the prison—and the capitalist system that it upheld—Debs counterposed the democratic solidarity of the inmates. Seventy years later, we are accustomed to stories of racial and personal animosities among the American prison popula-tion. But in Debs's experience, the sources of tensions in prison were institutional. Where the inmates were most free from the brutal guards and the arbitrary rules, the greatest harmony prevailed. The radical democrat found his ideal practiced in an unlikely spot:

> The cell in which I had settled assumed the institutional form of a
> perfect little democracy. We had all things in common—or would
> have had if we had had the things. . . . The incentive to greed which
> dominates in the other world was lacking there, and human nature,

unalloyed, had a chance to express itself, and it did so in a spirit of mutual kindness and understanding which greatly impressed me and which I shall never forget.[63]

So impressed was Debs by the potential for democratic solidarity among the inmate population that he prescribed it as a cornerstone of prison reform. He proposed that the inmates be "organized upon a basis of mutuality of interest and self-government." A minority of genuinely dangerous prisoners were incapable of self-government, but this was no reason to subject the majority to despotic rule. "Any honest warden," Debs argued, "would admit that 75 per cent of the prison population consists of decent, dependable men, and with this for a foundation I would proceed to build up the superstructure of the prison's self-determination." He recommended a parliament and executive council that could, with the approval of the prison authorities, establish rules and adjudicate disputes among the inmates. On the basis of his own experience, Debs was confident that most inmates would respond favorably to such a "direct appeal to their honor, their self-respect, as well as their intelligent self-interest." If the prison acknowledged the democratic dignity of its inhabitants, many of its worst evils would, he predicted, be mitigated. Most Americans today, fearing the explosive potential of the "underclass" that fills our prisons, would likely regard these views as the chimera of a naïve radical. But Debs was only asking for a test of one of America's oldest and grandest hypotheses: that republicanism could tap our underutilized potential for civic virtue, that self-government could educate us about our better selves.[64]

The impact that his sojourn in federal prison had upon Debs was matched by the impact that he had on his fellow prisoners. His departure from the penitentiary, after his sentence was commuted by President Harding in December 1921, was the occasion for a remarkable tribute. It is hard to improve upon Salvatore's description:

> On Christmas afternoon Theodore [his brother] and a group of Socialist comrades met Debs at the gates of Atlanta Penitentiary. As they joyfully and tearfully embraced and fervently kissed one another, a low rumbling in the background intensified. Warden Fred Zerbst, in violation of every prison regulation, had opened each cell block to allow the more than 2,300 inmates to throng to the front of the main jail building to bid a final good-bye to their friend. Turning away from the prison, Gene started down the long walkway to the parked car. As he did, a roar of pain and love welled up from the prison behind him. With tears streaming down his face, he turned

and, hat in hand, stretched out his arms. Twice more, as he walked
to the car, the prisoners demanded his attention. Twice more he
reached to embrace them. At the car, a terribly thin and drained
Debs offered one final good-bye and quickly entered.[65]

Atlanta Penitentiary was the nadir of Debs's life. Toward the end of
Walls and Bars, he cried out: "I hate, I abominate the prison as it exists today as the most loathsome and debasing of human institutions."
Yet Debs refused to let the horror of his prison experience overpower
the redemptive lessons he had drawn about democratic dignity. Instead, his prison memoirs were a personal surety for his vision of a
democratic society.[66]

Conclusion

In the few years left to him after prison, Debs often seemed a shadow
of his former self. Broken in health, he tried futilely to revive an
equally debilitated Socialist party. To many of those in the audiences
who came to hear the aged martyr of the American left, Debs sounded
stale—a tired echo of the old prewar radicalism. The revolutionary left
regarded him as a sentimental socialist, out of joint with the hard-
edged American Bolsheviks. Writing to the Socialist party's national
secretary, Bertha Hale White, in June 1925, Debs had to acknowledge
the failure of his postprison efforts: "The great mass of our ex-
members and socialists in general believe that the Socialist party is
dead and that it cannot be resurrected." Still, he could not relinquish
his life's dream. Almost as an incantation, he reaffirmed that dream in
a letter to George Viereck five months before his death: "I am as militant as ever in the international struggle for industrial freedom and
social justice and . . . I have the same unrelaxing faith in the ultimate
triumph of the people over all the powers of oppression and exploitation."[67]

Apart from his admirers on the left, Debs has become something of
a historical curiosity to most Americans who recall anything about
him. He is known chiefly as the most popular vote getter in the history of American radicalism. But if Debs's electoral accomplishments
remain notable, his public career is readily dismissed as quixotic.
Debs was the leader of a party that dwindled and the prophet of a vision that never came to pass. The American political mainstream is
not impressed by failure—and in the terms it normally favors, Debs
was a failure.

The blasted dreams of American socialism and the bleakness of Debs's final years should not, however, prevent us from reappropriating him as an exemplary figure in the history of American political leadership. In his passion to educate and empower his working-class followers, and in his ability to incorporate the experiences of those followers into his own, Debs demonstrated how a deeply committed democrat could act as a "true leader." Unfortunately, he often rejected his own insight into this possibility, instead insisting—out of a horror of self-aggrandizement and corruption—on a repudiation of the very idea of leadership. "A poor politician," in Kate O'Hare's description, Debs showed that even the most radical democratic cause cannot dispense with the political motives and skills of strong leadership.

Debs is instructive for the substance of his democratic vision as much as for the style of his dissenting leadership. His rhetoric refracted Marx's conception of a classless society through the original American dream of free, equal, and virtuous citizens. As industrial capitalism transformed the American polity into a bureaucratic, hierarchical order, Debs reworked classical republican ideals to formulate a protest that is still haunting. So long as American society fostered the degradation of working people, blacks, and women, Debs insisted that it could not be truly democratic. So long as it did not recognize the dignity of its lowliest members, it was a society willing to disavow its own conscience and to destroy its own ideals.

Proponents of democratic leadership might have as much to learn from those conventionally regarded as historical losers as from those whose triumphs we are accustomed to celebrate. Whatever failures we can ascribe to Eugene V. Debs, he lived a life of democratic value. In 1906, remembering "Old Bill" Robinson, one of many forgotten labor pioneers whom he eulogized, Debs wrote: "His career was a failure, but his life a success." The same might be said of Debs himself.[68]

Franklin D. Roosevelt

Democratic Leadership and the Modern State

A PPEARING BEFORE A CONVENTION OF THE DAUGHTERS OF THE AMERI-
can Revolution in April 1938, Franklin D. Roosevelt was a beleaguered president. The dramatic failure of his court-packing
plan the previous year had exposed a clumsy hand in the erstwhile political magician. A severe recession, currently in its ninth month, was
calling into question the entire New Deal approach to the economy.
Harried by his critics, particularly on the right, Roosevelt could not
resist the opportunity for a gibe at the primly conservative women of
the D.A.R. After informing his audience that he shared with them a
distinguished American lineage, he drove home his message in one
deliberately provocative sentence: "Remember, remember always that
all of us, and you and I especially, are descended from immigrants
and revolutionists."[1]

Meeting with newspaper editors in a special press conference later
that day, Roosevelt regaled them with an account of how he had dis-
comfited the "dear ladies" of the D.A.R. In his retelling, his American
pedigree was superior to that of most of his audience:

> I said that I probably had a more American ancestry than nine out
> of ten of the D.A.R. I had various ancestors who came over in the
> Mayflower and similar ships . . . and furthermore that I did not have
> a single ancestor who came to this country after the Revolutionary
> War; they were all here before the Revolution. And out of the whole
> thirty-two or sixty-four of them, whichever it was, there was only
> one Tory.[2]

This minor tale introduces several facets of a remarkably ambiguous political character. It shows the playful leader—an incurable tease and an exuberant devotee of political humor. It shows the serious Jeffersonian democrat, the aristocrat who sides with the many and who denounces his fellows among the privileged for denying to others the dignity they claim for themselves. But the democratic charm of this tale is partially offset by the tinge of boastfulness and the intimation of superiority. Beneath the modest, egalitarian link to immigrants and revolutionaries, we glimpse the leader who needs to be the star.

There was not much ambiguity in the immediate crises that demarcated Roosevelt's tasks as president. The Great Depression was a crisis of unprecedented suffering and demoralization, an unparalleled epidemic in an economy that had long been a marvel of vitality. Nazism and fascism threatened to choke off democratic liberties everywhere and inaugurate a new age of civilized barbarism. But there were also longer-term crises bound up with the depression and the war. In question during these years was the shape of the modern American polity—the role of the state, the structure of economic and military power, the relationship between classes and groups, the dimensions of the presidency, the possibilities and limits of democratic leadership. No president since Lincoln had arrived at the White House in a moment so freighted with consequences for the future of democracy.

Franklin D. Roosevelt was well suited to supply compelling democratic leadership. He brought to the presidency a complex balance of strong qualities: a radiant ego, a sometimes ruthless political savvy, a capacity for nurturance, an identification with Jefferson's brand of popular democracy. To a confused and dejected mass audience, he provided an inspiriting political education, drawing on older religious and democratic traditions to teach new lessons in interdependence and national community. Although Roosevelt could not vanquish the Great Depression, his administration relieved the worst of the mass distress, while restoring confidence in the power of a democracy to meet both the material and the moral needs of its citizens. Although he did little to stem the rise of Nazi and Fascist militarists, he effectively mobilized Americans and united allies to defeat them decisively once the war began.

It is with respect to the longer-term crises of the era that Roosevelt's leadership appears more shadowed. An authentic democratic leader, Roosevelt nonetheless fostered a number of developments that would plague modern American democracy: an overweening presidency, a massive bureaucratic state riddled with special-interest fiefdoms, a military leviathan. The fault lay in part with Roosevelt himself, with his desire for center stage, his blitheness about power, his inattention to the long-term consequences of emergency measures. It lay in part with his enemies, with the institutional actors and larger social/economic forces that, battling the New Deal across the entire landscape of politics, propelled it to reach for whatever instruments of power it could command. And it lay in those instruments, paradoxical tools of the modern state that dwarfed ordinary citizens even as it served them. In generating a democracy of bureaucratic organization, mass consumerism, and global military power, Roosevelt's leadership during the New Deal and war years, guided in large measure by a democratic spirit, ushered in conditions that would significantly sap a democratic spirit in their aftermath.

The Would-Be Hero and the Democratic Character

Franklin D. Roosevelt had perhaps the most elusive personality of any political leader in twentieth-century America. His associates and his biographers have left vivid pictures of his many public surfaces but have confessed to bafflement at the composition of his private core. Frances Perkins is representative of Roosevelt's associates: "He was the most complicated human being I ever knew." Arthur Schlesinger, Jr., is representative of the biographers: Beneath the "mask of cheer, . . . the real Roosevelt existed in mystery, even to himself." The subject of this bafflement delighted in his own "mystery," gleefully telling an audience in 1940 that "I, myself, am supposed to be a self-made riddle—in fact, sort of a cross between a riddle and a Santa Claus."[3]

Although we cannot penetrate Roosevelt's deeper "mystery," it remains essential to make sense of the central elements in his complex political identity. I approach Franklin D. Roosevelt's political identity by comparing him with his first political hero and role model, Theodore Roosevelt. Franklin Roosevelt's distinctive political identity can be clarified by examining how he set out to be another TR and why he turned out to be so different from his illustrious cousin. I emphasize four seemingly discordant elements that combine in Franklin Roosevelt's political identity: intense egotism, political cunning, a "feminine" capacity for nurturance, and a commitment to a populist democracy modeled after the philosophy of Thomas Jefferson. The first two link FDR to TR; the second two underline his fundamental difference. Ego and a will to political mastery propelled Theodore Roosevelt to a heroic brand of leadership that, I argued in an earlier chapter, is ultimately unhealthy for a democratic polity. Balancing a similar ego and will to power with more "feminine" and democratic qualities, Franklin Roosevelt became a democratic leader rather than the heroic leader he had originally intended to be.

His intense egotism was formed during his Hyde Park childhood. That golden childhood is an oft-told tale, in which a young mother and a considerably older father doted on their only child, the center of their tranquil and happy world. Leaving this world only at the age of fourteen, Roosevelt entered the prep school and college environments in which he would no longer be the object of adoration. At Groton, the frail adolescent could not win the athletic distinction that was most prized by his peers; moreover, his classmates mistrusted his smiling affability. At Harvard, his application to join Porcellian, the most prestigious of social clubs (both his father and Theodore Roosevelt had been members), was blackballed. Yet these blows could not shake Roosevelt's underlying egotism. Instead, he sought a new arena for satisfying his ego. As Geoffrey Ward has observed in his psychologically insightful study of the young Roosevelt: "He had been *the* boy throughout his most formative years, and it seems likely that his fascination with politics, with winning the approval of the voters and attaining the highest possible office, was at least in part an effort to replicate what would always seem to him the natural order of things."[4]

If politics was a vehicle for regaining center stage for young Franklin Roosevelt, the model for political stardom was readily at hand. Since his days at Groton, he had looked to Theodore Roosevelt as his political hero. Already restless as a young lawyer, he planned a political ascent that would copy exactly his kinsman's career. First, he told several of the other young lawyers with whom he worked, he would seek election to the New York State Assembly, then rise to become assistant secretary of the navy and governor of New York, and ultimately reach the presidency. Young Franklin's conception of emulating Theodore's heroic leadership was, at this point, relentless and unimaginative. Thus, when military intervention in Mexico briefly seemed likely in 1913, Roosevelt, the new assistant secretary of the navy, talked about resigning his position and organizing a regiment of "roughriders."[5]

Franklin Roosevelt shared with his first political hero the desire to display his ego. "When he discovered," Geoffrey Ward writes, "that the Assistant Secretary of the Navy had no distinctive flag—only the President of the United States and the Secretary then had them—he designed his own, and made sure it was flown whenever he arrived at a Navy yard or boarded a naval ship." Like Theodore, Franklin delighted in hobnobbing with European royalty. As president, he liked to invite visiting monarchs to Hyde Park, where picnics, complete with hot dogs, would be served on the lawn. It is hard to avoid the suspicion that Roosevelt was tutoring his European friends on how an elective monarch reigns—with a folksy touch.[6]

Although Franklin Roosevelt was the equal of Theodore Roosevelt in egotism, his ego usually took a different political form. Where Theodore was flamboyant and overpowering, Franklin was warm and ingratiating. Rather than trying to dazzle with an electrifying persona, he was more inclined to make other people feel welcome and appreciated. He scorned political figures who assumed airs. During World War II, for example, he came to detest Charles de Gaulle as a "prima donna," contrasting de Gaulle's hauteur with his own "normal simplicity." It was not simplicity, however, that separated Franklin Roosevelt from a de Gaulle or a Theodore Roosevelt; it was an egotism that was more subtle, sinuous, and calculating.[7]

One mark of the subtlety of Roosevelt's ego was his exceptional ability to understand and play to the large egos that surrounded him as president. The "secret diary" of his secretary of the interior, Harold Ickes, provides inadvertent testimony to a skill not ordinarily found in individuals with outsize egos. Ickes, whose combination of high-minded public service and peevish vanity recalled John Adams, remained under Roosevelt's spell despite repeated frustrations with his boss. Roosevelt first captured the heart of this self-proclaimed "curmudgeon" with gestures of friendliness and solicitude, leading Ickes to confide to his diary that "I have never been given to hero worship, but I have a feeling of loyalty and real affection for the President that I have never felt for any other man." Subsequently, Ickes came to suspect that his hero was repeatedly "selling me down the river" on the bureaucratic matters dearest to the secretary of the interior. Yet each time Ickes attempted to resign, Roosevelt would woo him back with a fresh gust of warmth: "It is pretty hard to keep a mad on with a man who makes such friendly gestures as the President does on occasion." The egotistical Ickes served his more subtly egotistical chief in splendid fashion for twelve years.[8]

This subtlety of ego allowed Roosevelt to dominate and yet not alienate a variety of subordinates. The public face of his ego, however, was more straightforward. His radiant self-assurance was perhaps his greatest political asset. In 1933 and again in 1942 it warmed and rallied a despondent American public. Roosevelt made his own cheerfulness and vibrancy a model for his followers. He made the best use of egotism that a democratic leader can—employing it, in the words of William E. Leuchtenburg, for "the instillation of hope and courage in the people."[9]

But self-assurance could slip into hubris: egotism was a factor in Roosevelt's greatest political failures as well as in his most magnificent successes. Perhaps the paramount instance of his hubris came in 1936–37. Roosevelt began the election year by defining the coming campaign as a struggle between the reform majority of the New Deal and the reactionary minority of "entrenched greed." But as the campaign progressed, the issue became personalized: the election pitted not the many against the few, but Roosevelt against the few. Routed by the first Roosevelt administration, the advocates of "government by organized money" had mobilized to bring down their scourge: "Never before in all our history have these forces been so united against one candidate as they stand today. They are unanimous in their hate for me—and I welcome their hatred." Roosevelt thus saw his 1936 landslide as a highly personal victory. It was this triumphant figure who, soon after the election, launched his secretive and devious plan to remove the supreme court as an impediment to the New Deal. The court-packing fiasco was the work of a president whose normal political acumen had been supplanted by the overconfidence of the resplendent ego.[10]

The blundering of that affair has long fascinated observers precisely because it was so uncharacteristic of the most supple politician of his age. No account of Roosevelt's political identity can be complete without examining his mastery of the professional politician's craft. Franklin Roosevelt not only emulated Theodore Roosevelt by pursuing a career in politics; far more than his model, he made politics his exclusive vocation. If he could never hope to equal his predecessor in heroics, he came to be more than his match as a politician. Theodore wrote extensively about his own political skills, vacillating in his essays on practical politics between an eagerness to substantiate his masculine toughness in the rough-hewn world of politicians and an anxiety to retain a reputation for moral rectitude. Franklin spoke little about his own political art, but he was less morally ruffled than Theodore as a politician, shrewder in his calculations, and ultimately more ruthless. Where Theodore squirmed to make politics and morality cohere, Franklin compartmentalized the two. Serious about his moral ends, Franklin Roosevelt was casual about his political means.

The contrast between the two Roosevelts was most evident in their respective relationships with political bosses. Theodore Roosevelt's collaboration with machine chieftains was marked by obvious distaste and moral unease, along with elaborate efforts to justify these inescapable liaisons. Franklin Roosevelt, after quickly learning that he had no political future in New York so long as he did not make peace with Tammany Hall, worked easily and comfortably with political bosses. As president, he funneled huge amounts of patronage to the Democratic urban machines in exchange for their reliable vote totals. Even when Roosevelt dealt with a boss as repulsive to him as was Frank Hague of Jersey City, the political advantages kept the patronage flowing. But when an urban boss no longer suited his needs (as was the case with Mayor James Curley of Boston), or had become a political embarrassment (as was the case with Thomas Pendergast of Kansas City), the president had no compunctions about abandoning him. Beneath his mask of affability, Roosevelt's code of politics was as hard-boiled as that of the political bosses that he so effectively exploited.[11]

Franklin Roosevelt was also more canny than Theodore Roosevelt in dealing with demagogues. Where Theodore had waxed hysterical about William Jennings Bryan and John Peter Altgeld in 1896, Franklin approached the more genuinely demagogic challengers of the 1930s in a quiet tone. So long as Father Charles Coughlin, the fiery radio priest with an estimated audience of ten million, supported the efforts of the New Deal, Roosevelt and his aides courted and charmed him. But when Coughlin began to repudiate the principal policies of the administration, the White House responded by playing political hardball. Roosevelt's men pored over Coughlin's finances in search of improprieties and even prodded the Immigration and Naturalization Service to ascertain whether the Canadian-born priest was residing in the United States illegally.[12]

For someone sympathetic to his ends, Roosevelt's hard-boiled political tactics can evoke a confusing mix of admiration and queasiness. But there were less morally ambiguous dimensions to Roosevelt's political art. Observing Woodrow Wilson's stiff-necked stance toward politicians, Roosevelt mused about the emotional needs of political professionals. As he later told Frances Perkins, "They'd rather have a nice jolly understanding of their problems than lots of patronage. A little patronage, a lot of pleasure, and public signs of friendship and prestige—that's what makes a political leader secure with his people and that is what he wants anyhow." To Roosevelt, politicians were not just competitors for power; they were people like any others, with a desire for recognition and respect that had to be understood and satisfied.[13]

Perhaps Roosevelt's most distinctive art as a politician was his appreciation of the difference between the logic of politics and the logic of economics. Advisers might concentrate only on economic consequences; Roosevelt looked always to the political meaning of New Deal policies. When Luther Gulick, an adviser in the area of public administration, complained to the president that the taxes that financed his social security program were draining needed purchasing power from a depressed economy, Roosevelt retorted:

> I guess you're right on the economics, but those taxes were never a problem of economics. They are politics all the way through. We put those payroll contributions there so as to give the contributors a legal, moral, and political right to collect their pensions and their unemployment benefits. With those taxes in there, no damn politician can ever scrap my social security program.[14]

Franklin Roosevelt had an ego worthy of Theodore Roosevelt's and a political cunning that outstripped his. Yet there was more than this to Franklin Roosevelt as a political leader. His ego and political savvy were the chief sources of his political strength (and sometimes of his political errors), but they were not the sources of his deeper appeal as a democratic leader. To understand that appeal, we must turn to the qualities that balanced egotism and political cunning: the capacity for nurturance and the commitment to a populist and participatory democracy.

That Franklin Roosevelt evolved from a would-be heroic leader in the mold of Theodore Roosevelt to a leader with a more democratic style can be explained in part by his incapacity for the hero's role. Certainly by the standards of Theodore and his Oyster Bay clan of Roosevelts, their young cousin had none of the stern masculine stuff of which heroes were made. When the slender, dandified Franklin visited Oyster Bay as a college student, Theodore's children laughed at him behind his back and nicknamed him "Miss Nancy." Despite doubts about Franklin's masculine prowess, Theodore Roosevelt took a benevolent interest in the budding political career of the husband of his favorite niece. But when he urged Franklin to follow his heroic 1898 example and rush to the front with the onset of American involvement in World War I, Franklin instead allowed himself to be dissuaded by his superiors from leaving his civilian post at the Navy Department. The hypermasculine heroism of Theodore Roosevelt was never a real possibility for Franklin Roosevelt. Instead, his temperament and his experience led him toward a different kind of strength and toward a lesson in nurturance that Theodore Roosevelt never learned.[15]

The pivotal experience in Franklin Roosevelt's life was not the triumph of a San Juan Hill but the anguish of infantile paralysis. It is easy, of course, to sentimentalize Roosevelt's courageous battle with polio, to view it as working, in the words of Frances Perkins, "a spiritual transformation" in him. The impact of infantile paralysis on his identity was, however, more complex. Polio did not make him any less ambitious, devious, or manipulative. Indeed, as Hugh Gregory Gallagher (himself a victim of polio and former resident of Warm Springs) has pointed out, the sense of dependence and physical helplessness that his disease brought with it only intensified Roosevelt's primary character traits. "By means of various tricks that actors use," Gallagher writes, "Roosevelt was able to project from his wheelchair a personality that dominated all others. . . . Trapped in a chair, he had to rely upon others to do things for him. Thus, whether to order, beg, or cajole, he was caused to be manipulative to get things done, to enforce his will."[16]

In his unsuccessful seven-year struggle to regain the use of his legs, Roosevelt displayed an astonishing persistence and pluck. Refusing to let his disability defeat his spirit, he exhibited a courage that represented to him a different route to masculine self-confidence than going to war. No one could think of him now as a "Miss Nancy." Indeed, the visual image of Roosevelt after his return to politics in 1928 was decidedly masculine. As his legs withered, his upper torso grew stocky and powerful; with a taboo imposed on pictures that might reveal his disability, he appeared in photographs and cartoons as a pillar of masculine strength.[17]

The battle with polio strengthened both the masculine and the feminine in Roosevelt's political identity. The capacity for nurturance that American culture designated as predominantly feminine first appeared in Roosevelt at Warm Springs, the sleepy Georgia spa that he developed into the first American rehabilitative center for the victims of infantile paralysis. At Warm Springs, the self-centered scion of privilege reached out in empathy to those whose suffering he shared. Roosevelt became teacher, therapist, friend to the "polios" who flocked to the center he was establishing. He led them through exercise sessions in the warm waters, soothed their frustrations, revealed to them the physical weakness that he concealed so carefully from the outside world.[18]

When Roosevelt purchased Warm Springs in 1926, he committed over two-thirds of his personal fortune to the spa. His goal was not to run a profitable business but to construct a community. Roosevelt's Warm Springs drew "polios" who had experienced social stigmatization as well as physical incapacitation. It set out deliberately to heal psyches as much as bodies, to restore self-respect along with self-locomotion. Reflecting Roosevelt's personality, the atmosphere was cheery and sociable. Picnics, parties, and other frolics, Gallagher observes, not only offered relief from the exercise sessions but also "provided a way for polio patients to relearn their social skills." Initially seeking only his own recovery from the ravages of infantile paralysis, Roosevelt came to provide a haven of dignity for others whose terrible ordeal he so fully understood. In the community of "polios" that he created at Warm Springs, the most humane and nurturing qualities of the New Deal were prefigured.[19]

Somewhat like Abraham Lincoln, Franklin Roosevelt developed a masculine/feminine political identity. He could not completely escape the need to prove his masculinity. But the preoccupation with masculine force that is the hallmark of heroic leadership was never pronounced in the mature Franklin Roosevelt. To Theodore Roosevelt, the promoter and practitioner of the "strenuous life," masculine toughness was the most serious of subjects. Franklin Roosevelt could turn toughness into a joke. Returning to Washington from a fishing trip in the Bahamas in April 1934, he told a congressional delegation that came to welcome him at the train station: "I did have a wonderful holiday and I have come back with all sorts of new lessons which I learned from barracuda and sharks. I am a tough guy. So, if you will come down and see me as often as you possibly can, I will teach you some of the stunts I learned."[20]

Franklin Roosevelt came to differ fundamentally from Theodore Roosevelt not only in his masculine/feminine balance but also in the political allegiances that defined his understanding of American democracy. Where Theodore Roosevelt admired Alexander Hamilton and despised Thomas Jefferson, Franklin Roosevelt's choice of political models and foils was precisely the reverse. The allure of Hamilton initially attracted Franklin as much as it had Theodore. Some time early in the 1920s, he wrote a romanticized (and highly inaccurate) sketch of Hamilton that was never published. In Roosevelt's enchanted imagination, Hamilton was no less than *the* Founding Father.[21]

In 1925, however, Roosevelt repudiated Alexander Hamilton and everything he represented and embraced Thomas Jefferson instead. At the request of the author, he wrote the only book review of his life, an enthusiastic endorsement of Claude Bowers's *Jefferson and Hamilton*. In the course of writing this review, the dramatic opposition between Jefferson and Hamilton was etched into Roosevelt's imagination. Decrying "the romantic cult" of Hamilton, Roosevelt praised Bowers for depicting Hamilton in his true colors as an "aristocrat and convinced opponent of popular government." What thrilled him even more was the portrait of a Jefferson who had much in common with his fellow patrician from Hyde Park: "In Jefferson we see not only the savior of the deeper ideals of the Revolution, but also the man with human failings, the consummate politician." As Roosevelt turned to Bowers's account of the Jefferson-Hamilton conflict of the 1790s, he pictured a struggle between the few and the many in terms that he would self-consciously reenact in the New Deal:

> Jefferson, eclipsed in the Cabinet by Hamilton, the natural democrat against the natural aristocrat, began then the mobilization of the masses against the autocracy of the few. It was a colossal task. With Hamilton were the organized compact forces of wealth, of birth, of commerce, of the press. With him at heart was Washington, the President. Jefferson could count only on the scattered raw material of the working masses, difficult to reach, more difficult to organize.

In concluding the review, Roosevelt confessed to "a breathless feeling." He wondered "if, a century and a quarter later, the same contending forces are not again mobilizing. Hamiltons we have today. Is a Jefferson on the horizon?"[22]

There is much to criticize in this new Jefferson. Roosevelt's Jeffersonianism was simplistic, drawing uncritically on the exaggerated polarities of Progressive historians. It was awkward; on a number of occasions in the next two decades, Roosevelt had to struggle mightily to transform the eighteenth-century Jefferson of local government and states' rights into a twentieth-century Jefferson of centralized power and national action. It was self-righteous; by the terms of discourse that Roosevelt adopted, his stance was automatically equated with democracy, his opponents' with aristocracy. Yet Roosevelt's new identification with Jefferson and Jeffersonian democracy was also the essential shift in political identity that made possible his later democratic leadership. His presidential aid to the disadvantaged has often been traced back to the sense of noblesse oblige that he absorbed in his upper-class upbringing. Noblesse oblige, however, was the common property of Roosevelt's upper-class peers—and most of them became vociferous critics of the New Deal. It was the link to Jefferson that encouraged Roosevelt to transform aristocratic duty into public responsibility. Siding with Jefferson against Hamilton, he aligned his sympathies and his political fortunes with the masses, ensuring that those who abhorred mass mobilization would some day call him what Theodore Roosevelt had called Thomas Jefferson: "that slippery demagogue."[23]

When Roosevelt reentered public life in 1928 as the Democratic candidate for governor of New York, it was as a dedicated Jeffersonian. On the eve of the presidential election, he lashed out at Republican candidate Herbert Hoover as a Hamiltonian. According to Roosevelt, Hoover had written in his book on American individualism that "the crowd, that is to say, 95 percent of all the voters who call themselves average citizens, that the crowd is credulous, that it destroys, that it hates, that it dreams, but that it never builds, that it does not think, but only feels." Roosevelt placed himself and his party's standard-bearer on the side of popular capacity and self-government. "Governor [Al] Smith," he proclaimed, "has given undoubted proof of the definite fact that the mass of humanity does think, that it can make up its own mind on the pros and cons of all public questions; that it often originates, and that there is a very definite relationship between what Mr. Hoover calls the crowd and the continuation of modern progress."[24]

Still, even as he identified with Jefferson and denounced a Hamiltonian Hoover, Roosevelt could never fully suppress his own sense of superiority, of belonging to the few. Four months before he attacked Hoover as an elitist, Roosevelt set down on paper, apparently for his own satisfaction, several aphorisms and queries about leadership. The first of these was in keeping with the spirit of Jefferson (and expresses one of the central themes of this book): "There is no magic in Democracy that does away with the need of leadership." The second, however, sounded more like Hamilton: "The danger of our Democracy lies in our tendency to select leaders who are similar to the rank and file of us, whereas the hope of Democracy seems to lie in our selecting leaders who are superior to the rank and file of us." Franklin Roosevelt was a genuine Jeffersonian, popular democrat, who nonetheless always bore an unacknowledged affinity with Alexander Hamilton.[25]

"The Greatest Duty of a Statesman Is to Educate"

Franklin D. Roosevelt set the twentieth-century standard for effective communication between president and people. Every facet of his complex political identity was called into play to win over the public. He disarmed the White House press corps with his personal warmth, his sensitivity to journalistic needs, his mastery of political details, his flair for supplying dramatic copy. He captivated radio audiences with his fireside chats, establishing an unprecedented tone of intimacy between leader and followers. Roosevelt's radio voice, in particular, was an exceptional political instrument. Clear, firm, buoyant, it exuded candor and plain truth. Yet it also possessed a seductive charm; New York Mayor Fiorello La Guardia once teased Roosevelt that "he had the best 'necking voice' in the world."[26]

Roosevelt's techniques were central to his hold on public opinion, but his appeal was rooted in the content as much as in the style of his public discourse. To evaluate Roosevelt by the substance of his messages to the public is to judge him by the standard that he himself proposed in 1932: "The greatest duty of a statesman is to educate." By this standard Roosevelt was, in the main, impressive; his discourse of the New Deal years functioned as a powerful—even if ultimately limited—form of democratic political education.[27]

Before turning to Roosevelt as a public educator, two potential objections to this portrayal should be confronted. The first concerns the issue of mystification. New Left critics of the 1960s, in particular, suggested that the rhetoric of the New Deal was far more egalitarian and humane than its performance. Soaring democratic phrases, they complained, often concealed service to established interests and a slighting of the weak and unorganized. Although the objection was legitimate and pointed to one of the deeper failures of the New Deal, it nevertheless gave too little credence to the importance of political discourse. Roosevelt's discourse was not "mere" rhetoric, a linguistic overlay obscuring political and economic realities. It played a major role in shaping the democratic political culture of the New Deal, in mobilizing mass support for it, and in constructing a synthesis of interest politics and democratic responsibility that is still of value.[28]

The second objection focuses on the question of shallowness. Queried by a reporter about his political philosophy, Roosevelt replied, "Philosophy? I am a Christian and a Democrat—that's all." This remark has sometimes been cited to demonstrate Roosevelt's intellectual vacuity. Yet if his public discourse was often superficial as political philosophy, it was deep in its resonances, in its evocations of Christian and democratic themes from the American tradition. With the assistance of some unusually able speech writers, Roosevelt tapped the power of vocabularies that had been largely cast aside in the march of American individualism, materialism, and capitalism. He revived the idioms of the Bible and the old republic to speak about social justice and the public good.[29]

James MacGregor Burns has observed of Roosevelt: "Probably no American politician has given so many speeches that were essentially sermons rather than statements of policy." For Roosevelt, political education was, above all, an instruction in democratic morality. "The presidency," he told a reporter shortly before assuming office, "is predominantly a place of moral leadership." His presidency began with a flurry of words as well as actions, words that take on a dramatic structure: the early New Deal was a morality play.[30]

In Roosevelt's morality play, the American people had lost their way in the Babylon of the 1920s. Speculators, promoters, and opportunists had set the tone of the decade, leading the people on "a mad chase for unearned riches." Social responsibilities had been disregarded in the spread of "the general attitude, 'Every man for himself; the devil take the hindmost.'" Material comfort came to define the American dream, as "the leaders of finance celebrated and assured us of an eternal future for [an] easy-chair mode of living." The stock market crash and ensuing depression left this deluded people stunned and increasingly frightened. As the fantasies of the 1920s turned to dust, as the false leaders floundered in confusion, the people were gripped by "fear itself—nameless, unreasoning, unjustified terror which paralyzes needed efforts to convert retreat into advance."[31]

Like a biblical prophet, Roosevelt railed at the idolaters who had misled the people. Setting the scene for his presidency, he borrowed imaginatively from the Old and New Testaments. Leaders of business, he thundered in his first inaugural address, "know only the rules of a generation of self-seekers. They have no vision, and when there is no vision the people perish. The money changers have fled from their high seats in the temple of our civilization." Roosevelt called upon the people to reclaim their abandoned temple by recovering their ancestral faith. "Our task of reconstruction," he said in 1934, "does not require the creation of new and strange values. It is rather the finding of the way once more to known, but to some degree forgotten, ideals and values."[32]

Roosevelt's early presidential speeches were rich in imagery that evoked older American values largely shoved aside by a self-seeking individualism. He spoke often of the spirit of the pioneers, of neighborliness, of "the old principle of the local community, the principle that no individual, man, woman, or child, has a right to do things that hurt his neighbor." He invoked the classical republican term for the common good: "I like that word 'Commonwealth.' All over this nation we are hewing out a Commonwealth." And against the psychological appeal of upward mobility, he preached a sermon on democratic affiliation. Speaking to the graduating class of the Naval Academy in June 1933, Roosevelt urged the midshipmen "to avoid an exclusive relationship to your own clan. . . . Remember to cultivate the friendship of people, not alone your own class or profession, but the average run of folks."[33]

The final act of Roosevelt's morality play told the story of the people's redemption. The depression had been an economic evil but also a moral purgative: "A great adversity has chastened us." In a rhetorical voice appropriate to both a Christian and a Jeffersonian leader, Roosevelt claimed only a modest role for himself, while hailing the people's return to the path of personal and public virtue. "Leadership

I have tried to give," he said in October 1933, "but the great and the outstanding fact . . . has been the response—the wholehearted response—of America. As we have recaptured and rekindled our pioneering spirit, we have insisted that it shall always be a spirit of justice, a spirit of teamwork, a spirit of sacrifice, and, above all, a spirit of neighborliness." These words elided some of the central realities of the early New Deal. There was little of the spirit of justice, teamwork, sacrifice, and neighborliness, for example, in the logrolling and grabs for power within the National Recovery Administration. Out of moral enthusiasm and even naïveté, rather than cynicism, the early New Deal overestimated its power to curb the pursuit of self-interest. But it was not so naïve in reviving the ideal of community as its necessary counterpoise. The greatest change produced during his first term in office, Roosevelt thus proclaimed in his second inaugural address, "has been the change in the moral climate of America."[34]

The popular and electoral appeal of the New Deal rested, of course, less on this uplifting moral drama than on the concrete benefits that the Roosevelt administration supplied to so many different groups. Roosevelt spoke to the people's better selves but never forgot their most pressing needs. He was pleased as a politician, but sometimes taken aback as a moralist, by the primal, desperate loyalties that New Deal assistance to the suffering could evoke. After a campaign swing in October 1936, he remarked, as Harold Ickes recounts, that "there was something terrible about the crowds that lined the streets along which he passed. He went on to explain what he meant, which was exclamations from individuals in the crowd, such as 'He saved my home,' 'He gave me a job,' 'God bless you, Mr. President,' etc."[35]

Were these voices from the crowd emblematic of the meaning that most Americans found in the New Deal? Indeed, was Roosevelt's real message moral or material? Richard Hofstadter and Daniel Rodgers have argued that the New Deal abandoned the moralistic discourse of the Progressives for a new, pragmatic discourse of interests. As the harmony and good will of the early New Deal gave way to growing political controversy, Roosevelt did begin to talk less of neighborliness and more of contending interests. There was still a moral edge to the rhetoric of class conflict that he began to employ in 1935, but he also began to speak in the dispassionate analytical terms of the emerging pluralist theory in political science: "The science of politics, indeed, may properly be said to be in large part the science of the adjustment of conflicting group interests."[36]

The language of interest became more common after 1934; it was the preferred vocabulary of the more unsentimental, hard-boiled New Dealers. But for Franklin Roosevelt, interest and morality were never set in opposition to one another. Instead, his discourse integrated pluralistic interests into a larger structure of interdependence that was moral as well as economic. One can see Roosevelt as the Jeffersonian moralist, first excluding the privileged, then weaving the fragmented constituencies of the middle and working class into a democratic majority, in the following typical, homespun piece of rhetoric from the later New Deal. On a tour of the Western states in September 1937, Roosevelt talked extemporaneously at Cheyenne, Wyoming:

> Out here in the cattle country and the sugar beet country, of course, I am interested in the prosperity of the raisers of cattle and the growers of beets. Perhaps somewhere down in my heart, I am a little bit more interested in the ten men who have a hundred head of cattle apiece, than I am in the one man who has a thousand head of cattle. And perhaps I am a little more interested in the ten men who have a hundred acres of beets than I am in the one man who has a thousand acres of beets. . . .
>
> In these next few years—four years, eight years, twelve years, twenty years—I am very firmly convinced that the people of the Nation will have, more and more, a national point of view. You people out here, for example, realize far better than you did four years ago that your prosperity is tied up very intimately with the prosperity of the cotton growers of the South and with that of the industrial workers of the East. And, in the same way, those people in the great factories of the East and Middle West, and on the cotton farms of the South, in the corn belt and in the wheat belt, know that their prosperity is affected by your prosperity out here.[37]

Roosevelt appealed to the interests of diverse economic groups and regions, but he always reminded each to be cognizant of its bond to the others. His discourse always grounded interdependence in hardheaded economic calculation, but it was graced by the language of the family and religion. "I like to think of our country," he said in 1936, "as one home in which the interests of each member are bound up with the happiness of all." He reached back beyond the language of liberal individualism to the communitarian idiom of the Puritans. Sounding like a John Winthrop for an industrial age, his 1938 Labor Day speech was "a sermon, if you will, on that ancient text 'We are all members one of another.'" If the early New Deal was a morality play for a bewildered people, the later New Deal offered a fusion of interest and morality for a democratic majority on the rise.[38]

Democratic political education teaches people about their economic, political, and moral interdependencies. It also summons them to apply what they have learned through active ventures in self-government. The discourse and the policies of the New Deal opened up new spaces—in Agricultural Adjustment Administration (AAA) and union elections, for example, or in Works Progress Administration (WPA) cultural projects—for public involvement. They also heightened awareness of the economic *and* moral stakes in political life. Franklin Roosevelt repeatedly expressed his pride that the New Deal had reawakened the public spirit of Americans and displaced the privatizing obsessions of the 1920s. As he put it in a 1936 campaign address at Boston: "The average American as I have met him . . . is no longer indifferent to the problems of Government. And it is my opinion that there is more downright political intelligence than ever before in our entire history. In a world which in many places has gone undemocratic, we have gone more democratic." Roosevelt had not inspired all of the political fervor of the 1930s; some of it, of course, was directed against him. Yet at least for a time, his New Deal had fostered an outpouring of popular democratic energy.[39]

Roosevelt's faults as democratic educator are readily apparent. He could be maddeningly cautious and evasive with the public when the political risks were high. The issue of civil rights for black Americans was a case in point. Blacks had legitimate reasons for shifting their political allegiance to the Democratic party in the brave symbolic gestures of Eleanor Roosevelt and the welfare-state assistance won for them by such stalwart racial liberals as Harold Ickes, Harry Hopkins, and Aubrey Williams. But Franklin Roosevelt, ever mindful of the place of the South in his electoral coalition and the dominance of Southerners in congressional leadership posts, shied away from a public discourse about racial justice. When the National Association for the Advancement of Colored People (NAACP) pressed its campaign for antilynching legislation, the president repeatedly gave private assurances of his sympathy. Just as repeatedly, Roosevelt cited the priority of economic recovery and the necessity of working with the Southerners in Congress as excuses for his public silence. The black masses might adulate the president, but civil rights leaders, smarting at his obeisance to Southern power on the antilynching issue, saw him differently. In words that recalled Frederick Douglass's description of Lincoln as "the white man's President," Roy Wilkins of the NAACP remarked: "'Mr. Roosevelt was no friend of the Negro. He wasn't an enemy, but he wasn't a friend.'"[40]

There were limitations in the depth as well as the range of Roosevelt's political education. His New Deal discourse was often too fragmented and underdeveloped to serve as a sophisticated guide to democratic citizens. Strongly evocative of moral hope, it was, as

James MacGregor Burns laments, too "soft and shapeless" when it came to practical action. Nevertheless, there was valuable democratic instruction in Roosevelt's discursive blend of American vocabularies, his mixture of liberal self-interest, a classical republican sense of the common good, a Jeffersonian romance of the people, a biblical idiom of penitence and compassion. He reworked old images into a new discourse—into a democratic message of interdependence and communal responsibility that is still relevant, especially to a later generation that has largely forgotten it.[41]

The Institution-Builder

In proclaiming that "the greatest duty of a statesman is to educate," Franklin Roosevelt professed his allegiance to a classical maxim of democratic leadership. As a modern democratic leader, he was equally concerned with building the institutions—party, presidency, administrative apparatus—appropriate to a new, positive state in America. Roosevelt the institution builder is, however, a figure rife with ambiguity. We see forming in the Roosevelt administration some of the most productive instruments of a new democratic state, but we also observe the genesis of some of its most troubling pathologies.

Political scientists have reached widely differing conclusions about Franklin Roosevelt's impact on the American party system. He has been portrayed as a party wrecker, who displaced political parties from their previous centrality by building up the national executive as the new locus of power and patronage; as a failed party reformer, who worked too cozily with the conservative Democratic establishment and then lashed out in a belated and ineffectual effort to "purge" it in 1938; as the overseer of a historic partisan realignment, which owed less to his leadership, however, than to the overwhelming force of the Great Depression as a realigning issue. Each of these views is instructive about Roosevelt's limitations as a party builder. Despite his failures in the realm of partisan politics, however, he may still be the most effective architect of a majoritarian party that twentieth-century American politics has produced.[42]

To a Jackson Day gathering of Democrats in 1940, Roosevelt admitted that "I hold to party ties less tenaciously than most of my predecessors in the Presidency." This lack of loyalty to the traditional Democratic party is easily understood. The party whose leadership Roosevelt had won in 1932 was a ramshackle structure, in which business-oriented conservatives, states' rights Southerners, and Wilsonian progressives were uncomfortably allied. Naturally, Roosevelt hoped to move beyond this jumbled party to a stronger, more coherent vehicle of governance. Not surprisingly, he dreamed of a "system of party responsibility" emerging in the United States, based on the requirement "that one of its parties be the liberal party and the other be the conservative party."[43]

Roosevelt hoped to be a builder of a "responsible" liberal party. His greatest deficiency in the partisan realm therefore lay in his halting, halfhearted efforts at reforming the Democratic party. The pragmatic politician was too wedded to the existing configuration of power to run the risks needed for party reform: He would not challenge the agricultural interests that undergirded Southern conservatism or the big city bosses who reined in New Deal sentiments in the North. Still, the impediments to the formation of an ideologically coherent Democratic party in the 1930s were formidable. Anthony Badger points out that Roosevelt had little choice at the outset of the New Deal but to work with the established leadership of his party; the president could not jeopardize his emergency legislative program for the sake of long-term party building. Further, given the strong local roots of party politicians, the president's ability to sponsor successful New Deal challengers to entrenched officeholders was circumscribed. Due to structural as well as personal limitations, then, Roosevelt left the Democratic party still jumbled, still substantially mortgaged to its conservative elements.[44]

Although Roosevelt's hopes for a liberal party were never realized, although the Democratic party remained riddled with incongruent elements, a significant reshaping of partisan conflict did occur in the 1930s, and it continued to dominate American politics until the 1980s. Large historical forces in demographics and political economy were at play here—but in recognizing these forces we should not minimize the role of Franklin Roosevelt. His personality became a lightning rod for a political generation, a symbolic carrier of political loves and hates. Even more important, the policies that he sponsored (or that became associated with his name) penetrated more deeply into the lives of more people than had those of any previous president and thereby gave a clearer content to partisan preferences than had previously been the case. Roosevelt could not "purge" the Democratic party, could not make it fully "responsible"—but he left a huge mark on that party and on the party system in general.

While political scientists might debate Franklin Roosevelt's impact on the party system, few would dispute his enormous impact on the presidency. Theodore Roosevelt and Woodrow Wilson are generally accorded the status of forebears of the "modern" presidency, but

Franklin Roosevelt is generally regarded as its true founding father. Under his leadership, American government was transformed from a political order that revolved around Congress to a more dynamic, presidency-centered polity.[45]

From the 1940s through the 1960s, Roosevelt's model of the strong presidency was widely praised, with only old-fashioned, checks-and-balances conservatives offering a vocal dissent. The twin presidential disasters of Vietnam and Watergate, however, uncovered the problematic relationship between presidential power and democratic values. From the standpoint of democratic leadership, Roosevelt's presidency building appears today as a deeply ambiguous accomplishment. Some of the ambiguities were present already in his own practices; others emerged as later chief executives followed in his footsteps.

Roosevelt liked to think of himself as a president in the tradition of Thomas Jefferson, battling on behalf of the people against a Hamiltonian elite. Yet his view of the president as the only man in the political order with a national vantage point and as the driving force in the expansion of government capacity belonged equally to the tradition of Alexander Hamilton. When he jokingly quoted Theodore Roosevelt as remarking "Sometimes I wish I could be President and Congress too," the humor was tinged with empathy. It pointed, too, to the role of opposition forces in driving Franklin Roosevelt to aggrandize the presidency. Local political and economic elites, nestled in the party system and shielded by the tenets of federalism, frequently frustrated the national policies of the New Deal. Congress, although subject to radical currents during Roosevelt's first few years in office, became after 1935 a forum where antilabor and segregationist Southern Democrats combined with business-oriented Republicans to form a powerful "conservative coalition." Even earlier the Supreme Court's majority made plain its adherence to the law of the old regime, stigmatizing the New Deal as constitutional usurpation. In Roosevelt's eyes, the elites who had once looked to Hamilton's presidency to serve them were now the sworn foes of executive action, while the new Jefferson could make headway against their entrenched power only by transforming Hamilton's preferred instrument into his own.[46]

As president, Roosevelt strove to make himself the center of the web of government. With great skill, he reached out for the multifarious pieces of information that would keep important decisions in his own hands and executive power centered in his own office. In an often-quoted passage, Arthur Schlesinger, Jr., limned the master of information and power in the White House:

He deliberately organized—or disorganized—his system of command to insure that important decisions were passed on to the top. His favorite technique was to keep grants of authority incomplete, jurisdictions uncertain, charters overlapping. The result of this competitive theory of administration was often confusion and exasperation on the operating level; but no other method could so reliably insure that in a large bureaucracy filled with ambitious men eager for power the decisions, and the power to make them, would remain with the President.[47]

It was an appealing image: the president who knows more than anyone else in American government, the president who exercises power for the sake of progressive change, the president who offers the gift of national vision to a fragmented and decentralized polity. But the drive for information and power could easily turn into the proclivity for secrecy and covert action. If this proclivity would turn into a nightmare in later administrations, its dangerous tendencies were already present in Roosevelt's presidency. Richard Gid Powers describes Roosevelt's close tie to J. Edgar Hoover and the FBI:

> The personal relationship between Hoover and Roosevelt erased any limit set by custom or law to the requests the president might make of the FBI director, or to the favors the director might do for the president. Hoover passed along political gossip about Roosevelt's friends and enemies, information about the plans of possible election opponents, and background material that might spare the president involvement in embarrassing situations. For his part, Roosevelt was not reluctant to ask Hoover to trace any piece of information he might need; he asked him to run down the source of unfriendly rumors or news stories and to fill him in on the background of citizens who wrote him letters or opposed his policies.[48]

A presidency-centered government taxed the capacity even of a Franklin Roosevelt. In 1936 he appointed three experts in public administration, Louis Brownlow, Charles Merriam, and Luther Gulick, to study the reorganization of the executive branch. One of the principal findings of the Brownlow Committee was that "the President needs help"; the committee recommended that he be provided with at least six assistants "possessed of high competence, great physical vigor, and a passion for anonymity." These assistants became the core of an expanding White House staff, which was, in turn, part of a newly formed Executive Office of the President, established by Roosevelt in 1939 after considerable resistance from Congress.[49]

The growth of a large White House staff and Executive Office of the President was necessary for the president to fulfill the mushrooming duties of his office. The dangerous bureaucratic potential in these structures was held in check by Roosevelt, with his extraordinary range of contacts in government and his personal involvement in important decisions. His successors in the White House, however, would not always be so adept at using the institutionalized presidency without being used by it. In later administrations a staff that had grown far beyond Roosevelt's initial expansion would become a set of buffers insulating a president from jarring contacts with people outside the White House. Unelected power brokers and zealous loyalists would, from the glamorous vantage point of the White House, exercise vast influence in the president's name. Constructing an institutionalized presidency to make democratic government more efficient, Roosevelt may in the long run have made democratic leadership from the White House more difficult.[50]

From the standpoint of democratic leadership, the most paradoxical of Roosevelt's effects on the presidency was the symbolic connection he drew between president and public. In one light, his bond with the American people was rich in democratic sustenance. Not only did Roosevelt rally the dispirited with his radiant self-confidence; he encouraged and praised the active citizenship that the New Deal presented as alternative to the failed privatism of the 1920s. Yet the bond was too tight, too exclusive; the people were becoming too dependent on the person of the president. A president in the Roosevelt mold might make occasional gestures of sponsorship for citizen participation, but his underlying message was that he was the people's surrogate, the practical embodiment of their theoretical sovereignty. With the advent of television, a more powerful medium than the radio at which Roosevelt had excelled, the White House became a giant publicity machine, aiming to shape a presidential image of action and power that dwarfed the political activities of ordinary citizens. As presidents came to monopolize the visible space of national politics, many Americans came to regard themselves as nothing but passive onlookers to the spectacle of presidential leadership.[51]

Roosevelt's creation of the modern presidency was greeted with a fusillade of criticism from the enemies of the New Deal. When he tried to secure congressional approval for his executive reorganization program in 1938, the criticism became so fierce that he felt compelled to issue a statement assuring the American people that "I have no inclination to be a dictator." Roosevelt was no dictator. He was, however, insensitive to the darker side of presidential power. Abraham Lincoln, too, had been reviled as a dictator for the way he stretched

presidential powers. He responded with powerful intellectual arguments for his emergency actions and with a pledge that presidential
power would be moderated once the emergency ceased. Lacking Lincoln's depth of understanding, Roosevelt approached presidential
power with his usual blithe spirit. When he pushed the presidency
into questionable domains, he excused his actions with rationalizations or else concealed them altogether.[52]

Those who branded Roosevelt as a dictator were referring not only
to his personal quest for power but also to the bureaucratic leviathan
that they saw him breeding. The conservative attack on the New Deal
administrative state as oppressive "big government," with its regi-
menting bureaucrats and dependent citizens, was to be a lasting and
increasingly potent one. A second attack came later, from more neutral, academic observers: the central flaw in the New Deal state was
not unconstrained government but compromised government; the alleged leviathan was actually a menagerie of hybrid creatures—narrow
administrative agencies bred with narrow interest groups. Thus, New
Deal liberalism became, in Theodore Lowi's influential phrase, "interest-group liberalism."[53]

If the conservative attack was vitiated by ideological nostalgia and
partisan excess, the academic critique was telling. Before we seize
upon the genuine pathologies of the New Deal state, however, we
need to acknowledge that Roosevelt and his associates were engaged
in a generally honorable effort to make bureaucracy serve democracy.
New Deal state building was a complicated process, in which the Roosevelt administration sought to incorporate established groups into a
new national regime, to extend recognition to previously excluded
groups, and even to serve the needs of the disadvantaged. It was not
entirely the fault of the administration that the most democratic of its
objectives was fulfilled the least.[54]

The administrative state that Roosevelt envisioned was not staffed
by meddlesome or self-seeking bureaucrats. It was, on the contrary,
an exciting new arena of public service for dedicated New Dealers. As
he put it in 1939: "We are handling complicated problems of administration with which no other party has ever had to wrestle. To do that,
we are constantly recruiting lieutenants who will give intense and
genuine devotion to the cause of liberal government." Dedicated administrators, he argued, were more capable of redressing the grievances of ordinary citizens than were the traditional mechanisms of
the legal process. Vetoing the Walter-Logan Bill in 1940 (a bill
through which congressional conservatives attempted to curb the use
of administrative tribunals), Roosevelt suggested that lawyers were
among the chief opponents of the New Deal administrative state:

"Many of them prefer the stately ritual of the courts, in which lawyers play all the speaking parts, to the simple procedure of administrative hearings which a client can understand and even participate in." Other, more ominous interests were also behind the Walter-Logan Bill: "Wherever a continuing series of controversies exist between a powerful and concentrated interest on one side and a diversified mass of individuals . . . on the other side, the only means of obtaining equality before the law has been to place the controversy in an administrative tribunal." Maintaining the administrative tribunal through his veto, he was guarding "the very heart of modern reform administration."[55]

"Modern reform administration" assumed a special responsibility for the disadvantaged. Louis Brownlow, whom Roosevelt tapped to head his committee on executive reorganization, was typical of many administrative reformers in pursuing through technocratic means what he regarded as "an essentially humanitarian, egalitarian, and libertarian dream." Among the recommendations of the Brownlow Committee, enthusiastically endorsed by Roosevelt, was a proposal to establish two new cabinet departments, a Department of Social Welfare and a Department of Public Works. Institutionalizing central aspects of New Deal policy, the proposal would have strengthened administrative agencies serving working people and the poor. But establishment of the two new departments was opposed by foes of the New Deal (and by some New Deal administrators protecting their own departmental turf) and was jettisoned during the political storm over Roosevelt's reorganization plan.[56]

The conception of an administrative state in which dedicated public servants made government accessible to average citizens and showed humane concern for citizens in distress was fulfilled in such New Deal agencies as the Works Progress Administration and the National Youth Administration. Unfortunately, the predominant character of the New Deal administrative state was shaped less by these democratic objectives than by the structural realities of economic power and bureaucratic organization. Particularly in the agencies patrolling the diverse realms of economic life in America, the state became ally, partner, sometimes captive to powerful interests. The most notorious case of "interest-group liberalism" in the New Deal involved agriculture. In the name of grass-roots democracy as well as economic efficiency, Roosevelt proclaimed that "a sound farm policy must be a policy run by farmers." The farmers doing the running, however, were hardly the Jeffersonian yeomanry that Roosevelt loved to hymn. New Deal agricultural policy brought the American Farm Bureau Federation, the organization of the largest and most prosperous farmers, to a new position of dominance. Theda Skocpol and Kenneth Finegold write that large commercial farmers "were ultimately able to use well-institutionalized farm programs to beat back all challenges from the agricultural underclasses and to gain an enduring governmental niche within the post–New Deal political economy."[57]

The webs of bureaucratic and interest-group power that the New Deal wove became one of the principal pathologies of the modern democratic state in America. Yet the New Deal's creation of "interest-group liberalism" seems to have been more inadvertent than planned, more a capitulation to immediate pressures for action than a deliberate recasting of liberal thought. Facing an unparalleled domestic emergency with a traditionally weak state, the Roosevelt administration lacked sufficient administrative capacity to monitor and manage the economy in an autonomous fashion. The expedient of alliance with interest groups allowed the New Deal to cope with the most urgent issues of economic reconstruction. But the cost was high, as Anthony Badger observes: "The New Deal fostered interest groups that in the long run obstructed its reforming designs."[58]

The ambiguous character of New Deal state building was brought home to Roosevelt during World War II. His calls for wartime sacrifice were blunted by the effective lobbying efforts of interest groups that had been strengthened by the New Deal. In his 1944 State of the Union address, he railed at these interests: "There are pests who swarm through the lobbies of the Congress and the cocktail bars of Washington, representing these special groups as opposed to the basic interests of the Nation as a whole." Roosevelt was vexed by the entrenchment of interest-group politics that the New Deal had effected, contrary to its discourse of the public good. The modern American administrative state, of which he was the foremost builder, would be not so much a Jeffersonian, majoritarian democracy made national and efficient as an interest-group democracy of the well organized and well connected.[59]

Democratic Leadership and the Modern Political Economy

From 1933 through 1939 the Great Depression dominated the presidency of Franklin D. Roosevelt. Judged by the standard of economic policy-making, his struggle to extricate the United States from the depression was marked more by failure than by success. Shifting policy erratically in accordance with conflicting prescriptions from his advisers, he managed to stimulate a gradual economic upturn until 1937. But the recession of 1937–38, caused by postelection cuts in public spending, wiped out many of the gains and revealed the confusion at the heart of Roosevelt's economic policy-making. Although a resumption of public spending ended the recession, there were still nine million unemployed in 1939. It took war production to end the depression in America.

Analysts of Roosevelt's economic policy have, however, detected a political logic beneath the economic illogic. "There was neither unity nor meaning to Roosevelt's economic eclecticism. . . ," writes Albert Romasco, "if these policies are analyzed and judged from an economic standpoint. His objectives, from first to last, were political, and Roosevelt's performance in pursuit of his political purposes was nothing less than masterful." The separation here between economics and politics is too neat; the recession of 1937–38, for example, was a political as well as an economic disaster for the administration. Still, it is as politics that Roosevelt's efforts in the political economy are best understood, though not merely as a concern for public approval or reelection support. Roosevelt's presidency raised fundamental questions about the place of democratic leadership in the modern American political economy. I will concentrate on two of these questions: the relationship of democratic leadership to the power of business and the role of democratic leadership in the rise and transformation of organized labor.[60]

A desperate business community initially welcomed Roosevelt's efforts. He was conciliatory in turn, despite the rhetoric of his first inaugural address, offering business an opportunity to shape codes of self-regulation under government aegis in the National Recovery Administration (NRA). The result was a reprise of what his rhetoric had condemned: by the fall of 1933, Ellis Hawley notes, "the realization began to dawn that essentially the codes reflected the interests of the larger and more highly organized businessmen, that the NRA was busily promoting cartels in the interests of scarcity profits." Yet even the corporate victors in the NRA were not happy, complaining of intrusive bureaucracy and gains for labor and fearing that this new instrument of centralized planning might someday be turned against them by the state.[61]

By 1934 many members of the business community had begun to excoriate Roosevelt. But some continued to support him and became major players in the New Deal coalition. Thomas Ferguson has pointed to the pivotal role of capital-intensive firms and international financiers in the New Deal; Steve Fraser has emphasized the importance of emerging industries oriented to mass consumption, such as housing, credit, and large-scale retailing. If business backers of the New Deal are not hard to find, neither are business beneficiaries. For instance, under Roosevelt the Reconstruction Finance Corporation, headed by Texas businessman Jesse Jones, bailed out banks, insurance companies, railroads, and other businesses to the tune of $10.5 billion, matching in outlays relief spending for the unemployed and the poor.[62]

Roosevelt repeatedly voiced his irritation that his critics in the business community had failed to comprehend the relationship between the New Deal and American capitalism. Like Theodore Roosevelt, he emphasized that his sponsorship of reform had been the alternative to far more radical possibilities. Describing his first presidential term in a 1936 speech, he reminded conservatives: "We were against revolution. Therefore, we waged war against those conditions which make revolutions—against the inequalities and resentments which breed them." Fending off radicalism, the New Deal had rescued capitalism from its own blundering. As Roosevelt put it in another 1936 campaign speech, "It was this Administration which saved the system of private profit and free enterprise after it had been dragged to the brink of ruin by these same leaders who now try to scare you." In short, Roosevelt knew himself to be what later historians would credit him as being: the savior of American capitalism in its most desperate hour.[63]

He was a savior, though, who brought some ill tidings to American capitalists. In the New Deal as morality play, capitalists were the principal sinners; in the New Deal as power play, they were the largest potential losers. Roosevelt was saving capitalism, but in a manner that challenged hidebound business assumptions and historical business dominance. It was not a radical challenge—to the lasting dismay of the American left. And even in Roosevelt's moderate terms, the challenge was pressed more strongly in his discourse than in his policies. Nonetheless, Roosevelt's questioning of business dominance in America went further than that of any of his predecessors or successors in the White House. He expressed, in ways that are still instructive, the unease of a democratic leader with the undemocratic tendencies in modern corporate capitalism.[64]

Heralding a revival of the ethics of cooperation and the politics of communal responsibility, the New Deal as morality play called upon members of the business community to reform their mores. Capitalists had to accept the premise, Roosevelt said in his Commonwealth Club address during the 1932 campaign, "that private economic power is, to enlarge an old phrase, a public trust as well." Repeatedly during his presidency he bemoaned their resistance to the brand of morally responsible capitalism he was preaching. One sign of Roosevelt's frustration with the blinkered ethics of business was his focus on the problem of tax avoidance and tax evasion. Anecdotes about how the rich escaped their fair share of taxation were a staple of his press conferences. After telling several such tales to a special press conference for the editors of trade papers in 1938, Roosevelt chided them: "Now, there is no moral indignation among you business men, among you people who represent them, when you hear about these things."[65]

Roosevelt also raised questions about the division of rewards under capitalism: A fairer spread of economic resources was central to a more morally responsible capitalism. Even more important, Roosevelt believed that a wider distribution of purchasing power was the key to economic recovery. "Again," he emphasized in his 1938 annual message, "I revert to the increase of purchasing power as an underlying necessity of the day. If you increase that purchasing power for the farmers and for the industrial workers, you will increase the purchasing power for the final third of our population." It was, he insisted, prudent even for the prosperous to favor economic redistribution: "When one-third of the nation hasn't got any buying power, it ought to be to the interest of every business man to try to help that one-third of the country to get buying power." The purchasing-power thesis anticipated later Keynesian, demand-side economics, but policy indecision and conservative opposition guaranteed that the New Deal would produce little in the way of genuine economic redistribution.[66]

Roosevelt toyed at times with alternatives to an economy dominated by giant corporations and financial institutions. In June 1936 he sent a delegation to Europe to study the functioning of cooperative enterprises. Announcing this delegation at a press conference, he disclosed his interest in learning more about the Swedish "middle way" between capitalism and socialism. Later that year he expressed his admiration for New England as an American "middle way" between outmoded individualism and economic giantism: "New England has traditionally been a land of moderate-sized independent business, a land of economic democracy. Its far-seeing statesmen have always understood that democracy was impossible under the relentless pressure of concentration and monopoly wielded by the new power of high finance." Sympathetic to Louis Brandeis's call for restoring an economy of competitive economic units and sharing, too, Jefferson's rural dislike for the dense industrial city, Roosevelt groped for a way out of the trend toward economic concentration.[67]

Economic concentration worried Roosevelt, and he thought it ought to worry all American democrats. He sounded the alarm in a 1938 message to Congress: "The liberty of a democracy is not safe if the people tolerate the growth of private power to a point where it becomes stronger than their democratic state itself." He drove home the threat with startling statistics: "Of all corporations reporting from every part of the nation, one-tenth of 1 per cent of them owned 52 per cent of the assets of all of them." Roosevelt had no effective means at hand to halt or reverse this trend toward corporate concentration. Calling for a thorough study of the issue by Congress, he was, as Ellis Hawley suggests, mostly postponing action to some uncertain future date. Policy indecision and political evasiveness marked Roosevelt's warning on economic concentration, but they did not altogether diminish its historical significance. This was perhaps the last time that a president raised in a serious manner the problem of corporate power in a democracy.[68]

If Roosevelt could not change the nature of corporate capitalism much, he could do something to challenge its political dominance. That enhancement of the power of the state to counter business that Theodore Roosevelt had unsuccessfully urged during his Progressive period was achieved in large measure by Franklin Roosevelt. If Wall Street had had the upper hand in public policy before the New Deal, Roosevelt claimed, "we have returned the control of the Federal Government to the City of Washington." But the challenge to business dominance required more than the New Deal elaboration of an administrative state (which was, as already noted, subject to penetration by business interests). It also required state sponsorship of the rise of organized labor.[69]

At first glance, state sponsorship of the rise of organized labor during the New Deal owed little to Roosevelt personally. Paying surprisingly scant attention to the labor upsurge of the 1930s, Roosevelt displayed more interest in wages-and-hours legislation than in the self-organization of workers. His endorsement of Senator Robert Wagner's National Labor Relations Act of 1935 came only at the last moment, after the Senate had already passed the bill. In the labor wars of the depression, James MacGregor Burns argues, Roosevelt's "part was not much more than that of an onlooker." Yet this "onlooker" did perform a crucial service to organized labor during the 1930s. Roosevelt's predecessors in the White House had generally sided with business and employed the power of the national government against strikes that aimed to win recognition for the organization of labor. A new presidential stance toward labor was evident in Roosevelt's responses to two of the fiercest strikes of the 1930s: the San Francisco "general strike" of 1934 and the Flint autoworkers' "sit-down strike" of 1937.[70]

In July 1934 a strike by Pacific Coast longshoremen led to bloody street fighting between police and workers in San Francisco, leaving two killed and sixty-seven injured. Refusing to allow the fledgling dockers' organization, led by Harry Bridges, a young Australian-born radical, to be destroyed by intransigent employers backed by the armed force of the state, San Francisco unions responded with a general strike. President Roosevelt, cruising in the Pacific aboard the USS *Houston*, was besieged by California authorities asking for federal intervention to put down the strike. Senator Hiram Johnson, thundering about revolution in the streets, wanted federal troops; Governor Frank Merriam urged the arrest and deportation of alien radicals. As Roosevelt later described the situation in sarcastic tones: "Everybody demanded that I sail into San Francisco Bay, all flags flying and guns double shotted, and end the strike. They went completely off the handle." Instead, Roosevelt listened to voices of calm among his own trusted advisers. At the prompting of Secretary of Labor Frances Perkins and political sage Louis Howe, he issued a deliberately bland statement, expressing "my confidence that common sense and good order will prevail on both sides of the controversy." Roosevelt's calm was rewarded: both sides soon agreed to arbitration, and the result was a landmark victory for the longshoreman's union.[71]

Six weeks after his refusal to intervene in San Francisco, Roosevelt reflected on the incident at one of his press conferences. Although he blamed both sides for the general strike, he presented the two parties in sharply contrasting images. Labor had been guided by "hot-headed young leaders" without organizing experience; their adversaries were "the old conservative crowd just hoping that there would be a general strike, being clever enough to know that a general strike always fails." If Roosevelt's underlying sympathy toward labor was evident in this comment, his conception of the future of labor was apparent in another statement about San Francisco:

> The general strike started; and immediately the strikers, being young, did silly things. . . . Of course they learn by things of that kind. They have got to learn by going through the actual processes, actual examples, and not by interference from the Federal Government or the President or the United States troops. . . . We have to . . . educate labor to their responsibility.

Unafraid of labor radicalism, Roosevelt looked to the gradual maturation of a "responsible" labor movement. Both paternalistic and prescient, he wanted to give "young" labor the time and space it needed to grow in his direction.[72]

In the closing days of 1936, autoworkers at several of the huge General Motors plants in Flint, Michigan, began a sit-down strike, attempting to force recognition of the new United Auto Workers on an industry that had fiercely resisted unionization in the past. Roosevelt was surprised and troubled by the tactic. There was much greater alarm in the middle class: the White House was flooded by letters demanding that the president uphold the rights of property in this strike. But Roosevelt took the same calm—and prolabor—stance that he had assumed during the San Francisco strike. Working behind the scenes with a close political ally, Michigan governor Frank Murphy, he backed the governor's refusal to employ troops to eject the strikers from the Flint factories and joined with him in successfully pressing management to meet with the representatives of the union. In February 1937 General Motors agreed to terms that amounted to a decisive victory for the United Auto Workers. The sit-down strike, Roosevelt said later, had been a manifestation of labor's "growing pains." But capital, he was quick to add, had demonstrated in its periods of growth "the same kind of faults, the same excesses, the same irresponsibility—even in greater degree."[73]

Alexander Hamilton had advocated a government that appeared as a "Hercules" by using its armed forces to cow unruly citizens. Theodore Roosevelt was lightning quick in dispatching troops to suppress labor conflicts. Franklin Roosevelt wrote: "I consider the calling out of Federal troops during a strike, except in a national emergency, one of the most dangerous things that can happen in a democracy." Both his Jeffersonian allegiance and his abhorrence of fascism told Roosevelt he must not use military force to protect the interests of the privileged. His nonintervention was his democratic service to American workers struggling for the legitimacy of labor-union representation, especially in the mass-production industries.[74]

Roosevelt's democratic service, however, was not matched by a thorough democratic understanding of what was at stake in the labor upheaval of the 1930s—his paternalism precluded such understanding. Frances Perkins has observed of Roosevelt:

> I doubt that he understood what solidarity really means in the trade union movement. He tended to think of trade unions as voluntary associations of citizens to promote their own interests in the field of wages, hours, and working conditions. He did not altogether grasp that sense of their being a solid bloc of people united to one another by unbreakable bonds which gave them power and status to deal with their employers on equal terms.

Roosevelt saw the labor battles of his administration as the prelude to the emergence of a "responsible" labor movement. The hallmark of this movement would not be the solidarity of its membership but the stability it would bring to industrial relations. Equally important, a mature labor movement would boost the purchasing power of workers, contributing thereby to the economic health of a reformed and restored capitalist system.[75]

The rise and transformation of labor was one of the most profound democratic ambiguities of the New Deal. Through the union gains of the New Deal and World War II, Steve Fraser writes, "labor ceased to be a great question or even a mass movement containing within it the seeds of a wholly new future. As an institutionalized interest group it had become part of the answer, contributing to and drawing its just deserts from the cornucopia of American mass production and consumption." According to such students of New Deal labor relations as Fraser and Stanley Vittoz, the integration of organized labor into the emerging system of consumer capitalism was a complex process, neither planned by wily businessmen nor managed by duplicitous New Dealers. That the rank-and-file militancy of the 1930s gave way to the conservative unionism of the postwar era owed much to bureaucratic labor leadership and to the conventional dreams of most American workers. In the process of labor's gain in economic security and loss in political vision, Franklin Roosevelt played only a modest part. Yet the postwar labor movement—its leaders no longer "hot-headed," its members now fueling economic growth with their enhanced purchasing power—was almost exactly what he had envisioned.[76]

World War II and Democratic Leadership

Foreign policy generally took a back seat to domestic concerns during the New Deal years. The exigencies of the depression compelled Roosevelt to concentrate on economic and social policy. The strength of isolationist sentiments in the United States made such concentration politically advantageous as well. Students of Roosevelt's foreign policy have argued over whether he accommodated an isolationism with which he fundamentally disagreed or was influenced by an isolationism whose paramount fear—of American involvement in another global war—he shared. There is less dispute, however, over Roosevelt's limited accomplishments in foreign policy before World War II. As the forces of Nazi and Fascist aggression hurtled Europe and

Asia toward war, the United States watched from the sidelines, occasionally criticizing but never acting with effect.[77]

In his personal correspondence, Roosevelt evinced an impressive awareness of the Nazi and Fascist threat. Writing to a friend in Paris in February 1936, for example, he rejected the false optimism of the isolationists: "One cannot help feeling that the whole European panorama is fundamentally blacker than at any time in your life time or mine." But as a political educator in matters of foreign policy, Roosevelt's record in the 1930s was unimpressive. Preoccupied with the fate of his domestic agenda, fearful of tangling with the isolationist bloc in Congress, he let slide numerous opportunities for alerting the American people to the dangers abroad.[78]

Finally, on October 5, 1937, in a major address in Chicago, Roosevelt took what appeared to be a bold stand against the forces of aggression: "It seems to be unfortunately true that the epidemic of world lawlessness is spreading. When an epidemic of physical disease starts to spread, the community approves and joins in a quarantine of the patients in order to protect the health of the community against the spread of the disease." Having shaken free from political timidity to rouse the American public, Roosevelt almost immediately began to blur his message. The day after his Chicago speech, when reporters tried to elicit from him the meaning of his proposed quarantine, he gave one of the classic demonstrations of his evasiveness. Asked whether his proposal renounced American neutrality, he responded, "Not for a minute. It may be an expansion." Questioned about whether he intended to call for economic sanctions against aggressors, he said, "Look, 'sanctions' is a terrible word to use." Several years later Roosevelt ascribed the failure of his quarantine proposal to public opinion, asserting that his idea "fell upon deaf ears." In fact, public reaction to the Chicago speech had been favorable. It was not the people's deafness but Roosevelt's muffled voice that subverted his lone attempt before 1939 to make public the realities that filled his personal correspondence.[79]

The coming of the war changed everything. Stymied by a "conservative coalition" of Republicans and Southern Democrats during his second presidential term, Roosevelt had a second chance to assert his leadership during World War II. In a number of respects, he was a superb wartime leader. As a military strategist, Roosevelt displayed greater coherence than he had in combating the depression. Armed with his usual self-confidence, he became, in the words of Robert Dallek, "the principal architect of the basic strategic decisions that contributed so heavily to the early defeat of Germany and Japan." Yet he gave his generals and admirals ample latitude. Picking talented commanders, he refrained from meddling in their decisions and achieved a workable division of labor with them. At a press conference in December 1943, Roosevelt talked of how "Old Dr. New Deal" had turned over his patient to "Dr. Win-the-War." The new physician proved to be an effective specialist.[80]

The much-argued questions about Roosevelt and World War II center not on the commander in chief but on the statesman. He has often been presented as a seat-of-the-pants improviser during the war, unable to come to grips with the larger diplomatic issues that would determine the shape of the postwar international order. Warren Kimball has convincingly argued, however, that Roosevelt did have an overarching conception of the postwar order, that he planned for a liberal democratic world and a globalization of the New Deal. But in a world where conflict between nations was the rule, he sought a more powerful source of order than anything the New Deal had created at home. To patrol the new international regime, Roosevelt looked to the Four Policemen.[81]

These would be the victorious allies: the United States, Great Britain, the Soviet Union, and China. Once the war was over, they would enjoy a monopoly of force, disarming not only defeated enemies but smaller nations as well, and for a vaguely defined transitional period, until a new organization of the United Nations took over the task, they would impose peaceful resolutions of disputes between countries. Roosevelt's conception of the Four Policemen, expressed only in private so as not to alarm either internationalists or isolationists, combined the diplomatic perspectives of his two presidential mentors, aiming to be more practical than Woodrow Wilson, more benign than Theodore Roosevelt. It rested on two critical assumptions: that cooperation between the Western allies and the Soviets could be perpetuated in the postwar era, and that Franklin Roosevelt himself would be around to coordinate and harmonize four heavily armed global gendarmes.[82]

Roosevelt hoped that the benign reign of the Four Policemen would foster the emergence of a more democratic and peaceful world. In some respects, his postwar vision resembled Henry Wallace's image of the "century of the common man," with European dominion and exploitation replaced by decolonization and New Deal–style public projects for the less developed nations. Roosevelt seemed genuinely outraged by the poverty and suffering that he had witnessed during his wartime visits to European colonies in Africa and the Middle East. He was convinced, too, that colonial rivalries were a source of war that had to be eliminated. Roosevelt as anticolonialist spoke promisingly of a world marked by greater equality and mutual respect. As he told

Congress in September 1943: "The policy of the Good Neighbor has shown such success in this hemisphere that its extension to the whole world seems to be the logical next step." A few months earlier, on a brief visit to Monterrey, Mexico, he had proclaimed: "We know that the day of the exploitation of the resources and the people of one country for the benefit of any group in another country is definitely over."[83]

But Roosevelt's version of "the century of the common man" also had something in common with a rival vision, Henry Luce's "American Century." A world redesigned along liberal democratic lines would be a world open to the superior resources of American commerce, the superior moral influence of American culture, the superior political/military might of American statecraft. The economics of the new postwar order were suggested in one of Roosevelt's 1944 letters: "While we shall not take advantage of any country, we will see that American industry has its fair share in the world markets." Its politics was implicit in his talk of extending the Good Neighbor Policy from Latin America to the world; the United States was to be the model state. Its military balance could be discerned beneath the facade of great power parity; with Britain and Russia counterposed in Europe, and with China remaining an American client, the United States was to be the most powerful policeman of all.[84]

Roosevelt's postwar order was a projection of his own complex political identity. In its hopes for peace, liberation of the colonized, and material progress, it reflected his generosity and capacity to nurture as well as his faith in Jeffersonian democracy. In its unspoken expectation that the United States, and Roosevelt himself, would occupy center stage, it reflected his egotism and love for political maneuver. At times during the war Roosevelt reached heights of hubris that would be comic had they not been so prophetic of what America's new military power would bring after the war. Thus, he proposed to a visiting British official that a new nation named "Wallonia" should be carved out of parts of the Low Countries and France. Such outbursts of grandiose imagination led British Foreign Secretary Anthony Eden to observe that the American president "seemed to see himself disposing of the fate of many lands, allied no less than enemy."[85]

Even before Roosevelt's death, it was apparent that a global New Deal would be even harder to install than the domestic version had been. Although he exercised great skill in holding the wartime coalition with Stalin and Churchill intact, neither was about to be maneuvered to help Roosevelt build the postwar world he wanted. Roosevelt's misreading of Stalin is the more notorious, although the subsequently embarrassing public paeans to the friendly "representative of the heart and soul of Russia" concealed his proclivity to pursue postwar cooperation with the Soviets in a skeptical and tough-minded fashion. But Churchill, too, as an unyielding pillar of imperialism, blocked Roosevelt's path. A bone of contention between them was French Indochina, which Roosevelt fixed upon as an egregious example of the evils of colonialism. He insisted that France, defeated in the war and deprived of its prior international standing, must relinquish its colony, which would be turned over to an international trusteeship and prepared for self-government. Churchill adamantly opposed this proposal, regarding it as a fatal precedent for the breakup of the British Empire. After the Yalta Conference in February 1945, as the French moved to retake their colony, Roosevelt conceded to reporters that his trusteeship scheme for Indochina had been thwarted: "Stalin liked the idea. China liked the idea. . . . As for the British, it would only make the British mad. Better to keep quiet just now."[86]

Despite such frustrations, Roosevelt remained optimistic that he could maintain concord among the Four Policemen after the war. In his optimism, he failed to consider what the American policeman's role abroad might imply for democracy at home. Proclaiming his Good Neighbor approach to Latin America in 1933, he had announced that "the definite policy of the United States from now on is one opposed to armed intervention." But when he extended the Good Neighbor Policy to the rest of the world during the war, it was with the understanding that a postwar America would go abroad heavily armed to enforce the peace. The war was giving rise to a military-industrial complex in the United States and spawning the greatest military behemoth in history. Roosevelt's intentions may have been benign, but this president who had refrained from using troops at home to break strikes oversaw the birth of a militarized state willing to intervene abroad time and again against any threats to property and order.[87]

On the home front, as abroad, Roosevelt's wartime leadership brought impressive immediate results while setting the stage for longer-term democratic setbacks. He sparked a remarkable mobilization of American resources. Criticisms of administrative chaos, of a wartime "mess" in Washington, were rampant. Yet this untidy government at war coaxed extraordinary results from a previously depressed economy. At the apex of wartime production in 1944, David Brody notes, "the country was producing for the military effort alone at a rate nearly as high as the gross national product in 1929." Restoring prosperity, the production boom threatened runaway inflation. Through herculean efforts, the president and his aides struggled with some success to hold wage and price increases to manageable levels.[88]

"Dr. Win-the-War" was single-minded in pursuit of that end. "In time of war," Roosevelt said in November 1942, "the American people know that the one all-important job before them is fighting and working to win. Therefore, of necessity, while long-range social and economic problems are by no means forgotten, they are a little like books which for the moment we have laid aside in order that we might get out the old atlas to learn the geography of the battle areas." Holding, in John Morton Blum's phrase, a "necessitarian view of the war," Roosevelt laid aside the books of economic and social reform. He also laid aside the fundamental American texts of civil liberties and humanitarian concern, relocating Japanese Americans from the West Coast to what he acknowledged were concentration camps and restricting himself to small-scale efforts to rescue European Jews out of a fear of offending allies and anti-Semites.[89]

As Roosevelt's moral failures in the cases of Japanese Americans and European Jews flagrantly belied the democratic pretensions of the American war effort, so his "necessitarian" approach to the war also involved more subtle setbacks to democracy. While Roosevelt was laying aside the books of economic and social reform, the enemies of the New Deal were mobilizing against him. The powerful blocs that had felt aggrieved by the New Deal and that had begun to gain ground at the time of the court-packing disaster and the recession of 1937–38 were in an even better position to strike at Roosevelt during the war. Bankers, industrialists, Southern conservatives sought to use the war emergency to revoke New Deal advances in the areas of business regulation and antitrust, labor relations, social welfare, and racial equality. They fought for control of a state and economy that the war had drastically enlarged, aiming to be the masters of a nation primed by the war for a masterful position in international affairs. Against this conservative mobilization stood the dispirited ranks of the New Dealers, whom Roosevelt, preoccupied with the war, seldom tried to rally. The president was concerned enough to fight off the fiercest of the conservative assaults. Ineluctably, though, and with profound consequences for the postwar polity, the democratic achievements of the New Deal began to unravel during the war years.[90]

To mobilize American industry for military production, Roosevelt felt compelled to turn to the corporate managers whom he had only recently denounced. Dollar-a-year men, still salaried by their corporations, assumed most of the key posts in the defense effort. Roosevelt was troubled by his dependence on his old adversaries, as he wrote in a March 1941 memorandum to Wayne Johnson: "I do think things are beginning to click pretty well but I am somewhat appalled by the fact that at least nine out of ten men being brought here by the Production people are not only Republicans but are mostly violent anti-Administration Republicans." He would not jeopardize the war machine, however, by reining in the corporate managers and their new allies in the military hierarchy.[91]

A defense production effort dominated by big business guaranteed war contracts and profits steered mostly to big business. The figures, reported by Blum, are startling:

> In 1940, when the defense program began, approximately 175,000 companies were providing some 70 per cent of the manufacturing output of the United States, and one hundred companies produced the remaining 30 per cent. By March 1943, even though twice as much was being produced, that ratio had been reversed. The one hundred companies previously holding only 30 per cent now held 70 per cent of war and civilian contracts, and were still gaining in proportion to the others.

In 1938 Roosevelt had warned Americans that growing economic concentration posed a threat to democratic governance. During the war, this Jeffersonian who had emphasized the connection between economic and political inequality became an inadvertent Hamiltonian who oversaw a spectacular furtherance of corporate concentration.[92]

To Bruce Catton, a disenchanted New Dealer who had worked under defense production chieftain Donald Nelson, the ascendancy of big business in World War II signaled the demise of democratic hopes. On the back cover of his 1948 book, *The War Lords of Washington,* Catton wrote: "Democracy means change, and the men to whom the President had entrusted the conduct of our war-time affairs were, for the most part, men who dreaded change above all things. So we won the war, but we didn't win anything else." Catton was particularly insightful in seeing that the resurgence of big business was a matter of values as much as of power. Roosevelt had not only welcomed his old enemies into his citadel; he had also allowed them to redesign its banners. "Fighting for its life," Catton lamented, "democracy drew its war cries from the philosophy of the salesman."[93]

As Catton perceived it, America's war effort had come to be defined by the advertising industry more than by the president. Before Pearl Harbor, Roosevelt had articulated grand democratic goals with his Four Freedoms and his Atlantic Charter. Yet this rhetoric remained ethereal and vague, unconnected to specific objectives, and pollsters soon determined that it had little impact on public opinion. Facing a resurgent conservatism that scored dramatic gains in the 1942 congressional elections, fearful, too, of recapitulating Woodrow Wilson's sad fate, Roosevelt eschewed the task of educating the American people on the democratic issues at stake in the war. Instead, he largely turned the job of inspiring the public over to advertising experts. Predictably, the messages they crafted projected a war fought primarily for the consumer comforts of home. The advertisers' war was mocked by Henry Pringle, head of the writers' division at the Office of War Information (and an irreverent biographer of Theodore Roosevelt). When a Coca-Cola adman became head of the graphics division, a disgusted Pringle designed a poster showing an American flag wrapped around a Coke bottle and a text that read: "'Step right up and get your four delicious freedoms. It's a refreshing war.'"[94]

Tasting prosperity (albeit restricted by wartime shortages and rationing) after years of hardship, a large number of Americans seemed to want these "delicious freedoms." As a democratic politician, Roosevelt was naturally attuned to the new consumer desires. But the preoccupation with consumption did not fit with the democratic morality that he had articulated in the years before the war. An Office of War Information report informed Roosevelt that the majority of Americans looked forward to a postwar era "'compounded largely of 1929 values and the economics of the 1920s.'" That "mad chase" after wealth and privilege that the New Deal morality play had scorned was about to begin again. This time, though, Roosevelt would not be among its critics. His economic advisers, most notably Alvin Hansen, were telling him that a prudent, Keynesian mix of government spending and consumer purchasing power could provide the kind of continuous economic growth that economists of the previous decade had despaired of achieving. By 1944 Roosevelt was ready to unveil his own vision of an affluent postwar America.[95]

Roosevelt's vision pledged an expansion of the New Deal's previously limited steps toward equality and dignity for the mass of Americans. In his 1944 State of the Union address, he called for an "economic bill of rights," including in his list the right to "a useful and remunerative job," "a decent home," "adequate medical care," and "a good education." This was less a legislative program than a campaign manifesto, rallying liberal New Dealers to another electoral crusade. Still, no president had ever gone as far in addressing the material bases essential for democratic dignity.[96]

Yet the Roosevelt of the 1944 campaign promised more than an economics of decency. As Blum observes of this campaign, the president "promised what wartime advertising had displayed." In a radio address from the White House a few days before the election, Roosevelt heralded a glittering future of mass consumption: "I look forward to millions of new homes, fit for decent living; to new, low-priced automobiles; new highways; new airplanes and airports, to television; and other miraculous new inventions and discoveries." The Roosevelt of the 1944 campaign spoke as the advocate of both social progress and individual pleasure. But it would be the dream of an expanding consumer cornucopia and not the thrust for greater social justice through a broadened New Deal that would dominate American politics after the war.[97]

Conclusion

When Franklin Roosevelt died of a cerebral hemorrhage on April 12, 1945, there was a massive outpouring of grief in the United States and around the world. Political commentators and editorialists rushed out testimonials to his accomplishments mixed with regrets that he had died before finishing his great work. Typical was the *Chicago Daily News:* "The journey ends at a tragic moment, just when Roosevelt's matchless diplomacy, his skill, his charm, his stubborn Dutch courage will be most needed to fashion that dream of his life—and America's—a permanent peace." Grief and heartfelt tributes were America's predominant reaction to Roosevelt's death—but there was also an undertone of disorientation. Broadcasting on CBS radio on the night of April 12, a British correspondent in New York, Alastair Cooke, captured this unsettling undertone:

> I walked across town, towards Broadway, and exchanged glances with hundreds of people who looked stonily back. You could only say the sentence ["Roosevelt is dead"] over in your mind and feel chilled and empty. . . . Down in the flowered square of Rockefeller Plaza strangers met in little knots. They looked sullen, and, then, because there was nothing they could do they drifted helplessly apart.[98]

Both the grief and the disorientation were fitting responses to Roosevelt's death. Contemplating a run for a precedent-shattering third term in the White House, Roosevelt had written to a supporter: "Under our political system it would be a great pity if the continuance of liberal government were dependent on one person in the Presidency." When he died, it was the supporters of his brand of democratic liberalism who especially experienced this "great pity." As Richard Hofstadter observed a few years later, Roosevelt's "passing

left American liberalism demoralized and all but helpless." He had
made the liberal democratic future too dependent on the personal
charm and political appeal of one man.[99]

Roosevelt's career exemplified the possibilities and the paradoxes
in modern democratic leadership. Egotistical and politically cunning,
he was saved from being merely a great political operator by seemingly antithetical qualities: a capacity for nurturance and a commitment to a Jeffersonian democratic faith. A moralist and preacher of
interdependence and communal responsibility, he was also, under the
pressure from powerful economic forces and persisting American individualism, a sponsor of interest-group selfishness and consumer
self-absorption. A builder of the strong presidency and the modern
administrative state as vital agencies of a national democracy, he also
foreshadowed the arbitrary executive power and bureaucratic pathol-
ogy that are banes of American democracy half a century later. A
critic of corporate power and a benign patron of labor unions, he was
also a participant in the wartime resurgence of big business and a
prophet of the postwar decline of labor's political fervor. An eloquent
advocate of an anticolonial course for an internationalist America, in
the guise of the Good Neighbor, he may also have been—as a proponent of the global spread of American capitalism under the aegis of a
heavily armed police power—an inadvertent forerunner of American
postwar imperialism.

There were many shortcomings in Roosevelt's record and many
democratic disappointments in his leadership. He compromised often
with entrenched structures of privilege, power, and prejudice, and
even when he battled them it was too often with hierarchical instruments of rule that held unfortunate consequences for a democratic future. Nonetheless, Roosevelt pushed democratic change farther than
any of his twentieth-century predecessors or successors in the presidency. He gave dramatic voice to the goal of a more egalitarian and
democratic polity and, in his politically calculated and compromising
way, led a majority of Americans toward that polity. There is much to
be gleaned from Roosevelt's story about the limits of modern democratic leadership. But there is also much to teach those who might
hope to revive the democratic spirit that his leadership, at its best,
inspired.

8

John F. Kennedy

Heroic Leadership for
a Television Age

THE MOST CELEBRATED LINE IN JOHN F. KENNEDY'S INAUGURAL ADdress was his challenge to the public: "And so, my fellow Americans: ask not what your country can do for you—ask what you can do for your country." These words seemed to summon Americans to a new era of political involvement and sacrifice for the common good. But when Alicia Patterson, editor and publisher of *Newsday*, wrote to the new president in May 1961, requesting specifics to match the soaring rhetoric, Kennedy's public response was no longer so inspiring. Apart from the Peace Corps, he was reduced to suggesting such sacrifices as a curb upon expense accounts and an acceptance of higher postal rates. The most important role that Kennedy had in mind for the American people was revealed near the end of the public letter to Patterson: "Each time we make any move or commitment in foreign affairs, I am in need of the support of the American people, their understanding, their patience, their willingness to endure setbacks and risks and hardships in order that this country can regain leadership and initiative."[1]

Kennedy continued to depict his presidency as an adventure in mass participation and public service. Yet the mass participation was mostly vicarious, the public service primarily reserved for an elite. The spotlight was on the heroic leader in international affairs, who, if he could count on the backing of a largely unquestioning nation, could evoke its power and personify its greatness. Presented as a revitalization of democracy, the Kennedy presidency was in reality a refashioning of heroic leadership for an age of global conflict and television spectacle.

Political values in the United States have often been personified by leaders. Even movements of dissent and opposition depend in part on leadership that exemplifies their causes—as with Elizabeth Cady Stanton and women's self-assertion, Eugene V. Debs and labor's demand for dignity, Martin Luther King, Jr., and blacks' struggle for racial justice. The important questions for a democratic polity are how leaders earn the right to personify a cause or a people, and whether leaders use the distinction they have attained to educate or to awe followers. John Adams insisted that leaders had to earn distinction through past services to the republic; Abraham Lincoln demonstrated how distinction could be linked to a democratic cause and why political education required an engagement of both leader and people with the deepest roots of their collective life. John F. Kennedy found an alternative—and more modern—path to distinction. His claim to personify the American people rested neither on a prior record of distinguished services nor on an identification with any particular democratic cause. Instead, he rose as a political celebrity, famous for *who* he was, a cynosure for his personal charm and his heroic masculine virtues. Dazzled contemporaries compared him to a movie star, seldom noticing that the images and fantasies suitable to the screen are not the stuff of democratic politics.

Kennedy reached the White House as a celebrity, with a heroic image more manufactured than earned. But he was determined to bring reality closer to image and to assume his place in the history books as a "great" president. This chapter will describe Kennedy's heroic conception of the presidency and will show the hero on the offensive in cold war politics, on the defensive in relations with the business community, and in tension with a civil rights movement that refused to play by the hero's script. In depicting Kennedy as a modern exemplar of heroic leadership, I link him to a tradition of American political leadership that was begun by Alexander Hamilton in explicitly aristocratic terms and adapted by Theodore Roosevelt to a democratic age.

Skeptical where Hamilton had been serenely certain, detached where Roosevelt had been morally combative, Kennedy nonetheless shared many of their distinctive qualities as leaders: the aristocratic sense of superiority, the preoccupation with masculinity, the longing for a heroic destiny. Like Theodore Roosevelt, Kennedy understood how the heroic leader could keep his actual distance from the people while offering them appealing images to consume. But Roosevelt's flamboyant persona would have sounded shrill in the electronic media. With a "cool" air of self-mastery, a disarming wit, a rhetoric of laconic idealism, Kennedy was television's hero.

The Modern Hero

When John F. Kennedy captured the Democratic presidential nomination in 1960, his record of substantive political accomplishments was unimpressive. Many of his party's elders resented him as an impatient upstart, whose appeal reflected little more than telegenic good looks and the profuse spending of his father, Joseph. John Kennedy deserved more credit than these elders were willing to grant: he had a gritty courage that vanquished ceaseless physical debility and pain, a driving energy (more evident in campaigns than in legislative work) that led him to outpace his rivals for the presidency, and a charm that rivaled Franklin Roosevelt's in winning supporters and disarming potential adversaries. But the two brightest facets to his public persona were even more suspect than the elders surmised. Like Theodore Roosevelt, John F. Kennedy presented himself to the electorate as a war hero and a man of letters. Roosevelt had artfully burnished his own real deeds. Kennedy had considerable help from others in manufacturing an image that he did not yet deserve.

Several researchers have uncovered the processes through which Kennedy's prepresidential image as the medal-winning war hero and prize-winning scholar was constructed. Joan Blair and Clay Blair, Jr., painstakingly disassembled the legend of *PT 109*. Reconstructing the events in which the patrol boat that Kennedy commanded was rammed and sunk by a Japanese destroyer, wounded sailors towed to a nearby island, and the crew ultimately rescued, the Blairs discovered that Kennedy had been inept before he was brave. His was the only one of the light, maneuverable boats ever rammed by a destroyer during the war in the Pacific. The most likely explanation for the unprecedented disaster was that Kennedy did not have his crew at a proper state of alert. After his craft sank, Kennedy exhibited authentic heroism in towing an injured crew member ashore—although this deed was enlarged in subsequent tellings to include two other injured men. The eventual rescue of the entire crew, attributed in legend to Kennedy's pluck, was in fact due to the efforts of others. The story of *PT 109*—with Kennedy's courageous exploits highlighted and exaggerated and his failures at naval command concealed—was soon celebrated in popular magazine articles and later became one of the principal bases for his political celebrity. The Blairs concluded that "it was wartime censorship and Joe Kennedy's contacts at *Reader's Digest* that were primarily responsible for Jack receiving so much credit during this episode. He was, in effect, a 'manufactured' war hero."[2]

Kennedy's prepresidential reputation as a man of letters with an intellect to equal his bravery rested principally on his book, *Profiles in*

Courage, awarded a Pulitzer Prize in 1957. Herbert Parmet's research exploded the long-standing belief that Kennedy had actually authored the book. Examining manuscript drafts and tapes at the Kennedy Library, Parmet determined: "There is no evidence of a Kennedy draft for the overwhelming bulk of the book; and there is evidence for concluding that much of what he did draft was simply not included in the final version." Kennedy did supervise the project, but the research and writing had been the handiwork of his chief aide, Theodore Sorensen, and assorted scholarly helpers. The book's popularity and prestige were given an immeasurable boost from the Pulitzer Prize. Absent from the recommendations of the Pulitzer's academic advisers, *Profiles in Courage* was selected by the Pulitzer's advisory board, which had been lobbied by an associate of Joseph Kennedy. Most contemporary politicians employ ghostwriters, but few gain from them the image of prize-winning man of letters. The construction and concealment in *Profiles in Courage,* Parmet observes, were "as deceptive as installing a Chevrolet engine in a Cadillac."[3]

Glittering images transformed an attractive but flawed young politician into the rising political star of his generation—and made it all the harder to detect the real personality underneath. Kennedy's original chroniclers, intent upon dramatizing the character of the heroic leader, were not much help. More candid commentators offer an interesting admission, however: John F. Kennedy was guarded and distant, very hard to know well, with an inner self nearly as elusive— perhaps to himself as well as to others—as that of Franklin D. Roosevelt. Journalist Benjamin Bradlee, a close friend of Kennedy during his presidency, wrote of Jack and Jackie: "They are the most remote and independent people we know most of the time." Harris Wofford, a presidential aide for civil rights, observed: "About the most important things, he was a man of few words—even with those closest to him." Diplomat George F. Kennan told an interviewer that "I had the impression of a person who guarded his inner self quite tightly from revealing. He had, of course, the sort of politician-actor's countenance. What Freud called the 'persona.'"[4]

If the "politician-actor" is to be credited for skill in the presentation of self, Kennedy deserves high praise. His brightness and charm are so engaging that even after all the criticisms have been leveled, he remains likable. From an early age, Kennedy was playful and prankish, embracing life with humor and zest. His wit was quick and penetrating, most disarming when it became self-deprecating. His intellect was practical and skeptical, alert to resist clichés (though not, unfortunately, to question deeper presuppositions). His ego was strong, but he did not need to dominate every scene; unlike a Theodore Roosevelt, he was, numerous associates testified, a good listener. Kennedy's successors in the White House, Lyndon Johnson and Richard Nixon, raged in frustration that they could never reproduce his successes at image making, unable to acknowledge that on the most basic level Kennedy simply had a more appealing personality.

Kennedy's warmth was genuine, but there was the hint of a chill underneath. Whatever passions resided in him, they were apparently not for democratic causes or moral pursuits. The judgment of biographer Thomas Reeves is caustic but accurate: "Beneath the surface . . . Jack was pragmatic to the point of amorality; his sole standard seemed to be political expediency. . . . Jack's character, so much a reflection of his father's single-minded pursuit of political power and personal indulgence, lacked a moral center, a reference point that went beyond self-aggrandizement." Kennedy seemed to have the passion for distinction that has driven so many American political leaders—but not the democratic disciplining of this passion that characterized the best of those leaders.[5]

For John Kennedy, politics was mostly about power, because politics was above all an arena for masculine competition. Like Theodore Roosevelt, Kennedy could not appreciate the masculine/feminine balance of qualities found in an Abraham Lincoln and a Franklin D. Roosevelt. He too admired men who had proved their mettle in warfare or sporting competition—but there were also new standards of masculinity since the days of Theodore Roosevelt. Kennedy thus wanted an administration staffed by technocratic warriors, intellectual mandarins who knew their way around the corridors of power. Recruitment forms for the administration listed "toughness" as one of the prerequisites for joining the Kennedy bureaucracy. Political figures who talked too effusively about morality or peace or political associates deemed insufficiently tough were objects of Kennedy's scorn—and sometimes his contemptuous imputations of homosexuality. When Theodore Roosevelt's ego and fame were threatened by the posthumous letters of John Hay, Roosevelt called Hay's manhood into doubt. His hold over the liberal wing of the Democratic party threatened by Adlai Stevenson, Kennedy responded in a similar spirit, ridiculing Stevenson's virility with the comment to friends that "he must be a switcher."[6]

The language that Kennedy used when out of the public eye reflected his hard-edged masculinity. Benjamin Bradlee's memoir quotes numerous instances of Kennedy's profane disparagement of other political figures; the secret White House tapes of the president's phone conversations now available at the Kennedy Library contain similar remarks. There is nothing surprising in the fact that Kennedy swore like the sailor he had been in World War II. What is revealing about Kennedy's private profanity, however, is its tone of hostility, of scoring points, of getting even. For instance, during his confrontation with the heads of the steel corporations in 1962, he told Bradlee: "They fucked us, and we've got to try to fuck them." Political life to Kennedy was agonistic male conflict, and its fundamental question, who screwed whom. Talking profane and tough was a badge of manliness and a requisite credential for politics.[7]

Women did not fit into this picture. There were no women in Kennedy's political circle or among his high-level appointments. (Thanks to the efforts of a lower-level appointee, Esther Peterson, Kennedy did create a new Commission on the Status of Women.) Kennedy's attitude toward women appears to have been modeled on both the behavior of his father and the manners of the British aristocracy that he so admired. The Blairs have written about the young Kennedy: "Women were secondary and primarily sex objects. He relished the chase, the conquest, the testing of himself, the challenge of numbers and quality." The mature Kennedy was an even more relentless womanizer by the time he reached the presidency. Sex, to him, was the secret prerogative of power. But in the White House, Garry Wills points out, there were "political implications [in] large-scale satyriasis." One of the few similarities between John Kennedy and Martin Luther King, Jr., was that both men allowed their sexual appetites to make them vulnerable to the blackmail of FBI chief J. Edgar Hoover.[8]

If Kennedy's private stance was profane and libidinous, the public stance he favored, while far more lofty, was no less masculine in style. He was willing at times to invoke the legacy of Franklin Roosevelt for political purposes, but the New Deal reformer (and wartime foe of his father) never appealed to Kennedy. His preferred model was British: the heroic demeanor of Winston Churchill. Positioning himself for a presidential bid after 1956, Kennedy frequently drew parallels between Churchill's efforts in the 1930s to warn a complacent Britain of the Nazi menace and his own campaign to awaken an equally complacent America to the gravity of the Soviets' global challenge. At times, as in the conclusion to his well-publicized "missile gap" speech in the Senate in 1958, his identification with Churchill was complete:

> No Pearl Harbor, no Dunkirk, no Calais is sufficient to end us permanently if we but find the will and the way. In the words of Sir Winston Churchill, in a dark time of England's history: "Come then—let us to the task, to the battle and the toil—each to our part, each to our station. . . . There is not a week, nor a day, nor an hour to be lost."[9]

We can hear further self-conscious Churchillian echoes in Kennedy's presidency. We can also hear an unconscious echo of an American heroic precursor. Speaking the year after his triumph in Cuba, Theodore Roosevelt called Americans to a "strenuous life" of imperial dedication. Speaking in a darker mood, immediately following his administration's Bay of Pigs fiasco in Cuba, John Kennedy presented a cold war version of the "strenuous life":

> The message of Cuba, of Laos, of the rising din of Communist voices in Asia and Latin America—these messages are all the same. The complacent, the self-indulgent, the soft societies are about to be swept away with the debris of history. Only the strong, only the industrious, only the determined, only the courageous, only the visionary who determine the real nature of our struggle can possibly survive.[10]

The heroic atmosphere of a near-apocalyptic global struggle fused Kennedy's private and public fixations on masculinity. During his presidency, as we shall see, he continued to cultivate his heroic image, but he also aimed to give it historic substance. In deed as well as in rhetoric, his would be the leadership of the strong, the industrious, the determined, the courageous, the visionary. Theodore Roosevelt had presented himself as a heroic leader to a nation in the first flush of imperial enthusiasm. John Kennedy would present himself as a young, sexy, masterful, aggressive leader to a nation at its pinnacle of imperial danger and greatness.[11]

"The Vital Center"

At one of his final press conferences, John Kennedy explained to the assembled reporters and to the mass television audience why he was happy in the presidency. The office, he said, allowed him to live up to "the definition of happiness of the Greeks"—that is, "full use of your powers along lines of excellence." Kennedy's deft invocation of ancient Greece was characteristic of his effort to portray his administration as a rebirth of political life at its highest. Some of the most thoughtful political observers in America were impressed. Hannah Arendt, the political philosopher who had revived the Athenian polis as a shining model for modern democrats, thus commented after Kennedy's death that he had bestowed on the political realm in the United States "a kind of dignity and intellectual splendor . . . which it had never had before."[12]

Excellence, in the rhetoric and gestures of the Kennedy administration, was available to the public as well as the president. Public interest in the arts was encouraged, while the status of artists was boosted through presidential patronage. The flabbiness of the "affluent society" was challenged by a campaign for physical fitness; vigorous New Frontiersmen led the way with fifty-mile hikes. Most important, indifference toward political matters, especially among the much-lamented "silent generation" of the young, was countered with a ringing summons to public service.

The results of these gestures toward democratic excellence were hardly as dramatic as Kennedy chroniclers were later to claim. But if the gestures had a limited impact on the citizenry, they still enhanced the stature of the leaders who made them. That such gestures redounded to the credit of the president and his circle offers a clue to the conception of excellence that Kennedy actually held. In Kennedy's view, excellence could not be a phenomenon of the masses, for its defining quality was precisely its uncommonness. Like Alexander Hamilton, Kennedy believed in the aristocratic superiority of "a few choice spirits"—but he was too schooled in the rhetoric of democracy to express this belief so directly. His hope for national excellence did not presume an elevation of ordinary Americans so much as it counted on their guidance by a leadership of uncommon qualities. Garry Wills has observed that from the time of his senior thesis at Harvard on the sluggishness of British public opinion in the face of the Nazi threat, Kennedy "had not thought of power as the recruiting of people's opinion, but as the manipulation of their response by aristocrats who saw what the masses could not see. Relying on his own talent and will, the leader prods them, against their instincts, toward duty and empire."[13]

As Wills indicates, Kennedy had little interest in educating the American public. He had the talent for political education—as we shall see when we consider his superb speeches of June 1963 on foreign policy and civil rights—but rarely the inclination. Genuine political education requires leadership that takes ordinary people seriously, that cares about the state of their political awareness and aims to increase their opportunities for political participation. Kennedy was astute at gauging public sentiment and calculating electoral prospects. But he regarded the public more as spectators than as participants in the political drama of his presidency. He wanted the people's approval and backing, not their judgment or their action.

Kennedy has often been credited with inspiring the renewed excitement about political matters that assumed more unconventional and radical forms after his death. No doubt some young people were moved to political action by the memory they carried of Kennedy—although the revival of youthful political activism that became the hallmark of the 1960s owed more to the black students who sat in at segregated lunch counters as Kennedy was running for the presidency. Yet if Kennedy's lofty and vague discourse of participation seemed to presage the political movements of the 1960s, another discourse of his would be precisely what these movements would challenge. This was a technocratic discourse, a discourse of expertise.

As Kennedy entered the presidency, many social commentators were hailing the "end of ideology" and its replacement by a moderate, practical politics dominated by experts. Kennedy adopted their language of nonideological expertise, not only because it provided useful ammunition against critics to his right and left, but because it squared with his conception of the appropriate distance between leaders and followers. Questions of foreign policy, he told the American Foreign Service Association, "are so sophisticated and so technical that people who are not intimately involved ... reach judgments which are based upon emotion rather than knowledge of the real alternatives." Questions of economic policy, he told participants in a White House Conference on National Economic Issues, demanded a similar expertise: "Most of the problems ... that we now face are technical problems, are administrative problems. They are very sophisticated judgments which do not lend themselves to the great sort of 'passionate movements' which have stirred this country so often in the past." A "sophisticated" leader in the White House, with the finest technical expertise at his command, needed relief from popular pressures if he was to save the public from its own emotion and ignorance.[14]

The White House was the natural headquarters for both technical and political expertise. Intellectuals of the day were extolling not only the "end of ideology" and the wonders of technocratic managerialism but the virtues of the strong presidency as well. Writers on the presidency divorced Franklin Roosevelt from the heated ideological wars of the 1930s and transfigured him into an idealized model for an age of consensus and cold war. Their confidence in presidential power was untouched by doubt. In his popular work, *The American Presidency*, Clinton Rossiter warned that "any major reduction now in the powers of the presidency would leave us naked to our enemies." In an even more influential work, *Presidential Power*, which Kennedy read, Richard E. Neustadt assured Americans that "one can say of a President what Eisenhower's first secretary of defense once said of General Motors: What is good for the country is good for the President, and vice versa." Most academic advocates of the strong presidency were skeptical of the allegedly inept Eisenhower. Sharing their skepticism, Kennedy was eager to offer himself as precisely what the new cult of the presidency was prescribing for the nation.[15]

Decrying the passivity of the Eisenhower presidency, Kennedy launched his bid for the presidency in January 1960 by setting forth his own heroic conception of the office in a speech to the National Press Club. The model he implicitly invoked was the presidency of Franklin D. Roosevelt. But Kennedy made claims for presidential power that Roosevelt—who had had to battle charges of "dictatorship"—would never have articulated. The fate of the American people, he announced in this speech, hinged on whether the next president had a bold or a timid conception of his role. "The history of this nation—its brightest and its bleakest pages—has been written largely in terms of the different views our Presidents have had of the Presidency itself." American history centered on the presidency because the Constitution relied on presidential power. Kennedy's Constitution was Hamilton's version, not Madison's, less an arrangement of checks and balances than a platform for presidential energy: "We will need . . . [in the years ahead] what the Constitution envisioned: a Chief Executive who is the vital center of action in our whole scheme of government." For the president who understood his role as the "vital center," the assertion of power was not self-aggrandizement but duty: "He must above all be the Chief Executive in every sense of the word. He must be prepared to exercise the fullest powers of his office—all that are specified and some that are not."[16]

Kennedy's speech was replete with romantic imagery. With his awesome responsibility and burdens, the president was "alone, at the top." This image of isolation, of withdrawal from the ranks of other political leaders, was balanced by a contrary one of reimmersion in political warfare and the thrill of combat for the public good. "In the decade that lies ahead. . . ," Kennedy proclaimed, "the American Presidency will demand more than ringing manifestos issued from the rear of the battle. It will demand that the President place himself in the very thick of the fight, that he care passionately about the fate of the people he leads, that he be willing to serve them at the risk of incurring their momentary displeasure."[17]

The American people, Kennedy suggested, would back this heroic chief executive once they understood how faithfully he served their interests. All other elected officials had limited vantage points and represented special interests. "Only the President represents the national interest." Given his identification with the common good, the president was, properly, the dominant policymaker in both foreign and domestic affairs. "It is the President alone," Kennedy claimed, "who must make the major decisions of our foreign policy." Congress would play a larger role in domestic affairs, yet here, too, the president had the superior claim. The times, he averred, "demand a vigorous proponent of the national interest—not a passive broker for conflicting private interests."[18]

Two years of experience in the White House tempered this grandiose posture. During a nationally televised interview in December 1962, Kennedy admitted that "there are greater limitations upon our ability to bring about a favorable result than I had imagined them to be." In particular, he noted with rueful humor, "Congress looks more powerful sitting here than it did when I was there in Congress." In this qualified fashion, the ideas and images found in the "vital center" speech continued to shape Kennedy's self-conception as president. He was relatively successful in pulling off his initial claim to monopolize foreign policy. The dramatic symbol of this dominance became the Cuban missile crisis, in which the president and his handpicked advisers led the nation to the brink of nuclear war with the acquiescence of an impotent Congress and a hushed public. But Kennedy's heroic conception of the presidency broke down, as we shall see, in the central domestic battles of his administration.[19]

In setting forth his conception of the president as the "vital center" of the American political system, Kennedy had said nothing about the medium of presidential leadership. Admiring accounts of his career would compensate for this omission, making much of his pioneering role as the first television president. As Carl Brauer puts it, "It was under and because of Kennedy that television became an essential determinant—probably *the* essential determinant—of a president's ability to lead the nation." Kennedy's mastery of the possibilities in television was indeed impressive. Yet upon closer inspection, there were dimensions to his television accomplishments that were hardly unproblematic for a democratic polity.[20]

Presidential press conferences were, even more than prime-time speeches, the height of Kennedy's television art. As the first president to permit live television coverage of his news conferences, Kennedy used this forum to demonstrate to the press and public his mastery of facts, quick intelligence, and sense of humor. Elaborate preparatory briefings for each news conference allowed him to project an air of spontaneous mastery. Reporters were charmed by Kennedy's grace during the press conferences, even though they were being reduced to props in a televised spectacle beamed to a larger audience. They asked relatively few challenging questions and allowed Kennedy to evade queries he did not want to answer. The public, too, was charmed—but it was not always well informed. "Although given facts and statistics and judgments," Henry Fairlie has observed, "the reporters for three years barely extracted from the President one significant statement about the American involvement in South Vietnam."[21]

His press conferences reflected the combination of democratic closeness and aristocratic distance that was the underlying message in Kennedy's masterful use of television. On television, with its immediacy and its illusion of familiarity, Kennedy offered his mass audience a sense of engagement and involvement with his policy-making in the White House. Yet the medium was simultaneously distancing; Kennedy's followers participated with the passive gaze, not the political act. They watched a larger-than-life figure, who enacted qualities of decisiveness, intellect, and toughness in magnitudes far beyond what ordinary citizens could imagine themselves possessing. Kennedy appeared as confident and masterful before spectators whose very position as onlookers denied the possibility of confidence and mastery.

Television also provided Kennedy a new vehicle for politicizing the personal (or, at least, the image of the personal) and personalizing the political. The youthful, gallant president, his attractive, cultured wife, and their winning children became the closest equivalents Americans had ever found to the British royal family. The television Kennedy was a regal head of state—but also a professional, knowledgeable, dispassionate chief executive. He was the familiar celebrity—and also the expert decision maker who ran highly secret, mysterious forums where national-security policies were determined. The president and his aides seized upon television to win the hearts of the public, but they used it in ways that subtly buttressed Kennedy's aristocratic distance from his audience.

Dramatic action has always been central to political leadership, and the rise of the modern media has made it ever more powerful in its effects. But the dramas of leadership can vary greatly in their impact upon a democratic polity. Martin Luther King, Jr., and his Southern Christian Leadership Conference, for example, used collective drama to mobilize and educate masses of ordinary citizens and offered them the opportunity to participate in the struggle for their own freedom. John Kennedy's drama also spoke of collective action, but its core was the power and grace of the hero and the admiring acquiescence of his followers. His television presidency was less a model of democratic education than one of presidential self-aggrandizement. Americans may have been more fortunate than they have realized in the often-lamented fact that none of Kennedy's successors, save Ronald Reagan, has been able to match his performance on television.[22]

"The Hour of Maximum Danger"

"In the long history of the world," John Kennedy proclaimed in his inaugural address, "only a few generations have been granted the role of defending freedom in its hour of maximum danger. I do not shrink from this responsibility; I welcome it." With such words, he pledged to steer the nation through an international crisis far more grave than most of his audience, reassured by the words of the outgoing President Eisenhower, had imagined to exist. Kennedy's calls for a reinvigorated cold war struggle against the global forces of communism supplied his presidency with the purpose and passion it lacked toward most matters of domestic policy. The struggle would be perilous, Kennedy declared, yet America would thereby conclusively affirm its greatness: "While no nation has ever faced such a challenge, no nation has ever been so ready to seize the burden and the glory of freedom." To Kennedy, an intensified cold war demanded an inspired, heroic effort. If the American people, lulled into complacency by Eisenhower, did not yet fully appreciate this fact, he was ready, as the nation's leader, to take on himself "the burden and the glory."[23]

As a presidential candidate, Kennedy had promised to replace Eisenhower's "soft sentimentalism" toward foreign policy with his own "tough-minded plans and operations." Broadcasting his superiority to his predecessor in both brains and guts, Kennedy entered office with a far-reaching strategy for the conduct of American foreign policy. At the heart of this strategy was a conception of a world haunted by ceaseless conflict. In the eyes of Kennedy and his chief foreign policy advisers, the relentless advance of the Soviet Union and the communist camp after the launching of the *Sputnik* satellite in 1957 had turned every corner of the globe into an East-West battlefield. Communist tactics in this ominous new phase of the cold war were dual: nuclear blackmail by the Soviets and subversive, guerrilla warfare by its allies and agents at the most vulnerable margins of the free world. Both tactics were designed to accomplish the same objective: a shift in the global balance of power, an erosion of Western security, and, ultimately, the international reign of Marxism-Leninism. The Kennedy administration devised responses for both aspects of the communist challenge. Soviet nuclear blackmail was to be frustrated by a massive buildup of American strategic forces and by displays of American resolve in superpower confrontations. Communist "nibbling" in the Third World was to be countered by projects in nation building and modernization, which would overcome the poverty and instability upon which communist agitation fed; and to protect the process of modernization from those who would seek to subvert it, a new military approach would be developed: counterinsurgency.[24]

Kennedy's global strategy had sweep and boldness. But these were more deficiencies than virtues, signs of arrogance rather than prudence. His foreign policy repeatedly inflated the import of events, transforming localized affairs into critical battles in a global struggle. Conflicts in Berlin, Cuba, and Vietnam were taken as challenges to American nerve, determination, courage. Each brought about a crisis of will, a decisive moment when the United States either proved its mettle or else watched freedom inexorably begin to vanish. Crisis, for Kennedy, was the hallmark of his time—and the field for his heroic leadership. It was not altogether an accident that the most frightening crises of the cold war occurred during his presidency.

Kennedy predicted these crises at the outset of his presidency. The language of his first State of the Union address bordered on the apocalyptic:

> No man entering upon this office . . . could fail to be staggered upon learning . . . the harsh enormity of the trials through which we must pass in the next four years. Each day the crises multiply. Each day their solution grows more difficult. Each day we draw nearer the hour of maximum danger, as weapons spread and hostile forces grow stronger.

This rhetoric, repeated often during Kennedy's first months in office, reached a crescendo after the Bay of Pigs disaster. Kennedy seemed to know what lay ahead for his leadership: "There can be no doubt . . . that this determined and powerful system [that is, communism] will subject us to many tests of nerve and will in the coming years—in Berlin, in Asia, in the Middle East, in this hemisphere. We will face challenge after challenge."[25]

There was, of course, political calculation behind this rhetoric. Talking much tougher than Eisenhower, Kennedy shielded himself from anticommunist zealots on the right. His summons to cold war heroics rallied a citizenry that had given him one of the slimmest victories in the history of presidential elections. But the rhetoric came too often and was too intense, too close to what Kennedy and his advisers were saying in private, to be written off as posturing for public consumption. Kennedy basically believed his own pronouncements. He dismissed signals during this period from the Soviet leader, Nikita Khrushchev, that looked to a possible détente between the superpowers. Instead, he focused on a Khrushchev speech of January 1961, praising "wars of national liberation" in the Third World (and aimed, apparently, at placating hardliners in the Kremlin and China rather than at challenging the United States), as the true indicator of the communists' intent. Seizing upon the speech as a vindication of his foreign policy strategy, Kennedy matched his rhetorical buildup with a military one. Despite knowledge that his campaign charge of a "missile gap" in favor of the Soviets was erroneous, and that the United States already enjoyed a substantial margin of strategic superiority over the Russians, he urged Congress to launch the most rapid increase in peacetime military spending in American history.[26]

Rankled by the militant rhetoric, the military buildup, the American-sponsored invasion of Cuba, the volatile Khrushchev in turn began to adopt a bellicose tone and, at a summit meeting with Kennedy in Vienna, set the stage for a Soviet-American confrontation over the unsettled status of Berlin and the two Germanys. Faced with a prior Khrushchev ultimatum over Berlin in 1958, Eisenhower had rejected Soviet threats but had defused the situation with a low-key approach and willingness to negotiate. Kennedy, as Michael Beschloss has written, "lacked the Eisenhowerian instinct to muffle foreign policy crises." He, too, was willing to negotiate over the German question—but only after he had made a public show of American determination and toughness. In a dramatic televised speech on July 25, 1961, he depicted West Berlin as "the great testing place of Western courage and will." Even though the military balance around the city was unfavorable, he did not shrink from such a test: "Any dangerous spot is tenable if men—brave men—will make it so." After the communists built the Berlin Wall, Khrushchev backed away from confrontation and settled for inconclusive negotiations. But the Berlin conflict of 1961 sped up the arms race and intensified the mood of crisis that now infected both superpowers. It was a prelude to the most dangerous crisis in the entire history of the cold war.[27]

The Cuban missile crisis of 1962 has, ever since, been narrated, analyzed, picked over in seemingly endless detail. Yet fresh revelations have continued to alter, and sometimes subvert, the version of the story that most Americans initially learned. In the last decade the publication of previously classified documents and a series of conferences bringing together American, Soviet, and Cuban participants have produced a new version of the crisis that centers on the dangerous misperceptions and miscalculations on both sides. Soviet participants now concede that Khrushchev's dispatch of medium-range missiles to Cuba—a clandestine move that was insensitive to the status of Cuba as a political sore point for President Kennedy—was reckless. At least some of the American participants (and most American scholars) now admit that the Soviet leader's gambit was defensive rather than aggressive, a response to the Kennedy administration's prior actions in threatening Castro's Cuba and in embarrassing Khrushchev with public statements of American nuclear superiority.[28]

The most direct evidence to date of Kennedy's mind-set and conduct during the crisis comes from transcribed recordings of the president's Executive Committee (ExComm) meetings. We have recordings for only the first and last full days of the missile crisis (October 16 and October 27), thus leaving us with an incomplete picture. Nevertheless, the comparison of Kennedy at the beginning of the crisis and at its end produces a surprise twist—a climax that had been concealed by the original accounts of a triumphant American hero. It shows us the bold risk taker of the outset of the crisis turning into a frightened, cautious, and ultimately more admirable figure at its end.

During the first day's meetings of ExComm (October 16), Kennedy rejected a private, diplomatic response to the Soviet missiles in Cuba and pondered a series of military options. Three options were presented to him: a limited air strike against the missile sites, a general air strike against all Soviet/Cuban air defenses, and an invasion of the island. In response, he told ExComm: "I don't think we got much time on these missiles. . . . [W]e can't wait two weeks while we're getting ready to roll. . . . We're certainly going to do number one; we're going to take out these missiles." His special assistant for national security, McGeorge Bundy, immediately cautioned him: "You want to be clear, Mr. President, whether we have *definitely* decided *against* a political track." Kennedy had so decided. While alert to "the dangers of the world-wide effects" if he chose a general air strike, his focus was almost entirely on military measures. Kennedy set an agenda for the ExComm in which the central question would not be whether to take military action but rather what kind of military action to take.[29]

An unwittingly humorous moment in the first day's deliberations indicated how blinkered was Kennedy's initial perception of the crisis. Speculating on Khrushchev's motives for installing missiles in Cuba, he said: "It's just as if we suddenly began to put a major number of MRBMs [Medium-Range Ballistic Missiles] in Turkey. Now that'd be goddam dangerous, I would think." Bundy interjected: "Well, we *did*, Mr. President," to which Kennedy lamely replied: "Yeah, but that was five years ago." The heroic leader could not acknowledge that both sides might have similar motives or take similar actions; he had too large a personal stake in viewing the crisis as a struggle between good and evil. Acknowledging the symmetry between United States missiles in Turkey and Soviet missiles in Cuba might have provoked some deeper self-questioning and, in turn, led him to confront the role of his own prior cold war actions in Khrushchev's reckless gamble.[30]

Many of the participants in the October 16 meetings assumed roles in keeping with their institutional positions and perspectives. Secretary of State Dean Rusk worried about the diplomatic costs to NATO and the Organization of American States if the United States initiated military action without consulting them. Secretary of Defense Robert McNamara voiced his frank judgment that the missiles in Cuba did not materially diminish American strategic superiority: "I don't think there *is* a military problem here. . . . [T]his is a domestic, political problem." President Kennedy's unique contribution to the dialogue was the perspective of heroic leadership. Puzzled that the Soviets were departing from their normal caution with such an adventurous stroke, he still had no doubt that this was a historic moment in which the nation and its leadership must prove their determination and courage. "I don't think," he told ExComm, "there's any record of the Soviets ever making this direct a challenge . . . since the Berlin Blockade."[31]

After several more days of deliberation, Kennedy and the ExComm agreed on a public confrontation to force the removal of the missiles from Cuba. While some ExComm members held to the hawkish sentiments of the first day's meetings and continued to favor an air strike, the president and the advisers closest to him personally sought a more prudent course, fixing on a naval blockade of Cuba as their first step. The naval "quarantine" was a more restrained response, but nonetheless a military one—and it set up the potential for violent confrontation at sea. Soviet sources have suggested that an angry Khrushchev came close to forcing that confrontation before he cooled down and began to contemplate the nightmare of a nuclear exchange. The tension of the blockade and the unresolved problem of Soviet missiles already in Cuba also began to tell on Kennedy, as the missile crisis moved, with seeming inexorability, toward some sort of climax. When he met with ExComm on October 27, his role in the deliberations was quite different from what it had been on October 16. Having provoked Khrushchev with his threats against Cuba and his brandishing of America's huge nuclear lead, having eschewed diplomacy for a public confrontation, Kennedy, Thomas Paterson notes, "in the end . . . frightened himself." It proved to be a fortunate fear.[32]

When ExComm convened on October 27, it puzzled over how to respond to two consecutive letters from Khrushchev, the first offering to remove the missiles in Cuba in exchange for an American pledge not to invade the island, the second upping the ante by insisting on a trade of Turkish for Cuban missiles. The first Soviet proposal was deemed acceptable, but almost all the members of ExComm strongly opposed the idea of a missile trade, assuming that it would be interpreted as a sign of weakness, especially by America's NATO allies.

President Kennedy, however, repeatedly steered the conversation to the option of a trade. Facing the responsibility for millions of deaths if the crisis got out of hand and led to the use of nuclear weapons, he now seemed desperate to avoid taking military action. In a moment like the Cuban missile crisis, Joseph Nye points out, fear "can lead to a heightened sense of prudence." So it was with Kennedy, who urged ExComm to consider Khrushchev's proposed swap from the standpoint of world opinion. "We're going to be in an insupportable position on this matter if this becomes his proposal. In the first place, we last year tried to get the missiles out of [Turkey] because they're not militarily useful. . . . Number 2 . . . , to any man at the United Nations or any other rational man it will look like a very fair trade."[33]

McGeorge Bundy spoke for the majority of ExComm in predicting that a trade of missiles would undermine the credibility of the United States: "If we sound as if we wanted to make this trade, to our NATO people and to all the people who are tied to us by alliance, we are in *real* trouble." But Kennedy looked further down the barrel of the crisis and glimpsed a frightening prospect that America's allies did not yet comprehend:

> You see, they haven't had the alternatives presented to them. They'll say, "Well God, we don't want to trade [the Turkish missiles] off." They don't realize that in two or three days we may have a military strike [against Cuba] which could bring perhaps the seizure of Berlin or a strike on Turkey, and then they'll say "By God we should have taken it."

More than anyone else in the room, Kennedy was, at this moment, attuned to the pitfalls in the cold war obsession with credibility. During a nuclear crisis, he realized, a pacific stance that risked the appearance of accommodation was wiser than a hard-line stance that brought a substantial risk of disaster.[34]

In the nerve-racking atmosphere of October 27, a number of Ex-Comm members persisted in talking tough, and the Joint Chiefs of Staff pressed for a massive air strike against Cuba within forty-eight hours, to be followed by an invasion of the island a few days later. On the first day of the crisis Kennedy had adopted a hawkish tone with hardly a second thought; now he quailed at the consequences of starting the shooting. "I think we're better off," he said, "to get those missiles out of Turkey and out of Cuba, because I think the [military] way of getting them out of Turkey and out of Cuba is going to be very grave . . . and very bloody, one place or another." The most recent information to come to light suggests that Kennedy's fear that an American strike against Cuba would unleash an uncontrollable escalation on both sides was realistic. At a Havana conference in January 1992, Russian participants informed their American counterparts that Soviet commanders in Cuba had had tactical nuclear weapons at their disposal and were authorized to fire them against an American invasion force. Horrified by the revelation, Robert McNamara commented: "It meant that had a U.S. invasion been carried out, if the missiles had not been pulled out, there was a 99 percent probability that nuclear war would have been initiated."[35]

Kennedy was finally persuaded by ExComm to delay raising the prospect of the Turkish trade and to pressure the Soviets to accept a deal based on the no-invasion pledge instead. Coupled with secret assurances to the Soviets that the missiles in Turkey would be removed in a matter of months, this bargain was accepted by a frightened Khrushchev. Because Kennedy did not have to offer a public trade and settled the crisis on terms that looked more favorable to the United States, his willingness to consider the missile swap was concealed in the most influential early accounts of the crisis. Theodore Sorensen, a member of ExComm, gave no indication that Kennedy had spoken favorably of the missile trade during the deliberations of October 27; Arthur Schlesinger, Jr., who had not been at the meetings, wrote: "Kennedy regarded the idea as unacceptable, and the swap was promptly rejected." Concealing the president's interest in a trade, they preserved the picture of a strong and masterful leader at the climax of the missile crisis. They also provided fuel for a later generation of "revisionist" commentators who, misled by the original accounts, castigated Kennedy for risking nuclear war over obsolete missiles in Turkey. In actuality, Kennedy had been neither the dauntless hero nor the reckless cold warrior as the crisis climaxed; he had been more frightened than his admirers admitted, more responsible than his detractors knew. For the moment the specter of nuclear war had shown him the shallowness of heroic leadership. (The transformation in Kennedy was, however, far from complete. Subsequent to the missile crisis, with public applause building for his triumph over Khrushchev, the president boasted to friends: "I cut his balls off.")[36]

Sobered by the missile crisis, both Kennedy and Khrushchev moved toward a relaxation of tension between the superpowers. To pave the way for a limited nuclear test ban, Kennedy delivered a magnificent speech at American University on June 10, 1963. With language that was as novel for him as for his audience, he asked the public to reexamine cold war clichés about the Soviet Union. He warned Americans "not to see only a distorted and desperate view of the other side." And he pointed out that both sides "have a mutually deep interest in a just and genuine peace and in halting the arms race." There is support, therefore, for the claim of Kennedy's admirers that he grew as a statesman during his final year—but it must be set alongside other evidence that he still remained wedded to cold war orthodoxy and posturing. If the Kennedy administration was shifting toward a policy of détente with the Soviet Union, it did not slow its strategic buildup or its counterinsurgency campaigns in the Third World. And the president was still addicted to heroic images. His rhetoric at the end echoed his rhetoric at the beginning: "We in this country, in this generation, are, by destiny rather than choice, the watchmen on the walls of world freedom."[37]

"Defending freedom in its hour of maximum danger" was a global enterprise, demanding intensified efforts in the Third World as well as public showdowns with the Soviet Union. Superpower confrontations were occasions for public displays of nerve and will; the grim, protracted struggle in the Third World called for the private heroics of the covert warrior. Kennedy and his advisers prided themselves on their tough-minded readiness to engage in clandestine activities that the squeamish public would never approve. Their most fervent secret war, code-named Operation MONGOOSE, was aimed at Cuba's Fidel Castro. One of the largest CIA projects of the cold war, MONGOOSE sought to harass the Castro regime by burning sugar cane fields, blowing up factories, and sabotaging imported equipment meant for Cuba's economic development. President Kennedy was vexed by the halting progress of this secret war, complaining to its planners, through his brother Robert, that "more priority should be given to trying to mount sabotage operations."[38]

The covert warrior was also the counterinsurgent. Convinced that Khrushchev and his allies aimed to pick off the most exposed areas in the Third World through "wars of national liberation," Kennedy established counterinsurgency as the military speciality of his administration. The president made the development of an antiguerrilla force a personal project, studying guerrilla warfare in the texts of Mao and Che Guevara, rapidly expanding the Army Special Forces, and bestowing on them the elite green beret over the Pentagon's objections. Counterinsurgency became a fad on Kennedy's New Frontier because it reflected Kennedy's heroic self-image of intelligence, élan, and, above all, toughness. The fruit of this fascination with counterinsurgency was a deepening American involvement in Vietnam.[39]

Like Theodore Roosevelt, John Kennedy justified American global expansion as an exercise in American beneficence. The covert warrior and counterinsurgent was also the modernizer, nation builder, democratic reformer. The idealistic side of Kennedy's approach to the

Third World was manifested in the Peace Corps, the gracious welcoming of the new nations of Africa, and, above all, the Alliance for Progress in Latin America. It was to the conservative elites of Latin America that Kennedy uttered his often-quoted admonition: "Those who make peaceful revolution impossible will make violent revolution inevitable." Yet his "peaceful revolution" through the Alliance for Progress was a failure by every political and statistical measure. Moreover, the forces that rendered it "impossible" were located in Washington as well as in Latin America. The Kennedy administration was too preoccupied with communism and too sensitive to the interests of American-based multinational corporations to promote fundamental social change in Latin America. The kind of contradictions that undermined Kennedy's Alliance for Progress—and his approach to the Third World in general—are evident in tragicomic miniature in the case of Honduras.[40]

Fancying himself one of the Latin American reformers that Kennedy was summoning, Ramón Villeda Morales, the president of Honduras, ardently embraced the Alliance for Progress. In keeping with Kennedy's rhetoric, Villeda Morales pushed a bill through the Honduran legislature that was primarily modeled on Venezuela's agrarian reform law. But whereas oil-rich Venezuela had the foreign currency to compensate American corporations for any land it expropriated, impoverished Honduras could offer only its own long-term bonds. Complaining that the law was cumbersome as well as financially inadequate, the largest American corporation operating in Honduras, the notorious United Fruit Company, ordered a halt to its banana planting and voiced its unhappiness over Villeda Morales's misguided enthusiasm to the Kennedy administration.

The problem was solved when Villeda Morales and his entourage visited Washington in November 1962. President Kennedy had been briefed by his aides to inform the Honduran president that his agrarian law "will require modification if its benefits are not to be offset by discouragement to badly needed private investment." Villeda Morales did not put up an argument, for his principal concern in his White House visit was personal. Prior to the trip, his wife had become obsessed by whether she would be welcomed at the White House by the now-legendary Jacqueline Kennedy. When Jackie greeted her with a bouquet of red roses and took her upstairs for a private chat, the success of the visit was assured. Villeda Morales was so happy for his wife and so star-struck by the Kennedys that he forgot what he and his aides had planned to ask for Honduras. Returning to Honduras after a stopover in Miami, where he visited United Fruit's corporate headquarters, Villeda Morales swiftly altered the agrarian reform law.

His modification made it, in the words of American Ambassador Charles Burrows, "livable for private interests."[41]

Disappointed hopes for social change in the Third World can be added to public demonstrations of will and covert wars as the marks of Kennedy's leadership in foreign policy. To his credit, Kennedy eschewed his heroic pose at the climax of the Cuban missile crisis and followed up with the beginnings of a détente with the Soviets. Yet his approach to foreign policy had exaggerated the perils that the United States faced, provoked the crises that he came into office prophesying, and overextended American power on behalf of an inflated sense of American virtue. Determined to carry out "tough-minded plans and operations," he limited himself far too often to a simplistic and dangerous conception of statesmanship.

The Hero and the Corporations

The stress on dynamism and expansion that characterized Kennedy's foreign policy was equally evident in his management of the American economy. He was a modern Hamiltonian in his belief that rapid economic growth necessitated an alliance between the state and private capital. Like Hamilton, Kennedy equated the public good with accelerated economic growth—and rooted both in the ability of political leaders to shape the investment decisions of capitalists. Unlike Hamilton, however, Kennedy found that a modern corporate capitalist economy left less room to maneuver businessmen than he had originally believed. In his relationship with the corporate sector, the heroic leader would prove to be less the master than the supplicant.

Kennedy was hardly unique among modern American political leaders in having to woo the heads of the nation's largest corporations. Both neo-Marxist and non-Marxist writers have pointed out that owners of private capital occupy a special position in the modern political economy because of the primacy of investment in determining the rate of economic development. State managers, responsible to the electorate for economic performance, cannot command a high rate of investment from private owners and must seek to coax it from them instead. Consequently, under most circumstances state managers will pursue policies that make private investment more attractive, while studiously avoiding measures that might arouse corporate ire and undermine "business confidence." We will see this logic at work in the Kennedy presidency, which offers a textbook illustration of the structural constraints felt by modern American leaders in the era of mature corporate capitalism.[42]

From the outset of Kennedy's administration, economic growth was the top domestic priority. The president and his economic advisers believed a more rapid rate of growth was essential for reducing the disturbingly high level of unemployment and for utilizing the slack potential of American industry. Economic growth was also a cold war issue: in the face of Khrushchev's boasts about superior Soviet performance, Kennedy was eager to bolster the international prestige of American free enterprise. Above all, accelerated growth was the linchpin of his domestic political strategy, which aimed to replace the class-based conflicts of the New Deal era with a politics of consensus through abundance. Ronald King explicates this strategy well:

> Kennedy was a president who spoke the end-of-ideology language .... A technically administered economic expansion would help suppress potentially divisive group and class cleavages, substituting prosperity for particularism and abundance for allocation. No fundamental change was required in either structures or processes. Neither power nor income would be redistributed. The goal was reinvigoration, not reform.[43]

To achieve accelerated growth, the corporate sector would have to increase its level of investment. Kennedy sought to promote this increase by directing both friendly words and favorable policies toward big business. At his first appearance before a major business group, the National Industrial Conference Board, he told the assembled corporate executives: "Our revenues and thus our success are dependent upon your profits and your success. . . . Whatever past differences may have existed, we seek more than an attitude of truce, more than a treaty—we seek the spirit of a full-fledged alliance." The centerpiece of Kennedy's 1961 tax bill, a tax credit for new investment in plant and equipment, was the administration's first token of this promise to pursue an investment-oriented (or, in a term widely used later, supply-side) approach.[44]

But the business community was suspicious of Kennedy and was even more mistrustful of his academic appointments to the Council of Economic Advisers. In an age of technocratic policy-making, businessmen feared that academic experts would critically influence a president unschooled in sophisticated economics. Hence, the administration's investment tax credit was derided by business publications as gimmicky and inadequate. Minor incidents—such as the insistence of Secretary of Commerce Luther Hodges that secret meetings between government officials and the elite Business Advisory Council be opened to reporters—were interpreted by corporate executives as signs of the administration's underlying animus toward business. Businessmen were even unhappy because they were not invited to the White House as frequently as they had been when Eisenhower was president.[45]

Persistent tension between business and the Kennedy administration boiled over in the spring and summer of 1962. The key incident was the famous "steel crisis"—in legend, the domestic counterpart to the Cuban missile crisis. As part of his administration's campaign to forestall inflation once economic growth began to accelerate, Kennedy had prevailed upon the steelworkers' union to accept a modest contract, with the tacit agreement of the steel corporations that they would thereby forgo a price increase. When Roger Blough, chairman of United States Steel, came to the White House on April 10, 1962, to inform the president that his company was raising prices by six dollars a ton, Kennedy felt duped. Seething, he mobilized all the resources of his administration to force a recision of the price rise. For the moment, he abandoned his usual talk of alliances for the brand of combative rhetoric that had been adopted by Theodore Roosevelt in 1907–8 and by Franklin Roosevelt in 1935–36: "The American people will find it hard, as I do, to accept a situation in which a tiny handful of steel executives whose pursuit of private power and profit exceeds their sense of public responsibility can show such utter contempt for the interests of 185 million Americans."[46]

When pressure from the administration forced the steel giants to back down, many businessmen were convinced that the mask of friendship had been dropped to expose Kennedy's true, antibusiness face. The unhappiness of the business community over the steel affair was exacerbated a month and a half later by a huge drop in the stock market, attributed by neutral observers to overvalued stocks but ascribed by Wall Street to a lack of business confidence in the administration. Bitterness toward Kennedy mounted among businessmen, and there was reluctance to risk new investment in an unfavorable political climate. Economists began to warn of an impending recession.

Kennedy chafed at the irrational business mood. His administration's policies had clearly been in the spirit of the alliance he had proposed: the investment tax credit promised corporations substantial tax savings for their new investments; the Treasury Department was preparing a new and more liberal depreciation schedule. Together, these measures offered business an 11 percent tax cut for 1962. No matter what Kennedy offered, though, businessmen continued to insist that he was their adversary. Venting his frustration, the president told journalist Hugh Sidey: "'I think maybe I ought to get a little tougher with business. . . . When I'm nice to them, they just kick me.'" In his calmer moments, however, the heroic leader knew he could not afford to be tough with the men who would make the investment decisions that would determine the rate of economic growth. So in the face of business hostility, with a recession possibly in the cards, the Kennedy administration redoubled its efforts to win over the corporate sector.[47]

At the president's request, Theodore Sorensen prepared a strategy paper, "The Kennedy Administration and Business." Sorensen observed that "most big businessmen are, by conviction, habit, and association Republicans or [conservative] Democrats inherently opposed to this Administration and its policies." It would be foolish, he pointed out, for the administration to jeopardize its support from the majority of the electorate by "policies designed to appease those who will never support us." But Sorensen was not calling for a resumption of New Deal–era conflict between a Democratic administration and the business elite. On the contrary, his strategy paper advocated a fourteen-point "psychological" campaign that sought to "soften the business hostility which reached an emotional peak during the steel price–stock market sequence of events." One of his proposals was for better public relations for the administration's investment-oriented policies; thus, he suggested a "major press build-up" for the impending announcement of the new depreciation guidelines. Other measures sought to create a warmer atmosphere for businessmen who felt excluded from the White House; in this vein, Sorensen proposed "a series of presidential luncheons or black-tie stag dinners for business leaders."

Above all, the administration was desirous of avoiding any further offenses to the business community. In his strategy paper, Sorensen asked:

> Can the President, or the Attorney General, or the Special Counsel, meet quietly and individually with the heads of the regulatory agencies, the anti-trust division, the wage-hour, Food-and-Drug, and other enforcement activities—to emphasize that there are times to steam ahead, to pursue, to be zealous, and there are times to be cooperative and understanding (and the latter is more appropriate now). [Also], to explore what they can do or refrain from doing. Can the SEC tone down its investigation? . . . Are there broad new areas of investigation planned that can be postponed?[48]

In accordance with this strategy, the business community became the recipient of both tangible benefits and symbolic gestures, of tax cuts and private ownership of the new communications satellite system, of White House dinners and New Frontiersmen flocking to business meetings. Eventually, all this solicitude did mitigate business hostility to the Kennedy administration. But corporate complaints did not die away completely, because businessmen were starting to perceive that their complaining gave them the upper hand. As Bernard Nossiter commented, businessmen "had learned that the President tried to relieve rather than resist pressure; the less support they admitted they were getting, the more he was likely to give."[49]

The administration's defensiveness in the face of business pressure did not pass unnoticed by organized labor. A member of the staff of the Council of Economic Advisers informed Walter Heller, chairman of the council, about organized labor's reactions in the fall of 1962 to the talk of a forthcoming Kennedy tax bill: "They think they will wind up next year, like this year, with the dirty end of the stick—big cuts for the fat cats, some crumbs for the little folk, and no reform. They wonder if they wouldn't do better if this so-called 'anti-business' Administration reversed itself and became violently 'anti-labor.'" But the Kennedy administration was able to keep the unions in line, despite their periodic rumblings. Presidential gestures of friendliness kept labor leaders happy, while warnings that if labor fought publicly with the administration it would get nothing from Congress served to keep the unions tamely behind Kennedy.[50]

Although Kennedy's economic policies directed more benefits and more ingratiating gestures toward the corporate sector than toward any other private interest, the president and his aides continued to cherish their self-image as impartial public servants. They knew that they were not tools of big business; they believed that they were doing what had to be done to achieve accelerated economic growth in the national interest. Only in facetious moments could they acknowledge how much they had yielded to corporate pressures. Thus, Walter Heller, the epitome of the neutral technocrat in the Kennedy administration, sent the president an article of his that was to be published in the liberal *New Republic* accompanied by a quip: "While making love to business, we must not neglect 'our opening to the left.'"[51]

It was largely due to Heller's educative efforts that Kennedy decided on a major tax cut for individuals as well as businesses in 1963—the proposal that made his reputation as a Keynesian innovator and overshadowed his struggling alliance with business in most subsequent accounts of his presidential economics. In proposing to stimulate the economy through deliberately planned deficits, Kennedy was charting new terrain in fiscal policy. In grounding his tax program in the sophisticated theorizing of the neo-Keynesians, he was shifting economic discourse in the United States in a more intelligent direction. Yet for all the talk of a "Keynesian revolution," what was at stake was essentially an advance in technique, whose impact on existing structures of wealth and power would hardly be radical. In fact, the 1963 tax cut was Kennedy's most successful ploy in finally securing the alliance with business that he had been advocating from the start.

Even though Heller had sold Kennedy on the desirability of a major tax cut during the summer of 1962, the president hesitated about proposing one until the business community gave its approval. Only after the favorable reception of his speech on taxation before the Economic Club of New York in December 1962—lamented by John Kenneth Galbraith as "'the most Republican speech since McKinley'"—was Kennedy willing to go forward as a tax cutter. Many businessmen rallied behind the 1963 tax bill, with lobbying efforts spearheaded by an administration-sponsored Business Committee for Tax Reduction, a prestigious collection of corporate notables cochaired by Henry Ford II. Their enthusiasm is understandable when the distribution of tax benefits in the bill is broken down by income categories: the wealthiest 2.4 percent of taxpayers received $2.3 billion in tax cuts, while the 39.6 percent of taxpayers at the bottom of the income ladder received only $1.5 billion. Since Kennedy's version of Keynesian fiscal policy proved so attractive for business's bottom line, the tax cut finally softened corporate hearts. As Allen Matusow remarks: "A late-blooming love affair between Wall Street and the White House was entering its first stage."[52]

Images of youth, of vigor, of idealism had diverted most businessmen from Kennedy's neo-Hamiltonian desire for a partnership between the two most powerful players in the American political economy. As Douglas Dillon, his secretary of the treasury, observed: "I don't think that there had been a President in a long time who had basically done as much for business . . . [but] it took the business community a long time to recognize this." Business was finally won over when the rewards of Kennedy's version of economic growth became unmistakable. Others, too, benefited from the accelerated growth that his economic policies generated. But the rewards were skewed in the direction of those who were already advantaged; corporate profits, for example, rose three times as fast as average weekly take-home pay. Kennedy had promised a democratic politics of abundance. To achieve that abundance, he furthered the concentration of wealth and power that remains one of the principal threats to democracy in America.[53]

The Hero and the Democratic Movement

A stirring civil rights speech and a far-reaching civil rights bill in 1963 were John Kennedy's greatest contributions to the furtherance of American democratic values. As his admirers have told the story, Kennedy was slowed for a time by political constraints but acted boldly at the pivotal moment and wound up as a hero of civil rights. "Operating within the bounds of a democratic political system," Carl Brauer writes, "Kennedy both encouraged and responded to black aspirations and led the nation into its Second Reconstruction." The legend of Kennedy as civil rights hero was touching—and true in parts—but it left out all of the ironies. The civil rights movement had been Kennedy's rival as well as his ally, presenting him with political dilemmas and moral choices that he sought, until 1963, to finesse or evade. The civil rights issue had been an intrusion rather than a priority for Kennedy—for there was nothing else in domestic politics to which his political style was so ill suited or which gave him such consistent headaches.[54]

For a shrewd politician like Kennedy, civil rights was a minefield. He had won the presidency by carefully balancing appeals to the white South and to blacks. Once elected, however, the power of the South loomed larger in his political calculations. Due to the seniority system, white Southerners held a disproportionate share of congressional committee chairs. On many issues, they held the balance of power in voting as well. Kennedy also had to be concerned about the Democratic party's traditional Southern base when he ran for reelection. That a strong party commitment to black rights might permanently alienate the white South—the historical shift that has eviscerated the Democratic party in presidential elections since 1964—was a likelihood upon which Kennedy always reckoned. Visiting with the president in 1962, James MacGregor Burns found him haunted by "this Southern problem." It was not the moral problem of the South that troubled him so much as the political problem. Kennedy was a politician attuned to his own power stakes—and the South meted out power to presidents largely on the basis of how quiet they kept the issue of race.[55]

Had Kennedy been a political leader deeply committed to the cause of racial justice, the political dilemma that he faced would have been enormously poignant. But civil rights was not a subject that aroused his passion. While believing that racial discrimination was wrong and should be eradicated from American life, he viewed the issue with detachment. Kennedy did not feel the emotional pull of the civil rights crusade, did not share its adherents' sense of urgency. He could admire the rhetorical force in the orations of Martin Luther King, Jr., but not the ethical intensity that carried over into King's private discourse. As Harris Wofford, his aide for civil rights in 1961–62, later recounted: "There was always a strain in his dealing with King, who came on with a moral tone that was not Kennedy's style and made him uncomfortable."[56]

It was not only the moral fervor of the civil rights movement that made Kennedy uneasy. If the white South threatened him with the loss of votes, the civil rights movement threatened him with the loss of control. Kennedy expected to be "the vital center of action" in the White House, the leader who would set the domestic political agenda. The civil rights movement refused him this role. Through the collective dramas of sit-ins, freedom rides, and mass marches, participants in the movement forced the pace of change faster than Kennedy had calculated. With their courage and willingness to suffer, they seized the initiative on the racial question, they defined it. Introducing into the political arena new actors who refused to play by Washington's rules of adjustment and compromise, and who spoke in the urgent language of "freedom now," the movement brought a democratic challenge to the heroic leader from below.

At the outset of his administration, Kennedy assumed a low profile on civil rights. Responsibilities in the civil rights field were delegated to White House aides and to the Justice Department, with the president's personal involvement kept to a minimum. Legislation was deferred in favor of quieter efforts in litigation and executive action. Public statements on the issue were infrequent and cautious; every presidential comment on civil rights was weighed for its probable reception in the South. Kennedy wanted gradual progress to end racial discrimination—and please blacks—without controversy that would agitate white Southerners. Too remote from the issue to have much inkling of either black or white passions, he thought he could keep both camps satisfied.[57]

The flaw in Kennedy's strategy first became apparent with the freedom rides in May 1961. Sending interracial groups of riders to challenge segregation in bus terminals, the Congress of Racial Equality (and later the Student Non-violent Coordinating Committee) uncovered the brutality of Southern racism. When the freedom riders were savagely beaten in Anniston, Birmingham, and Montgomery, Alabama, the Kennedy administration responded by sending federal marshals to protect them. The president properly fulfilled his responsibility to safeguard citizens exercising their constitutional rights. But in private he was irate at the freedom riders for embarrassing him as he prepared for a summit meeting with Khrushchev in Vienna. "Tell them to call it off," he ordered Harris Wofford. "Stop them!"[58]

At this juncture, Kennedy was not about to address the moral issues raised by the freedom riders affair. His only public statement during the height of the mob violence was a terse six sentences, asking Alabama residents to refrain from provocative acts and local officials to perform their legal duties. Kennedy's words disappointed civil rights supporters, who saw the racist violence as the occasion for a president to point out to a shocked nation the evils of segregation. A racially mixed delegation respectfully urged the president to release a statement that would go beyond the cautious talk of law and order, with Eugene Rostow (brother of Kennedy aide Walt Rostow) arguing the case most forcefully. Kennedy fended off the civil rights supporters and, after they had left his office, complained to Wofford about Rostow: "What in the world does he think I should do? Doesn't he know I've done more for civil rights than any President in American history?"[59]

Kennedy's behavior in the freedom riders affair established a pattern that he would follow for the next two years. His administration attempted to avert further civil rights confrontations through behind-the-scenes maneuvering. It acted belatedly but effectively when its efforts failed and large-scale racial violence exploded, as at Ole Miss in 1962. The president continued to deflect pressures for major new civil rights legislation and to shy away from the moral vocabulary that might educate national public opinion at the cost of offending Southern power holders. Through this period Kennedy was successful at mollifying the white South. His standing in the polls in 1962 was only a few points lower in Dixie than elsewhere.

He was also largely successful during this period in retaining the allegiance of the majority of blacks in spite of the paucity of civil rights gains. Kennedy's popularity among blacks resembled Franklin Roosevelt's under similar circumstances. Both benefited from the contrast with a predecessor whose icy attitude toward racial equality was well known. Both knew the political value of charm in personal dealings with black delegations and of symbolic appointments of black public officials. Both received more credit for their commitment to racial justice than their records warranted.

Civil rights leaders, however, were increasingly frustrated with the slow pace of progress. Martin Luther King, Jr., in particular, pondered how to impel Kennedy to move faster—and to bear presidential witness to the righteousness of the civil rights cause. Although the immediate target of the Birmingham campaign that King and his staff launched in the spring of 1963 was that city's business elite, the ultimate target was the administration. The civil rights leader and his aides hoped to initiate a civil rights confrontation in Alabama that the president could not ignore or finesse. King's words in his "Letter from Birmingham Jail" were directed to local white clergymen, but their message also challenged the White House: "Nonviolent direct action seeks to create . . . a crisis and establish such creative tension that a community that has constantly refused to negotiate is forced to confront the issue." The words would have fallen short, however, if they had not been backed by masses of mostly young blacks who went into the streets to demand their freedom. Once Birmingham's "Bull" Connor assaulted the black demonstrators with firehoses and police dogs—and provided graphic images of brutality that were shown across the nation and internationally—Kennedy found himself in the middle of the civil rights dilemma he had always tried to evade.[60]

Most of the president's senior advisers urged a cautious response to Birmingham and the kindred campaigns it inspired in other cities. But with prodding from Robert Kennedy, John Kennedy decided that the time had arrived for strong words and actions on civil rights. Thanks to the secret recordings that the president made of his meetings and phone conversations during this period, there is direct evidence to help us uncover the reasons behind Kennedy's dramatic shift to major legislation and moral exhortation on civil rights.

Fear played a significant role in Kennedy's decision making on civil rights in the late spring of 1963, as it had during the Cuban missile crisis. While King's organization had conducted the Birmingham campaign with nonviolent discipline, black bystanders had heaved rocks and bottles at police, and the black community had erupted into a riot after bombings by the Ku Klux Klan. As demonstrations spread to other cities, the specter of racial violence began to preoccupy Kennedy and his aides. At a White House meeting on May 20, 1963, there was much worried conversation about black anger and antagonism toward whites. The foreboding figure of Malcolm X was invoked as the alternative should King be perceived as failing. Speaking to other white leaders during this period, Kennedy shared his alarm. When the governor of Louisiana complained to him over the phone about civil rights demonstrations in Jackson, Mississippi, the president replied: "It isn't just Jackson. . . . It's Philadelphia, and it's going to be Washington, D.C. this summer, and we're trying to figure out

304 ICONS OF DEMOCRACY

what we can do to put this stuff in the courts and get it off the streets because somebody's going to get killed."[61]

Kennedy also felt impelled to take strong action because his leadership was now in question. The civil rights movement had raised the stakes, had driven its cause beyond the reach of Kennedy's tepid gestures; to continue in his old course would make the president, the "vital center of action," look feckless and devitalized. At a White House meeting on June 1, 1963, Robert Kennedy told his brother that new civil rights legislation was imperative:

> I don't think we have even an alternative. We couldn't go on and not have legislation. . . . Just the fact that we have a major crisis. Congress will have a lot of Republicans and a lot of Democrats that put legislation in. Everybody will be saying, "Where is your legislation?" I couldn't possibly defend that position.[62]

Beyond the fear of racial violence and the concern for his image, Kennedy was now more receptive to the arguments that the civil rights movement had been presenting all along; the crisis finally penetrated his customary detachment. In meetings with his aides, and in White House sessions with business, labor, religious, and other group leaders, he echoed some of the urgency and passion about civil rights that he had previously found discomforting. Kennedy was educated by Birmingham. The kind of civil rights demonstrations he had always tried to forestall became the most valuable learning experience of his presidency.

To introduce his civil rights legislation, Kennedy went on national television on June 11, 1963. Gone from his televised speech were the cautious phrases that assuaged Southern white sensitivity. Accepting the political risks, Kennedy was, at last, ready for rhetoric that could match the moral power of the civil rights struggle:

> We are confronted primarily with a moral issue. It is as old as the Scriptures and is as clear as the American Constitution. . . . One hundred years of delay have passed since President Lincoln freed the slaves, yet their heirs, their grandsons, are not fully free. . . . And this nation, for all of its hopes and all its boasts, will not be fully free until all its citizens are free.[63]

Kennedy's speech and legislation were the highpoints of his growth toward democratic leadership. Yet his conversion to the civil rights cause was never as complete as later legend portrayed it. Although he had finally adopted the moral vocabulary of the civil rights move-ment, the movement nonetheless remained a rival to him for control of the direction the struggle would now take. When he sent his legisla-tion to Congress on June 19, the special message that accompanied it contained a stern warning to civil rights forces that the time for "di-rect action" was over. Kennedy conceded that demonstrations had been necessary to dramatize the issue when "no other remedy was in sight." But now they were dangerous: "As feelings have risen in recent days, these demonstrations have increasingly endangered lives and property, inflamed emotions, and unnecessarily divided communities. . . . I want to caution against demonstrations which can lead to vio-lence." The president and the Congress were now considering legal remedies for black grievances, so a movement that persisted with "un-ruly tactics or pressures" would only harm its own cause.[64]

The president's concern to prevent violence and to guard against a political backlash were understandable. His rebuke of continuing demonstrations was politically astute, since polls showed a majority of whites becoming apprehensive about them. Yet his blast at demon-strations on June 19 undercut some of the educational impact of his speech of June 11. Instead of focusing attention on the ugliness of a white racism whose champions bombed homes and churches and murdered black leaders, he laid the responsibility for future violence upon the black freedom movement. Instead of alerting the public to the possibility that civil rights struggles would continue even if the Kennedy bill was passed by Congress, he created the impression that elected officials had the matter in hand and that the movement's chief tactics were no longer necessary. John Kennedy had, as his admirers have claimed, become something of a hero of civil rights. His version of racial progress, however, did not leave room for the mass heroism of the civil rights movement.

Conclusion

In a 1983 Gallup poll respondents ranked John F. Kennedy as the greatest president in the history of the United States. Five years later, a poll of seventy-five scholars and journalists in *American Heritage* judged Kennedy to be the most overrated figure in American history. Scholarly critiques of Kennedy's presidential policies are numerous, revelations of his sexual antics and seamy covert wars are widely broadcast, yet his image has remained curiously untarnished in the eyes of the mass audience. The heroic leader has not entered the history books as he had hoped, but decades after his death he is still television's hero.[65]

November 22, 1963, remains the foundation for Kennedy's enduring mystique of greatness. The horror of his assassination instantly marked the most memorable day in the life of a generation. It froze Kennedy in his youth and grace, a leader of eternal promise. That promise extended to the people as well as the president, through their vicarious participation in his televised spectacles. Kennedy offered Americans the most flattering of self-images: of a people ambitious for the affluent life yet dedicated to the welfare of their country, of a nation in the full maturity of its global power yet still characterized by youthful vitality and generosity, of leadership that was tough and pragmatic yet lofty, excellent, and ennobling.

Kennedy's death came to organize popular understanding of modern American history. Before his death, in this understanding, America was on the ascendant. After his assassination, the nation found itself spiraling downward, into race riots, overseas catastrophes, and economic stagnation. When Americans treasure the grace and glamour in stories or visual images of Kennedy, they treasure an imagined time when America, too, was suffused with grace and glamour. Nostalgia for Kennedy is nostalgia for an American dream that the decade of the 1960s first magnified and then exploded.

Kennedy's successors are blamed for destroying the dream, but he, too, was responsible for some of what went wrong after his death. A bold and incautious globalist, he pushed America's postwar power to heights that inevitably provoked the Soviet adversary and stirred the nation to a flush of overconfidence in its ability—and its right—to guide the rest of the world. A neo-Hamiltonian advocate of corporate-led economic growth, he sponsored a prosperity that profited and strengthened the business community more than it did the constituencies that had elected and supported him. An educator after much delay and evasion on the moral imperative of racial justice, he tried to head off further civil rights demonstrations with rhetoric that fed white incomprehension of the black movement's passions and struggles. Kennedy's vitality and drive were not balanced by a sense of the limits of American power and American virtue. His exclusively masculine conception of politics lacked that deeper commitment to democratic ends and that "feminine" counterpoise to heroic willfulness that marked the democratic leadership of an Abraham Lincoln and a Franklin Roosevelt.

Even after his flaws are elucidated, Kennedy remains a figure of considerable charm, especially in contrast to the presidents who came after him. But charm should not be mistaken for democratic leadership. Kennedy's charm beguiled more than his words and actions enlightened. It cloaked the aristocratic claim to superior talent and wisdom in its most attractive guise, calling forth the admiring gaze of passive spectators. A democratic polity needs active and questioning citizens more than it needs charming leaders.

Martin Luther King, Jr.

Dissenting Leadership and Democratic Redemption

IN THE 1950S AND EARLY 1960S AMERICAN POLITICAL THOUGHT AND CUL-
ture celebrated the successes of democracy. Material abundance
seemed the fulfillment of a democratic capitalism. Class politics
declined and the "end of ideology" was proclaimed. With the acces-
sion of John F. Kennedy to the presidency, the reign of sophisticated
and confident problem solvers was at hand. But a complacent society
was in the process of learning that American democracy had unfinished business: race was at its core. The struggle for civil rights made
historic gains, only to open up increasingly intractable dilemmas of
power and justice. Central to the democratic advances and anguish of
the era was the dissenting leadership of Martin Luther King, Jr.

Since his death—and increasingly since the initiation of a national
holiday celebrating his birthday—King has been anointed as the
source of the civil rights movement's democratic achievement. But we
have been admonished by Clayborne Carson, among others, that the
civil rights movement was a *collective* struggle for democracy; Carson
reminds us that there was political danger at the time, as well as the
danger of distorted historical understanding now, in the preoccupation with a single great leader. As we shall see, Martin Luther King,
Jr., had an impulse to grandiosity, to playing the role of this great
leader. But he also had the opposing impulse of humility, and in this
latter mood he recognized that he was only one element of a much
larger movement. Six weeks before his death, he explained to a group
of black ministers being trained for the upcoming Poor People's Campaign in Washington that "this struggle is not a struggle with one

actor by the name of Martin Luther King, but it is a drama with many, many actors, each playing their parts exceedingly well." The most marvelous quality of this drama, King said in 1965, was that the public stage had been taken over by those who previously had been the most invisible Americans: "In the deep South in some insignificant towns and cities some extremely insignificant people came abruptly to the end of their patience."[1]

It is an error to reduce the civil rights movement to Martin Luther King, Jr.; it is equally an error to fail to appreciate the value of his leadership. As important as the continuing debate is over King's place in the real history of the civil rights struggle, it is important as well to examine his place in the history of American political leadership.

Unique among the nine figures studied in this book, Martin Luther King, Jr., couched his leadership predominantly in religious terms. He defined his civil rights leadership as an expression of his ministry and derived much of his message and style from the African American religious experience. If leadership was often a painful burden to King, it was a task to which he felt called by God. By the conventional standards of American politics, King was an ethereal leader in his desire to introduce Christian love and Gandhian nonviolence as a force in public life. But religiosity has seldom been a barrier to political influence in America. Like many other figures in American history, King was empowered by a religious idiom with enormous evocativeness for his audience. He managed to avoid, as some of those predecessors had not, the dangers to democracy of religious intolerance and dogmatism.[2]

King was also unique among the dissenting leaders we have considered in understanding and acquiring some of the essential skills of the democratic politician. Far more than Elizabeth Cady Stanton or Eugene V. Debs, he learned to seek the always precarious balance between the moral and the political dimensions of dissenting leadership. His civil rights career was marked by a developing sense of how to make the American political process work for the sake of black liberation. King faced squarely the perplexing political choices that presented themselves to a dissenting leader, particularly about the pragmatic uses of white racist violence and the functions of charismatic leadership in a democratic movement. If his choices sometimes entailed compromise and moral ambiguity, they also made him the most instructive American exemplar of effective dissenting leadership.

Successful in the battle against segregation and black disfranchisement in the South, King ran up against the limits of dissenting leadership when he moved North and confronted racism, economic inequality, and imperialism on a more fundamental plane. His story can be told as a progression from a stirring but somewhat naïve idealism to a politically astute idealism to a tragic wisdom that recognized the limits of the American political order and the profound resistances to racial justice and democratic dignity. In his final years King was driven to the margins, where dissenting leadership normally resides. The most prophetic—and moving—period of his public career was its end, with his last, desperate effort to promote radical democratic change, as former supporters scorned him, old enemies moved in to destroy him, and the violent fate he had long anticipated finally tracked him down.

The Drum Major

A single sentence can sometimes tap the deepest vein of a people's anguish. In his first major political address, launching the Montgomery bus boycott, Martin Luther King, Jr., aroused his audience with just a few words, words that both crystallized centuries of suffering and pointed to their transcendence. "And you know, my friends, there comes a time when people get tired of being trampled over by the iron feet of oppression."[3]

King's career as a public person began in an astonishing moment for both himself and his people. We have seen the sudden, unexpected emergence of a leader expressing the grievances and passions of an excluded group once before. What the Wesleyan chapel in Seneca Falls, New York, was to Elizabeth Cady Stanton on July 19, 1848, the Holt Street Baptist Church in Montgomery, Alabama, was to King on December 5, 1955: a place where the first utterances of a new public voice burst into American politics with a dissenting vision bound to transform it. Both Stanton and King spoke of sufferings that the powerful had long managed to ignore. Yet where Stanton grounded her dissent in a feminist reconstruction of republicanism and democracy, King tied these same American political traditions to the religious tradition of his own people, finding in African American Christianity images of both collective liberation and personal calling. To comprehend King as a political leader, I begin with his public persona, with questions of voice, calling, and self-transformation.

The story of the Montgomery bus boycott has been told many times, and most authors are careful to point out that Martin Luther King, Jr., did not play a role in originating the boycott. That King became the boycott leader on December 5, 1955, was largely fortuitous. Participants' accounts differ, but it appears that King was selected to head the new Montgomery Improvement Association because he was well educated and articulate. Perhaps more important, he was a newcomer to town—as such, not identified with any of the competing factions in the black community or compromised by past favors from the white elite. From the start, King was something of a reluctant leader. Andrew Young, King's close associate later on in the Southern Christian Leadership Conference (SCLC), has remarked: "I'm convinced that Martin never wanted to be a leader. . . . [E]verything he did, he was pushed into."[4]

When King was chosen as leader by a meeting of his fellow ministers, he had less than an hour to prepare his first speech before the crucial mass meeting that would determine the future of the bus boycott. Only twenty-six, his personality and thought were still in flux. He had only recently returned to the black South after immersion in the white world of Northern seminaries and universities. Insecure in that world, he had experienced the arcane language of theology as alien to his background and his concerns, and had fallen into a persistent pattern of plagiarism to obtain the academic credentials he desired. Commenting on this plagiarism, David Thelen looks beyond the question of moral condemnation to observe that King could not find his own voice in a white school of theology—and would have to find it, instead, in his encounter with an aroused black community.[5]

King discovered his voice in the mass meeting at the Holt Street Baptist Church. Before an audience overflowing in numbers—and in long-suppressed emotions—King unloosed the sorrow and pride of his people. He claimed for the mass struggle of the bus boycott the highest of secular and sacred authority: "We are not wrong in what we are doing. If we are wrong, then the Supreme Court of this nation is wrong. If we are wrong, the Constitution of the United States is wrong. If we are wrong, God Almighty is wrong." He spoke of Christian love but also of justice, of "the tools of persuasion" and "the tools of coercion." Most remarkable, he prophesied the history of the civil rights movement to come: "When the history books are written in the future, somebody will have to say, 'There lived a race of people, of black people, . . . who had the moral courage to stand up for their rights, and thereby they injected a new meaning into the veins of history and of civilization.'"[6]

Recalling the event in *Stride toward Freedom*, King wrote that the victory his people were seeking had already, in a sense, been won, regardless of what happened on the buses: "The real victory was in the mass meeting, where thousands of black people stood revealed with a new sense of dignity and destiny." Those thousands spoke to King in a way that would forever change him. Their "new sense of dignity and destiny" was what he felt and expressed, in a self-revelation both personal and collective. At this mass meeting at Holt Street Baptist Church, King found his vocation as a dissenting leader. He also found the followers who would continue to inspire him, as he would inspire them.[7]

The vocation King assumed that night was initially rooted in the deepest of democratic bonds between a leader and followers. There was also another bond that he experienced, one even more profound to him. "I realized," he wrote, "that this speech had evoked more response than any speech or sermon I had ever delivered, and yet it was virtually unprepared. I came to see for the first time what the older preachers meant when they said, 'Open your mouth and God will speak for you.'" If the assembled people were speaking to him, the God of love, justice, and deliverance from bondage was speaking through him. Sometimes in tension, more often in combination, democratic commitments and divine obligations would together drive King's entire public career.[8]

King's sense of religious vocation as a civil rights leader began in the mass meeting, but, as David J. Garrow has emphasized, its touchstone was a more private epiphany. Two months into the bus boycott, King experienced a personal crisis. Arrested on a trumped-up traffic charge, harassed by death threats over the telephone, a sleepless King sat in his kitchen at midnight and poured out his fear and foreboding to his Lord. His prayer was answered:

> And it seemed that that moment that I could hear an inner voice saying to me, Martin Luther, stand up for righteousness. Stand up for justice. Stand up for truth. And lo, I will be with you. . . . I heard the voice of Jesus saying still to fight on. He promised never to leave me, never to leave me alone. No, never alone.

As the demands of leadership multiplied, as the physical dangers of leadership intensified, King would be sustained by this sense of divine companionship. "God has been profoundly real to me in recent years," he wrote in a 1960 article. "In the midst of outer dangers I have felt an inner calm."[9]

King understood his role as a leader within the framework of a providential mission for the liberation of his people. He understood the meaning of leadership itself in terms drawn from the African American religious experience. What seemed most unusual and idiosyncratic about King as a political figure were often, in fact, the characteristics of black Baptist ministers. The black Baptist minister typically claimed divine ordination and charismatic authority. Thus, when the young King took over his first position as a pastor, at Dexter Avenue Baptist Church in Montgomery, he was quick to insist upon "the unconditional willingness of the people to accept the pastor's leadership." Within the church, he reminded his congregants, "Leadership never ascends from the pew to the pulpit, but it invariably descends from the pulpit to the pew." Yet if the black Baptist minister's claims tended toward charismatic authority, there was a countervailing pull toward democratic openness. Even in his exalted position, the minister shared with his congregation the legacy of oppression and the dream of deliverance. The preacher thus was expected to empathize with individual congregants, to identify with his entire flock, to give voice to his people's sorrows and their hopes for freedom.[10]

Experiencing leadership as a divine calling, and developing a leadership style out of the religious traditions of his people, King, in one of his last sermons, provided a gloss on John Adams's "passion for distinction" that we have not encountered before. Agreeing with Adams that everyone harbors the "same basic desires for recognition," King said: "It's a kind of drum major instinct—a desire to be out front, a desire to lead the parade, a desire to be first." After detailing the destructive manifestations of this instinct—living above one's means, boasting, tearing down others—King, like Adams, turned to its constructive potential. Jesus' message, according to King, was: "Don't give up this instinct. . . . Keep feeling the need for being important. Keep feeling the need for being first. But I want you to be first in love. I want you to be first in moral excellence. I want you to be first in generosity."[11]

In this sermon, King rejected the conventional forms of the "drum major instinct," including that passion for political distinction that Adams had regarded as the best hope for republican virtue in America. He seemed to resemble more closely Eugene V. Debs, who feared the power of political distinction to subvert egalitarian humility. Yet King, unlike Debs, did not reject the value of leadership as a public role. To him, leadership was a religious calling, an opportunity for serving God by serving others. At the end of the sermon, he imagined a eulogy for his own funeral—and captured his own paradox as the humble drum major:

> I'd like somebody to mention that day, that Martin Luther King, Jr., tried to give his life serving others. I'd like for somebody to say that day, that Martin Luther King, Jr., tried to love somebody. . . . Yes, if you want to say that I was a drum major, say that I was a drum major for justice; say that I was a drum major for peace; I was a drum major for righteousness.[12]

A political leadership grounded in the claim of a divine visitation and couched in the language of scriptural authority naturally makes democrats uneasy—religious certainty can, of course, produce an intolerant and exclusionary leadership. But as King's religious assurance deepened, he seemed to grow more humble—and more capable of reaching those who did not share his faith. His vision came to appeal as much to non-Christians and nonbelievers as to Christians, perhaps because his was a God whose message was the democratic equality and dignity of all His children.

Religion provided King with a vocabulary not only for redirecting the "passion for distinction" but also for registering the fundamental tensions between his public and his private selves. On a conscious level, King embraced antitheses. "The strong man," he wrote in an early sermon, "holds in a living blend strongly marked opposites." The theme of this sermon was the need to balance "a tough mind" with "a tender heart." This was King's formulation of the New Testament counsel: "Be ye therefore wise as serpents, and harmless as doves." King advocated and exemplified the kind of masculine/feminine synthesis that, I argued earlier, characterized the political leadership of a Lincoln, Stanton, Debs, and Franklin Roosevelt. His version, however, came not from gender but from Jesus.[13]

The "strongly marked opposites" in King's character were not always so conscious—or so desirable. Throughout his life, he remained a paradoxical blend of pride and humility. His critics were not altogether off the mark in castigating him for grandiosity. As the son of one of the most prominent black ministers in the South, King grew up with the sense that he was special. Arriving in Montgomery for his first pastorate, his ambitions were couched in youthfully pompous terms: his first lengthy communication to his congregation predicted that once "great leadership" and "great followship" were united, "Dexter will rise to such heights as will stagger the imagination of generations yet unborn, and which even God himself will smile upon." As a civil rights leader, King frequently compared himself to the Old Testament prophets and modeled his epistles after those of St. Paul. Above all, he identified himself with Moses, depicting the symbolic geography of his public career as the exodus, the wilderness, the mountaintop, and the promised land.[14]

King's grandiosity was balanced by a painful sense of guilt. A number of those who met the famous Dr. King for the first time have commented that they were surprised by how modest and unpretentious he turned out to be in private settings. Beneath the grand public exterior, King was a deeply sensitive man. As he grew in fame, his sensitivities were increasingly troubled by the acclaim he was accorded. To J. Pius

Barbour, an old friend from his seminary days, he confided: "The Martin Luther King that the people talk about seems . . . somebody foreign to me." Stanley Levison, King's closest white friend and adviser, observed that the civil rights leader was a "guilt-ridden man," who "didn't feel he deserved the kind of tribute that he got." To Levison, King was a man "tortured by the great appreciation that the public showed for him. If he had been less humble, he could have lived with this kind of acclaim, but because he was genuinely a man of humility, he really couldn't live with it."[15]

On a still more private level, King was racked by the opposition of sin and goodness, of giving in to temptation and overcoming the most common of human failings. In public, he preached: "Man is more than a dog to be satisfied by the bones of sensory pleasure and showy materialism. He is a being of spirit, born for the stars and created for eternity." Routinely, he decried "a world rife with sexual promiscuity." But King had a secret life as a womanizer, where sexual pleasure was the recompense for political pain. This temptation he could not resist, even though it brought him recurrent pangs of guilt, as well as continuing fears that the eavesdropping FBI would expose him, at incalculable cost to his career and to the civil rights movement with which he was identified.[16]

King could acknowledge his sexual sinfulness. But he did not realize that his womanizing was related to a chauvinistic attitude that contradicted his belief in universal human dignity and damaged his ability to unify the civil rights movement. Steeped in the male chauvinism common to black preachers of his generation, King was a democrat who denied the potential contributions of half of his followers. He could not treat as equals some extraordinary black women. He thereby alienated Ella Baker, one of the founders of SCLC and a skilled civil rights organizer. She became one of his most powerful critics and, through her influence on black student activists, an important source of their skepticism about King's leadership. Even the gentle Septima Clark, who continued to work for King as director of SCLC's Citizenship Education Program—and to admire his qualities as a man and a leader—was troubled by the treatment of women in SCLC. "I don't think women's words had any weight whatsoever," Clark noted of the organization headed by a man who gave us some of the most eloquent words about equality that we possess.[17]

Dogged by the guilt of being a sinner in his own religious terms, King perhaps did not give himself enough credit for the self-transformation he had managed in other dimensions of his life through the vehicle of nonviolence. He remarked in a 1964 interview that nonviolence possessed a "strange power to transform and transmute the individuals who subordinate themselves to its disciplines." He was referring to the dignity and courage that nonviolent black demonstrators had displayed in the face of police clubs, dogs, and fire hoses. That same "strange power" was operating in King's life—and producing effects even more unusual than sublime dignity and courage.[18]

King's own nonviolence was measured by his reaction to physical attacks on his person. At the 1962 SCLC convention in Birmingham, Alabama, a young Nazi party member attacked him as he was speaking, repeatedly punching him in the face. "After being knocked backward by one of the last blows," Taylor Branch recounts, "King turned to face him while dropping his hands. It was the look on his face that many would not forget." Septima Clark, who "would not have been shocked to see the unloosed rage of an exalted leader, marveled instead at King's transcendent calm." When members of the audience came to King's aid and surrounded his assailant, King cried, "'Don't touch him. We have to pray for him.'"[19]

That nonviolent purgation of hatred that King constantly urged upon his followers was a process to which he fully submitted himself. His talk of love was not a mere borrowing from the Gospels and Gandhi; it was the hard-won wisdom of brutal experience. To the black advocates of violence who were increasingly scoffing at his non-violent approach after 1965, King retorted: "I've seen hate on the faces of too many Klansmen and too many White Citizen's Councilors in the South to want to hate myself, because every time I see it, I know that it does something to their faces and their personalities and I say to myself that hate is too great a burden to bear." Responding to hate with hate, he insisted, was a form of self-violence that produced an escalating cycle of public violence. Only nonviolence could mend "the broken community."[20]

Nonviolence also helped King to become a more democratic character in his relationships with the people who worked with and for him. Critics sometimes bemoaned his passivity and willingness to tolerate considerable chaos within his own organization. Yet his gentle, nonviolent approach to his staff, with all its real drawbacks for organizational efficiency, was a productive source of democratic learning. King managed to hold together a corps of talented but fractious subordinates. By patiently extracting from their ongoing battles his own syntheses, he reached decisions that drew on a wide range of arguments and insights, while assuring staff members that they had been heard. Andrew Young observed in amusement that King "would want somebody to express as radical a view as possible and somebody to express as conservative a view as possible. . . . He figured . . . the wider variety of opinions you got, the better chance you had of extracting the truth from that." Like Abraham Lincoln, King was strengthened by his kindness; he was shrewder because he listened so patiently to his staff.[21]

Finding a public voice and calling that he had never anticipated or sought, transforming the self through the arduous discipline of nonviolence while failing to escape recurrent bouts of guilt over both uncontrolled lust and undeserved fame, Martin Luther King, Jr., paid a price for his political leadership. The further he elaborated his public persona, the more he was trapped by it. It was a persona that required the suppression of some of his most appealing private qualities. Politicians such as Franklin Roosevelt and John Kennedy could show off their playful sense of humor, projecting a charm that was an important part of their public appeal. King's public persona was reserved and formal; his rollicking sense of humor and talent for mimicry were known only to his intimates. Solemnity was dictated to King by his religious role; it may also have stemmed from his fear that displays of humor would be taken as confirmation of white stereotypes about blacks. So King had always to be soberly uplifting before the public.[22]

Constantly on the run, much of his time was spent in the indispensable but draining task of fundraising for the SCLC. He was freed from this mundane duty only when he entered the realm of danger, in tense civil rights confrontations where his life and those of his followers were on the line. King's counterpart in political time, John Kennedy, was celebrated for his radiant vigor. Weariness was the more notable motif in King's public career. Twenty-six when he found his public voice, thirty-nine when he died, he was, in reality, very young to be so prominent. But he never seemed young again after December 5, 1955.

Freedom Songs

"Freedom songs are the soul of the movement," King wrote in 1964:

> They are adaptations of the songs the slaves sang—the sorrow songs, the shouts for joy, the battle hymns and the anthems of our movement. . . . We sing the freedom songs today for the same reason the slaves sang them, because we too are in bondage and the songs add hope to our determination that "We shall overcome, Black and white together, We shall overcome someday."

Singing freedom songs, King the leader found communion with his people. The spirit of those songs came to infuse his own rhetoric.

Although King's oratory took its power from synthesizing the democratic themes of American civil religion and the prophetic themes of black Christianity, the music of his most memorable oratorical flights suggested that King was composing new freedom songs.[23]

Words were a critical source of power to King, but what made his rhetoric extraordinary was not its originality in the conventional sense of the word. Keith Miller has demonstrated how King borrowed extensively for his sermons and political speeches, drawing particularly on the writings of liberal white preachers and the oral tradition of the African American church. Following a practice common to both white and black preachers, he adopted the phrases of others to make his own points about racial justice. Through secondhand metaphors, he found a new way across the American racial divide. Miller argues that King's borrowing does not detract from his rhetorical achievement: "Like folk preachers who preceded him, he expertly blended others' voices with his own; in his public discourse, no matter how much he borrowed, he invariably sounded exactly like himself."[24]

His choice of words was complicated by the duality of his audience. Needing to inspire and mobilize blacks, he also needed the sympathy and support of whites. The first of these tasks was perhaps the simpler. Speaking in the familiar terms and cadences of black Christianity and clothed in the traditional authority of the black ministry, King creatively expanded on a long-standing discourse to meet the purposes of political activism. (The same shared rhetorical background that so appealed to Southern blacks was much less effective in the Northern ghettos, however.) When speaking before mainly black audiences, in mass meetings or sermons, his language became looser and less grammatical, more redolent of ordinary black people than of the academic diction he had learned in the North. Echoing the sorrow songs and hymns of hope, he refurbished the African American discourse of bondage and liberation.

With white audiences unaccustomed to hearing black voices, King found words that reassured and words that challenged. Keenly attuned to whites' fears of black rage over racial injustice, he believed that white audiences required reassurance before they could hear black grievances. His talk of nonviolence provided that reassurance: "Only through our adherence to love and nonviolence will the fear in the white community be mitigated." King's call for racial integration demanded that whites change both their behavior and their attitudes, but it promised as well that blacks were seeking reconciliation with whites rather than power over them. Before his final, radical phase, his vision of integration—that blacks aspired to join white society—even seemed to flatter white America.[25]

Yet King's appeal to white listeners should not be reduced to mere reassurance. More than any other leader in American history, he staked out a common rhetorical ground of democratic and Christian symbols that united the values and aspirations of both blacks and whites. Like Abraham Lincoln and Franklin Roosevelt, King spoke to ancestral American ideals of a democratic community. Unlike Lincoln or Roosevelt, King defined this community as not merely incomplete, but as corrupted, without the full presence of African Americans. King's essential message to whites was that the "soul" of America was under judgment in the civil rights struggle and that only love and justice could save it.

King's freedom songs can be heard in his most famous address, the "I have a dream" speech at the March on Washington in 1963, and in a second address less celebrated (but no less memorable according to those who heard both)—the speech climaxing the march from Selma to Montgomery in 1965. As was the case with Lincoln, King's most familiar words deserve close attention. We can observe in these two speeches how he reached for rhetoric that fitted emotion to occasion and substance to form. We can also observe the integration of black and white discourses, signifying King's central point that black liberation was necessary to complete American democracy.

Much of what King said at the March on Washington he had said many times before; even the great "dream" passage had been used before, during a speech in Detroit. It was the setting that initially supplied special drama to King's words: appearing before the Lincoln Memorial to an interracial throng of unprecedented size and to a national television audience, he found the kind of stage for his oratory ordinarily available only to presidents. It was also the passion of the occasion that led King to discard his planned peroration and to end his speech with extemporaneous fire.[26]

Until the peroration, King's speech was undistinguished. It began with an obvious connection to the Gettysburg Address: "Fivescore years ago, a great American, in whose symbolic shadow we stand today, signed the Emancipation Proclamation." It moved on to an awkward metaphor, in which freedom was symbolized in monetary terms: "In a sense we've come to our nation's capital to cash a check. When the architects of our republic wrote the magnificent words of the Constitution and the Declaration of Independence, they were signing a promissory note to which every American was to fall heir." King began to pick up steam as he voiced the "fierce urgency" of the civil rights struggle: "Now is the time to make real the promises of democracy." His words were unsettling to the white majority: "There will be neither rest nor tranquility in America until the Negro is granted his citizenship rights." Then he was reassuring: "But there is something that I must say to my people who stand on the warm threshold which leads into the palace of justice. In process of gaining our rightful place we must not be guilty of wrongful deeds."[27]

Only with the "I have a dream" passage did the speech soar. In lines that have become as familiar today as those of the Gettysburg Address, King hymned a vision of racial reconciliation that fulfilled the promise of American democracy, even as it negated the reality of American history. His images spoke to the sacred even more than to the secular. "When King had a dream," Garry Wills has written, "it was of the millennium, when Isaiah's lamb, and a little child shall lead them." King's images conjured the reign of gentleness after an era of violent turmoil, of the "sons of former slaves and sons of former slave-owners" supping together at "the table of brotherhood," of "little black boys and black girls . . . join[ing] hands with little white boys and white girls as sisters and brothers." The millennium King imagined was played out on Southern ground—in Georgia, Mississippi, Alabama. In his dream, racist hells were transformed into heavens of racial harmony and human dignity.[28]

Among the hallowed texts of American civil religion, King's speech made reference to the Declaration of Independence and the Gettysburg Address. But there were some suggestive parallels between the exaltation of the "I have a dream" passage and the more somber lines of Lincoln's second inaugural address. King's images of reconciliation recalled Lincoln's "With malice toward none; with charity for all." His, too, was a vision of a nation that had to undergo the painful encounter with its own past sins before it could hope for redemption. Both men evoked a providential history for America. Yet King's dream surpassed Lincoln's. Where Lincoln's words aimed to reconcile North and South, King envisioned the more daunting reconciliation of white and black.

King was not done when he concluded his dream. He followed it with music, with his hymn for

the day when all of God's children will be able to sing with new meaning—"my country 'tis of thee; sweet land of liberty; of thee I sing; land where my fathers died, land of the pilgrim's pride; from every mountain side, let freedom ring"—and if America is to be a great nation, this must become true.

So let freedom ring from the prodigious hilltops of New Hampshire.

Let freedom ring from the mighty mountains of New York. . . .

But not only that.

Let freedom ring from Stone Mountain of Georgia.

Let freedom ring from Lookout Mountain of Tennessee.

Let freedom ring from every hill and molehill of Mississippi, from every mountainside let freedom ring.

And when we allow freedom to ring, when we let it ring from every village and hamlet, from every state and city, we will be able to speed up that day when all of God's children—black men and white men, Jews and Gentiles, Catholics and Protestants—will be able to join hands and to sing in the words of the old Negro spiritual, "Free at last, free at last; thank God Almighty, we are free at last."

King's freedom song at the March on Washington merged two other songs—one an all-American tune, the other an "old Negro spiritual." The two songs flowed together, the American anthem finished—and fulfilled—by the black spiritual.[29]

The speech that King delivered in Montgomery on March 25, 1965, at the conclusion of the Selma to Montgomery voting-rights march was as powerful as the March on Washington speech—and perhaps even more musical. Brutally beaten back at the Pettus Bridge in Selma, the voting-rights campaign of the SCLC had enlisted the shocked conscience of the nation, the protection of the federal judiciary, and the political endorsement of the president. It was marching into Montgomery in high spirits, to consecrate its inevitable victory on the steps of the Alabama state capitol, the political habitation of Governor George Wallace. In his speech to the marchers, King gave eloquent testimonial to this triumph before moving on to a call for further militancy:

Once more the method of nonviolent resistance was unsheathed from its scabbard and once again an entire community was mobilized to confront the adversary. And again the brutality of a dying order shrieks across the land. Yet Selma, Alabama, became a shining moment in the conscience of man. There never was a moment in American history more honorable and more inspiring than the pilgrimage of clergymen and laymen of every race and faith pouring into Selma to face danger at the side of its embattled Negroes. Confrontation of good and evil compressed in the tiny community of Selma generated the massive power to turn the whole nation to a new course.[30]

What was extraordinary about this speech, however, was not the new words King skillfully crafted but the old ones he transfigured.

James H. Cone, an African American theologian, has pointed out that "in the black church, the meaning is found not primarily in the intellectual content of the spoken word but in the *way* the word is spoken and its effect upon those who hear it." Cone's point is applicable to the closing of King's Montgomery speech. In print, it is unremarkable. Heard or seen on film, it is electrifying.[31]

The peroration began with a call-and-response sequence common to the black church: "I know you are asking today, 'How long will it take?'. . . . How long? Not long, because no lie can live forever. How long? Not long, because you still reap what you sow. How long? Not long, because the arc of the moral universe is long but it bends toward justice." The audience was with King now, first affirming his statements with "yes, sir," then picking up his rhythm and chanting "not long" with him. Then, he was off into song: "Not long, 'cause mine eyes have seen the glory of the coming of the Lord, trampling out the vintage where the grapes of wrath are stored. He has loosed the fateful lightning of his terrible swift sword. His truth is marching on." King's "Battle Hymn" did not follow the Civil War original. His cadence was different, more fierce and urgent, with his accents on the words "glory," "wrath," and "terrible." In King's rendition, the millennial rhymes of the Civil War became a new holy battle cry. Montgomery, Alabama, the "Cradle of the Confederacy," was finally being forced to admit its defeat and to bear witness to what Lincoln had proclaimed at Gettysburg: "a new birth of freedom."[32]

Militancy gave way to exaltation. "Glory, hallelujah!" King cried, and flung his arm out toward the crowd. He repeated the line four times. Each time, his baritone became louder, more vibrant, more intense. Each time, his arm moved closer to the heavens. By the final "hallelujah," the emotional effect was overwhelming. The way King spoke this one word crystallized Selma, the voting rights campaign, the whole civil rights history to this moment of travail and triumph. In Montgomery, as in Washington, King redefined America's democratic dream and breathed into it a new spiritual fire. His finest words functioned not as descriptions of reality, but as hymns of hope—freedom songs.[33]

A Political Man

His words so resonant and his voice so powerful—King was the undeniable orator of the civil rights movement. To his critics within the movement, however, impressive words concealed an unimpressive record of actions. King was viewed by these critics largely as a "symbolic" leader, enthroned by the press and adulated by the black masses, yet indecisive and ineffectual in the heat of actual civil rights battles. There were plenty of failed SCLC campaigns to provide ammunition to King's detractors. But the historic SCLC successes in Birmingham in 1963 and Selma in 1965 suggest that he could be highly effective in the strategic and tactical aspects of leadership. A religious leader, moralist, and orator, King also became a political man, adding political prudence to his spiritual force. The combination of morality and politics that he developed was difficult, unstable, sometimes even disturbing. Yet he made it work to brilliant effect at critical junctures in the history of the civil rights movement. Rejecting the notion that moral integrity necessitated political innocence, King demonstrated how a dissenting leader might turn to political techniques that verged on the Machiavellian without losing his soul.[34]

King recognized from the start that political power had a rightful place in a struggle for social justice. In his December 5, 1955, speech in Montgomery, as we have already seen, he characterized the bus boycott as one of the legitimate "tools of coercion" that a civil rights movement could employ. Yet in his initial civil rights campaign, King was not particularly astute or calculating about politics. In March 1956, when he insisted that the civil rights crusade in Montgomery was "a spiritual movement," the phrase referred to strategy as well as to ultimate ends. Nonviolence, he explained in *Stride toward Freedom*, "does not seek to defeat or humiliate the opponent, but to win his friendship and understanding." The tactics of nonviolence were "merely means to awaken a sense of moral shame in the opponent. The end is redemption and reconciliation."[35]

King held on to this conception of nonviolence for several years after the victory in Montgomery. We hear it at its height of moral splendor and political naïveté in his statement about the student lunch counter sit-ins in February 1960: "As we sit down quietly to request a cup of coffee, let us not forget to drink from that invisible cup of love, which can change a segregationist into an integrationist." King never abandoned the hope for ultimate reconciliation expressed in this statement—and many others like it. But the mounting brutality of white resistance to integration taught him the limitations of that "invisible cup of love" and the unlikelihood of converting segregationists. When the Freedom Riders, an interracial group testing segregated interstate transportation facilities in the South, were greeted with bus burnings and beatings in the spring of 1961, King understood how violence on this scale changed the context for nonviolent action. Speaking at a rally for the riders in Montgomery, with a crowd

of angry whites surrounding the church and threatening mass bloodshed, he drew a crucial political lesson from the "ugly and howling
mobs." Moral shame, he now recognized, would not constrain the opponents of black freedom: "The deep South will not impose limits
upon itself. The limits must be imposed from without."[36]

If limits on the system of segregation were to be imposed from without, the real target of nonviolent struggle ceased to be the Southern
segregationists and came to be a Northern audience with the democratic influence to compel action from the federal government. It
would not be through shaming the conscience of the recalcitrant that
the civil rights movement could break down segregation; rather, it
would be through dramatizing immorality to the conscience of the
unaware. Writing in October 1961 to Harold Courlander, a white
critic of the movement, King defended what would increasingly become his definitive political strategy of contriving Southern moral
dramas for Northern public consumption:

> Public relations is a very necessary part of any protest of civil dis-
> obedience. The main objective is to bring moral pressure to bear
> upon an unjust system or a particularly unjust law. The public at
> large must be aware of the inequities involved in such a system.

To the charge that the civil rights movement was intentionally seeking
to draw media attention, King pleaded guilty. But the civil rights
movement, he argued, had perfect extenuating reasons: "Without the
presence of the press, there might have been untold massacre in the
South."[37]

Two months after this letter, King and SCLC were drawn, without
advance preparation, into a mass movement for desegregation in Albany, Georgia. There they learned precisely what *kind* of moral drama
they would have to stage. Albany seemed to offer favorable conditions
for a confrontation with segregation: its black community, from the
youngest to the oldest members, was mobilized and full of fervor. But
there were hidden divisions within the local Albany movement, and
the young activists of SNCC (Student Non-violent Coordinating Committee), who had first organized the city's blacks, were resentful of
King and SCLC. Most important, King and SCLC faced a canny white
adversary whose dramatic instincts more than matched their own.

Albany's chief of police, Laurie Pritchett, studied King's nonviolent
philosophy and tactics in preparation for coping with the movement
he would lead. The chief insight he gleaned was that the force of
King's nonviolent demonstrations would be blunted if the police responded with courtesy rather than brutality. This approach denied

SCLC the drama it sought. Although Albany was a typical bastion of deep-South segregation, the national press lauded Pritchett's decorum and the Kennedy administration refused to intervene, even in the face of violations of federal law, so long as order was maintained. The frustrations of Albany taught King and SCLC that the injustice of segregation was not, by itself, sufficient to engage the conscience of the North and to compel action on the part of the federal government. Chief Pritchett wore the polite mask that concealed the vicious face of segregation. In future confrontations, King and SCLC would seize the attention of America by revealing the face behind the mask.[38]

The major successes of King and SCLC—Birmingham in 1963, Selma in 1965—were great dramas of unmasking. In both cases, public outrage, federal intervention, and, ultimately, national civil rights legislation were the products of tableaux in which nonviolent civil rights demonstrators—representing justice—were brutalized by violent defenders of the segregationist system—palpable emblems of injustice. After Albany, King and SCLC tried to select battlegrounds where their principal adversary was known for racist intransigence and violence. Their selection methods were hardly infallible; the campaign in St. Augustine, Florida, in 1964, for example, was largely a flop. But the political payoff from the flamboyant racist brutality of Birmingham's police commissioner, Eugene "Bull" Connor, and Sheriff Jim Clark of Dallas County, Alabama (in which Selma was located), was not a stroke of luck but a calculated effect on SCLC's part. Starting with Birmingham, King, the champion of nonviolence, turned to the politically astute—but also morally complex—strategy of inviting white racist violence in order to dramatize his larger moral point.[39]

Naturally, King and his SCLC aides did not like to talk about the place of white violence in their political strategy. Yet there is ample evidence that such violence was central to their dramaturgy. The evidence is strongest in the case of the Selma voting-rights campaign of 1965. Selma offered SCLC talented local black leadership, an aroused community, an easily demonstrable pattern of black disfranchisement. Its prime attraction, however, was Sheriff Jim Clark. Andrew Young of SCLC described Clark as "a near madman." Violent and volatile, indeed almost a caricature of racist rage, Clark was an ideal foil for the movement.[40]

When SCLC staged its first mass march in Selma, Clark disappointed the movement by displaying unexpected restraint. Worried SCLC leaders decided to give the sheriff one more try; should he again emulate Laurie Pritchett, they would move the main voting-rights operation to one of the adjoining Black Belt towns where segregationist violence could likely be coaxed into the open. Clark's patience was only a veneer, however, and he snapped back into his anticipated role the next day, manhandling Amelia Boynton, a Selma civil rights leader, in full view of the national press. From this point on, King and SCLC knew that they had the right dramatic ingredients in Selma. To an exasperated Wilson Baker, Selma's prudent director of public safety, SCLC's exploitation of Clark's violent temper was a work of art: "They played him just like an expert playing a violin." But SCLC's art was a dangerous one: the instrument they were playing commanded guns, clubs, electric cattle prods. Ralph Abernathy, King's closest friend and comrade in nonviolent battle, captured both the strategy of inviting racist violence and the personal risks it entailed in his recollection of Selma: "With any luck we would be visibly abused without being maimed or killed. The line we walked was increasingly thin in these matters."[41]

SCLC knew that the white racists could easily cross over their own line during the voting-rights campaign in Selma. When SCLC attempted a night march in the nearby town of Marion, state troopers turned off the streetlights, denying the national press any chance for pictures, and proceeded to attack civil rights demonstrators with billy clubs. A young black, Jimmie Lee Jackson, tried to protect his mother from a clubbing and was mortally wounded by a trooper. In protest of Jackson's death, SCLC announced a march from Selma to Montgomery. When the marchers set out on Sunday, March 7, they were blocked at the Pettus Bridge at the edge of Selma and then hurled back, tear gassed, and beaten by state troopers and Sheriff Clark's mounted posse. This time, however, there were no fatalities or permanent injuries. Even better for the movement, vivid film footage of the police violence stunned the nation and made federal voting-rights legislation a political imperative.

King and his aides had not scripted these particulars. But the drama of Selma, climaxing with "Bloody Sunday" on the Pettus Bridge, unfolded largely as they had intended. President Johnson's superb speech introducing his voting-rights bill ensured the ultimate success of the drama. A triumphant King provided a rare and rather impolitic elaboration of his successful strategy:

> The goal of the demonstrations in Selma, as elsewhere, is to dramatize the existence of injustice and to bring about the presence of justice by methods of nonviolence. Long years of experience indicate to us that Negroes can achieve this goal when four things occur:
> 1. Nonviolent demonstrators go into the streets to exercise their constitutional rights.
> 2. Racists resist by unleashing violence against them.

3. Americans of conscience in the name of decency demand federal intervention and legislation.
4. The administration, under mass pressure, initiates measures of immediate intervention and remedial legislation.[42]

The second point in this list, David Garrow has observed, constituted a public admission that "racial violence is crucial to the movement's progress." Even before this admission, King's opponents in the South and elsewhere accused him of provocation. The real instigator of violence, they charged, was the supposedly nonviolent Martin Luther King. King's favorite retort to such accusations was an analogy: to blame nonviolent demonstrators for the violence they encountered was like "condemning a robbed man because his possession of money precipitated the evil act of robbery." But the analogy was weak: individuals with money do not go looking for robbers, as SCLC went looking for "Bull" Connor and Jim Clark. Fortunately, King had a second and more cogent defense against the charge that he was the cause of violence in the South. Racist violence, he pointed out, was an everyday reality in the South, thriving in the shadows under which it normally found protection. The nonviolent movement brought this violence into the light, where its perpetrators could be witnessed and held accountable. The dramas King and SCLC staged were the only way to reveal to the nation the hidden brutality of segregation.[43]

King thus had moral as well as political grounds for inviting racist violence. Yet he also had to grapple with the moral perplexities of deliberately exposing followers to anticipated attacks by the minions of a "Bull" Connor and a Jim Clark. King handled this dilemma by alerting civil rights recruits to the dangers they faced—those who joined the movement knew that they were in for a "season of suffering"—and by sharing these dangers himself. On a practical level, he and his staff worked to limit suffering. It was no accident, Adam Fairclough suggests, that there were relatively few fatalities in King's campaigns: "By staging its protests in carefully contrived, highly public situations, SCLC tried to evoke white violence while keeping casualties to a minimum. . . . [E]xtensive press coverage caused law enforcement officials to proceed with caution. When they did resort to violence, they usually stopped short of lethal force."[44]

Becoming a political man exposed King to other moral dilemmas as well. To maintain his political tie to the White House and Northern white liberals, King at times had to stomach political compromises that did not square with his conscience. When the integrated Mississippi Freedom Democratic Party (MFDP) challenged the segregated regular party at the 1964 Democratic convention at Atlantic City,

President Johnson and his supporters, fearful of losing Southern electoral votes, brought intense pressure to bear on the MFDP delegation to accept a token gesture of two at-large convention votes. King, a backer of the MFDP, was pressed to lobby the disillusioned Mississippi civil rights forces to accept the presidential offer. Knowing that he would need White House sympathy for his planned voting-rights campaign in Alabama, he acceded. But his heart plainly was not with the compromise, and his lobbying of the MFDP delegation was mild, awkward, and ambivalent.

Writing racist violence into his civil rights dramas and compromising with established political power when he saw no other choice, King developed another of those "strongly marked opposites" in his character: moral integrity and political craftiness. Perhaps the highest testimonial to his success as a political man was that he got the better of two masters of the political profession, John Kennedy and Lyndon Johnson. With Birmingham in 1963 and Selma in 1965, King and the civil rights movement compelled presidents who had hoped to follow the path of political caution and to protect their Southern political base to come out for bold civil rights legislation. Kennedy and Johnson wanted King to go slower; he maneuvered them to move faster.

The irony in this history was that the strategic defeat Kennedy and Johnson suffered at the hands of King turned into personal triumphs for them as well as for him. After SCLC's campaign in Birmingham had stirred the nation and generated a score of similar movements throughout the South, Kennedy went on television to propose a sweeping equal-accommodations law. He told the country: "We are confronted primarily with a moral issue. It is as old as the Scriptures and is as clear as the American Constitution." After "Bloody Sunday" in Selma, Johnson embraced not only the movement's ideas for a voting-rights law but also its fundamental truths: "Their cause must be our cause too. Because it's not just Negroes, but really it's all of us who must overcome the crippling legacy of bigotry and injustice. And we *shall* overcome." Historians regularly cite these speeches of Kennedy and Johnson as the most memorable moments in the domestic policies of their respective presidencies. Because King's political craft was used in the service of his moral vision, he prodded two presidents to take moral stands beyond anything they had previously imagined. His political victory was not only the landmark civil rights legislation he helped bring into being. It was also the remarkable—albeit brief—seasons when political power in America spoke in his moral terms.[45]

"De Lawd"

King the political man had to face squarely the issue of making pragmatic use of white racist violence. He also had to confront an even more fundamental question: was his type of charismatic leadership consistent with the values of a democratic movement for equality and freedom? The question was raised by the young black militants of SNCC. It was sharpened and made painfully personal by the mocking sobriquet they hung on King: "De Lawd."

When members of SNCC made fun of "De Lawd," they were jeering at King's public persona. In their eyes, King was too bourgeois in dress and manner, too fame-struck, too cautious politically, too pompous in his intimation of divine authority—and too appealing to the religious instincts of the black masses in the South. SNCC resentments toward SCLC as an organization also rubbed off personally on King. The mild-mannered King was held responsible for the abrasive demeanor of SCLC's executive secretary, Wyatt Tee Walker. SNCC activists also complained, often with good reason, that while they did the time-consuming and dangerous work that laid the basis for successful local movements, King and SCLC swept onto Southern civil rights battlegrounds at the last minute to capture the attention of the media and the bulk of the financial contributions from sympathetic Northerners.

Most important, SNCC's appellation for King carried a critique of his mode of leadership itself. SNCC was engaged in a brave, democratically motivated attempt to avoid hierarchy and to create a community of equals. It assailed King from this radical-democratic standpoint, fearing leadership from the top and charismatic authority as destructive to democratic movement building. James Forman of SNCC put it simply during the Selma campaign: "We don't believe in leadership." SNCC's critique of King's leadership deserves respectful attention, both where it uncovered weaknesses and where it failed to grasp democratic strengths. It was all the more poignant a critique because SNCC itself could not escape the inherent dilemmas of leadership.[46]

In his autobiography, Forman explained why he had opposed the plan to bring King into the Albany struggle in 1961: "A strong people's movement was in progress, the people were feeling their own strength grow. I knew how much harm could be done by interjecting the Messiah complex—people would feel that only a particular individual could save them and would not move on their own to fight racism and exploitation." SNCC's commitment was to building local "people's movements" throughout the deep South. It hoped to identify and nurture indigenous leaders, who would organize their communities for a protracted struggle against segregation and inequality. To SNCC, when King and SCLC came from outside to take over the freedom struggle in a black community, they undermined the most important resources fueling that struggle. Indigenous leaders were overshadowed and shunted aside by King and his men. Black participants forgot their brief experience of strength and dignity in freeing themselves from submission to white power and were swept up in a new form of dependence on a powerful black leader above them.[47]

According to SNCC, King and SCLC had an agenda incompatible with local movement building. They were using—and, in effect, sacrificing—local communities to capture national media attention. Once King and his organization squeezed all the drama they could out of towns like Albany, St. Augustine, or Selma, they departed, leaving the local movement demoralized and adrift. SCLC left no lasting black organizations at the scenes of its most famous campaigns. To SNCC, this emphasis on national media over indigenous movement represented King's fatal dependence on the good will of distant, unreliable white liberals. SNCC was more suspicious than SCLC of white assistance; the young militants believed that black freedom would have to be won almost exclusively by African Americans themselves. To SNCC activists, "De Lawd" sadly shared the gullibility of the black masses who adored him about the eventual beneficence of white America.

The SNCC critique cut to the heart of King's weaknesses as a charismatic leader. As we have seen, SCLC deliberately selected Southern black communities that offered the most favorable stage for dramatizing injustice and disturbing the complacency of Northern public opinion. Of course, the federal legislation that this strategy sometimes induced was a strong justification for SCLC's approach. Yet the black communities involved often felt exploited and abandoned once SCLC departed for new stages. Further, SCLC's failure to build lasting local organizations retarded black possibilities for capitalizing on the political opening created by the 1965 Voting-Rights Act. By 1967 King had to concede that this part of SNCC's critique was correct:

> In candor and self-criticism it is necessary to acknowledge that the tortuous job of organizing solidly and simultaneously in thousands of places was not a feature of our work. . . . Many civil rights organizations were born as specialists in agitation and dramatic projects; they attracted massive sympathy and support; but they did not assemble and unify the support for new stages of struggle. . . . Support

waxed and waned, and people became conditioned to action in crises but inaction from day to day.[48]

In his final years King also acknowledged that he had been overly dependent on the good will of Northern whites. Responding to the political phenomenon of the "white backlash" against civil rights for blacks, King insisted that it was nothing new: "There has never been a single, solid, determined commitment on the part of white America where genuine equality is concerned for the black people of this nation." Racist brutality had won King the backing of the white majority for equal-accommodations and voting-rights laws. But white support for the black cause fell away after 1965, as King and other civil rights advocates turned to the more explosive agenda of redistributing economic and political power.[49]

While the SNCC critique highlighted the principal flaws in King's leadership, it failed to credit his principal democratic accomplishments as a leader. As SNCC alleged, charisma was potentially dangerous for a democratic movement. Yet the essential question was how King used his own charisma. He did not use it to seek domination over the entire civil rights movement. Advocating "the tireless, creative building of alliances . . . with all democratic minded sections of the population," King always favored a broad and diverse civil rights coalition. If anything, he was not aggressive enough in promoting the place of his own organization within that coalition. Out of deference to the long-established NAACP, SCLC never sought a mass membership. Aware of the jealousies that his national celebrity inspired, King graciously raised funds for the other civil rights groups. If King and SCLC sometimes took advantage of SNCC's unheralded labors for their own media dramas, there were also occasions where SNCC exploited the drawing power of "De Lawd" for its own purposes.[50]

A modest man (despite his moments of grandiosity), plagued by guilt over his fame, King never sought to employ his charismatic appeal for the purpose of dominating followers. Instead, he used it to draw them into a mass struggle, in which they could participate fully and grow in self-respect and democratic dignity. As Aldon Morris writes:

> King could attract large segments of oppressed blacks from the poolrooms, city streets, and backwoods long enough for trained organizers to acquaint them with the workshops, demands, and strategies of the movement. Blacks would come from near and far to get a glimpse of King and to hear him speak. Once exposed to the organizational activities of the movement, the chance was greater that

they too would soon be boycotting, . . . singing movement songs, and creating political leverage by fostering social disruption. What resulted was the "collective power of masses."[51]

King asked a great deal of those who would be his followers. His effectiveness as a leader depended on the choices ordinary blacks made to practice his nonviolent approach and to emulate his readiness to suffer. If they were not prepared to go out into the streets under the banner of nonviolent self-discipline, or even more daringly, to go to jail, his power would be exposed as hollow. King's followers were not called heedlessly to accompany a charismatic leader into peril; they were asked to confront the difficult decision to risk themselves for their own liberation.

The SNCC image of "De Lawd" thus distorted King's style of leadership. His was not the spectacle of heroic leadership, in which an active leader presents himself before a passive mass as their surrogate and savior. Rather, King produced a collective drama, in which leaders and followers shared in commitments, risks, losses, and triumphs. King's democratic modesty was apparent even to some of the SNCC militants when they finally saw "De Lawd" up close. During the Mississippi march against fear in 1966, Cleveland Sellers of SNCC was surprised to discover that the cardboard saint he was accustomed to deride turned out to be friendly, good-humored, and open to the young militants. SNCC's fear of leadership had blinded it to the democratic possibilities that King's leadership exemplified.[52]

Indeed, SNCC's antileadership bias trapped the young radical democrats in a series of conundrums that plagued the organization. Although its philosophy called for bottom-up mobilization rather than top-down leadership, the approach to the grass roots depended heavily on local, indigenous *leaders*. SNCC was often successful in identifying and training these local leaders. Yet local leaders, Clayborne Carson observes, often had "more pragmatic concerns" than the SNCC organizers who had recruited them. While increasingly angry and alienated SNCC cadres moved toward the stance of self-proclaimed revolutionaries, local leaders were often more interested in concrete improvements for their communities. Even worse from SNCC's standpoint, the attempt to establish indigenous leadership as the alternative to King's top-down leadership was sometimes subverted by the local leaders themselves. It was indigenous leaders in Albany, Birmingham, St. Augustine, and Selma who invited King and SCLC to enter their cities and lead their movements.[53]

That King had to defend his mode of leadership against the young militants strengthened him in the end. Barbs about "De Lawd" bothered the sensitive King. Criticisms from the brave activists who spent more time on the firing line and in jail than he had raised inner doubts about his own courage. But King did not turn away from his SNCC critics. With an openness and tolerance that impressed his SNCC detractors, he listened to them in gripe sessions and promised to redress their complaints. Humility and a nonviolent democratic character helped King to enter into a dialogue with his radical-democratic critics; so, too, did his awareness that the young activists of SNCC had something to teach him. Vincent Harding has noted of the relationship between SNCC and King that "they helped radicalize him, helped keep him pressed against the hard and jagged edges of the struggle." If SNCC, in conjuring up the figure of "De Lawd," failed to credit the democratic bearing of King as a leader, they deserve some credit for contributing to that democratic bearing.[54]

Chicago

In March 1968 King was recruiting in the deep South for SCLC's upcoming Poor People's Campaign in Washington, D.C. Speaking to a group of impoverished rural blacks in Clarksdale, Mississippi, he candidly warned of what awaited them if they journeyed North to protest economic injustice:

> I've been up North, you don't know how to deal with it, because . . . you can't quite get your target. He'll sit up there and smile in your face. You go down to see the official and they'll serve you cookies and tea, and shake your hand and pose for a picture with you. And at the same time, keeping Negroes in ghettoes and slums.

King's main experience "up North" had been the failed Chicago Freedom Movement of 1966. The experience revealed to him as well as to others his limitations as a political man. But the deeper and more disturbing failures of the Chicago campaign owed less to King than to the forces that defeated him. Chicago sent King crashing up against the limitations of dissenting leadership in America.[55]

King and SCLC had to move North. By the time of the Selma voting-rights campaign early in 1965, it was as apparent to them as to many others that the civil rights victories in the South had brought heightened aspirations but no genuine improvements to the black masses of the Northern ghettoes. The Northern ghetto riots during the summer of 1964 punctuated the point, but it was the Watts riot in

August 1965, hard on the heels of presidential signing of the Voting-Rights Act, that shook King the most. He was moved by the anguished cries of the Watts rioters—and fearful that their turn to violence presaged the end of the nonviolent phase in the black struggle for freedom. So King and SCLC turned their focus to the North, the ghetto, the economic problems of exploitation and poverty. The move, King wrote in the fall of 1965, was fated: "The rushing history of change has been late to reach the North but it is now on a fixed northerly course. The urban slums need not be destroyed by flames; earnest people of good will can decree their end nonviolently—as atrocious relics of a persisting unjust past."[56]

Andrew Young emphasized to his colleagues in SCLC that the opponents they would face in the North were "more sophisticated and subtle" than the blundering Southern cops whose flagrant brutality had played into the hands of the movement. Yet if SCLC entered Chicago, to which it had been invited by a local civil rights coalition, with its eyes at least partly open, the daunting immensity of the city's population and problems seemed to generate a compensatory need for extravagant visions. Thus, James Bevel, the principal SCLC organizer in Chicago, reported to King in October 1965 that "our task is not to patch up the ghetto, but to abolish it." When King officially kicked off the Chicago Freedom Movement in January 1966, his agenda was equally sweeping: "Our primary objective will be to bring about the unconditional surrender of forces dedicated to the creation and maintenance of slums." King and SCLC hoped to use Chicago, like Selma, to shake the nation. SCLC's battle plan for Chicago characterized the city as "the prototype of the northern urban race problem." Dramatizing the evils of the ghetto in Chicago was expected to create pressure for federal action, including "comprehensive legislation which would meet the problems of slum life across this nation."[57]

SCLC's initial focus in Chicago was on organizing the population of the black ghetto into a nonviolent army that could be deployed against slum conditions. According to its battle plan, it hoped separately to mobilize African American ministers, high school and college students, tenants of slum apartments, the unemployed, and even the youth gangs and then unite them into an unstoppable force for change. Small-scale demonstrations, designed to "reveal the agents of exploitation," would build confidence and enthusiasm and lead toward "the phases of massive action." What these phases might be necessarily remained vague: "Just as no one knew on January 2, 1965, that there would be a march from Selma to Montgomery by March of that year, so now we are in no position to know what form massive action might take in Chicago."[58]

Events did not develop in accordance with SCLC's strategy. Under-staffed from the start, the organizing campaign ran up against not only the apathy and social disorganization of the vast ghetto but also the competitive resources of Mayor Richard J. Daley and his legendary political machine. When King and his SCLC lieutenants attempted to dramatize the horrors of the slums, Daley countered with his own dramatic gestures of amelioration. Alan B. Anderson and George W. Pickering, authors of the most comprehensive study of the Chicago Freedom Movement, describe some of the mayor's ploys:

> He promised to end slums himself by 1968 and invited King to join with him in this effort. Daley turned every wheel of his machine to neutralize the issue and its constituency. A hundred building inspectors were dispatched to the West Side. The Welfare Department suspended rent payments to forty owners of slum buildings. A rat control program was introduced. Garbage collections were doubled.[59]

Frustrated in their efforts to organize the ghetto, SCLC and its local allies switched to a strategy of trying to break out of it. By the summer of 1966 the official goal of the Chicago Freedom Movement had become the "Open City." The movement now sought to dramatize the practices of housing discrimination that kept blacks confined to an inner city, where they paid exorbitant rents and food prices and were distant from the job opportunities they needed. In reality, the Open City approach, even if successful, was likely to help only a minority of ghetto dwellers in the immediate future. But after a riot erupted in the black West Side neighborhoods on July 12, with King powerless to calm it, he was increasingly desperate to win *something* in Chicago through nonviolent action. Announcing plans for open-housing marches into all-white neighborhoods, he made a plaintive cry to Chicago's white establishment that the future of nonviolent social change—and of his own leadership as the alternative to violent extremists—was at stake: "I need help. I need some victories; I need some concessions."[60]

When the Chicago Freedom Movement began its marches into the white ethnic neighborhood of Gage Park–Chicago Lawn at the end of July, it hoped to dramatize how a discriminatory real-estate market trapped the black population in the slums. Unlike in Selma, however, SCLC had not counted on a violent white reaction in Chicago—and was stunned by the ferocity of its reception. Recalling what happened in Gage Park, Andrew Young observed: "The violence in the South always came from a rabble element. But these were women and children and husbands and wives coming out of their homes becoming a mob—and in some ways it was far more frightening." The mob stoned nuns and cheered when they were knocked to the ground, spat upon any demonstrator it could get near, and screamed that the white participants in the march were communists, sexual perverts, and "white niggers." One of these white participants captured a particularly chilling scene: "Boys wearing Catholic high school football jerseys pranced along the curb opposite us carrying an oversized noose and chanting: 'I'd love to be an Alabama trooper / That is what I'd really like to be / For if I were an Alabama trooper / Then I could hang a nigger legally.'" Refusing to be intimidated, the civil rights forces continued the marches under police protection. When King arrived to lead another foray into Gage Park, he was almost immediately felled by a large rock; regaining his feet, he resumed the march to chants of "Get the witch doctor" and "Kill him." He commented afterward: "I've been in many demonstrations all across the South, but I can say that I have never seen—even in Mississippi and Alabama—mobs as hostile and as hate-filled as I've seen in Chicago."[61]

By evoking such violence, nonviolent protest in Chicago created a civic crisis, forcing white economic and political elites to come to the bargaining table with the Chicago Freedom Movement. The economic elites were disturbed by the unfavorable national publicity; Mayor Daley was perhaps more worried by the threat to his machine from ethnic voters angry that he had not kept the marchers away from their doorsteps. Yet if the "hate-filled" mob of Gage Park–Chicago Lawn served, in this sense, as the functional equivalent of "Bull" Connor's or Jim Clark's brutal troops, there was also an ominous difference in Chicago. King had been able to interpret the resistance of Southern segregationists as the violent spasms of a dying social order. But the Gage Park mob exposed a bedrock white racism that showed no sign of eroding. (In retrospect, it is evident just how prophetic the bigotry in Gage Park proved to be.) In their frenzied defense of property values, neighborhoods, low self-esteem, the working-class, ethnic mob was voicing the fears of huge numbers of Northern whites. Their violence aided the civil rights movement for the moment; their representativeness, as the explosive emblem of the "white backlash," spelled political weakness for the Chicago Freedom Movement on a more fundamental level.[62]

If white resistance in Chicago was more powerful than any King and SCLC had encountered in the South, black support was more frail. In the South, King had mobilized a significant segment of the black population in his local campaigns. But in Chicago the black masses were not behind King. As Kathleen Connolly notes, "King had not succeeded in channeling the indignation of poor Negroes into a political organization. In fact, the inroads of his organization into the black ghetto were embarrassingly unsuccessful, especially because this fact was known to City Hall." The open-housing marches failed to appeal to ghetto residents, most of whom had neither the economic means nor the personal desire to move to white neighborhoods. At their height, the marches attracted fifteen hundred participants, half of them white. An estimated 80 percent of the black marchers were middle class.[63]

The "summit negotiations" produced by the violence in the white neighborhoods brought together the mayor, leaders of the Chicago business community, representatives of the realtors, religious leaders, and other influential whites with the Chicago Freedom Movement. In the two summit sessions, King was both forceful and conciliatory, a goad to white action and a bridge to white conscience. One of his strongest moments came in response to the argument of the realtors that they were merely agents for sellers and thus powerless to overcome discriminatory instructions. King retorted to the realtors: "You are men confronted with a moral issue. . . . People will adjust to changes but the leadership has got to say that the time for change has come. The problem is not the people in Gage Park, the problem is that their leaders and institutions have taught them to be what they are." What King was asking of the realtors in Chicago was what he was asking of white leadership in general as the depths of America's racial dilemma became increasingly manifest. The realtors would not be the only white leaders who no longer wished to hear him.[64]

With the city desperate to stop the marches, and the Chicago Freedom Movement close to the end of its limited resources, a "summit agreement" was reached on August 26, 1966. Suppressing his misgivings, King hailed the open-housing pact as a victory for nonviolent protest in the North. But the agreement was vague and porous, substituting pledges of good faith action for the specific timetable of implementation that some in the Chicago Freedom Movement had demanded. The civil rights militants who scoffed at the agreement as paper promises were soon proved correct. The city and the realtors dragged their feet after the agreement, and housing segregation continued as before. The civil rights movement in Chicago sank into demoralization and confusion. In the spring of 1967 Mayor Daley was reelected in a landslide, while the Chicago Freedom Movement, denouncing its betrayal at the hands of the white elite, faded from view.[65]

The false victory of the open-housing pact and the palpable defeat that attended its nonimplementation suggest that King and SCLC seriously underestimated what they were facing in Chicago. The problems of the Northern ghetto were vaster and more intractable than the system of segregation that they had defeated in the South. White hostility to integration had greater political strength; black enthusiasm for integration was substantially weaker. Deep structural forces stymied King in Chicago. But he was also defeated by specific political leaders. Foremost among them was the machine politician who out-maneuvered the moral politician. "Like Herod," Ralph Abernathy wrote in his autobiography, "Richard Daley was a fox, too smart for us, too smart for the press, too smart for the white leaders who sat in the room and signed the agreement in good faith, too smart to give any credence to dreams, too smart for his own good and for the good of Chicago. He was the essential politician of our time."[66]

Mayor Daley's silent accomplice was President Lyndon Johnson. The end result of the campaign in Chicago, in the thinking of King and his organization, was to be federal action against the slums. Action by the federal government had, in fact, been the key to King's major victories in the past: a U.S. Supreme Court decision in the case of Montgomery, presidential proposals for civil rights legislation after Birmingham and Selma. But King and SCLC badly miscalculated in expecting to use Chicago to force the federal government to the side of massive changes in urban America. Not only was President Johnson preoccupied with Vietnam (and furious with King for his still-muted opposition to the war); he was in addition closely allied with Mayor Daley and sensitive to the growing white political backlash. King and SCLC had seized propitious political moments in Birmingham and Selma, and won over national leaders to their terms. In Chicago, the moment was no longer theirs for the seizing.

King went North to demonstrate that his method of nonviolence—and his leadership—were relevant to the next stage of black liberation after the accomplishment of civil rights. Chicago cast doubt on both his nonviolent approach and his leadership abilities. With the triumph in Selma in the spring of 1965, King had appeared at the apex of his influence as a dissenting leader; a year and a half later, with the evident failure of the Chicago "summit agreement," he had to contend with a growing chorus of both black and white voices intoning that his day was over. Ralph Abernathy wrote of Chicago: "It was an embittering experience, and I'm not sure that Martin ever got over it." After Chicago, there was a new edge—and a scarred wisdom—to King's leadership.[67]

"Hellhound on My Trail"

In the year and a half left to him after the defeat in Chicago, King was progressively marginalized as a leader by a society that he felt increasingly powerless to change. The choices he made during this period—to condemn the war in Vietnam, to elaborate a radical critique of American society, to push the problem of poverty upon an indifferent nation—were politically damaging to him. But they were morally right and prophetically apt. In failure as well as in success, King remained true to his vocation as a dissenting leader. The price he paid for this integrity was immense. At the end, he was a weary, haunted figure, living out the eerie lyrics of Robert Johnson, the great Mississippi Delta bluesman: "I got to keep moving, / Blues falling down like hail, / And the days keep on 'minding me / There's a hellhound on my trail."[68]

King had tangled only indirectly with President Johnson in Chicago, but eventually he had to confront the power of the presidency over the war in Vietnam. When Johnson escalated the war early in 1965, King was distressed by the increasing violence and repeatedly called for a negotiated peace settlement. He muted his criticisms in September 1965, however, in the face of mounting opposition from within the civil rights movement and pressure from the Johnson administration. As a political man, King was concerned to protect his fund-raising capacity among white liberals, his alliance with more conservative civil rights groups, his access to the White House. But as he held back from fully voicing his feelings about Vietnam over the next year and a half, his moral anguish festered. What finally pushed him to speak out in the spring of 1967, he told his colleagues in SCLC, was a magazine story featuring photos of Vietnamese children burned by American napalm. With Birmingham and Selma, King had been able to combine morality and political pragmatism; Vietnam finally forced him to choose morality over politics. A dissenting leader who had come to appreciate and utilize many of the insights of the democratic politician, King never forgot the fundamental disparity between these two types of leadership.[69]

When King came out strongly against the war in Vietnam in a series of speeches, climaxed by his well-publicized address at the Riverside Church in New York on April 4, 1967, he set off a firestorm of criticism. Much of the media, including the *New York Times* and the *Washington Post*, lambasted him for reckless comments on the war that tarnished his stature and thereby harmed the cause of civil rights. Conservative black leaders repudiated his position. The White House, seething, arranged for a black surrogate, Carl Rowan, to rip him in print. King was taken aback by the vehemence of the response, but he was unrepentant about his decision to break his silence. "I was politically unwise but morally wise," he argued to Stanley Levison in defense of his Riverside Church speech. To a SCLC staff retreat in May, he explained how his new stance on Vietnam was another inescapable moment in his life's mission:

> When I took up the cross I recognized its meaning. . . . The cross is something that you bear and ultimately that you die on. The cross may mean the death of your popularity. It may mean the death of your bridge to the White House. It may mean the death of a foundation grant. It may cut your budget down a little, but take up your cross and just bear it. And that is the way I have decided to go. Come what may, it doesn't matter now.[70]

Once King chose morality, he chose to be bravely impolitic about the war, in a way that no professional politician would dare. Most American political leaders have demonized the nation's wartime enemies; King humanized them. As he had first sought to be a public voice for his own people back in Montgomery, now he assumed a larger responsibility: "We are called to speak for the weak, for the voiceless, for victims of our nation and for those it calls enemy, for no document from human hands can make these humans any less our brothers." King tried to show to Americans a human visage in "that strangely anonymous group we call VC or Communists." He tried to strip from them the appearance of evil and to place their deeds in the context of American actions: "Surely we must understand their feelings even if we do not condone their actions. Surely we must see that the men we supported pressed them to their violence. Surely we must see that our own computerized plans of destruction simply dwarf their greatest acts."[71]

King was equally impolitic and brave in refusing to treat the war in Vietnam as an aberration in an otherwise beneficent American foreign policy. The Vietnam War, he insisted, was "but a symptom of a far deeper malady within the American spirit": imperialism. Needing "to maintain social stability for our investments" in the Third World, the United States was placing itself "on the wrong side of a world revolution." Forgetting their revolutionary heritage, American foreign policymakers pursued overseas profits at the expense of impoverished, nonwhite peoples. Vietnam demonstrated how far they would go to preserve this imperial system. In a line sure to produce an apoplexy in the White House, King assailed "the greatest purveyor of violence in the world today—my own government."[72]

Knowing that he was cutting all remaining ties to the White House by excoriating the war in this fashion, King steeled himself to cross swords with Lyndon Johnson. Speaking privately to his SCLC colleagues, his moral vocation took on the edge of personal conflict: "I'm not gonna allow Mr. Johnson to destroy the soul of the nation." In public settings, he swiped at the president by contrasting Johnson's self-proclaimed "consensus" leadership with King's own dissenting brand. "I'm not a consensus leader," King orated in what became one of his oft-repeated passages. "I do not determine what is right and wrong by looking at the budget of the Southern Christian Leadership Conference or by taking a Gallup Poll of the majority opinion. Ultimately, a genuine leader is not a searcher for consensus but a molder of consensus."[73]

Yet King could not be altogether comfortable asserting his personal moral superiority, even in the face of Johnson's war in Vietnam. In June 1967, amid his mounting denunciations of the president and the war, he delivered a sermon at his own Ebenezer Baptist Church in Atlanta on "Judging Others." As had Lincoln in his second inaugural address, King turned to the scriptural admonition: "Judge not that ye be not judged." He told his congregation that "in criticizing another, Jesus is saying, you'd better be careful, because in the process you are probably criticizing yourself." There was another danger in the posture of judgment, one particularly threatening to King's personal philosophy: "Judging others widens the gulf which Christian love should bridge." Preaching to his flock, King was reminding himself to balance his fierce commitment to end the war with compassion toward those whom he had to oppose.[74]

Balancing righteousness with humility, and anger with sorrow, King joined the ranks of American radicalism that the war was swelling. In 1964 he had depicted the civil rights struggle as "a revolution, not to liquidate the structure of America, but a revolution to get into the mainstream of American life." Chicago and Vietnam signaled to King that this mainstream was not the good society into which he and his people ought to be integrated. Speaking before a "New Politics" convocation of radicals in Chicago in August 1967, he recast the apocalyptic rhetoric of the New Left into the more traditional form of the Christian jeremiad:

> We have come here because we share a common concern for the moral health of our nation. We have come because our eyes have seen through the superficial glory and glitter of our society and observed the coming of Judgment. Like the prophets of old, we have read the handwriting on the wall.

It was no longer enough, King now insisted, to demand that the nation live up to its own rules. Those rules had to be changed; America had to undertake "a revolution of values."[75]

The moral evils that must be overcome, King stressed, were the intertwined trio of "racism, economic exploitation, and militarism."
These were sins too deep to be reformed: "What America must be
told today is that she must be born again. The whole structure of
American life must be changed." King called for "a radical redistribution of economic and political power." Racism would persist so long
as integration was understood as the inclusion of a few blacks in
white-dominated structures. "Integration in its true dimensions,"
King now argued, "is shared power." Economic exploitation and militarism would persist so long as American capitalism was not supplanted by a more humane and just political economy. Fearful of
being labeled a communist, King spoke gingerly before the public
about a new economic system, depicting it as "a socially conscious
democracy which reconciles the truths of individualism and collec-
tivism." Before his SCLC staff, he was more forthright: "We are
treading again in very difficult waters, because . . . we are saying that
something is wrong with the economic system of our nation. . . .
Something is wrong with capitalism. . . . There must be a better distribution of wealth, and maybe America must move toward a democratic socialism."[76]

King's radicalism was somewhat overshadowed by the more colorful and inflammatory rhetoric of the New Left and of black power in
the late 1960s. In reality, his radical vision shared much with the
white and black militants of his era. Yet it differed in two critical respects. While the white New Left and the black militants of SNCC and
its offspring were moving from a hopeful crusade for participatory
democracy to a despairing fantasy of guerrilla warfare against the
state, King held on to his commitment to nonviolence. And while
SNCC and other militant black organizations expelled their longtime
white activists and adopted a platform of black separatism, King refused to relinquish his dream of an interracial community. Wiser after
Chicago about the depth and intransigence of white racism, he
nonetheless delivered an emotional plea to his SCLC colleagues in November 1966 that they not give up on white America:

> In the final analysis there is no separate black path to power and
> fulfillment that does not intersect white roots. And there is no sepa-
> rate white path to power and fulfillment short of social disaster that
> does not share that power with black aspirations for freedom and
> human dignity. We are tied together. And in some strange way every
> Negro is a little white, and every white man is a little Negro. Our
> music, our cultural patterns, our material prosperity, our language,
> and even our food are an amalgam of black and white. And we have

come too far down the path now to turn back. There have been too many hymns of hope, too many anthems of expectation, too many deaths, too many dark days of standing over graves of those who fought for integration for us to turn back now. We must still sing: Black and white together, We shall overcome.[77]

As American society polarized along racial lines, King pursued his final dream of an interracial coalition of the poor. He had been deeply affected by the suffering he had witnessed in the rural South and the urban North. He had been touched, too, by the violent cries of ghetto rioters. King opposed their actions but listened to the pain and frustration that those actions expressed. Attuned to the voices of the rioters, he sought to give them a nonviolent translation and to "transmute the inchoate rage of the ghetto into a creative and constructive force." Reaching out to other minorities and to the white poor as well, King planned to bring representatives from every quarter of "the other America" to Washington, D.C., to bring the comfortable, affluent America face-to-face with its sins.[78]

Overriding the skepticism of many within SCLC, King threw himself almost desperately into preparations for the Poor People's Campaign, scheduled for the spring of 1968. His strategy was to bring three thousand poor people, from five rural and ten urban areas, to the nation's capital, to dramatize the problem of poverty and to pressure the federal government to take remedial action. King spoke of massive demonstrations, along the lines of Birmingham and Selma, that would disrupt national business until the poor had been heard. The campaign, he said in January 1968, "must be militant enough, assertive enough, aggressive enough to be as attention getting and dramatic as a riot, without destroying life or property in the process." Despite the bold words, however, the campaign's goals and tactics remained vague. Under pressure to scale down his plans, King eventually shifted from the radical tactic of seizing the streets to the more moderate tactic of constructing an encampment of the poor on the doorstep of the powerful.[79]

King knew that the political odds had shifted against him since Selma. "When we were struggling in Alabama," he reminded his SCLC associates in a planning session for the Poor People's Campaign,

it was often the federal government that came to our aid to restrain the brutality and the recalcitrance of local [and] state government. . . . In this instance, we will be confronting the very government, and the very federal machinery that has often come in as our aid. . . . The problem cannot be solved without a radical reordering

of national priorities. . . . I say all of these things because I want us
to know the hardness of the task.

Having failed to overcome economic injustice with the power of nonviolence in Chicago, King was gambling that he could accomplish it at
the national level. The gamble was based more on hope than on a calculation of political prospects. He was running mostly on hope now—
hope pitched over a widening despair.[80]

The despair of King's final year was the natural reaction of a man
whose path is blocked and whose enemies are gaining on him. After
his defeat in Chicago and his denunciation of the war in Vietnam,
David Lewis points out, there was "an open hunting season on Martin
King and the nonviolent movement." With black militants and white
leftists proclaiming his philosophy passé, with former liberal allies re-
proaching him for his break with the Johnson administration, King
felt increasingly isolated. He still had many admirers, black and
white, but they could not come close to matching the power of his enemies. At the White House, he was the target of vituperation and contempt. Presidential aide John Roche wrote in a memo to Johnson that
in coming out against the war, an "inordinately ambitious and quite
stupid" King had "thrown in with the commies." At the FBI, the smol-
dering desire of J. Edgar Hoover to discredit and destroy King took on
a fresh impetus. After King had announced plans for the Poor People's
Campaign, the Bureau circulated a new report to top federal officials
on King's alleged communist connections and sexual "aberrations."[81]

Committed to a religious vocation that he could not escape, doubtful that he could effect further change in the face of such furious opposition and such intractable social ills, King suffered several bouts of
depression during the last year of his life. Leadership had become an
endless ordeal to him. Andrew Young, who accompanied King on
many of his travels during these months, witnessed his anguish: "He
talked about death all the time. . . . He couldn't relax, he couldn't
sleep. . . . He was spiritually exhausted." King's friends were unable to
ease his despondency, as he drove himself on through an act of will
and faith.[82]

"As early as 1906," King stated in August 1967, "W. E. B. Du Bois
prophesied that the problem of the twentieth century will be the problem of the color line. Now as we stand two-thirds into this crucial period of history, we know full well that racism is still that hound of hell
which dogs the tracks of our civilization." In his final year, King's answer to "the problem of the color line" was no longer heard by the
angry proponents of repression on the one side and armed revolution
on the other. His enemies were on his trail, and he could sense that he

was nearing his end. Yet if this heartsick King is a sad figure to recall, he is also, in his refusal to abandon hope, moving and magnificent. Perhaps it is the King of his final year, in his tragic, aborted search for a democratic answer to America's most cruel dilemmas, who is the King Americans most need to understand and to honor.[83]

Conclusion

Departing Atlanta on April 3, 1968, for Memphis, where he was to lead a march of striking black garbage collectors and their supporters, King was delayed by a bomb threat. The experience seemed to trigger the emotional ending to his speech in Memphis that night:

> Well, I don't know what will happen now. We've got some difficult days ahead. But it doesn't matter with me now. Because I've been to the mountaintop. And I don't mind. Like anybody, I would like to live a long life. Longevity has its place. But I'm not concerned about that now. I just want to do God's will. And He's allowed me to go up to the mountain. And I've looked over. And I've seen the promised land. I may not get there with you. But I want you to know tonight, that we, as a people, will get to the promised land. And I'm happy, tonight. I'm not worried about anything. I'm not fearing any man. Mine eyes have seen the glory of the coming of the Lord.

After King's assassination the next day, these words became famous as his haunting prophecy of his own martyrdom. Seldom noted about the passage was the part of the prophecy that did not come true: for the majority of King's people, the promised land receded after his death.[84]

If American history did not parallel the Scriptures, if King could not, in the end, be a black Moses, his public career still offers one of the richest and most compelling images of leadership that Americans possess. There are many paths to leadership, and King's was one of the most unusual. An accidental leader, a minister as politician, a guilt-ridden drum major, King felt called to his public role by God, who consoled him but also demanded everything he could give. Beginning his career as a privileged member of his race, he found communion with the mass of ordinary blacks and merged his more educated voice with theirs to shape freedom songs that expressed the deepest of his people's—and America's—democratic longings. Practicing what he preached, he became a nonviolent man and a democratic character, tolerant of those who disappointed him, open to those who disagreed with him. King knew the burden and pain of leading the struggle of the most cruelly excluded and exploited of Americans. He also knew the exaltation.

King is especially instructive for practitioners of dissenting leadership. Eschewing electoral politics, he explored the potential of democratic change through nonviolent direct action. But the rejection of conventional politics did not lead King to a rejection of political prudence. He and his associates learned from their failures what it would take to move the political order. They staged artful dramas of white violence and black victimization that gripped public attention and forced the hand of cautious politicians in the White House. As the young militants of SNCC correctly charged, these dramas did not build lasting political organizations in the black community. But SNCC was in error in deriding these dramas as vehicles fit only for a star. Unlike a heroic leader such as Theodore Roosevelt or John Kennedy, King was intent on collective drama, on the story of black people displaying their dignity and their courage to a white majority who had never before really seen them. Montgomery, Birmingham, and Selma were democratic triumphs for a movement, not mere personal victories for King.

Although King knew how to unite moral vision and political craft, he also knew when political pragmatism had to stop. The war in Vietnam ate at him as he tried to maintain his crumbling position within the political mainstream. Recognizing that the cost to his integrity was too great, he went into opposition in the spring of 1967, denouncing the war in the most impolitic terms. In this move, he was true to his vocation as a dissenting leader, even as it took him toward an increasingly pessimistic radicalism. Dissenting leadership in America has to be concerned with the question of political effectiveness, but its ultimate standard must be the demands of its democratic vision. By this standard, King's bleak final years are as impressive as his years of success.

King's successes showed how much dissenting leadership and democratic movements could accomplish to move the nation closer to its democratic values. His failures showed how far "the soul of America" was from democratic redemption. Not only his "freedom songs," but his life and leadership as well, speak to Americans in the most profound democratic terms of what our redemption still requires of us.[85]

Democracy and
Leadership in America

The Terms of American Political Leadership

T HIS BOOK HAS EXAMINED NINE ICONS OF DEMOCRACY IN AMERICA,
seeking to read from their stories the possibilities, limitations,
and dangers of American political leadership. Running
throughout the book has been an argument directed simultaneously
at the elitist and the radical democratic views of leadership. American
devotees of leadership have trusted the nation's political salvation to
the hands of a leadership elite, while treating followers as a secondary
and inferior lot. Radical democrats have feared leadership as inherently destructive to democracy and have counted instead on the enthusiastic and capable efforts of leaderless equals. Against both of
these perspectives, I have looked for American leadership that, while
never free of tension with democratic principles and values, still nur-
tures and serves democratic possibilities.

If we recur to Richard Nixon's distinction between leaders and followers, we find the essence of the elitist perspective: active and strong-
willed leaders guide passive and wishful followers. This distinction is
seldom drawn so blatantly, with so little regard for democratic conventions, but it captures one of the most powerful and enduring

American traditions of leadership. As we have seen, Alexander Hamilton projected himself as the model of the aristocratic statesman, who would lead the nation with ability and strength and bring power and prosperity to a people otherwise given to a disordered and fruitless liberty. Adapting Hamilton's conception of leadership to a democratic political culture, his successors, such as Theodore Roosevelt and John F. Kennedy, projected heroic images that allowed the public the pleasures of vicarious participation, while maintaining the reins of power firmly in the hands of the leader and his circle of "a few choice spirits." The Hamiltonian tradition of leadership has produced many moments of splendor, brilliance, and bravery in American history. But these have largely been aristocratic triumphs, glorifying a few while diminishing the many. Threatened by active, questioning citizens, whose unruly demands disrupt the aristocrat's plans, Hamiltonian leaders in a democratic age seek admiring spectators rather than engaged followers. Ironically, it was John Adams, himself an advocate of aristocratic leadership (though in a form different from Hamilton's), who provided a warning against the deleterious impact of this brand of leadership on the virtues of citizenship, insisting that the people "must be taught to reverence themselves, instead of adoring their servants."

While the people should be taught to reverence themselves, they should not be taught to romanticize themselves. A democratic political life of active and committed citizenship is a difficult and often problematic endeavor. Advocates and theoreticians of participatory democracy have rightly called us to take seriously the democratic goal of self-government. They have exposed the costs to dignity and self-development when citizens are redefined as individualistic, nonpolitical consumers of government services and spectators to the adventures of a political elite. Put into practice, however, a pure participatory democracy has often appeared too demanding for most people, as the adherents of the New Left, SNCC, and the early women's movement of the 1960s and 1970s found out to their chagrin. Endless meetings, intrusions on personal life and privacy, and especially the draining but unsuccessful effort to avoid any trace of hierarchy and leadership made democracy in its highest form seem like an unattainable ideal, fit, as Rousseau once suggested, only for the gods.[1]

Committed democrats must confront not only the difficulties in citizen participation but also the limitations of citizens' understanding of the political world. When the scale of public action grew beyond the ward hymned by Jefferson and the township celebrated by Tocqueville, citizens were called to make judgments on matters of which they could have little experience or expertise. In the 1920s Walter Lippmann, perhaps the most penetrating American critic of democratic citizenship, emphasized that most people view the public world through "stereotypes," simplified images that reduce complex realities to manageable but distorted conventionalities of thought. The flow of information has accelerated dramatically since Lippmann wrote, but few would argue that the contemporary media substitute enlightened understanding for stereotyped thinking.[2]

A pessimistic minimalism in democratic thought and practice that focuses on such difficulties scales down expectations and settles for a free voting choice between competing elites. But this approach reinforces all of democracy's maladies. As the contemporary political scene demonstrates, declining citizen participation signals alienation rather than satisfaction. Instead of freeing leaders, in the Hamiltonian mold, for great services to the Republic, it tempts them to self-serving practices, abuses of power, and even corruption. The alternative to both a romanticized ideal and a pessimistic minimalism is a view of democracy as an experimental proposition, always up for grabs, always in the process of reconstruction. In this view, the character and quality of leadership are crucial to democracy's fate.

This book has emphasized that leaders can profoundly affect citizens' capacity to know about public matters, to care about them, to act upon them. Leaders can treat citizens as ignorant, to be excluded from the actual processes of decision making. They can treat them as spectators, to be impressed or entertained. But they can also approach citizens through processes of mutuality and education, as capable of greater ventures in self-government. The American tradition contains some notable instances of this latter kind of leadership: Lincoln's painful reexamination of American history in the second inaugural address, Franklin Roosevelt's exuberant call to a dispirited people to rebuild a "commonwealth," King's challenge to Chicago realtors to face up to their role in promoting racism. King's effort in that case was unavailing, but his words bear repeating as a credo of democratic leadership: "People will adjust to changes but the leadership has got to say that the time for change has come. The problem is not the people in Gage Park, the problem is that their leaders and institutions have taught them to be what they are."

As a young man, Abraham Lincoln had worried that the Founding Fathers, establishing for the first time in modern history "the capability of a people to govern themselves," had already harvested the American "field of glory," leaving only paltry remains for their political heirs. But he underestimated what it would take to maintain the American experiment in self-government, threatened as it perpetually was by the elevation of leadership and the diminution of citizenship.

He underestimated even more what it would take to extend and complete the experiment. Lincoln was right to suggest that American political leaders would always live in the shadow of the Founders. Yet there was much democratic glory still to be won in transforming their essentially aristocratic order into a more egalitarian, inclusive, and democratic polity. That democratic glory deservedly flowed to Lincoln himself in the crisis of the Civil War and to Franklin Roosevelt in the maelstrom of the Great Depression. It belonged as well to leaders who stood outside Lincoln's tradition and demanded its democratic completion, to the likes of Elizabeth Cady Stanton, Eugene V. Debs, and Martin Luther King, Jr.

If democracy is in need of nurturance by leaders committed to democratic values, then how Americans conceptualize leadership becomes all the more important. Unfortunately, the professional students of leadership—the political scientists—turn all too often to the vocabulary of economics in the quest for a more scientific understanding. Thus, Robert Dahl, in his influential *Who Governs?*, depicted the most effective kind of American leader by means of an analogy with the successful businessman in classical capitalist economics: "To the political entrepreneur who has skill and drive, the political system offers unusual opportunities for pyramiding a small amount of initial resources into a sizable political holding." More recently, adherents of rational-choice theory have, with sophisticated mathematics and primitive psychology, elaborated on the assumption, to quote Bryan Jones, that "voters are preference revealers" and "politicians are vote maximizers." These theoretical perspectives are not without value for students of democratic leadership, reminding us, for example, that the task of coalition building is one of the most intricate yet indispensable activities of the democratic politician. Yet their increasingly dominant position in academic circles threatens to drive out older and richer vocabularies, to supplant with mathematical formulas the symbols, meanings, and associations of a democratic discourse about American political leadership.[3]

The resources of the American tradition uphold more complex and more democratic conceptions of leadership than are available in theories that employ the classical capitalist market as the master model for politics. Foremost among these resources is the discourse of republicanism. For several decades a debate has been waged among historians and political scientists over whether the American polity was born republican, with a primary emphasis on civic virtue and the common good, or liberal, with primacy given to individual rights and self-interest. This debate shows signs of waning, with the increasing acknowledgment on both sides that both discourses played prominent roles in shaping American politics at its inception. There is little dispute that liberalism has come to dominate our understanding of private life, or that it characterizes most citizens' evaluations of government policies in terms of individual benefits or burdens. Yet liberalism has never been an adequate vocabulary for public life and political leadership in the United States. Even liberal citizens expect republican political leaders, servants of the public good rather than self-serving "utility maximizers."[4]

Classical republican codes of leadership, with their call to talent and virtue placed in the service of the public, continue to operate in the unclassical politics of modern America, even if more as symbol and hope than as reality. Although the standards they set are not often met, they function both as benchmarks for criticism and reminders of what American leadership has been at its best. At the time of the founding, classical republicanism was largely aristocratic in tone, assuming that the distance between leaders and followers should be great. Popularized, even radicalized by later leaders, however, the discourse of republicanism now can encompass a democratic dialogue between leaders and followers. The amalgam of republican codes of leadership and democratic expectations for citizenship is evident in Franklin Roosevelt's statement that "the greatest duty of a statesman is to educate." In the hands of a Lincoln, Stanton, Debs, Franklin Roosevelt, and King, a democratized discourse of republicanism has been the most fertile of all American languages of leadership.

Other discourses are also available to American leadership to supplement or deepen the discourse of republicanism. For some leaders, a scriptural discourse has been the principal vehicle to call followers to penitence, compassion, and justice. Secular democrats are uncomfortable with the invocation of religious authority in political debate. Yet some of the highest moments in American democratic speech have involved the application of the Scriptures to American political problems: Lincoln's second inaugural address, Franklin Roosevelt's first inaugural address, Martin Luther King, Jr.'s, address at the March on Washington. A religion that proclaims equal dignity and communal responsibility has been one of the most evocative and powerful mediums for democratic and dissenting leadership in America.

American concepts and discourses of leadership can also be enriched by newer modes of thought. Feminism, for example, serves as an important countervailing force to the tendency to regard leadership as a masculine competition for power and mastery. Feminist theorists, Susan Carroll observes, approach leadership in terms of "supportive and cooperative relationships rather than relationships based on domination." They emphasize how leaders, by listening to and nurturing followers, can empower them. This book has suggested that the best American leadership has always had a "feminine" side, even when the terms through which this side was expressed were not drawn from the conventions of gender. The best American leaders have not slighted the realities of power but have understood the tasks of leadership as demanding the empowerment of a democratic people.[5]

Types of American Political Leadership

Leadership in the American tradition has assumed a number of distinctive forms. I have presented four types of American political leadership: aristocratic, democratic, heroic, and dissenting. A review of the four types and their historical exemplars will show how they illuminate the range of leadership possibilities within the American political context.[6]

The prevalent type of leadership developed by the Founders was aristocratic. Leaders were viewed as an elite superior to the people in talent and wisdom, charged with the responsibility of guiding the Republic toward a higher public good. Alexander Hamilton and John Adams propounded differing, indeed rival, versions of aristocratic leadership. Hamilton's conception of aristocratic leadership was to have a lasting impact, as later leaders refurbished it with a democratic facade. Adams's conception sank into obscurity, a "lost" classical understanding of republican political leadership.

Central to the aristocratic type was a negative view of popular virtue. Both Hamilton and Adams had entertained grand hopes for civic virtue during the first flush of Revolutionary enthusiasm, only to be disenchanted by the failure of most Americans to measure up to the republican dream. Both turned to a small corps of superior actors, defined by Hamilton as "a few choice spirits" who sought higher ends than the mass of mankind. Hamilton thought that the "ruling passion" of these aristocrats would be "the love of fame." Adams agreed, while exploring much more fully and deeply than Hamilton the political meanings and uses of what he called "the passion for distinction."

Where Hamilton and Adams most diverged was on the relationship of aristocratic leadership to the people. Hamilton thought that the aristocratic leader, driven by a lofty "love of fame," could constitute a system of capitalism that would transmute the avaricious passions of lesser men into economic energy. Adams, as a classical republican, feared the corrupting effects of such an emphasis on wealth. He wanted a republic rich in symbols of public honor rather than a wealthy republic that prized private displays of affluence. The two differed in their fears as well as their hopes: Hamilton dreaded the demagogue who would dismantle the system he was constructing, while Adams feared the dissemblers of merit who would reap public honors through imposture and manipulation rather than through talent and virtue. Both men saw the executive as the central player in the American political order—but Hamilton's executive was an energetic actor who promoted national prosperity and imperial expansion, whereas Adams's executive was a mediating figure who opposed empire as fatal to republican values.

Although Hamilton's historical importance for American leadership is undeniably greater than that of Adams, it is Adams's ideas, I have suggested, that are the more instructive for proponents of democratic leadership. More than any other American thinker, Adams explored in depth the possibilities of a political leadership actuated by public motives and resistant to the temptations of private desire that proved so potent in a capitalist political economy—not only the temptation of monetary corruption but also the temptation of personal ambition indifferent to public values. Yet he failed utterly in his campaign for public honors that would foster higher public motives. His effort was bound to fail in the aristocratic terms that he employed, because the American people could not respect a lofty sphere of public action so condescending toward their own activities and aspirations.

In the nineteenth century the American republic developed a political culture that made possible a second type of leadership. Recapturing a faith in the potential for popular virtue, democratic leadership emphasizes mutuality in place of superiority, education in place of dominance. That "passion for distinction" that Adams explored becomes a legitimate motive for individuals from the humblest of circumstances. Yet this passion demands a democratic disciplining, a commitment to democratic ends and causes. That ego can be both served and democratically tempered is apparent in Lincoln's antislavery campaign and in Franklin Roosevelt's identification with the Jeffersonian masses.

Democratic leadership involves a difficult balance between closeness to the people and a political education that may challenge and discomfit the people. Democratic leaders respect and identify with followers, opening themselves to followers' grievances, insights, and dreams. Yet they also need to nurture and educate followers, to disrupt their complacency and to shake their stereotypes. The language of democratic leadership is deceptively simple. Speaking in accessible, even homely terms, democratic leaders, like Lincoln in his great wartime speeches and Franklin Roosevelt in his "morality play" for a bewildered people, can draw followers into the depths of democratic experience.

In both their practices and their rhetoric, Lincoln and FDR suggest another characteristic of the democratic leader, what I have termed the balance of masculine/feminine. The typical American politician has been steeped in the conventions of masculinity, but for the politician who would also be a democratic character it is necessary to transcend the conventional American dichotomy of gender qualities. Adept at the processes of power, the democratic leader must also be concerned about the processes of empowerment. Skilled at political maneuver and stratagem, the democratic leader must also develop the capacity for empathy and care.

At its best, democratic leadership not only serves people's interests but furthers their democratic dignity as well. Democratic leadership must sustain and promote the material well-being of the people. The pursuit of an egalitarian and decent economy is evident in Lincoln's commitment to "the right to rise" and Roosevelt's "economic bill of rights." Yet a leadership that fosters too exclusive a focus on material pleasures cannot nurture democratic public spirit and civic concern.

Even at its best, democratic leadership bears the marks of compromise and lives out the paradoxes of power. Lincoln and FDR were superb educators on many issues, but both shied away from the responsibilities of the most daunting political education when it came to the enduring American dilemma of race. Both also found that the instruments of democratic power entangled them in institutional practices that jeopardized democratic values. Lincoln's wartime violations of civil liberties foreshadowed Roosevelt's even more problematic elaboration of an overweening presidency, a bureaucratic state, and a military leviathan. Even more now than in the nineteenth century, the term "democratic leadership" is inescapably suffused with tension.

This tension is lacking in heroic leadership. Heroic leaders flatter the people, but their shibboleths serve mostly as legitimation of a spectacle that highlights the leader. Theodore Roosevelt proclaimed himself a representative of Lincoln's "plain people," and John Kennedy announced that he would ask Americans what they would do for their country—but behind these democratic disguises, both were neo-Hamiltonians. They harbored a sense of superiority and a desire to guide a public whose instincts and capacities they fundamentally distrusted.

Sharing the democratic leader's "passion for distinction," the heroic leader never submits this passion to a democratic disciplining. The heroic ego is magnified, leaving democratic commitments secondary and opportunistic. Heroic leaders are drawn to, and sometimes obsessed by, proofs of masculinity, regarding politics as an arena suitable only for what the young Eugene Debs labeled "masterful men." As both Theodore Roosevelt and John Kennedy suggest, heroic leaders are contemptuous of those who do not live up to the code of what Roosevelt called "the man in the arena." The masculine/feminine balance appears to the heroic leader as a symptom of weakness and perhaps a mark of effeminacy.

Since the heroic leader wishes to impress the public with the grandeur of his character and exploits, he must engage, to a greater extent than the democratic leader, in the art of image making. His political career revolves around spectacles that construct a larger-than-life persona before an admiring audience. Theodore Roosevelt was a genius at image making; John Kennedy was a manufactured hero whose talents at image making also proved substantial. Modern media make possible the politics of spectacle, with the televised drama of the Kennedy presidency surpassing, in both scope and illusory intimacy, the newspaper saga of Theodore Roosevelt.

Whereas Alexander Hamilton aimed to constitute American capitalism as the instrument for American national power, his heroic heirs have found capitalist elites to be irksome allies. Pursuing personal and national power, Roosevelt and Kennedy needed businessmen to fulfill their plans for economic dynamism. Roosevelt found himself increasingly frustrated by capitalist avarice and moved to install stronger state controls over business; Kennedy was plagued by irrational capitalist anxieties but, feeling himself more constrained by structural factors, had to placate the corporate sector with repeated tokens of affection. A freer field of glory for both heroic leaders was empire. For Roosevelt, American expansion was a test of national character and a bid for enduring fame. To Kennedy, global politics was the arena in which to demonstrate the will and nerve of American leadership. Both leaders called up the uglier side of American politics in their search for imperial glory: brutal wars against nonwhite peoples, the demonization of enemies, the chilling righteousness of power without humility.

At its most appealing, heroic leadership brings color and charm to American politics. But it does not nurture a more democratic public life. Indeed, heroic leaders have seen themselves as the alternative to mobilized masses, the defender of order and progress against democratic frenzy. Theodore Roosevelt aimed to trump, even more than to repress, the political energies of what he regarded as the dangerous classes. In a milder vein, John Kennedy hoped to manage and moderate the emancipatory passions of the civil rights movement. Despite his rhetoric, the heroic leader is not interested in encouraging new ventures in self-government. Instead, he hopes, in the name of the people, personally to monopolize the drama of democratic action.

Breaking monopolies in political life has been a central task of a fourth type of American leadership. To those for whom the model of democratic leadership has been unavailable or has seemed insufficient, dissenting leadership has presented an alternative set c̣ ˌpossibilities. Recognizing that the existing order denies freedom and dignity to the group to which they belong, dissenting leaders seek democracy for their followers rather than office for themselves. More than any other type of American leader, they attend to the unfinished business of democracy. Because they operate on the borders of democratic life, they encounter its most painful and intractable dilemmas.

Dissenting leaders serve as voices for their followers. They vocalize the anguish, passion, and aspirations of those whose oppression has previously gone unheard by the powerful. Thus, we have seen Elizabeth Cady Stanton pioneering a new discourse for women, Eugene V. Debs developing the terms to recapture dignity for working people, Martin Luther King, Jr., elaborating the African American freedom song of deliverance from bondage. In the lives of each of these three, the principal impetus to leadership was the experience of discovering a personal voice. From this experience they recognized a responsibility to spark followers to find their own voices in turn.

Since the leader is both teacher and model, the relationship with followers is most intense in this type of leadership. Dissenting leaders have tried to present to their followers exemplary public lives. Stanton embodied the complex dimensions of a new identity for women. Debs defied the existing order with radical convictions that led him to the federal penitentiary. King transformed himself through the discipline of nonviolence and made his practices as well as his words express racial justice and reconciliation.

There are enormous difficulties and risks in the stance of the dissenting leader. It is not easy to strike the precarious balance between morality and political effectiveness, between the impassioned rejection of injustice and the calculated compromises that advance the welfare of followers. Stanton was awkward at this task and Debs repudiated it altogether; only King saw, at least for a time, how to be the moral politician. Less morally ruffling, but more discouraging, are the obstacles that stand between dissenting leaders and their democratic hopes. Stanton battled for half a century against the resistance of men (and of many women as well) to a public life equally open to both sexes. Debs saw his dream of democratic socialism crumble at the end of his life. King won democratic victories only to learn how limited they were and spent his final days desperately attempting to outrun the hellhounds on his trail.

If we note the anguish of dissenting leadership, we also need to remember its triumphs. Dissenting leaders have been our true subversives and at times our truest democrats. By the subversive uses they have made of dominant discourses, they have exposed the mystifications and equivocations in those discourses, while turning their democratic core against the powers that deny democracy. It is dissenting leadership that most often recovers the radical democratic thrust inherent in the conventional idiom of American political discourse. Reappropriating American political discourse for the excluded, dissenting leaders appropriate political distinction for themselves. Lincoln democratized what John Adams had described as "the passion for distinction," but it was dissenting leadership, bringing glory to women, working people, and African Americans, that most fully revealed the potential for a public life of democratic honors.

The State of American Political Leadership

The early 1990s seem a particularly bleak time for American political leadership. The conditions of contemporary politics appear to militate against the development of leadership. A media politics of sound bites and negative campaigning renders political discourse superficial and sour. Many journalists are more concerned to uncover private peccadilloes than to evaluate political talents or past public service. The decline of political parties has weakened the institutional base for leadership and encouraged the rise of self-made politicians who are aptly captured by the economic term "entrepreneur." An alienated public thus has good reason to complain that there are hardly any impressive leaders left on the political scene.

Laments over the decline of political leadership are, however, an old American story. As we have seen, John Adams, concluding in his old age that America would recapitulate the decline of republican Rome, grumbled that "an aristocracy of wealth, without any check but a democracy of licentiousness, is our curse." Visiting the United States in the 1830s, during the era of Clay, Webster, and Calhoun, Alexis de Tocqueville insisted that "during the last fifty years the race of American statesmen has strangely shrunk." It was not only political aristocrats of the nineteenth century who sniffed at the inferiority of American leadership after the age of the Founders. Attacking the ascendancy of a "power elite" in the 1950s, C. Wright Mills, a radical democrat, sounded remarkably like John Adams: "The men of the higher circles are not representative men; their high position is not a result of moral virtue; their fabulous success is not firmly connected with meritorious ability."[7]

Although contemporary conditions make leadership difficult, Americans can move beyond both cynical complaints about politicians and pious exhortations to statesmanship. We possess a rich and complex tradition, and it includes exemplars of democratic and dissenting leadership that can, with suitable adaptations, still be emulated. In reappropriating the American tradition of leadership, it is crucial that the inherent tension between leadership and democracy be understood. It is tempting to look for a prospective leader who promises the energy, the air of mastery, the heroic spectacle of an Alexander Hamilton, a Theodore Roosevelt, a John Kennedy. But we have more to learn from the likes of John Adams, Abraham Lincoln, and Franklin Roosevelt, and from those dissenting leaders, like Elizabeth Cady Stanton, Eugene V. Debs, and Martin Luther King, Jr., who challenged American democracy to fulfill its deeper promise. The American tradition offers no blueprints for contemporary leadership, but it does offer some clues that are worth pondering. It seems appropriate to end this study with a couple of these clues.

A revival of American political leadership requires the restoration of honor to an American political realm currently mired in cynicism and alienation. Leadership will not regain honor, however, so long as the public is regarded as an ignorant, emotional force to be managed and manipulated. To make public life honorable for leaders, as John Adams wished, it would have to take on a new value for ordinary citizens. Only citizens who value their own political activity—who feel empowered to adopt public ways of addressing shared problems—can today bestow honor on public action in America. The classical "language of signs" that Adams wanted, to stimulate civic action and inspire talented individuals to seek political glory, can be made relevant to American politics, but only if these signs emerge out of a democratic encounter between leaders and active citizens. Greater American leadership rests on fuller American citizenship.

In looking for leaders, Americans should beware of those who equate leadership with power, mastery, and efficiency. Calling for "strong" leaders who can break through political impasses, we neglect those countervailing qualities that must balance strength if leadership is to have democratic effect. The best American leaders in the past have been brave enough to risk the appearance of softness. They have broken with the cultural conventions that define strength as masculine and denigrate nurturing as feminine, and they have demonstrated how the balance of these qualities is the characteristic of both male and female leaders who appreciate democracy's ways. When Americans are asked what qualities they admire in a leader, strength is usually ranked first. Understanding a Lincoln, Stanton, Franklin Roosevelt, or King, they might respond by raising compassion to an equal rank.

It has been our dissenting leaders, especially, who have encountered the formidable impediments to the full democratization of American life. Those leaders who have taken the dreams of American democracy most seriously have had the hardest political course to follow. But from them we learn how far leadership in America can travel. On the borders of democratic life that they explore, the identity of the American people becomes once more a matter for political contestation. Challenging the ruling stereotypes, dissenting leaders make us rethink our capacities as a free and self-governing people. To recollect their visions is to understand how leaders can educate citizens to aspire to Stanton's equality, Debs's dignity, King's love.

N O T E S

INTRODUCTION

1. Thomas Paine, *The Rights of Man* (1792; Baltimore: Penguin Books, 1969), p. 206.

2. Richard Nixon, *Leaders* (New York: Warner Books, 1982), p. 337.

3. Herman Melville, *Moby Dick* (1851; New York: W. W. Norton, 1967), p. 104.

4. James MacGregor Burns, *Leadership* (New York: Harper and Row, 1978), p. 18; Robert C. Tucker, *Politics as Leadership* (Columbia: University of Missouri Press, 1981), p. 15.

5. Robert Bellah et al., *Habits of the Heart* (Berkeley: University of California Press, 1985), p. 292.

6. Although historical research is at the center of this book, political theory also has an important place in it. I have learned a great deal from a number of theoretical approaches; among these are the works on leadership cited above, theories of symbols, signs, and discourses, the "republican" school of American history, and feminist theory. Readers familiar with these theoretical approaches will recognize some of their distinctive concerns in the chapters that follow. Yet I have not wanted the perspectives of political theory to define or prejudge the possibilities or dangers

in American political leadership. Hence, my principal focus and source of theoretical insight remains the materials from American history.

CHAPTER 1

Alexander Hamilton: The Aristocratic Statesman and the Constitution of American Capitalism

The following abbreviations are used in the notes for chapter 1:

FP   Clinton Rossiter, ed., *The Federalist Papers* (New York: New American Library, 1961).

PAH   Harold C. Syrett, ed., *The Papers of Alexander Hamilton* (New York: Columbia University Press, 1961–79).

1. *PAH*, 18, p. 310.
2. *PAH*, 18, p. 329.
3. Some readers may wonder why, in considering the founding era, I focus on the aristocratic leadership of Alexander Hamilton and John Adams rather than on the more democratic leadership of Thomas Jefferson. In my estimation, the most distinctive conceptions of leadership to emerge in the era of the American founding were aristocratic. Jefferson as a political leader does not fit easily into either an aristocratic or a democratic category. In his underlying trust in the American people, he foreshadows Abraham Lincoln's democratic approach to leadership. But Jefferson was a member of the gentry and shared many of its aristocratic assumptions; in this regard, he had more in common with Hamilton or Adams than his admirers have wanted to acknowledge. For a brilliant discussion of gentry assumptions about leadership that were shared by Hamilton, Adams, Jefferson, and others, see Robert H. Wiebe, *The Opening of American Society* (New York: Alfred A. Knopf, 1984), pp. 3–125.
4. *PAH*, 1, pp. 562–63. The seminal works on classical republican thought in America are Bernard Bailyn, *The Ideological Origins of the American Revolution* (Cambridge: Harvard University Press, 1967); Gordon S. Wood, *The Creation of the American Republic, 1776–1787* (New York: W. W. Norton, 1972); J. G. A. Pocock, *The Machiavellian Moment: Florentine Political Thought and the Atlantic Republican Tradition* (Princeton: Princeton University Press, 1975). For a discussion of historical scholarship that raises questions about these works, see Robert E. Shalhope, "Republicanism and Early American Historiography," *William and Mary Quarterly* 39 (April 1982): 334–56.
5. *PAH*, 1, pp. 568–69.
6. *PAH*, 1, pp. 580–81.
7. *PAH*, 1, p. 582.

8. *PAH*, 2, pp. 53, 167.

9. *PAH*, 2, p. 255.

10. *PAH*, 3, p. 103. While Hamilton lampooned the relevance of classical ideals, in his correspondence with Laurens he continued to use classical imagery. With peace in sight, he wrote to Laurens in August 1782: "Quit your sword, my friend, put on the *toga*, come to Congress." *PAH*, 3, p. 145.

11. *PAH*, 1, pp. 95, 53, 156. On the likely impact of Hamilton's childhood on his view of human nature, see James Thomas Flexner, *The Young Hamilton* (Boston: Little, Brown, 1978), pp. 3–33. On the influence of Hume, see Clinton Rossiter, *Alexander Hamilton and the Constitution* (New York: Harcourt, Brace and World, 1964), pp. 120–21; and Gerald Stourzh, *Alexander Hamilton and the Idea of Republican Government* (Stanford, Calif: Stanford University Press, 1970), pp. 77–78.

12. *FP* no. 6, p. 54; *PAH*, 4, p. 216.

13. *PAH*, 4, pp. 216–17.

14. *PAH*, 5, p. 43.

15. *PAH*, 4, pp. 181, 187.

16. *FP* no. 72, p. 437.

17. *PAH*, 3, p. 135.

18. *PAH*, 4, p. 193; *PAH*, 18, p. 496. On the Federalists' fears of Jacobinism in America, see Lance Banning, *The Jeffersonian Persuasion: Evolution of a Party Ideology* (Ithaca, N.Y.: Cornell University Press, 1978), pp. 210–11.

19. *PAH*, 25, p. 597.

20. *FP* no. 1, p. 35.

21. *PAH*, 5, pp. 265, 269.

22. *PAH*, 5, pp. 320–21.

23. *PAH*, 5, p. 299; *PAH*, 12, pp. 408, 480.

24. *PAH*, 25, pp. 271, 295.

25. *PAH*, 25, pp. 276, 296, 272.

26. *PAH*, 25, pp. 287, 292, 297. Hamilton's charge that Burr lacked principles is confirmed in a sympathetic biography of Burr. "No deep thought underlay the colonel's never well-defined political leanings. He was a doer, not a thinker." Milton Lomask, *Aaron Burr: The Years from Princeton to Vice-President, 1756–1805* (New York: Farrar, Straus, and Giroux, 1979), p. 150.

27. *PAH*, 25, pp. 297, 272, 276.

28. *PAH*, 25, pp. 280–81, 276. Faced with skepticism from the recipients of his letters that Burr was foolish enough to attempt usurpation, Hamilton was driven, in his final letter on Burr during this period, to concede that Burr's success was doubtful. "And tho' I believe he will fail, I think it almost certain he will attempt usurpation. And the attempt will involve great mischief." *PAH*, 25, p. 323.

29. Douglass Adair and Martin Harvey, "Was Alexander Hamilton a Christian Statesman?" in Trevor Colbourn, ed., *Fame and the Founding Fathers: Essays by Douglass Adair* (New York: W. W. Norton, 1974), p. 153n; *PAH*, 25, p. 323.

30.` *PAH*, 12, p. 408. On Hamilton's intentions in the duel, see *PAH*, 26, pp. 278–80.

31. *PAH*, 25, p. 597.

32. *PAH*, 2, p. 408; *FP* no. 36, p. 217.

33. *PAH*, 11, p. 439.

34. *PAH*, 22, p. 192; *PAH*, 25, pp. 515, 321.

35. *FP* no. 30, p. 191; *PAH*, 21, p. 454. For Hamilton's views on political theory and political science, see Rossiter, *Alexander Hamilton and the Constitution*, pp. 113–18.

36. *FP* no. 72, p. 437.

37. Gerald Stourzh has suggested that this passage "enlightens the whole edifice of [Hamilton's] mind." Stourzh, *Alexander Hamilton and the Idea of Republican Government*, pp. 101–2.

38. On the allure of fame to the American Founders, see Douglass Adair, "Fame and the Founding Fathers," in Colbourn, *Fame and the Founding Fathers*, pp. 3–26.

39. *PAH*, 4, pp. 203, 207–8.

40. *PAH*, 19, pp. 3–4.

41. *PAH*, 19, pp. 59–60.

42. Rossiter, *Alexander Hamilton and the Constitution*, p. 246. See also Morton J. Frisch, *Alexander Hamilton and the Political Order: An Interpretation of His Political Thought and Practice* (Lanham, Md.: University Press of America, 1991), pp. 63–78.

43. *PAH*, 8, pp. 102–5; *PAH*, 10, p. 303.

44. *PAH*, 19, p. 89.

45. *PAH*, 12, p. 616.

46. On the Federalists' inherent disadvantages in competing for public opinion, see Richard Buel, Jr., *Securing the Revolution: Ideology in American Politics, 1789–1815* (Ithaca, N.Y.: Cornell University Press, 1972), pp. 91–135.

47. *PAH*, 12, p. 161; *PAH*, 17, p. 135.

48. *PAH*, 21, p. 41; *PAH*, 25, p. 606.

49. *PAH*, 21, p. 467.

50. *PAH*, 21, p. 470; *PAH*, 25, p. 613.

51. *PAH*, 12, p. 618; *PAH*, 4, pp. 193–94, 208.

52. *FP* no. 68, p. 414.

53. *FP* no. 70, pp. 423, 424.

54. *FP* no. 71, p. 434.

55. *FP* no. 70, pp. 429, 430.

56. *FP* no. 72, p. 438.

57. *PAH*, 5, pp. 234, 335.

58. *PAH*, 5, p. 336. The description of Washington is quoted in Leonard D. White, *The Federalists: A Study in Administrative History, 1789–1801* (New York: Free Press, 1948), p. 109.

59. *PAH*, 15, p. 39.

60. John C. Miller, *Alexander Hamilton: Portrait in Paradox* (New York: Harper and Brothers, 1959), p. 323; *FP* no. 73, p. 444.

61. *PAH*, 15, p. 77.

62. *PAH*, 16, p. 136. Under Hamilton's influence, the presidency of George Washington demonstrated the possibilities of executive energy. Hamilton criticized Washington's successors, however, for failing to live up to his standards. He attacked John Adams for lacking the talent and drive needed for successful executive performance, as well as for his egregious vanity. With respect to Jefferson, Hamilton charged that the Virginian was guilty of making "a most prodigal sacrifice of constitutional energy, of sound principle, and of public interest, to the popularity of one man." On Adams, see *PAH*, 25, pp. 186–234; on Jefferson, see *PAH*, 25, pp. 453–57.

63. White, *The Federalists*, pp. 125–26. On Hamilton as administrator, see White, pp. 116–27; and Forrest McDonald, *Alexander Hamilton: A Biography* (New York: W. W. Norton, 1979), pp. 217–22.

64. *PAH*, 24, p. 238.

65. *PAH*, 19, p. 405; *PAH*, 24, p. 31.

66. On the relationship between popular participation and administration, see Harvey Flaumenhaft, "Hamilton's Administrative Republic and the American Presidency," in Joseph M. Bessette and Jeffrey Tulis, eds., *The Presidency in the Constitutional Order* (Baton Rouge: Louisiana State University Press, 1981), pp. 70–71.

67. *FP* no. 30, p. 188.

68. *PAH*, 7, pp. 306–7.

69. *PAH*, 10, p. 256; Banning, *The Jeffersonian Persuasion*, pp. 143–44.

70. *PAH*, 19, p. 196.

71. On Hamilton's attempt to join a classical conception of leadership with a modern conception of political economy, see Ralph Ketcham, *Presidents above Party: The First American Presidency, 1789–1829* (Chapel Hill: University of North Carolina Press, 1984), pp. 194–95.

72. *PAH*, 26, pp. 521–22; *PAH*, 10, pp. 266–67.

73. For Hamilton's discussion of the sources of capital for manufacturing, see *PAH*, 10, pp. 274–77.

74. Enlisting the aid of the governor of New Jersey and personally lobbying members of the New Jersey legislature, Hamilton secured an ample charter for S.E.U.M. When the corporation applied to the Bank of New York for a loan in May 1792, he wrote to the bank's William Seton that he had "a strong wish that the Directors of that Bank may be disposed to give

facilities to this institution upon terms of perfect safety to itself." The secretary of the treasury made it clear that a favorable response from the bank would earn favorable treatment from the national government: "I will not scruple to say *in confidence* that the Bank of New York shall suffer no diminution of its *pecuniary faculties* from any accommodations it may afford to the Society in question. I feel my reputation much concerned in its welfare." *PAH*, 11, pp. 424–25.

75. *PAH*, 8, p. 589.

76. *PAH*, 11, pp. 218–19.

77. For a sketch of Duer's character and financial schemes, see Broadus Mitchell, *Alexander Hamilton: The National Adventure, 1788–1804* (New York: Macmillan, 1962), pp. 155–57, 168–76. For an account of his entire sordid career, see Robert F. Jones, "William Duer and the Business of Government in the Era of the American Revolution," *William and Mary Quarterly*, 3d ser., 32 (July 1975): 393–416.

78. On the multiple reasons for S.E.U.M.'s failure, see Miller, *Alexander Hamilton*, pp. 308–10. Hamilton's reputation as the patron and prophet of American industrialization has come under attack by several scholars. Jacob E. Cooke has argued convincingly that Tench Coxe deserves a major share of the credit for both the *Report on the Subject of Manufactures* and the Society for Establishing Useful Manufactures. Jacob E. Cooke, "Tench Coxe, Alexander Hamilton, and the Encouragement of American Manufactures," *William and Mary Quarterly*, 3d ser., 32 (July 1975): 369–92. A far more radical attack on Hamilton's reputation can be found in John R. Nelson, Jr., *Liberty and Property: Political Economy and Policymaking in the New Nation, 1789–1812* (Baltimore: Johns Hopkins University Press, 1987), pp. 22–65. Nelson argues that Hamilton was not genuinely interested in manufacturing and that his advocacy of it was incidental to his fiscal stabilization program. This thesis is ingenious and well argued. Yet I am not convinced, in the final analysis, that Hamilton's efforts to promote American industrialization were completely subordinate to—and sometimes a smoke screen for—his fiscal program. Nelson's interpretation requires us to dismiss as facade or dissimulation Hamilton's elaborate theoretical apparatus in the report on manufactures and his indefatigable work on behalf of S.E.U.M. Further, his account of Hamilton's political economy unduly downplays Hamilton's concern for economic dynamism and for the political benefits it promised.

79. *PAH*, 5, p. 42.

80. *PAH*, 1, p. 4; *PAH*, 3, p. 461.

81. On the prevalent American fear of standing armies and fondness for militias, see Richard H. Kohn, *Eagle and Sword: The Federalists and the Creation of the Military Establishment in America, 1783–1802* (New York: Free Press, 1975), pp. 1–13.

82. On the military academy, see *PAH*, 24, pp. 69–75; on supplies, see

PAH, 23, pp. 15–19; on parades, see *PAH*, 23, pp. 122–23; on formations and tactics, see *PAH*, 24, pp. 135–53; on the pace, see *PAH*, 24, pp. 340–41.

83. *PAH*, 23, p. 122.

84. *FP* no. 28, p. 178; *PAH*, 22, pp. 552–53.

85. *PAH*, 17, pp. 13, 151. On the Whiskey Rebellion, see Leland D. Baldwin, *Whiskey Rebels: The Story of a Frontier Uprising* (Pittsburgh: University of Pittsburgh Press, 1968); and Thomas P. Slaughter, *The Whiskey Rebellion: Frontier Epilogue to the American Revolution* (New York: Oxford University Press, 1986). For highly favorable treatments of Hamilton's handling of the Whiskey Rebellion, see Mitchell, *Alexander Hamilton*, pp. 308–30; and McDonald, *Alexander Hamilton*, pp. 297–303.

86. *PAH*, 17, pp. 13, 18.

87. *PAH*, 17, p. 340.

88. *PAH*, 16, p. 272; *PAH*, 18, p. 499.

89. *PAH*, 22, pp. 154–55.

90. *PAH*, 22, pp. 192, 389.

91. *PAH*, 24, p. 557; Merrill D. Peterson, ed., *The Portable Thomas Jefferson* (New York: Penguin, 1975), pp. 470, 456.

92. For an insightful discussion of Hamilton's assault on the democratic conception of a body politic, see Sheldon S. Wolin, "The People's Two Bodies," *democracy* 1 (January 1981): 13–16.

93. *PAH*, 25, p. 544.

CHAPTER 2

John Adams: Merit, Fame, and Political Leadership

The following abbreviations are used in the notes for chapter 2:

AJL	Lester J. Cappon, ed., *The Adams-Jefferson Letters* (New York: Simon and Schuster, 1971).
AP	Adams Papers, Massachusetts Historical Society, Boston, Microfilm Collection.
DAJA	Lyman H. Butterfield, ed., *Diary and Autobiography of John Adams* (Cambridge: Harvard University Press, 1961).
JAMW	Charles Francis Adams, ed., *Correspondence between John Adams and Mercy Warren* (1878; New York: Arno Press, 1972).
SPUR	John A. Schutz and Douglass Adair, eds., *The Spur of Fame: Dialogues of John Adams and Benjamin Rush* (San Marino, Calif: The Huntington Library, 1966).
WAL	Worthington Chauncey Ford, ed., *Warren-Adams Letters* (Boston: Massachusetts Historical Society, 1917, 1925).

WJA   Charles Francis Adams, ed., *The Works of John Adams*
               (Boston: Charles C. Little and James Brown, 1851–56).

1. *DAJA*, 2, p. 351.

2. Bernard Bailyn, *The Ideological Origins of the American Revolution* (Cambridge: Harvard University Press, 1967); Gordon S. Wood, *The Creation of the American Republic, 1776–1787* (New York: W. W. Norton, 1972); J. G. A. Pocock, *The Machiavellian Moment: Florentine Political Thought and the Atlantic Republican Tradition* (Princeton: Princeton University Press, 1975). For the quotation from Pocock, see *The Machiavellian Moment*, p. 317; for the quotation from Wood, see *The Creation of the American Republic*, p. 53.

3. Pocock, *The Machiavellian Moment*, p. 459.

4. Harold C. Syrett, ed., *The Papers of Alexander Hamilton*, vol. 2 (New York: Columbia University Press, 1961–79), p. 244; *WJA*, 6, p. 249; *SPUR*, p. 119. John Patrick Diggins has challenged the view that John Adams should be considered a classical republican. Diggins effectively highlights those parts of Adams's political psychology that emphasize human selfishness and denigrate the potential for widespread civic virtue. But his rather narrow consideration of Adams's ideas slights those aspects of them that distinctly link Adams to classical republicanism, especially his belief in the primacy of politics. The John Adams who rooted his political hopes in the wisdom of republican Rome cannot easily be claimed, as Diggins attempts to do, for liberalism and against classical republicanism. See John Patrick Diggins, *The Lost Soul of American Politics: Virtue, Self-Interest, and the Foundations of Liberalism* (New York: Basic Books, 1984), pp. 69–99.

5. *WJA*, 4, p. 397. By interpreting John Adams as a theoretician of leadership, I am deviating from the most common scholarly reading of his ideas. Recent analyses of Adams generally concentrate on the sources and anachronisms of the institutional side to his thought. See Edward Handler, *America and Europe in the Political Thought of John Adams* (Cambridge: Harvard University Press, 1964); John R. Howe, Jr., *The Changing Political Thought of John Adams* (Princeton: Princeton University Press, 1966); Wood, *The Creation of the American Republic*, pp. 567–92 ("The Relevance and Irrelevance of John Adams"); Joyce Appleby, "The New Republican Synthesis and the Changing Political Ideas of John Adams," *American Quarterly* 25 (1973): 578–95.

6. *WJA*, 6, p. 279.

7. Robert S. Taylor, ed., *Papers of John Adams*, vol. 4 (Cambridge: Harvard University Press, 1979), p. 124.

8. *WJA*, 9, p. 539.

9. *WJA*, 6, p. 57; Adams's marginal comment on Mary Wollstonecraft's *Historical and Moral View of the Origin and Progress of the*

French Revolution quoted in Zoltan Haraszti, *John Adams and the Prophets of Progress* (New York: Grosset and Dunlap, 1952), p. 198.

10. *WJA*, 6, pp. 232, 248. Because Adams borrowed and paraphrased so extensively from one chapter in Adam Smith's *Theory of Moral Sentiments* in deriving his basic psychology, most recent commentators have given short shrift to the *Discourses on Davila*. Yet Adams traced the complexities of "the passion for distinction" with far greater persistence than did Smith in his chapter, "Of the Origin of Ambition, and of the Distinction of Ranks." More important, Adams developed the political implications of "the passion for distinction" in a manner that went well beyond anything in Smith's text.

11. *DAJA*, 1, pp. 23, 8, 24–25. Adams's fascination with the issue of fame was hardly idiosyncratic. On the appeal of fame for Adams's generation of American leaders, see Douglass Adair, "Fame and the Founding Fathers," in Trevor Colbourn, ed., *Fame and the Founding Fathers: Essays by Douglass Adair* (New York: W. W. Norton, 1974), pp. 3–26. On the importance of this theme in seventeenth- and eighteenth-century thought, see Arthur O. Lovejoy, *Reflections on Human Nature* (Baltimore: Johns Hopkins University Press, 1961).

12. *DAJA*, 1, p. 222.

13. *DAJA*, 1, pp. 100, 52, 53.

14. *WJA*, 6, p. 246.

15. *WAL*, 2, p. 73.

16. *JAMW*, p. 474; *DAJA*, 2, p. 260; AP, microfilm reel 377.

17. *WJA*, 6, p. 318; *WAL*, 2, p. 73.

18. *WJA*, 6, pp. 270–71.

19. *WJA*, 6, p. 105.

20. Wood, *The Creation of the American Republic*, p. 572. On the powerful appeal of the idea of merit to four of Adams's contemporaries in the generation of 1776, Samuel Adams, Isaac Sears, Thomas Young, and Richard Henry Lee, see Pauline Maier, *The Old Revolutionaries: Political Lives in the Age of Samuel Adams* (New York: Alfred A. Knopf, 1980), especially pp. 40–41, 97, 134, 198–200.

21. *WJA*, 6, p. 243.

22. The Constitution of Pennsylvania (1776), Article 13 is quoted in Samuel Eliot Morison, ed., *Sources and Documents Illustrating the American Revolution, 1764–1788* (New York: Oxford University Press, 1965), p. 167; *DAJA*, 3, p. 411.

23. *WJA*, 7, pp. 249–51. On Adams's interest in and identification with Cicero, see Peter Shaw, *The Character of John Adams* (Chapel Hill: University of North Carolina Press, 1976), pp. 270–72.

24. *DAJA*, 2, p. 35; *AJL*, p. 349; *WJA*, 9, p. 540.

25. *WJA*, 6, p. 242.

26. *JAMW*, p. 438. In letters written during the period of the titles con-

troversy, Adams was in fact flirting with the notion that electoral corruption might someday compel Americans to take refuge in hereditary institutions.

27. *JAMW*, p. 439; AP, microfilm reel 364.

28. *WJA*, 6, p. 249.

29. *WJA*, 6, pp. 249–50, 251.

30. *WJA*, 6, p. 256.

31. *WJA*, 5, p. 489; *WJA*, 6, p. 241; *WAL*, 2, p. 216.

32. *WJA*, 6, p. 158; *WAL*, 2, p. 275. It was not only the "public mind" that had a difficult time discerning "real merit." The young John Adams, in an essay entitled "On Self-Delusion," recognized something that he was loath to admit in later years: the political actor was inevitably biased in estimating the relative merits of himself and his rivals. "Let not writers nor statesmen deceive themselves. The springs of their own conduct and opinions are not always so clear and pure, nor are those of their antagonists in politics always so polluted and corrupted, as they believe, and would have the world believe too. Mere readers and private persons can see virtues and talents on each side." *WJA*, 3, p. 436.

33. *AJL*, p. 457.

34. *DAJA*, 3, p. 336.

35. *WAL*, 2, p. 175; *SPUR*, p. 59; *JAMW*, p. 334.

36. *SPUR*, p. 61.

37. *WAL*, 2, pp. 71–72. Adams had earlier complained of the kind of delegate to the Continental Congress who served the selfish interests of a "phalanx" of supporters in order to make them "trumpeters of his praise." L. H. Butterfield, ed., *Adams Family Correspondence*, vol. 2 (Cambridge: Harvard University Press, 1963), p. 99.

38. *WAL*, 2, pp. 209, 211. For a penetrating analysis of Adams's feelings toward Franklin, see Shaw, *The Character of John Adams*, pp. 115–27. Page Smith has noted that while Adams's "dislike of Franklin was certainly an obsession," it was "shared by every American envoy with the exception of the unhappy Silas Deane." Smith, *John Adams*, vol. 1 (Garden City, N.Y.: Doubleday, 1962), p. 570.

39. *DAJA*, 4, p. 69; *WAL*, 2, pp. 210, 211.

40. *SPUR*, p. 217; *JAMW*, p. 474.

41. *SPUR*, pp. 97–98.

42. *DAJA*, 2, p. 363; *SPUR*, p. 98. In a later letter to Rush, Adams credited Washington with a different kind of talent: "If he was not the greatest President, he was the best actor of presidency we have ever had." Washington's farewell addresses, Adams wrote, "were all in a strain of Shakespearean and Garrickal excellence in dramatical exhibitions." *SPUR*, p. 181.

43. *SPUR*, pp. 35, 59. On the Federalists' use of Washington as an icon, see Joseph Charles, *The Origins of the American Party System* (New York:

Harper and Row, 1961), pp. 39, 48–53; and Stephen G. Kurtz, *The Presidency of John Adams* (Philadelphia: University of Pennsylvania Press, 1957), pp. 27, 58, 203, 303.

44. *SPUR*, p. 135.

45. *AJL*, p. 488.

46. Butterfield, *Adams Family Correspondence*, vol. 2, pp. 289–90.

47. AP, microfilm reel 115.

48. *DAJA*, 1, p. 25; *WJA*, 6, p. 500.

49. AP, microfilm reel 364. Josiah Quincy remembered the elderly Adams telling him that "vanity is the cordial drop which makes the bitter cup of life go down." Quincy quoted in Smith, *John Adams*, vol. 2, p. 1103.

50. *WJA*, 4, p. 380.

51. *AJL*, pp. 351–52.

52. *AJL*, p. 371; *WJA*, 6, p. 451.

53. *AJL*, p. 398.

54. *WJA*, 6, pp. 491–92; *WJA*, 5, p. 24. A strong claim can be advanced that Adams deserves the title of America's first major elite theorist. Indeed, the force of his analysis was recognized by America's preeminent modern elite theorist, C. Wright Mills. Mills coupled Adams with Thorstein Veblen as students of the role of prestige in American society and credited Adams with the superior understanding of how social status is translated into political influence. See Mills, *The Power Elite* (New York: Oxford University Press, 1956), pp. 89–91.

55. *WJA*, 4, p. 290. For the Federalist perspective on the Senate during the ratification debates, see Wood, *The Creation of the American Republic*, pp. 553–62.

56. *AJL*, p. 213; AP, microfilm reel 115.

57. *WJA*, 6, p. 530; *SPUR*, p. 108.

58. *AJL*, pp. 388, 391.

59. *SPUR*, p. 24.

60. *WJA*, 6, p. 68.

61. *WJA*, 6, pp. 39, 484.

62. Adams's marginal comment on Turgot's letter to Dr. Price of March 22, 1778, quoted in Haraszti, *John Adams and the Prophets of Progress*, p. 147.

63. *WJA*, 5, p. 457.

64. *WJA*, 6, pp. 165, 473.

65. *WJA*, 9, p. 570.

66. Handler, *America and Europe in the Political Thought of John Adams*, pp. 66–67; *WJA*, 6, p. 340; *WJA*, 4, p. 585.

67. For his description of appropriate executive powers, see *WJA*, 6, pp. 430–31.

68. Max Farrand, ed., *The Records of the Federal Convention*, vol. 1 (New Haven: Yale University Press, 1937), p. 65; Clinton Rossiter, ed., *The*

Federalist Papers (New York: New American Library, 1961), p. 423; *WJA,* 4, pp. 585, 586.

69. *WJA,* 6, pp. 533, 340, 341.

70. *WJA,* 5, p. 473.

71. On the Alien and Sedition Acts, see John C. Miller, *Crisis in Freedom: The Alien and Sedition Acts* (Boston: Little, Brown, 1951); and James Morton Smith, *Freedom's Fetters: The Alien and Sedition Laws and American Civil Liberties* (Ithaca, N.Y.: Cornell University Press, 1956). For a sympathetic treatment of Adams's role with respect to the Alien and Sedition Acts, see Smith, *John Adams,* vol. 2, pp. 975–78.

72. Adams on "oligarchic influence" quoted in a letter from Theodore Sedgwick to Alexander Hamilton in Syrett, *The Papers of Alexander Hamilton,* vol. 22, p. 503; Richard H. Kohn, *Eagle and Sword: The Federalists and the Creation of the Military Establishment in America, 1783–1802* (New York: Free Press, 1975), p. 272. For Alexander Hamilton's bitter evaluation of the Adams presidency, see Bruce Miroff, "John Adams and the Presidency," in Thomas E. Cronin, ed., *Inventing the American Presidency* (Lawrence: University Press of Kansas, 1989), pp. 319–22.

73. *JAMW,* pp. 332–33; *AJL,* p. 249.

CHAPTER 3

Abraham Lincoln: Democratic Leadership and the
Tribe of the Eagle

The following abbreviations are used in the notes for chapter 3:

CW   Roy P. Basler, ed., *The Collected Works of Abraham Lincoln,* vols. 1–9 (New Brunswick, N.J.: Rutgers University Press, 1953–55).

HLL   Paul Angle, ed., *Herndon's Life of Lincoln* (Greenwich, Conn.: Fawcett Publishers, 1961).

RAL   Allen Thorndike Rice, ed., *Reminiscences of Abraham Lincoln by Distinguished Men of His Times* (New York: North American Review, 1888).

1. Robert H. Wiebe, *The Opening of American Society* (New York: Alfred A. Knopf, 1984).

2. Hay quoted in Edmund Wilson, *Patriotic Gore: Studies in the Literature of the American Civil War* (New York: Farrar, Straus and Giroux, 1977), p. 119.

3. *HLL,* p. 374; William Carlos Williams, *In the American Grain* (New York: New Directions, 1956), p. 234; George Forgie, *Patricide in the House*

Divided: A Psychological Interpretation of Lincoln and His Age (New York: W. W. Norton, 1979), p. 255; *RAL*, p. 314.

4. *HLL*, p. 374; *RAL*, p. 365; *CW*, 5, p. 346; *CW*, 4, p. 341.

5. Judging by the books he read and the friends he made, Lincoln did not develop a feminine side to his character out of contact with the sentimental, feminized culture of his era, brilliantly depicted in Ann Douglas, *The Feminization of American Culture* (New York: Avon Books, 1977). His qualities of tenderness and nurturance seem to have grown out of his own brooding temperament and his response to tragic experience. My interpretation of Lincoln as a masculine/feminine figure is, in most respects, antithetical to Robert Wiebe's provocative essay, "Lincoln's Fraternal Democracy," in John L. Thomas, ed., *Abraham Lincoln and the American Political Tradition* (Amherst: University of Massachusetts Press, 1986), pp. 11–30. Wiebe convincingly situates the Lincoln of the 1840s and 1850s in a male culture of politics and law that was more emotionally expressive than in earlier (and later) periods of American history. But he neglects to consider the ways in which Lincoln grew beyond his male comrades. And in suggesting that Lincoln's wartime compassion extended only to suffering males (soldiers), he fails to confront the meaning of "charity for all."

6. *CW*, 1, pp. 108, 109, 113–14.

7. Wilson, *Patriotic Gore*, pp. 129, 108; Dwight G. Anderson, *Abraham Lincoln: The Quest for Immortality* (New York: Alfred A. Knopf, 1982), pp. 115, 193; Harry V. Jaffa, *Crisis of the House Divided: An Interpretation of the Issues in the Lincoln-Douglas Debates* (Chicago: University of Chicago Press, 1982), p. 217; Forgie, *Patricide in the House Divided*, pp. 86, 262.

8. Anderson's case for a "demonic" Lincoln is based on a series of strained interpretations and misreadings of Lincoln's words. For an account of one of the most egregious of the misreadings, see Don E. Fehrenbacher, *Lincoln in Text and Context* (Stanford, Calif.: Stanford University Press, 1987), pp. 282–83.

9. Lincoln did not treat Douglas as a "towering genius." On the contrary, he often cut down the "Little Giant" with belittling barbs. Among these was his comparison of Douglas to a "cuttlefish, a small species of fish that has no mode of defending itself when pursued except by throwing out a black fluid, which makes the water so dark the enemy cannot see it and thus it escapes." *CW*, 3, p. 184.

10. Some of the language in the "towering genius" passage echoed—and parodied—phrases uttered by Martin Van Buren. See Major L. Wilson, "Lincoln and Van Buren in the Steps of the Fathers: Another Look at the Lyceum Address," *Civil War History* 29 (September 1983): 197–211.

11. *CW*, 6, pp. 78–79.

12. *CW*, 3, p. 29; *CW*, 2, p. 126.

13. *CW*, 2, pp. 382–83.

14. *CW*, 2, p. 482.

15. *CW*, 2, p. 547.

16. *CW*, 1, pp. 178–79.

17. *CW*, 2, p. 352; *CW*, 4, pp. 190, 193, 226.

18. See chapter 2.

19. *CW*, 8, pp. 1, 96.

20. *HLL*, pp. 407–8; Richard Hofstadter, *The American Political Tradition* (New York: Vintage Books, 1948), p. 136. While citing Speed's account here, I acknowledge Don Fehrenbacher's point that recollections by his associates of what Lincoln said do not carry the evidentiary weight of words that can be authenticated as Lincoln's own. See Fehrenbacher, *Lincoln in Text and Context*, pp. 270–86.

21. *HLL*, pp. 326–29; J. G. Randall, *Lincoln the Liberal Statesman* (New York: Dodd, Mead and Company, 1947), pp. 66–67.

22. David Donald, *Lincoln Reconsidered* (New York: Vintage Books, 1956), pp. 65, 71; Richard N. Current, *The Lincoln Nobody Knows* (New York: Hill and Wang, 1958), p. 211.

23. *CW*, 7, p. 398. Particularly valuable here is Don E. Fehrenbacher, *Prelude to Greatness: Lincoln in the 1850s* (Stanford, Calif.: Stanford University Press, 1962).

24. *CW*, 1, pp. 65–66.

25. *CW*, 1, pp. 48, 507.

26. *CW*, 1, p. 272.

27. *CW*, 4, p. 64.

28. *CW*, 1, pp. 440, 446; *CW*, 2, pp. 12, 13. Recent historical scholarship has called into question the older view that Lincoln's stance on the Mexican War was so unpopular as to drive him from politics in 1849. My point here is not that Lincoln's critique of Polk condemned him to political "exile" but that this situation raised for him in a new way the conflict between popular wishes and fundamental principles.

29. *CW*, 3, p. 27.

30 *CW*, 2, p. 385; *CW*, 3, p. 423.

31. *CW*, 2, pp. 256, 282. Clay had asked in 1842: "What man, claiming to be a statesman, will overlook or disregard the deep-seated and unconquerable prejudices of the people?" Quoted in George M. Fredrickson, "A Man but Not a Brother: Abraham Lincoln and Racial Equality," *Journal of Southern History* 41 (February 1975): 43.

32. *CW*, 4, p. 437.

33. *CW*, 4, p. 438.

34. *CW*, 5, p. 535; Herndon quoted in Roy P. Basler, "Abraham Lincoln's Rhetoric," *American Literature* 11 (1939): 167. For an interesting elaboration of Herndon's point, see James M. McPherson, *Abraham Lincoln and the Second American Revolution* (New York: Oxford University Press, 1991), pp. 93–112.

35. James Hurt, "All the Living and the Dead: Lincoln's Imagery," *American Literature* 52 (November 1980): 377; *CW*, 7, p. 23. For an interpretation of the Gettysburg Address as linking "domestic" to public images, see Hurt, "All the Living and the Dead," pp. 376–80. For interpretations that emphasize Christian imagery in the speech, see John P. Diggins, *The Lost Soul of American Politics: Virtue, Self-Interest, and the Foundations of Liberalism* (New York: Basic Books, 1984), pp. 297–98; and Anderson, *Abraham Lincoln*, pp. 186–90. Garry Wills's impressive study of the Gettysburg Address, *Lincoln at Gettysburg: The Words That Remade America* (New York: Simon and Schuster, 1992), arrived after my manuscript was completed.

36. *CW*, 7, p. 23.

37. *CW*, 7, p. 23.

38. *CW*, 7, p. 23.

39. *CW*, 8, p. 333.

40. *CW*, 8, p. 361. On the jeremiad as an American rhetorical form, see Sacvan Bercovitch, *The American Jeremiad* (Madison: University of Wisconsin Press, 1978).

41. *CW*, 7, pp. 169, 24.

42. *CW*, 8, p. 356.

43. Carol Gilligan, *In a Different Voice: Psychological Theory and Women's Development* (Cambridge: Harvard University Press, 1982), pp. 164, 21–22, 30, 16.

44. *RAL*, p. 242.

45. Wilson quoted in *HLL*, p. 374; Lincoln quoted in Stephen B. Oates, *With Malice toward None: The Life of Abraham Lincoln* (New York: New American Library, 1978), p. 266.

46. *CW*, 6, p. 414.

47. *RAL*, p. 339.

48. Current, *The Lincoln Nobody Knows*, p. 175.

49. *CW*, 7, p. 255.

50. *CW*, 6, p. 538.

51. *CW*, 5, p. 346; *CW*, 8, p. 333.

52. *CW*, 8, p. 429.

53. *CW*, 2, pp. 87, 88.

54. *CW*, 6, pp. 73, 76.

55. *CW*, 6, p. 559.

56. *CW*, 4, p. 78.

57. *CW*, 8, p. 308.

58. Fletcher's letter to Lincoln quoted in *CW*, 8, pp. 319–20n.

59. Lincoln quoted in Tyler Dennett, ed., *Lincoln and the Civil War in the Diaries and Letters of John Hay* (1939; New York: Da Capo Press, 1988), p. 108. For the older historical view, see T. Harry Williams, *Lincoln and the Radicals* (Madison: University of Wisconsin Press, 1941); Randall,

Lincoln the Liberal Statesman, pp. 69–74; Benjamin Thomas, *Abraham Lincoln* (New York: Alfred A. Knopf, 1952), pp. 290–91, 405, 438–40. For the more recent view, see Donald, *Lincoln Reconsidered*, pp. 103–27; Hans L. Trefousse, *The Radical Republicans: Lincoln's Vanguard for Racial Justice* (New York: Alfred A. Knopf, 1968), pp. 168–304; LaWanda Cox, *Lincoln and Black Freedom: A Study in Presidential Leadership* (Columbia: University of South Carolina Press, 1981), pp. 3–43; and Stephen B. Oates, *Abraham Lincoln: The Man behind the Myths* (New York: New American Library, 1985), pp. 94–111, 115–19, 136–46.

60. *CW*, 6, pp. 231, 504.

61. Richard Hofstadter has written that Lincoln "was chastened and not intoxicated by power." Hofstadter, *The American Political Tradition*, p. 135. See also Fehrenbacher, *Lincoln in Text and Context*, pp. 157–63.

62. *CW*, 1, p. 454. The Whig congressman was a satirist of presidential pretensions and rationalizations: "An honest laborer digs coal at about seventy cents a day, while the president digs abstractions at about seventy dollars a day. The *coal* is clearly worth more than the *abstractions*, and yet what a monstrous inequality in the prices!" *CW*, 1, p. 484.

63. *CW*, 2, p. 60.

64. *CW*, 4, p. 271; *CW*, 5, p. 241.

65. Mark E. Neely, Jr., *The Fate of Liberty: Abraham Lincoln and Civil Liberties* (New York: Oxford University Press, 1991), pp. 3–138, 232–35; *CW*, 4, p. 430.

66. Clinton Rossiter, *Constitutional Dictatorship: Crisis Government in the Modern Democracies* (New York: Harcourt, Brace, and World, 1963), pp. 236–37. See also Herman Belz, "Lincoln and the Constitution: The Dictatorship Question Reconsidered," *Congress and the Presidency* 15 (Autumn 1988): 147–64.

67. J. G. Randall, *Constitutional Problems under Lincoln*, rev. ed. (Urbana: University of Illinois Press, 1951), p. 184.

68. Donald, *Lincoln Reconsidered*, pp. 187–208. For a critique of the argument that Lincoln retained a Whig view of executive power, see Stephen B. Oates, "Abraham Lincoln: *Republican* in the White House," in Thomas, *Abraham Lincoln and the American Political Tradition*, pp. 98–110.

69. *CW*, 8, p. 152.

70. Lincoln's comment to Browning quoted in *CW*, 7, p. 283n.

71. *CW*, 7, p. 281.

72. *CW*, 7, p. 282.

73. *CW*, 1, p. 64. On Lincoln's early, Whig economic perspective and activities, see G. S. Boritt, *Lincoln and the Economics of the American Dream* (Memphis: Memphis State University Press, 1978), pp. 1–152.

74. Fehrenbacher, *Prelude to Greatness*, p. 7.

75. Boritt, *Lincoln and the Economics of the American Dream*, p. 160; *CW*, 5, p. 52.

76. *CW*, 1, p. 412. On the Republican ideology of "free labor," which Lincoln shared, see Eric Foner, *Free Soil, Free Labor, Free Men: The Ideology of the Republican Party before the Civil War* (New York: Oxford University Press, 1970), pp. 11–39.

77. *CW*, 7, p. 259.

78. Hofstadter, *The American Political Tradition*, p. 106. See also Foner, *Free Soil, Free Labor, Free Men*, pp. 38, 316–17; and Boritt, *Lincoln and the Economics of the American Dream*, pp. 179–80. For a suggestion that Lincoln might not be so innocent of Gilded Age capitalist evils, see Phillip S. Paludan, "Commentary on 'Lincoln and the Economics of the American Dream,'" in Gabor S. Boritt, ed., *The Historian's Lincoln: Pseudohistory, Psychohistory, and History* (Urbana: University of Illinois Press, 1988), pp. 116–23.

79. Michael Kammen, *A Season of Youth: The American Revolution and the Historical Imagination* (New York: Oxford University Press, 1980), pp. 96–97.

80. *CW*, 3, pp. 145–46. For the historical iconoclasm, see Hofstadter, *The American Political Tradition*, pp. 107–20. The views of white bigots and black militants are discussed in Oates, *Abraham Lincoln*, pp. 21–30.

81. For scholarly defenses of Lincoln against the charge of racism, see Jaffa, *Crisis of the House Divided*, pp. 363–86; Cox, *Lincoln and Black Freedom*, pp. 19–22; Don Fehrenbacher, "Only His Stepchildren: Lincoln and the Negro," *Civil War History* 20 (December 1974): 302–5. For a more skeptical approach to Lincoln's racial views, see Fredrickson, "A Man but Not a Brother," pp. 46–55.

82. Fehrenbacher, "Only His Stepchildren," pp. 307–8; Oates, *With Malice toward None*, p. 338; Benjamin Quarles, *Lincoln and the Negro* (New York: Oxford University Press, 1962), p. 116; *CW*, 5, p. 372.

83. *CW*, 7, p. 191; *CW*, 8, p. 325.

84. *CW*, 6, p. 410; *CW*, 7, p. 243.

85. *RAL*, p. 193; Philip S. Foner, ed., *The Life and Writings of Frederick Douglass*, vol. 4 (New York: International Publishers, 1955), p. 312.

86. Foner, *Life and Writings of Frederick Douglass*, vol. 4, pp. 313, 316.

87. *CW*, 3, p. 6.

88. *CW*, 2, p. 4. Lincoln's views here were shared by most Whigs. See Daniel Walker Howe, *The Political Culture of the American Whigs* (Chicago: University of Chicago Press, 1979).

89. *CW*, 1, p. 473.

90. *CW*, 3, p. 357.

91. On Lincoln as a pragmatist, see Donald, *Lincoln Reconsidered*, pp. 128–43.

92. On presidential invocations of Lincoln, see Richard Nelson Current, *Speaking of Abraham Lincoln: The Man and His Meaning for Our Times* (Urbana: University of Illinois Press, 1983), pp. 126–45; and Michael Paul Rogin, *Ronald Reagan, the Movie and Other Episodes in Political Demonology* (Berkeley: University of California Press, 1987), pp. 81–114.

CHAPTER 4

Elizabeth Cady Stanton: Dissenting Leadership and Feminist Vision

The following abbreviations are used in the notes for chapter 4:

ECS	Theodore Stanton and Harriot Stanton Blatch, eds., *Elizabeth Cady Stanton as Revealed in Her Letters, Diary and Reminiscences, vol. 2* (New York: Harper and Brothers Publishers, 1922).
ECSP	Elizabeth Cady Stanton Papers, Vassar College Library, Poughkeepsie, New York.
ECS/SBA	Ellen Carol Dubois, ed., *Elizabeth Cady Stanton/Susan B. Anthony: Correspondence, Writings, Speeches* (New York: Schocken Books, 1981).
EYM	Elizabeth Cady Stanton, *Eighty Years and More: Reminiscences, 1815–1897* (1898; New York: Schocken Books, 1971).
HWS	Elizabeth Cady Stanton et al., *History of Woman Suffrage*, vols. 1–4 (Rochester, N.Y.: Susan B. Anthony, 1881–1902).
REV	*The Revolution.*

1. *ECS*, p. 75.

2. Richard Hofstadter, *The American Political Tradition* (New York: Vintage Books, 1948), pp. 138–40; Garry Wills, *Confessions of a Conservative* (New York: Penguin Books, 1980), p. 167.

3. Reliance on a division of labor between dissenting leaders and politicians may also place too much trust in a kindly political Providence, which supplies both types of leadership just when the American republic most needs them.

4. Nancy Cott, *The Bonds of Womanhood: "Woman's Sphere" in New England, 1780–1835* (New Haven: Yale University Press, 1977), p. 57. On domesticity and movements for moral reform, see Paula Baker, "The Domestication of Politics: Women and American Political Society, 1780–1920," *American Historical Review* 89 (June 1984): 620–47. On do-

mesticity and female friendships, see Carroll Smith-Rosenberg, "The Female World of Love and Ritual: Relations between Women in Nineteenth-Century America," in Smith-Rosenberg, *Disorderly Conduct: Visions of Gender in Victorian America* (New York: Oxford University Press, 1986), pp. 53–76.

5. ECSP, Scrapbooks, vol. 2. On Stanton's childhood, see Elisabeth Griffith, *In Her Own Right: The Life of Elizabeth Cady Stanton* (New York: Oxford University Press, 1984), pp. 3–13; and Alma Lutz, *Created Equal: A Biography of Elizabeth Cady Stanton* (New York: John Day Company, 1940), pp. 3–12.

6. See Griffith, *In Her Own Right*, pp. 14–42.

7. *EYM*, p. 147; ECSP, box 1.

8. *EYM*, pp. 147–48.

9. *EYM*, p. 148.

10. *HWS*, 1, pp. 68, 70.

11. For descriptions of the Seneca Falls Convention, see Eleanor Flexner, *Century of Struggle: The Woman's Rights Movement in the United States*, rev. ed. (Cambridge: Harvard University Press, 1975), pp. 75–77; and Griffith, *In Her Own Right*, pp. 55–57.

12. *ECS/SBA*, p. 28.

13. *HWS*, 1, p. 71. The male monopoly on public speech had been boldly challenged a decade earlier by the abolitionist Grimké sisters.

14. *HWS*, 1, p. 75.

15. *HWS*, 1, pp. 75, 810.

16. *HWS*, 1, p. 72.

17. Ellen Dubois, "The Radicalism of the Woman Suffrage Movement: Notes toward the Reconstruction of Nineteenth-Century Feminism," in Anne Phillips, ed., *Feminism and Equality* (New York: New York University Press, 1987), pp. 130, 131; *HWS*, 1, p. 495.

18. *HWS*, 1, p. 804.

19. ECSP, box 1.

20. *ECS*, p. 41.

21. *ECS*, pp. 42, 71.

22. *HWS*, 3, pp. 47, 118.

23. *ECS*, p. 95.

24. *HWS*, 2, pp. 52, 51, 152.

25. *HWS*, 2, p. 382.

26. *ECS/SBA*, p. 81; *HWS*, 2, pp. 267, 267–68.

27. *HWS*, 2, p. 319, 153, 368.

28. *HWS*, 2, p. 188; *ECS*, p. 120.

29. On the American Equal Rights Association and the Kansas campaign of 1867, see Ellen Carol Dubois, *Feminism and Suffrage: The Emergence of an Independent Women's Movement in America, 1848–1869* (Ithaca, N.Y.: Cornell University Press, 1978), pp. 53–104.

30. *REV*, January 29, 1868; *ECS*, p. 119.

31. *HWS*, 2, p. 181; *REV*, December 24, 1868; *REV*, February 4, 1869.

32. *REV*, January 29, 1868. Writing to the *Revolution* in response to this attack on Garrison, Jane Elizabeth Jones, a feminist and abolitionist, hoped to avoid becoming another target of Stanton's cutting prose: "I own to a little fear of her sharp points." *REV*, April 9, 1868.

33. *HWS*, 2, p. 152.

34. My analysis of the connection between Stanton's racist rhetoric and her class bias was developed in the course of conversations with Melinda Lawson.

35. *ECS*, p. 292. As if to make amends for her racist statements during Reconstruction, Stanton's autobiography lovingly described Peter, a black Cady family servant, as one of the most benevolent influences of her childhood. Rising above paternalistic sentiment, she lamented the racial prejudice that led her church to discriminate against Peter, "the grandest specimen of manhood in the whole congregation." *EYM*, p. 17.

36. Griffith, *In Her Own Right*, p. 124; *HWS*, 2, pp. 322, 319.

37. Dubois, *Feminism and Suffrage*, p. 164.

38. Lutz, *Created Equal*, p. 194.

39. Griffith, *In Her Own Right*, pp. 143, 163.

40. *ECS*, pp. 255, 131.

41. *ECS*, p. 31. For instances of Stanton's self-presentation as a super-mother, see *EYM*, pp. 122–26, 271–72. For an illustration of her piercing humor, see *EYM*, pp. 300–301.

42. ECSP, Scrapbooks, vol 2. On the interest of nineteenth-century reformers in hygiene, see William Leach, *True Love and Perfect Union: The Feminist Reform of Sex and Society* (New York: Basic Books, 1980), pp. 19–37.

43. *HWS*, 4, p. 58.

44. *HWS*, 1, p. 685; *ECS*, pp. 45, 61. Some men would, of course, object to Stanton's claim of male incapacity to experience the "bliss" of parent-hood. The claim should be seen, however, as a search for compensation by women denied access to the realms of male pleasures.

45. *ECS*, p. 58.

46. *HWS*, 3, p. 56.

47. *ECS*, p. 252. On the opposition to women's suffrage, see Flexner, *Century of Struggle*, pp. 304–18.

48. *ECS*, p. 125.

49. *HWS*, 3, p. 81; *HWS*, 1, p. 595; *ECS/SBA*, p. 43. The militant republi-canism that Stanton voiced during the Civil War remained a constant pas-sion. So fervent was she in this regard that she not only welcomed the as-sassination of Tsar Alexander of Russia in 1881 as "a telling blow" to despotism, but she also expressed her "hope that the son too will soon re-pose in Abraham's bosom." When, a few months later, President Garfield

was assassinated, her first concern was that "such tragedies do not speak well for a republic." Stanton's republicanism reproduced the founding generation's anxious comparisons of Europe and America. *ECS,* pp. 183, 185.

50. ECSP, Scrapbooks, vol. 1. On the idea of "republican motherhood," see Linda K. Kerber, *Women of the Republic: Intellect and Ideology in Revolutionary America* (New York: W. W. Norton, 1986), pp. 269–88.

51. ECSP, Scrapbooks, vol. 2. On Henry Stanton's opportunism, see Griffith, *In Her Own Right,* pp. 89–90.

52. *ECS,* pp. 239, 251.

53. *ECS,* p. 289; ECSP, Scrapbooks, vol. 3.

54. Nancy Cott, "Feminist Theory and Feminist Movements: The Past before Us," in Juliet Mitchell and Ann Oakley, eds., *What Is Feminism?* (New York: Pantheon Books, 1986), p. 50; *HWS,* 1, p. 72; *ECS/SBA,* p. 35; *HWS,* 1, p. 811.

55. *HWS,* 2, pp. 190, 307; *REV,* September 24, 1868.

56. *ECS,* p. 160; Stanton quoted in Griffith, *In Her Own Right,* p. 11; Elizabeth Cady Stanton et al., *The Woman's Bible,* pt. 1 (New York: European Publishing Company, 1895), p. 21.

57. *HWS,* 2, pp. 189–90.

58. *HWS,* 1, p. 15; *HWS,* 4, pp. 176, 177. On the conflicting liberal and radical feminist strains in Stanton's thought, see Zillah Eisenstein, "Elizabeth Cady Stanton: Radical-Feminist Analysis and Liberal-Feminist Strategy," in Phillips, *Feminism and Equality,* pp. 77–102.

59. *HWS,* 1, p. 680; *HWS,* 4, p. 41.

60. *ECS/SBA,* p. 132; *HWS,* 1, pp. 22, 722.

61. *ECS,* p. 49; Stanton quoted in Griffith, *In Her Own Right,* p. 157; Ellen Dubois, "On Labor and Free Love: Two Unpublished Speeches of Elizabeth Cady Stanton," *Signs* 1 (Autumn 1975): 266.

62. *ECS,* p. 82; Ellen Dubois, "The Nineteenth-Century Woman Suffrage Movement and the Analysis of Women's Oppression," in Zillah Eisenstein, ed., *Capitalist Patriarchy and the Case for Socialist Feminism* (New York: Monthly Review Press, 1979), pp. 148–49.

63. *ECS,* pp. 281–82.

64. *ECS/SBA,* pp. 247, 251, 253–54.

65. *ECS/SBA,* p. 247. Stanton seemingly intended her feminist individualism to be more of a moral than an economic or political prescription. While telling women that they must confront their existential solitariness, she wanted to relieve their actual isolation through "cooperative labor and cooperative homes." *HWS,* 1, p. 21.

66. *HWS,* 4, p. 114; *ECS/SBA,* p. 226.

67. *ECS,* p. 81.

68. ECSP, box 2.

69. Stanton et al., *The Woman's Bible,* pt. 1, pp. 24–25.

70. *ECS/SBA,* p. 264.

CHAPTER 5

Theodore Roosevelt: Heroic Leadership and Masculine Spectacle

The following abbreviations are used in the notes for chapter 5:

AUTO   Theodore Roosevelt, *An Autobiography* (1913; New York: Da Capo Press, 1985).

LTR   Elting E. Morison et al., eds., *The Letters of Theodore Roosevelt* (Cambridge: Harvard University Press, 1951–54).

RR   Theodore Roosevelt, *The Rough Riders* (1899; New York: Charles Scribner's Sons, 1924).

WTR   Hermann Hagedorn, ed., *The Works of Theodore Roosevelt*, national edition (New York: Charles Scribner's Sons, 1926).

1. John Morton Blum, *The Republican Roosevelt* (New York: Atheneum, 1964), p. 6. On popular idolization of Roosevelt, see Kathleen Dalton, "Why America Loved Teddy Roosevelt: Or, Charisma Is in the Eyes of the Beholder," in Robert J. Brugger, ed., *Our Selves/Our Past: Psychological Approaches to American History* (Baltimore: Johns Hopkins University Press, 1981), pp. 269–91.

2. Henry Adams, *The Education of Henry Adams* (1918; Boston: Houghton Mifflin Company, 1961), p. 417; Worthington Chauncey Ford, ed., *Letters of Henry Adams, 1892–1918* (Boston: Houghton Mifflin Company, 1938), pp. 418–19.

3. Bernard De Voto, ed., *Mark Twain in Eruption* (New York: Harper and Brothers, 1940), p. 49.

4. *Papers of Eugene V. Debs, 1834–1945* (New York: Microfilming Corporation of America, 1983), reel 8.

5. *WTR*, 13, p. 510. This passage has evidently been a favorite of Richard Nixon's. He ended his 1982 book, *Leaders*, by quoting it and took from it the title for his 1990 memoir, *In the Arena*.

6. Theodore Roosevelt, *Gouverneur Morris* (1888; New York: Theodore Roosevelt Association, 1975), p. 229; *WTR*, 13, p. 32.

7. *WTR*, 13, p. 323. For Roosevelt, feminine virtue was to be displayed in the home, not in the public arena. Obsessed with the prospect that a declining birth rate might cause the United States to lose the competition with more virile nations, he preached strenuous motherhood. As he put it in a 1911 lecture,

> I do not believe that the question of woman's voting is a thousandth or a millionth part as important as the question of keeping, and where necessary reviving, among the women of this country, the realization that their great work must be done in the home, that the ideal woman of the future, just like

the ideal woman of the past, must be the good wife, the good mother, the mother who is able to bear, and to rear, a number of healthy children. (*WTR*, 13, p. 635.)

Running for the presidency the following year as a Progressive, Roosevelt came out more strongly for women's suffrage. But the obsession with motherhood continued to dominate his view of women.

8. Roosevelt quoted in William H. Harbaugh, *The Life and Times of Theodore Roosevelt* (New York: Oxford University Press, 1975), p. 142.

9. T. J. Jackson Lears, *No Place of Grace: Antimodernism and the Transformation of American Culture, 1880–1920* (New York: Pantheon Books, 1981), pp. 98–139. On Roosevelt's preoccupation with masculinity as psychological compensation for his childhood, see Henry F. Pringle, *Theodore Roosevelt: A Biography* (New York: Harcourt, Brace and World, 1956), p. 4; and Richard Hofstadter, *The American Political Tradition* (New York: Vintage Books, 1948), pp. 209–11.

10. *LTR*, 2, pp. 1442–45.

11. *LTR*, 3, p. 663; *LTR*, 7, p. 343.

12. *LTR*, 2, p. 1334.

13. *LTR*, 2, p. 1387; *LTR*, 7, p. 676.

14. Hay quoted in Harbaugh, *The Life and Times of Theodore Roosevelt*, p. 272; Frederick S. Wood, ed., *Roosevelt As We Knew Him* (Philadelphia: John C. Winston Company, 1927), p. 163; Lee's comments cited in Frederick W. Marks III, *Velvet on Iron: The Diplomacy of Theodore Roosevelt* (Lincoln: University of Nebraska Press, 1979), p. 64; Edmund Morris, *The Rise of Theodore Roosevelt* (New York: Ballantine Books, 1980), p. 17.

15. Blum, *The Republican Roosevelt*, pp. 8–9; *LTR*, 4, p. 1279; *LTR*, 5, p. 517.

16. *LTR*, 3, pp. 343–44, 300. On the Philippines, see *LTR*, 3, pp. 276–77; on Panama, see *LTR*, 3, p. 652.

17. *LTR*, 3, pp. 362, 363.

18. *LTR*, 6, p. 1490.

19. *LTR*, 7, p. 526; *WTR*, 17, p. 322. A month later, discussing his Milwaukee speech in a letter to Edward Grey, Roosevelt insisted that he had only performed as any hardened man of action would have:

The average political orator or party leader, the average broker or banker or factory owner, at least when he is past middle age, is apt to be soft—I mean both mentally and physically—and such a man accepts being shot as a frightful and unheard-of calamity. . . . But a good soldier or sailor, or for the matter of that even a civilian accustomed to hard and hazardous pursuits, a deep-sea fisherman, or railwayman, or cowboy, or lumberjack, or miner, would normally act as I acted without thinking anything about it (LTR, 7, p. 648).

20. *LTR*, 1, pp. 100–101.

21. *LTR*, 5, p. 170; *LTR*, 7, p. 121.

22. *LTR*, 5, p. 351; Roosevelt, *Gouverneur Morris*, p. 106. For Roosevelt's letter to Oliver, see *LTR*, 5, pp. 350–53.

23. John Milton Cooper, Jr., *The Warrior and the Priest: Woodrow Wilson and Theodore Roosevelt* (Cambridge: Harvard University Press, 1983), pp. 28–29. On the transformation of newspapers, see George Juergens, *News from the White House: The Presidential-Press Relationship in the Progressive Era* (Chicago: University of Chicago Press, 1981), pp. 5–7; and Michael E. McGerr, *The Decline of Popular Politics: The American North, 1865–1928* (New York: Oxford University Press, 1986), pp. 107–37.

24. Walter Dean Burnham, *Critical Elections and the Mainsprings of American Politics* (New York: W. W. Norton, 1970), pp. 71–90. See also McGerr, *The Decline of Popular Politics*, pp. 138–83.

25. *WTR*, 1, pp. 379, 384, 390. The photograph of Roosevelt and his captives can be found in Morris, *The Rise of Theodore Roosevelt*, facing page 319. For an insightful analysis of Roosevelt's personal and historical myths of the American West, see Richard Slotkin, "Nostalgia and Progress: Theodore Roosevelt's Myth of the Frontier," *American Quarterly* 33 (Winter 1981): 608–37.

26. *LTR*, 2, pp. 803, 832. For the suggestion that Roosevelt's eagerness for war was rooted in familial guilt, see Morris, *The Rise of Theodore Roosevelt*, pp. 39–40; and Cooper, *The Warrior and the Priest*, p. 12.

27. For Roosevelt's cultivation of the media in Cuba, see Morris, *The Rise of Theodore Roosevelt*, pp. 629, 639, 642, 645–46.

28. *RR*, pp. 15, 11.

29. *RR*, pp. 19, 65, 29–30.

30. *RR*, pp. 75, 104. Roosevelt's scorn for the Cuban insurgents was widely shared among the American expeditionary forces. See Virgil Carrington Jones, *Roosevelt's Rough Riders* (Garden City, N.Y.: Doubleday, 1971), p. 100.

31. *RR*, pp. 117–39. A decade earlier, Roosevelt had described an American warrior who sounds exactly like the hero of San Juan Hill. In his *Winning of the West*, he wrote of General Anthony Wayne: "He felt very keenly that delight in the actual shock of battle which the most famous fighting generals have possessed. He gloried in the excitement and danger, and shone at his best when the stress was sorest. . . . But his head was as cool as his heart was stout. . . . By experience he had grown to add caution to his dauntless energy." *WTR*, 9, p. 323.

32. *RR*, pp. 126, 118, 124, 127; Joseph Campbell, *The Hero with a Thousand Faces* (Princeton: Princeton University Press, 1968), p. 97. For more of Roosevelt's narrow escapes, see *RR*, pp. 132, 144, 155.

33. *RR*, pp. 195–96.

34. *RR*, pp. 232, 235, 236.

35. Juergens, *News from the White House*, p. 16.

36. Ibid., pp. 65, 66.

37. *LTR*, 4, p. 1029.

38. Cooper, *The Warrior and the Priest*, p. 115.

39. *LTR*, 7, p. 143; *LTR*, 8, p. 1012; Cooper, *The Warrior and the Priest*, p. 218.

40. Willard B. Gatewood, Jr., *Theodore Roosevelt and the Art of Controversy* (Baton Rouge: Louisiana State University Press, 1970), p. 17.

41. On the modern manufacture of the hero, see Bruce Miroff, "The Presidency and the Public: Leadership as Spectacle," in Michael Nelson, ed., *The Presidency and the Political System*, 3d ed. (Washington, D.C.: CQ Press, 1990), pp. 289–313.

42. *LTR*, 5, p. 351.

43. Harbaugh, *The Life and Times of Theodore Roosevelt*, p. 222.

44. *WTR*, 14, p. 258.

45. *WTR*, 14, p. 258.

46. *WTR*, 14, pp. 261, 262.

47. *WTR*, 14, p. 264. In later years, as Bryan's threat faded, his place as a dangerous demagogue was assumed, for Roosevelt, by several others, particularly Eugene V. Debs. But Roosevelt's images of radical democratic horror were still imported from France. In 1911 he argued that Debs and his Socialist followers were "on a par with the creatures of the Paris Commune." *LTR*, 7, p. 423.

48. *AUTO*, p. 288.

49. *WTR*, 13, p. 28.

50. *LTR*, 1, p. 458.

51. *LTR*, 5, p. 83.

52. *LTR*, 1, p. 545; *LTR*, 6, p. 1387.

53. *AUTO*, pp. 372, 379.

54. *AUTO*, p. 419.

55. *AUTO*, p. 563; *WTR*, 10, pp. 308–9. For a detailed account of Roosevelt's presidency, see Lewis L. Gould, *The Presidency of Theodore Roosevelt* (Lawrence: University Press of Kansas, 1991).

56. *LTR*, 3, pp. 550–51.

57. On Roosevelt and Lincoln's "plain people," see *LTR*, 4, pp. 1037, 1083, 1132.

58. Stephen Skowronek, *Building a New American State: The Expansion of National Administrative Capacities, 1877–1920* (New York: Cambridge University Press, 1982), p. 172. On the emergence of the new class of professionals, see Robert H. Wiebe, *The Search for Order, 1877–1920* (New York: Hill and Wang, 1967), pp. 111–32, 145–63.

59. *LTR*, 4, p. 1201. For the congressional response to the Keep Commission, see Skowronek, *Building a New American State*, p. 185.

60. *LTR*, 6, p. 1388; Clinton Rossiter, ed., *The Federalist Papers* (New York: New American Library, 1961), p. 438 (no. 72).

61. Howard K. Beale, *Theodore Roosevelt and the Rise of America to World Power* (New York: Collier Books, 1962), pp. 393–94.

62. *WTR*, 8, p. 3; *WTR*, 9, p. 56; *WTR*, 14, p. 364. Hamilton and his

wing of the Federalist party had opposed westward expansion. Roosevelt considered this one of the few areas where Jefferson, normally a villain in his eyes, was preferable to Hamilton.

63. *LTR*, 2, p. 1104.

64. *WTR*, 11, p. 249.

65. *WTR*, 9, p. 57; *LTR*, 2, pp. 995, 1025.

66. *LTR*, 2, p. 1303; *WTR*, 13, p. 322.

67. *LTR*, 3, p. 8; *WTR*, 14, p. 317. Proud that Americans were proving in the Philippines that they could do their part "in policing the world, in keeping order in the world's waste spaces," Roosevelt railed at the Democrats' proposal to disengage from the islands, considering it a prescription for national dishonor. Indeed, by encouraging Aguinaldo with this proposal, the Democrats, he held, were primarily to blame for American casualties: "It is a terrible and most lamentable truth that our soldiers who are now facing death in the Philippines are forced to recognize in the Bryanistic Democracy their most dangerous foe. . . . The bullets that slay our men in Luzon are inspired by the denouncers of America here." *WTR*, 14, pp. 339, 381.

68. Stanley Karnow, *In Our Image: America's Empire in the Philippines* (New York: Random House, 1989), p. 194. On the brutalizing effects of the war on American forces, see Karnow, especially pp. 154–55, 178–80, 187–94; and Richard Drinnon, *Facing West: The Metaphysics of Indian-Hating and Empire-Building* (Minneapolis: University of Minnesota Press, 1980), pp. 307–32.

69. *WTR*, 15, p. 111.

70. Marks, *Velvet on Iron*, p. 140. For an argument that "strategic necessity, not imperialism nor the big stick, caused American intervention in the Philippines and Panama," see Richard H. Collin, *Theodore Roosevelt, Culture, Diplomacy, and Expansion: A New View of American Imperialism* (Baton Rouge: Louisiana State University Press, 1985), especially pp. 1–5, 95–153. Any reader doubting that Roosevelt was genuinely an imperialist should turn to a valuable earlier work: David H. Burton, *Theodore Roosevelt: Confident Imperialist* (Philadelphia: University of Pennsylvania Press, 1968).

71. *LTR*, 6, p. 1408.

72. *LTR*, 7, pp. 32, 66. In a lighthearted moment, Roosevelt imagined himself firming up the British Empire: "I should greatly like to handle Egypt and India for a few months. At the end of that time I doubtless would be impeached by the House of Commons but I should have things moving in fine order first." *LTR*, 7, p. 63.

73. *LTR*, 1, p. 707.

74. *WTR*, 13, pp. 160, 165.

75. *LTR*, 1, p. 412.

76. Martin J. Sklar, *The Corporate Reconstruction of American Capital-*

ism, 1890–1916: The Market, the Law, and Politics (New York: Cambridge University Press, 1988), p. 45.

77. *WTR*, 15, pp. 141–42; Richard Hofstadter, *The Age of Reform: From Bryan to F. D. R.* (New York: Vintage Books, 1955), p. 234; *LTR*, 5, p. 212.

78. *LTR*, 3, p. 108; *WTR*, 13, p. 620. On corporate contributions to Roosevelt in 1904, see Pringle, *Theodore Roosevelt*, pp. 249–52.

79. *LTR*, 3, p. 515; *LTR*, 4, p. 909.

80. *LTR*, 5, p. 183; *LTR*, 4, p. 1113.

81. *WTR*, 16, p. 17; *LTR*, 5, p. 535.

82. *LTR*, 5, pp. 755, 826. For a good analysis of the reasons behind Roosevelt's move to the left in 1907–8, see George E. Mowry, *The Era of Theodore Roosevelt and the Birth of Modern America, 1900–1912* (New York: Harper and Row, 1958), pp. 209–25.

83. *LTR*, 6, pp. 1580, 1582.

84. Sklar, *The Corporate Reconstruction of American Capitalism*, p. 244.

85. *WTR*, 16, p. 97; *WTR*, 17, pp. 170, 11.

86. *WTR*, 17, p. 17; *LTR*, 7, p. 113.

87. *WTR*, 17, p. 299. On the 1912 Progressive convention, see George E. Mowry, *Theodore Roosevelt and the Progressive Movement* (1946; New York: Hill and Wang, 1960), pp. 256–73; and Robert M. Crunden, *Ministers of Reform: The Progressives' Achievement in American Civilization, 1889–1920* (New York: Basic Books, 1982), pp. 200–224.

88. *AUTO*, p. 597. Once World War I began, Roosevelt's concerns largely shifted away from the domestic economy. Yet he did not back off from his Progressive commitments. In 1917 he predicted hopefully that "there can and will come—gradually and by evolution, not revolution—a shift in control which will mean that the competent workers become partners in the enterprise. This partnership must mean not only a sharing of profit, but a sharing in the guidance and management." *WTR*, 19, p. 80.

89. *LTR*, 7, p. 243.

90. *LTR*, 8, p. 820; *WTR*, 18, p. 4; *LTR*, 8, p. 817.

91. *LTR*, 8, p. 967; *WTR*, 18, p. 447. Predicting correctly that the United States would eventually enter the war, Roosevelt stormed against the pacifists who hoped to forestall that event. What most aroused his scorn were the collegiate pacifists. "The college boy who deliberately elects to be a 'sissy,'" he wrote in August 1915, "should be replaced in the nursery and spanked." He taunted these sons of the upper class (only the children of the affluent generally attended college in this era) who refused to follow the virile example of Roosevelt and his generation of 1898, as babies, fit only for the company of women. *WTR*, 18, p. 312.

92. *WTR*, 17, p. 410; *LTR*, 8, p. 1063.

93. *WTR*, 19, p. 190; *LTR*, 8, p. 1153.

94. *WTR*, 11, p. 295; *WTR*, 19, p. xxv.

95. *WTR*, 19, p. 301; *LTR*, 8, p. 1252; Theodore Roosevelt, *Roosevelt in*

the Kansas City Star: War-Time Editorials (Boston: Houghton Mifflin Company, 1921), p. 36.

96. Roosevelt, *Roosevelt in the Kansas City Star*, p. 136; *LTR*, 8, p. 1276. To read Roosevelt's wartime correspondence is a strange experience. Poignant letters from a loving father and charming anecdotes told by a doting grandfather alternate with brutal talk of repression from the chief scourge of America's evil Huns.

97. *LTR*, 8, p. 1263; *WTR*, 19, p. 347.

98. Roosevelt, *Roosevelt in the Kansas City Star*, p. 259; *LTR*, 8, p. 1422.

99. Michael Paul Rogin, *Ronald Reagan, the Movie and Other Episodes in Political Demonology* (Berkeley: University of California Press, 1987), p. xiii; *WTR*, 19, p. 350. Among scholarly admirers of Theodore Roosevelt, John Morton Blum has been the most stinging in his condemnation of Roosevelt's World War I activities. Blum writes that Roosevelt had much company in his crusade of intolerance but that "if he was not alone, he was also not often surpassed in his excursions into hate and his paeans to conformity." Blum, *The Republican Roosevelt*, pp. 157–58.

100. *WTR*, 13, pp. 3–4.

CHAPTER 6

Eugene V. Debs: Dissenting Leadership and Democratic Dignity

The following abbreviations are used in the notes for chapter 6:

PEVD   *Papers of Eugene V. Debs, 1834–1945* (New York: Micro-
            filming Corporation of America, 1983).
TAM   Eugene V. Debs Collection, Tamiment Institute, New
            York University, New York.
WAB   Eugene Victor Debs, *Walls and Bars* (1927; Chicago:
            Charles H. Kerr and Company, 1973).
WSEVD   *Writings and Speeches of Eugene V. Debs* (New York:
            Hermitage Press, 1948).

1. *PEVD*, reel 8.

2. Ray Ginger, *Eugene V. Debs: A Biography* (New York: Collier Books, 1962), p. 49. On the conservative unionism of the young Debs, see Nick Salvatore, *Eugene V. Debs: Citizen and Socialist* (Urbana: University of Illinois Press, 1982), pp. 23–55.

3. *PEVD*, reel 6.

4. David Montgomery, *The Fall of the House of Labor: The Workplace, the State, and American Labor Activism, 1865–1925* (New York: Cambridge University Press, 1987), p. 7.

5. *PEVD*, reel 1.

6. *PEVD*, reel 7, reel 1.

7. *WSEVD*, pp. 303–4.

8. *WSEVD*, pp. 308–9, 310. Combating bourgeois individualism in the working class, Debs observed that it was rampant even among socialist cadres. As he put it in 1913: "We need to grow out of the selfish, sordid, brutal spirit of individualism which still lurks even in Socialists and is responsible for the strife and contention which prevail where there should be concord and good will. The social spirit and the social conscience must be developed and govern our social relations before we shall have any social revolution." *PEVD*, reel 7.

9. *WSEVD*, pp. 37–38.

10. *WSEVD*, p. 128; *PEVD*, reel 7.

11. *WSEVD*, p. 120; "Lincoln Steffens Learns about Debs and Socialism," in Ronald Radosh, ed., *Debs* (Englewood Cliffs, N.J.: Prentice-Hall, 1971), p. 115.

12. *PEVD*, reel 7. On Debs's youthful practice at public speaking, see Ginger, *Eugene V. Debs*, p. 40. For an analysis of Debs's strengths and weaknesses as an orator, see Bernard J. Brommel, *Eugene V. Debs: Spokesman for Labor and Socialism* (Chicago: Charles H. Kerr, 1978), pp. 199–206.

13. "Elizabeth Gurley Flynn: A Remembrance of an IWW Leader," in Radosh, *Debs*, p. 98. Debs became celebrated not only for the emotional vibrancy of his speeches but also for his tirelessness in delivering them. His most prodigious feats of oratory were his presidential campaigns. The most famous of these came in 1908, when the Socialist party provided Debs with a three-car train that was promptly christened the "Red Special." Touring the country on the "Red Special" between late August and election day, the Socialist presidential candidate never paused to rest. Speaking 68 days straight, he delivered 560 campaign orations. On the "Red Special" campaign, see Ginger, *Eugene V. Debs*, pp. 291–302; and Salvatore, *Eugene V. Debs*, pp. 223–24.

14. Debs quoted in Ginger, *Eugene V. Debs*, pp. 399–400.

15. *PEVD*, reel 2.

16. *PEVD*, reel 7.

17. *PEVD*, reel 1.

18. *PEVD*, reel 6.

19. TAM, box 3.

20. *PEVD*, reel 1. On Debs's failure to "face Berger," see Salvatore, *Eugene V. Debs*, pp. 199–200, 247–51.

21. See H. Wayne Morgan, *Eugene V. Debs: Socialist for President* (Syracuse, N.Y.: Syracuse University Press, 1962), pp. 200–201; James Weinstein, *The Decline of Socialism, 1912–1925* (1967; New Brunswick, N.J.: Rutgers University Press, 1984), pp. 12, 26; Bert Cochran, "The Achievement of Debs," in Harvey Goldberg, ed., *American Radicals: Some*

Problems and Personalities (New York: Monthly Review Press, 1957), pp. 168–71.

22. Cochran, "The Achievement of Debs," p. 170. See also Salvatore, *Eugene V. Debs*, pp. 250–51, 258–61.

23. For various explanations of socialism's unhappy fate in the United States, see John H. M. Laslett and Seymour Martin Lipset, eds., *Failure of a Dream? Essays in the History of American Socialism*, rev. ed. (Berkeley: University of California Press, 1984).

24. Salvatore, *Eugene V. Debs*, p. 200.

25. TAM, box 3. For an insightful comparison of Debs and Lincoln, see Cochran, "The Achievement of Debs," pp. 164–66.

26. *PEVD*, reel 8.

27. Roosevelt quoted in Ginger, *Eugene V. Debs*, p. 268; *PEVD*, reel 7.

28. Debs quoted in Ginger, *Eugene V. Debs*, p. 260; *WSEVD*, p. 418.

29. On Paine's fear of leadership, see the Introduction.

30. *PEVD*, reel 7.

31. *WSEVD*, pp. 285, 286. Writing about the Haymarket "martyrs," the anarchists unjustly executed for a bombing in Haymarket Square, Chicago, in 1886, Debs prophesied about these selfless heroes of labor that one day "the parks of Chicago shall be adorned with their statues." *WSEVD*, p. 22.

32. *WSEVD*, p. 395.

33. On Debs's lack of theoretical study, see Ginger, *Eugene V. Debs*, pp. 33, 39, 186, 223, 335; and Brommel, *Eugene V. Debs*, pp. 208–10. Mark Kann has argued that Debs's thought poses a major challenge to Louis Hartz's thesis of an American liberal consensus. Mark E. Kann, "Challenging Lockean Liberalism in America: The Case of Debs and Hillquit," *Political Theory* 8 (May 1980): 203–22.

34. Dorothy Ross, "The Liberal Tradition Revisited and the Republican Tradition Addressed," in John Higham and Paul K. Conkin, eds., *New Directions in American Intellectual History* (Baltimore: Johns Hopkins University Press, 1979), pp. 116–31.

35. *PEVD*, reel 6.

36. *PEVD*, reel 7; *WSEVD*, p. 125; *PEVD*, reel 7.

37. *PEVD*, reel 7; William Appleman Williams, *The Contours of American History* (Chicago: Quadrangle Books, 1966), p. 487. On the jingoism of the young Debs, see Salvatore, *Eugene V. Debs*, pp. 64–65, 106–7.

38. *PEVD*, reel 7. As the subtitle of his book—*Citizen and Socialist*—indicates, Nick Salvatore highlights Debs's profound appreciation for the ideal of American citizenship. For Salvatore's treatment of this theme, see his *Eugene V. Debs*, especially pp. 85, 100, 107, 171–72, 224–25, 292.

39. *PEVD*, reel 7.

40. *PEVD*, reel 4.

41. Herman Melville, *Moby Dick* (1851; New York: W. W. Norton, 1967), p. 104.

42. *WSEVD*, p. 437.

43. *PEVD*, reel 6, reel 7.

44. *WSEVD*, p. 221.

45. *WSEVD*, p. 124.

46. *PEVD*, reel 7.

47. *WSEVD*, pp. 115, 129.

48. *PEVD*, reel 7.

49. *WSEVD*, pp. 64, 65. This 1903 defense of black equality (within the context of "the labor question") provoked an attack from an anonymous Socialist, who backed up his opposition to black rights by quoting Lincoln's endorsement of white superiority during the debates with Stephen Douglas. Debs's rejoinder demonstrated his capacity to appropriate the American political tradition in a critical fashion. "Abraham Lincoln," he wrote, "was a noble man, but he was not an abolitionist and what he said in reference to the Negro was with due regard to his circumscribed environs. . . , and we are not bound by what he thought prudent to say in a totally different situation half a century ago." *WSEVD*, p. 71.

50. *PEVD*, reel 8.

51. *PEVD*, reel 7.

52. Debs quoted in Ginger, *Eugene V. Debs*, p. 394. Debs was a Victorian sentimentalist on many subjects. Looking through his correspondence, full of references to "heart-throbs" and "loving heartbeats," the modern reader is struck by the mawkishness. See especially TAM, box 3.

53. *PEVD*, reel 7. For an insightful treatment of Debs's preoccupation with manhood, see Salvatore, *Eugene V. Debs*, pp. 23–26, 54–55, 63–65, 89, 215–16, 228–29.

54. *WSEVD*, p. 455.

55. Merrell R. Davis and William H. Gilman, eds., *The Letters of Herman Melville* (New Haven: Yale University Press, 1960), pp. 126–27.

56. Debs quoted in Ginger, *Eugene V. Debs*, p. 404.

57. Ginger, *Eugene V. Debs*, p. 406.

58. Weinstein, *The Decline of Socialism in America*, p. 232. On Debs's suffering in prison, see Salvatore, *Eugene V. Debs*, pp. 308–28.

59. *Walls and Bars* originated as a series of newspaper articles in 1922. Too weak to write, Debs dictated his prison memoirs to David Karsner, a young Socialist and journalist. See Ginger, *Eugene V. Debs*, pp. 444, 450–51.

60. *WAB*, pp. 83, 84, 54, 55.

61. *WAB*, p. 95.

62. *WAB*, pp. 202, 259.

63. *WAB*, pp. 107–8.

64. *WAB*, pp. 205–7.

65. Salvatore, *Eugene V. Debs*, p. 328.

66. *WAB*, p. 257.

67. *PEVD*, reel 4.

68. *PEVD*, reel 7.

CHAPTER 7

Franklin D. Roosevelt: Democratic Leadership and the Modern State

The following abbreviations are used in the notes for chapter 7:

FDRL	Franklin D. Roosevelt Library, Hyde Park, New York.
PL	Elliott Roosevelt, ed., *F.D.R.: His Personal Letters* (New York: Duell, Sloan and Pearce, 1947–50).
PPA	Samuel I. Rosenman, ed., *The Public Papers and Addresses of Franklin D. Roosevelt* (New York: Russell and Russell, 1969).

1. *PPA*, 7, p. 259.

2. *PPA*, 7, pp. 260–61.

3. Frances Perkins, *The Roosevelt I Knew* (1946; New York: Harper and Row, 1964), p. 3; Arthur M. Schlesinger, Jr., *The Crisis of the Old Order, 1919–1933* (Boston: Houghton Mifflin Company, 1957), p. 409; *PPA*, 9, p. 25.

4. Geoffrey C. Ward, *A First-Class Temperament: The Emergence of Franklin Roosevelt* (New York: Harper and Row, 1989), p. 91. On Roosevelt's childhood, see especially Ward, *Before the Trumpet: Young Franklin Roosevelt, 1882–1905* (New York: Harper and Row, 1985), pp. 109–77. On his Groton and Harvard frustrations, see Ward, *Before the Trumpet*, pp. 178–243.

5. On Franklin Roosevelt's youthful emulation of Theodore Roosevelt, see Ward, *A First-Class Temperament*, pp. 85–90, 133, 155, 202, 206, 208, 240–42.

6. Ward, *A First-Class Temperament*, pp. 212–13. On Roosevelt and royalty, see *PL*, 3, pp. 328–29; *PL*, 4, pp. 806, 824–26; Frank Friedel, *Franklin D. Roosevelt: A Rendezvous with Destiny* (Boston: Little, Brown and Company, 1990), pp. 316–17.

7. *PL*, 4, pp. 1453, 1362.

8. Harold L. Ickes, *The Secret Diary of Harold L. Ickes* (New York: Simon and Schuster, 1953–54), vol. 1, p. 122; vol. 2, pp. 345, 312.

9. William E. Leuchtenburg, *Franklin D. Roosevelt and the New Deal, 1932–1940* (New York: Harper and Row, 1963), p. 42.

10. *PPA*, 5, pp. 13, 568.

11. On Roosevelt and the bosses, see Lyle W. Dorsett, *Franklin D. Roosevelt and the City Bosses* (Port Washington, N.Y.: Kennikat Press, 1977).

12. For the hardball tactics against Coughlin, see Alan Brinkley, *Voices of Protest: Huey Long, Father Coughlin, and the Great Depression* (New York: Vintage Books, 1983), p. 127. Roosevelt was also shrewd in biding his time while the demagogues roared in public, confident that he could upstage them at the proper moment. As he wrote to Colonel House in March 1935: "On the whole, the diversion by the trinity of Long, Coughlin and [Hugh] Johnson was long overdue and it is vastly better to have this free side-show presented to the public at this time than later on when the main performance starts!" *PL*, 3, p. 468.

13. Roosevelt quoted in Perkins, *The Roosevelt I Knew*, p. 20.

14. Roosevelt quoted in Friedel, *Franklin D. Roosevelt*, p. 150.

15. On "Miss Nancy," see Ward, *Before the Trumpet*, p. 315; on Franklin's resistance to Theodore's urging that he go to war, see Ward, *A First-Class Temperament*, pp. 346–47.

16. Perkins, *The Roosevelt I Knew*, p. 29; Hugh Gregory Gallagher, *FDR's Splendid Deception* (New York: Dodd, Mead and Company, 1985), p. 213.

17. Gallagher writes: "Although there are over thirty-five thousand still photographs of FDR at the Presidential Library, there are only two of the man seated in his wheelchair. No newsreels show him being lifted, carried, or pushed in his chair. Among the thousands of political cartoons and caricatures of FDR, not one shows the man as physically impaired. In fact, many of them have him as a man of action—running, jumping, doing things." Gallagher, *FDR's Splendid Deception*, p. xiii.

18. On FDR's nurturing of other "polios" at Warm Springs, see Ward, *A First-Class Temperament*, pp. 722–25, 726–30; and Gallagher, *FDR's Splendid Deception*, pp. 40–43.

19. Gallagher, *FDR's Splendid Deception*, p. 56. On Warm Springs as a community, see Gallagher, pp. 45–58; and Ward, *A First-Class Temperament*, pp. 771–72. As president, Roosevelt talked proudly of the "spirit of Warm Springs," offering his community as a paradigm that demonstrated how the majority of disabled children "can be restored to useful citizenship." *PPA*, 2, pp. 502, 503.

20. *PPA*, 3, p. 182. Although Franklin Roosevelt held to many Victorian sentiments about women, he, unlike Theodore Roosevelt, was not obsessed with upholding their maternal and domestic roles. On the contrary, he was quite ready to welcome and utilize women in public service and, thanks largely to Eleanor's influence, recruited a number of talented female associates. According to Susan Ware, Molly Dewson, who served him with great effectiveness as director of the Women's Division of the Democratic National Committee, believed that Roosevelt "appreciated

women's native ability more than any other man she had ever known."
Susan Ware, *Beyond Suffrage: Women in the New Deal* (Cambridge: Harvard University Press, 1981), p. 58.

21. At the Philadelphia convention, Roosevelt wrote, Hamilton

> brought Washington, Benjamin Franklin and others to agreement with his
> principle that the Government should consist of three branches. . . . Hamilton, with no experience in statesmanship, had called upon his mind and out
> of this command had evolved that document that has been the model for
> other nations and the bulwark of our own, the Constitution of the United
> States. (FDRL, Family, Business, and Personal Papers, 1922–1932, folder
> 22.)

22. Franklin D. Roosevelt, "Is There a Jefferson on the Horizon?" in
Basil Rauch, ed., *The Roosevelt Reader* (New York: Holt, Rinehart and
Winston, 1957), pp. 44–47. The Bowers review was not the first time that
Roosevelt focused on the Jefferson-Hamilton conflict. After the election of
1924 Roosevelt, hoping to revive the Democrats' fortunes and to keep his
own name prominent in party circles, dispatched a letter on party rebuilding to the delegates from the most recent national convention. Describing
the responses of the delegates in a letter to Senator Thomas J. Walsh of
Montana in February 1925, he wrote: "My correspondents are overwhelmingly agreed that the Democracy must be unqualifiedly the Party representative of progress and liberal thought. In other words, the clear line of
demarcation which differentiated the political thought of Jefferson on the
one side, and of Hamilton on the other, must be restored." FDRL, General
Political Correspondence, 1920–1928, container 4.

23. For insightful treatments of Roosevelt's Jeffersonianism, see Graham J. White, *FDR and the Press* (Chicago: University of Chicago Press,
1979), pp. 143–62; and Philip Abbott, *The Exemplary Presidency: Franklin
D. Roosevelt and the American Political Tradition* (Amherst: University of
Massachusetts Press, 1990), pp. 3–5, 47–109.

24. *PPA*, 1, pp. 68, 69.

25. FDRL, Family, Business, and Personal Papers, 1922–1932, folder 40.

26. La Guardia quoted in Ickes, *The Secret Diary of Harold Ickes*, vol. 2,
p. 271. On Roosevelt's manner of handling the Washington press corps,
see White, *FDR and the Press*, pp. 5–24; and Betty Houchin Winfield,
FDR and the News Media (Urbana: University of Illinois Press, 1990),
pp. 27–77.

27. *PPA*, 1, p. 756.

28. For the New Left critique of Roosevelt, see, for example, Barton
J. Bernstein, "The New Deal: The Conservative Achievements of Liberal Reform," in Bernstein, ed., *Towards a New Past: Dissenting Essays
in American History* (New York: Vintage Books, 1969), pp. 263–88.

29. Roosevelt quoted in Perkins, *The Roosevelt I Knew*, p. 330.

30. James MacGregor Burns, *Roosevelt: The Lion and the Fox* (New York: Harcourt, Brace and World, 1956), p. 476; Roosevelt quoted in Friedel, *Franklin D. Roosevelt*, p. 94.

31. *PPA*, 3, pp. 313, 123; *PPA*, 1, p. 640; *PPA*, 2, p. 11.

32. *PPA*, 2, p. 12; *PPA*, 3, p. 288.

33. *PPA*, 2, p. 340; *PPA*, 3, p. 458; *PPA*, 2, p. 217. On Roosevelt's use of the images of pioneers and neighbors, see Abbott, *The Exemplary Presidency*, pp. 73–76.

34. *PPA*, 4, p. 406; *PPA*, 2, p. 380; *PPA*, 6, p. 3. On the appeal of the communitarian theme in the 1930s, see Richard H. Pells, *Radical Visions and American Dreams: Culture and Social Thought in the Depression Years* (New York: Harper and Row, 1973), pp. 96–150.

35. Ickes, *The Secret Diary of Harold Ickes*, vol. 1, p. 695.

36. *PPA*, 5, p. 148. On the New Deal as a discourse of interests, see Richard Hofstadter, *The Age of Reform* (New York: Vintage Books, 1955), pp. 316–28; and Daniel T. Rodgers, *Contested Truths: Keywords in American Politics since Independence* (New York: Basic Books, 1987), pp. 203–11. Hofstadter acknowledges that the New Deal had a "soft side" (pp. 324–25); Rodgers notes that FDR himself "never abandoned the rhetoric of the common good" (p. 204).

37. *PPA*, 6, pp. 382–83.

38. *PPA*, 5, p. 86; *PPA*, 7, p. 514.

39. *PPA*, 5, p. 518.

40. Wilkins quoted in Nancy J. Weiss, *Farewell to the Party of Lincoln: Black Politics in the Age of FDR* (Princeton: Princeton University Press, 1983), p. 222. On Roosevelt and the antilynching campaign, see Weiss, pp. 96–119, 241–49; and Harvard Sitkoff, *A New Deal for Blacks: The Emergence of Civil Rights as a National Issue* (New York: Oxford University Press, 1978), pp. 268–97.

41. James MacGregor Burns, *The Crosswinds of Freedom* (New York: Vintage Books, 1990), p. 125.

42. On Roosevelt's displacement of parties, see Sidney Milkis, *The Modern Presidency and the Transformation of the American Party System* (New York: Oxford University Press, forthcoming). On Roosevelt as a failed party reformer, see Burns, *Roosevelt: The Lion and the Fox*, pp. 375–80. On Roosevelt and partisan realignment, see James L. Sundquist, *Dynamics of the Party System: Alignment and Realignment of Political Parties in the United States* (Washington, D.C.: Brookings Institution, 1983), pp. 198–297.

43. *PPA*, 9, p. 28; *PPA*, 7, p. xxix.

44. Anthony J. Badger, *The New Deal: The Depression Years, 1933–1940* (New York: Noonday Press, 1989), pp. 271–83.

45. On Roosevelt and the creation of the "modern" presidency, see especially William E. Leuchtenburg, "Franklin D. Roosevelt: The First Modern President," in Fred I. Greenstein, ed., *Leadership in the Modern Presidency* (Cambridge: Harvard University Press, 1988), pp. 7–40.

46. *PPA*, 5, p. 215.

47. Arthur Schlesinger, Jr., *The Coming of the New Deal* (Boston: Houghton Mifflin Company, 1958), pp. 527–28.

48. Richard Gid Powers, *Secrecy and Power: The Life of J. Edgar Hoover* (New York: Free Press, 1987), p. 216.

49. Brownlow Committee quoted in Barry Dean Karl, *Executive Reorganization and Reform in the New Deal: The Genesis of Administrative Management, 1900–1939* (Cambridge: Harvard University Press, 1963), p. 230.

50. The work that first highlighted in dramatic fashion the pathologies of a swollen White House staff was George Reedy, *The Twilight of the Presidency* (New York: New American Library, 1970).

51. For an elaboration of the argument in this paragraph, see Bruce Miroff, "Monopolizing the Public Space: The President as a Problem for Democratic Politics," in Thomas E. Cronin, ed., *Rethinking the Presidency* (Boston: Little, Brown and Company, 1982), pp. 218–32.

52. *PPA*, 7, p. 179.

53. Theodore J. Lowi, *The End of Liberalism* (New York: W. W. Norton, 1969).

54. For the academic critique of the New Deal administrative state, see James A. Morone, *The Democratic Wish: Popular Participation and the Limits of American Government* (New York: Basic Books, 1990), pp. 129–42.

55. *PPA*, 8, p. 67; *PPA*, 9, pp. 618–19.

56. Brownlow quoted in Richard Polenberg, *Reorganizing Roosevelt's Government: The Controversy over Executive Reorganization* (Cambridge: Harvard University Press, 1966), p. 12. Polenberg's book provides an excellent account of the political struggle over executive reorganization.

57. *PPA*, 5, pp. 433–34; Theda Skocpol and Kenneth Finegold, "State Capacity and Economic Intervention in the Early New Deal," *Political Science Quarterly* 97 (Summer 1982): 258.

58. Badger, *The New Deal*, p. 309. See also Theda Skocpol, "Political Response to Capitalist Crisis: Neo-Marxist Theories of the State and the Case of the New Deal," *Politics and Society* 10 (1980): 155–201.

59. *PPA*, 13, p. 34.

60. Albert U. Romasco, *The Politics of Recovery: Roosevelt's New Deal* (New York: Oxford University Press, 1983), p. 243.

61. Ellis W. Hawley, *The New Deal and the Problem of Monopoly* (Princeton: Princeton University Press, 1966), p. 66.

62. Thomas Ferguson, "Industrial Conflict and the Coming of the New

Deal: The Triumph of Multinational Liberalism in America," in Steve
Fraser and Gary Gerstle, eds., *The Rise and Fall of the New Deal Order,
1930–1980* (Princeton: Princeton University Press, 1989), pp. 3–31; Steve
Fraser, "From the 'New Unionism' to the New Deal," *Labor History* 25
(Summer 1984): 405–30. On Reconstruction Finance Corporation lending
during the New Deal, see Romasco, *The Politics of Recovery*, pp. 52–66.

63. *PPA*, 5, pp. 386, 487.

64. C. Wright Mills observed that "the thirties was a political decade:
the power of business was not replaced, but it was contested and supplemented: it became one major power within a structure of power that was
chiefly run by political men." Mills, *The Power Elite* (New York: Oxford
University Press, 1956), p. 273.

65. *PPA*, 1, p. 753; *PPA*, 7, p. 200.

66. *PPA*, 7, p. 7; *PPA*, 6, p. 266.

67. *PPA*, 5, pp. 226–28, 520–21.

68. *PPA*, 7, pp. 305, 306; Hawley, *The New Deal and the Problem of Monopoly*, pp. 402–19. Although later presidents would shy away from talking about the problem of concentrated corporate power, that power still
troubled political theorists concerned for the health of democratic politics. As Charles Lindblom posed the issue: "The large private corporation
fits oddly into democratic theory and vision. Indeed, it does not fit." Lindblom, *Politics and Markets* (New York: Basic Books, 1977), p. 356.

69. *PPA*, 5, p. 13.

70. Burns, *Roosevelt: The Lion and the Fox*, p. 217.

71. *PPA*, 3, p. 399; FDRL, Official Files 407b. For an informative ac-
count of the San Francisco strike, see Irving Bernstein, *Turbulent Years: A
History of the American Worker, 1933–1941* (Boston: Houghton Mifflin
Company, 1969), pp. 252–98.

72. *PPA*, 3, p. 399.

73. *PPA*, 6, p. 272. Letters to the White House during the sit-down
strikes are contained in FDRL, Official Files 407b.

74. *PPA*, 6, p. 274. In a November 1940 letter to Samuel Rosenman,
Roosevelt expressed pride in the fact that, as both governor and president,
he had repeatedly resisted calls to settle labor disputes with "marching
troops." *PL*, 4, p. 1078. His record of nonintervention came to an end in
June 1941, when he sent twenty-five hundred troops to Inglewood, California, to break a strike, allegedly led by communists, at the North American Aviation Company.

75. Perkins, *The Roosevelt I Knew*, p. 325.

76. Steve Fraser, "The 'Labor Question,'" in Fraser and Gerstle, *The
Rise and Fall of the New Deal Order*, p. 57. On the New Deal role in trans-
forming labor, see Fraser, pp. 55–84; and Stanley Vittoz, *New Deal Labor
Policy and the American Industrial Economy* (Chapel Hill: University of
North Carolina Press, 1987), pp. 3–12, 165–73.

77. For a view of Roosevelt as accommodating isolationism out of political necessity, see Robert Dallek, *Franklin D. Roosevelt and American Foreign Policy, 1932–1945* (New York: Oxford University Press, 1979), pp. 101–68. For a view of Roosevelt as sharing the isolationist dread of war, see Robert A. Divine, *Roosevelt and World War II* (Baltimore: Penguin Books, 1970), pp. 1–23. A more caustic view of Roosevelt, as a secret appeaser of Hitler, can be found in Frederick W. Marks III, *Wind over Sand: The Diplomacy of Franklin Roosevelt* (Athens: University of Georgia Press, 1988), pp. 120–67.

78. *PL*, 3, p. 555.

79. *PPA*, 6, pp. 410, 423; *PPA*, 8, p. xxviii.

80. Dallek, *Franklin D. Roosevelt and American Foreign Policy*, p. 532; *PPA*, 12, p. 571. On Roosevelt's relationship with his military commanders, see James MacGregor Burns, *Roosevelt: The Soldier of Freedom, 1940–1945* (New York: Harcourt Brace Jovanovich, 1970), pp. 490–96.

81. Warren F. Kimball, *The Juggler: Franklin Roosevelt as Wartime Statesman* (Princeton: Princeton University Press, 1991), pp. 3–19, 185–200.

82. On the role of the Four Policemen in Roosevelt's thinking, see Kimball, *The Juggler*, pp. 83–105; and Divine, *Roosevelt and World War II*, pp. 56–65.

83. Wallace quoted in John Morton Blum, *V Was for Victory: Politics and American Culture during World War II* (New York: Harcourt Brace Jovanovich, 1976), p. 285; *PPA*, 12, pp. 405–6, 177.

84. *PL*, 4, pp. 1546–47.

85. Eden quoted in Freidel, *Franklin D. Roosevelt*, p. 466.

86. *PPA*, 12, p. 558; *PPA*, 13, p. 563. On Roosevelt's skepticism toward Stalin's intentions, see Dallek, *Franklin D. Roosevelt and American Foreign Policy*, pp. 410–17, 468–71.

87. *PPA*, 2, p. 545.

88. David Brody, "The New Deal and World War II," in John Braeman, Robert H. Brenner, and David Brody, eds., *The New Deal: The National Level* (Columbus: Ohio State University Press, 1975), p. 267.

89. *PPA*, 11, p. 483; Blum, *V Was for Victory*, p. 119.

90. On the struggle between conservatives and New Dealers during the war, see especially Bruce Catton, *The War Lords of Washington* (New York: Harcourt, Brace and Company, 1948); and Steven Fraser, *Labor Will Rule: Sidney Hillman and the Rise of American Labor* (New York: Free Press, 1991), pp. 441–540.

91. *PL*, 4, p. 1131.

92. Blum, *V Was for Victory*, p. 123. The war years were economically beneficial to organized labor as well as to big business. Labor union membership soared from 10.5 million to 14.75 million. Weekly earnings in

manufacturing industries rose by 80 percent, compared with a 30 percent rise in prices. See Blum, pp. 140–41; and Brody, "The New Deal and World War II," pp. 276–77.

93. Catton, *The War Lords of Washington*, "A Statement by the Author" (on the book's back cover), p. 80.

94. Pringle quoted in Blum, *V Was for Victory*, p. 39. On advertising's role in shaping the public meaning of the war, see Blum, pp. 15–52; Catton, *The War Lords of Washington*, pp. 66–80; Mark H. Leff, "The Politics of Sacrifice on the American Home Front in World War II," *Journal of American History* 77 (March 1991): 1306–13.

95. Office of War Information report quoted in Blum, *V Was for Victory*, p. 104. On Roosevelt's economic advisers and the dominant approach of economic growth through fiscal policy, see Alan Brinkley, "The New Deal and the Idea of the State," in Fraser and Gerstle, *The Rise and Fall of the New Deal Order*, pp. 85–121; and John W. Jeffries, "The 'New' New Deal: FDR and American Liberalism, 1937–1945," *Political Science Quarterly* 105 (Fall 1990): 397–418.

96. *PPA*, 13, pp. 41–42.

97. Blum, *V Was for Victory*, p. 298; *PPA*, 13, p. 388.

98. Donald Porter Geddes, ed., *Franklin Delano Roosevelt: A Memorial* (New York: Pocket Books, 1945), pp. 77, 21–22. I am grateful to my late uncle, Joseph Merlin, for bequeathing me his frayed copy of this book, published six days after Roosevelt's death.

99. *PL*, 4, p. 1011; Richard Hofstadter, *The American Political Tradition* (New York: Vintage Books, 1948), p. 315.

CHAPTER 8

John F. Kennedy: Heroic Leadership for a Television Age

The following abbreviations are used in the notes for chapter 8:

JFKL   John F. Kennedy Library, Boston.
PP   *Public Papers of the Presidents of the United States: John F. Kennedy* (Washington, D.C.: United States Government Printing Office, 1962–64).

1. *PP*, 1961, pp. 3, 377.

2. Joan Blair and Clay Blair, Jr., *The Search for JFK* (New York: Berkeley Publishing Corporation, 1976), p. 587. For the Blairs' account of the *PT 109* episode, see pp. 178–270.

3. Herbert S. Parmet, *Jack: The Struggles of John F. Kennedy* (New York: Dial Press, 1980), pp. 332, 323.

4. Benjamin Bradlee, *Conversations with Kennedy* (New York: Pocket Books, 1976) p. 203; Harris Wofford, *Of Kennedys and Kings* (New York: Farrar, Straus and Giroux, 1980), p. 129; George F. Kennan, oral history interview, JFKL, p. 139.

5. Thomas C. Reeves, *A Question of Character: A Life of John F. Kennedy* (New York: Free Press, 1991), p. 415.

6. Kennedy quoted in Parmet, *Jack*, p. 476. On the Kennedy administration's recruitment form, see Herbert Parmet, *JFK: The Presidency of John F. Kennedy* (New York: Penguin Books, 1984), p. 63.

7. Kennedy quoted in Bradlee, *Conversations with Kennedy*, p. 78. For other examples of Kennedy's private profanity, see Bradlee, pp. 97, 153, 172, 217; and Presidential Recordings, "Civil Rights, 1963," JFKL, dictabelt transcripts of October 28, 1963 and October 30, 1963.

8. Blair and Blair, *The Search for JFK*, p. 584; Garry Wills, *The Kennedy Imprisonment: A Meditation on Power* (Boston: Little, Brown and Company, 1982), p. 34. For Wills's insightful analysis of Kennedy's Don Juanism, see pp. 27–38. On Esther Peterson and the President's Commission on the Status of Women, see Irving Bernstein, *Promises Kept: John F. Kennedy's New Frontier* (New York: Oxford University Press, 1991), pp. 198–204.

9. John F. Kennedy, *The Strategy of Peace* (New York: Popular Library, 1961), p. 73. For Kennedy's views toward Franklin Roosevelt, see William E. Leuchtenburg, *In the Shadow of FDR: From Harry Truman to Ronald Reagan*, rev. ed. (Ithaca, N.Y.: Cornell University Press, 1985), pp. 63–120.

10. *PP*, 1961, p. 306.

11. John Milton Cooper, Jr., has observed that

> the twentieth-century presidency most closely modeled, albeit largely unconsciously, on Theodore Roosevelt's was . . . Democratic. When he put greatest stress on world leadership, advocated domestic reforms for the sake of strength and image abroad, and purveyed quasi-aristocratic cultural patronage, John F. Kennedy came closer to duplicating Theodore Roosevelt's viewpoint and approach than did any of his successors, even Franklin Roosevelt. (Cooper, *The Warrior and the Priest: Woodrow Wilson and Theodore Roosevelt* [Cambridge: Harvard University Press, 1983], p. 355.)

12. *PP*, 1963, p. 830; Arendt quoted in A. Alvarez, *Under Pressure* (Baltimore: Penguin Books, 1965), pp. 104–5.

13. Wills, *The Kennedy Imprisonment*, p. 258.

14. *PP*, 1962, pp. 533, 422.

15. Clinton Rossiter, *The American Presidency*, rev. ed. (New York: New American Library, 1960), p. 246; Richard E. Neustadt, *Presidential Power and the Modern Presidents* (1960; New York: Free Press, 1990), p. 156.

16. Theodore C. Sorensen, ed., *"Let the Word Go Forth": The Speeches, Statements, and Writings of John F. Kennedy* (New York: Delacorte Press, 1988), pp. 17, 20, 19.

17. Ibid., pp. 19, 18.

18. Ibid., pp. 22, 20, 18.

19. *PP*, 1962, pp. 889, 892.

20. Carl M. Brauer, "John F. Kennedy: The Endurance of Inspirational Leadership," in Fred I. Greenstein, ed., *Leadership in the Modern Presidency* (Cambridge: Harvard University Press, 1988), p. 119.

21. Henry Fairlie, *The Kennedy Promise* (New York: Dell Books, 1974), p. 175.

22. For a fuller comparison of Kennedy and King, see Wills, *The Kennedy Imprisonment*, pp. 297–301.

23. *PP*, 1961, pp. 2–3; *PP*, 1962, p. 15.

24. For a more extensive discussion of Kennedy's approach to the cold war, see Bruce Miroff, *Pragmatic Illusions: The Presidential Politics of John F. Kennedy* (New York: David McKay, 1976), pp. 35–166.

25. *PP*, 1961, pp. 22, 368–69.

26. On Kennedy's disregard for conciliatory feelers from the Soviets and his misreading of Khrushchev's speech of January 6, 1961, see Michael R. Beschloss, *The Crisis Years: Kennedy and Khrushchev, 1960–1963* (New York: HarperCollins, 1991), pp. 38–66.

27. Beschloss, *The Crisis Years*, p. 350; *PP*, 1961, p. 534.

28. For instructive versions of the new narrative of the missile crisis, see Beschloss, *The Crisis Years*, pp. 354–575; and James N. Giglio, *The Presidency of John F. Kennedy* (Lawrence: University Press of Kansas, 1991), pp. 189–216. For the multinational conferences, see James G. Blight and David A. Welch, *On the Brink: Americans and Soviets Reexamine the Cuban Missile Crisis* (New York: Noonday Press, 1990).

29. Presidential Recordings, Cuban Missile Crisis Meetings, JFKL, transcript of October 16, 1962, p. 27 (morning meeting), p. 23 (evening meeting).

30. Missile Crisis Meetings, transcript of October 16, 1962, p. 26 (evening meeting).

31. Missile Crisis Meetings, transcript of October 16, 1962, pp. 45–46 (evening meeting), p. 32 (evening meeting).

32. Thomas G. Paterson, "Fixation with Cuba: The Bay of Pigs, Missile Crisis, and Covert War against Castro," in Paterson, ed., *Kennedy's Quest for Victory: American Foreign Policy, 1961–1963* (New York: Oxford University Press, 1989), p. 151. On Soviet accounts of the near fighting at sea, see Blight and Welch, *On the Brink*, p. 306.

33. Nye quoted in Blight and Welch, *On the Brink*, p. 84; Presidential Recordings, Cuban Missile Crisis Meetings, JFKL, transcript of October

27, 1962, pp. 2–3.

34. Missile Crisis Meetings, transcript of October 27, 1962, pp. 19, 24.

35. Missile Crisis Meetings, transcript of October 27, 1962, p. 28; Mc-Namara quoted in the *New York Times,* January 15, 1992, p. A11.

36. Arthur Schlesinger, Jr., *A Thousand Days: John F. Kennedy in the White House* (Greenwich, Conn.: Fawcett Crest Books, 1967), p. 756; Kennedy quoted in Beschloss, *The Crisis Years,* p. 549. I was one of the "revisionists" who, drawing on the original "insider" accounts of the missile crisis, accused Kennedy of recklessness in ruling out the missile trade. See *Pragmatic Illusions,* pp. 96–100. Had Khrushchev rejected the no-invasion pledge as insufficient and insisted on the public trade of Cuban and Turkish missiles, Kennedy seemingly was prepared to accept this deal. Dean Rusk revealed in 1987 that Kennedy left himself a secret option for possible last-minute use in the missile crisis: "He instructed me to telephone the late Andrew Cordier, then at Columbia University, and dictate to him a statement which would be made by U Thant, the Secretary General of the United Nations, proposing the removal of both the Jupiters and the missiles in Cuba." Cordier was to forward the statement to U Thant only when signaled by Rusk. If Kennedy's only way of preventing war was the trade, he would have greater political cover acceding to a request from U Thant than appearing to knuckle under to a demand from Khrushchev. Rusk quoted in Blight and Welch, *On the Brink,* p. 83.

37. *PP,* 1963, pp. 461, 462, 894.

38. Select Committee to Study Governmental Operations with Respect to Intelligence Activities, United States Senate, *Alleged Assassination Plots Involving Foreign Leaders* (Washington, D.C.: United States Government Printing Office, 1975), p. 147. Operation MONGOOSE was coordinated with expanded military planning for a potential invasion of Cuba. See James G. Hershberg, "Before 'The Missiles of October': Did Kennedy Plan a Military Strike against Cuba?" *Diplomatic History* 14 (Spring 1990): 163–98.

39. On Vietnam as a test case for counterinsurgency, see Miroff, *Pragmatic Illusions,* pp. 142–66.

40. *PP,* 1962, p. 223. On the failures of the Alliance for Progress, see Jerome Levinson and Juan de Onis, *The Alliance That Lost Its Way* (Chicago: Quadrangle, 1970); Ruth Leacock, *Requiem for Revolution: The United States and Brazil, 1961–1969* (Kent, Ohio: Kent State University Press, 1990); Stephen G. Rabe, "Controlling Revolutions: Latin America, the Alliance for Progress, and Cold War Anti-Communism," in Paterson, *Kennedy's Quest for Victory,* pp. 105–22; Miroff, *Pragmatic Illusions,* pp. 111–42.

41. President's Office Files, JFKL, box 118; Charles Burrows, oral history interview, JFKL, p. 16. Part of the section on agrarian reform in the

briefing paper for Kennedy has been blacked out by a government censor. The details on Villeda Morales's White House visit can be found in the Burrows interview, pp. 20–24.

42. For a neo-Marxist view of the power of investment capital over state actors, see Fred Block, "The Ruling Class Does Not Rule: Notes on the Marxist Theory of the State," in Thomas Ferguson and Joel Rogers, eds., *The Political Economy* (Armonk, N.Y.: M. E. Sharpe, 1984), pp. 32–46. For a non-Marxist version of the argument, see Charles E. Lindblom, *Politics and Markets* (New York: Basic Books, 1977), pp. 170–88.

43. Ronald F. King, "Continuity and Change: Fiscal Policy in the Kennedy Administration," in Paul Harper and Joann P. Krieg, eds., *John F. Kennedy: The Promise Revisited* (Westport, Conn.: Greenwood Press, 1988), p. 180.

44. *PP*, 1961, p. 87.

45. For business reactions to the Kennedy presidency, see Jim F. Heath, *John F. Kennedy and the Business Community* (Chicago: University of Chicago Press, 1969).

46. *PP*, 1962, p. 316.

47. Kennedy quoted in Schlesinger, *A Thousand Days*, p. 589.

48. Papers of Theodore C. Sorensen, JFKL, box 29. A month later Sorensen sent memos to agency heads requesting "a complete list of the major actions undertaken or proposed by this Administration which might be termed 'pro-business' or 'pro-free enterprise.'" In response, extensive lists were compiled by each agency, demonstrating, as Sorensen later put it, "remarkable efforts by this Administration to help business." Sorensen Papers, box 29.

49. Bernard Nossiter, *The Mythmakers: An Essay on Power and Wealth* (Boston: Beacon Press, 1964), p. 41.

50. Papers of Walter W. Heller, JFKL, box 5.

51. Papers of Walter W. Heller, JFKL, box 5.

52. Galbraith quoted in Thedore C. Sorensen, *Kennedy* (New York: Bantam Books, 1966), p. 483; Allen J. Matusow, *The Unraveling of America: A History of Liberalism in the 1960s* (New York: Harper and Row, 1984), p. 56. For the statistics on the distribution of benefits from the 1963 tax bill, see Nossiter, *The Mythmakers*, pp. 35–36.

53. Dillon quoted in Sorensen, *Kennedy*, p. 521. For the data on corporate profits and take-home pay, see Herb Gebelein, "Economic Policy in Practice: Perspective on the 1960s," in Harper and Krieg, *John F. Kennedy*, pp. 186–89.

54. Carl M. Brauer, *John F. Kennedy and the Second Reconstruction* (New York: Columbia University Press, 1977), p. 320.

55. James MacGregor Burns, oral history interview, JFKL, p. 71.

56. Wofford, *Of Kennedys and Kings*, p. 128.

57. On the Kennedy administration's litigation strategy, see Brauer, *John F. Kennedy and the Second Reconstruction,* pp. 116–25. On its strategy of executive action, see Hugh Davis Graham, *The Civil Rights Era: Origins and Development of National Policy, 1960–1972* (New York: Oxford University Press, 1990), pp. 27–73. These strategies produced only token gains for blacks.

58. Kennedy quoted in Wofford, *Of Kennedys and Kings,* p. 153.

59. Ibid., p. 126.

60. James M. Washington, ed., *A Testament of Hope: The Essential Writings of Martin Luther King, Jr.* (San Francisco: Harper and Row, 1986), p. 291.

61. Presidential Recordings, "Civil Rights, 1963," meeting of May 20, 1963, dictabelt transcript of June 3, 1963.

62. Presidential Recordings, "Civil Rights, 1963," meeting of June 1, 1963.

63. *PP,* 1963, p. 469.

64. *PP,* 1963, p. 493. In Sorensen's drafts of the special message, the warning against demonstrations became sharper with each successive version. President's Office Files, JFKL, box 97.

65. The Gallup poll is cited in Giglio, *The Presidency of John F. Kennedy,* p. 282; the *American Heritage* poll is cited in Reeves, *A Question of Character,* p. 11. For an insightful treatment of Kennedy's scholarly and popular reputation since his death, see Thomas Brown, *JFK: History of an Image* (Bloomington: Indiana University Press, 1988).

CHAPTER 9

Martin Luther King, Jr.: Dissenting Leadership and
Democratic Redemption

The following abbreviations are used in the notes for chapter 9:

KP   King Papers, Martin Luther King, Jr., Center for Nonvio-
          lent Social Change, Atlanta.
KPBU   King Papers, Mugar Memorial Library, Boston Univer-
          sity, Boston.
TOH   James Melvin Washington, ed., *A Testament of Hope: The
          Essential Writings of Martin Luther King, Jr.* (San Fran-
          cisco: Harper and Row, 1986).

1. Clayborne Carson, "Reconstructing the King Legacy: Scholars and National Myths," in Peter J. Albert and Ronald Hoffman, eds., *We Shall Overcome: Martin Luther King, Jr., and the Black Freedom Struggle* (New York: Pantheon Books, 1990), pp. 244–48; KP, Series 3, box 14; KP, Series

3, box 8.

2. On the place of religion in American political life, see Garry Wills, *Under God: Religion and American Politics* (New York: Simon and Schuster, 1990).

3. KP, Series 3, box 1. For the audience's fervent response to these words of King's, see Taylor Branch, *Parting the Waters: America in the King Years, 1954–63* (New York: Simon and Schuster, 1988), pp. 139–40.

4. Young quoted in Howell Raines, *My Soul Is Rested: Movement Days in the Deep South Remembered* (New York: Penguin Books, 1983), p. 425. For thorough accounts of the Montgomery bus boycott, see David J. Garrow, *Bearing the Cross: Martin Luther King, Jr., and the Southern Christian Leadership Conference* (New York: Vintage Books, 1988), pp. 11–32, 51–82; and Branch, *Parting the Waters*, pp. 128–205. For King's own account, see Martin Luther King, Jr., *Stride toward Freedom: The Montgomery Story* (New York: Harper and Row, 1958).

5. David Thelen, "Becoming Martin Luther King, Jr.: An Introduction," *Journal of American History* 78 (June 1991): 20.

6. KP, Series 3, box 1.

7. King, *Stride Toward Freedom*, p. 64.

8. Ibid., p. 63.

9. KP, Series 3, box 13; KPBU, box 4. For Garrow's treatment of King's midnight epiphany, see *Bearing the Cross*, pp. 56–58; and idem, "Martin Luther King, Jr., and the Spirit of Leadership," in Albert and Hoffman, *We Shall Overcome*, pp. 18–21.

10. KPBU, box 77. On the leadership style of black Baptist preachers, see Aldon D. Morris, *The Origins of the Civil Rights Movement: Black Communities Organizing for Change* (New York: Free Press, 1984), pp. 4–11; and Lewis V. Baldwin, "The Minister as Preacher, Pastor, and Prophet: The Thinking of Martin Luther King, Jr.," in David J. Garrow, ed., *Martin Luther King, Jr.: Civil Rights Leader, Theologian, Orator*, vol. 1 (Brooklyn, N.Y.: Carlson Publishing, 1989), pp. 39–57.

11. *TOH*, pp. 260, 265.

12. *TOH*, p. 267.

13. Martin Luther King, Jr., *Strength to Love* (1963; Philadelphia: Fortress Press, 1981), pp. 13, 17, 13.

14. KPBU, box 77. One of King's most notable comparisons of himself to the Hebrew prophets and St. Paul was in his "Letter from Birmingham Jail." See Martin Luther King, Jr., *Why We Can't Wait* (New York: New American Library, 1964), p. 77. David L. Lewis argues that such comparisons were "redolent of the divinity-school seminar" and thus not as immodest as they might appear to lay readers. David L. Lewis, *King: A Critical Biography* (Baltimore: Penguin Books, 1971), p. 188.

15. King quoted in Garrow, *Bearing the Cross*, p. 289; Levison quoted in Garrow, *Bearing the Cross*, p. 588.

16. KPBU, box 7; King, *Strength to Love*, p. 22. On the FBI's obsession with King's sexual behavior, see David J. Garrow, *The FBI and Martin Luther King, Jr.* (New York: Penguin Books, 1983), pp. 101–72.

17. Septima P. Clark Interview, Oral History Collection, Martin Luther King, Jr., Center for Nonviolent Social Change, Atlanta, p. 39.

18. *TOH*, p. 349.

19. Branch, *Parting the Waters*, p. 654.

20. KP, Series 3, box 13; *TOH*, p. 148.

21. Young quoted in Garrow, *Bearing the Cross*, pp. 464–65. On King's "dialectical" method of reaching syntheses after listening to his staff, see Garrow, *Bearing the Cross*, pp. 463–65; and Adam Fairclough, *To Redeem the Soul of America: The Southern Christian Leadership Conference and Martin Luther King, Jr.* (Athens: University of Georgia Press, 1987), pp. 168–70.

22. On King's private humor, see Ralph David Abernathy, *And the Walls Came Tumbling Down: An Autobiography* (New York: HarperCollins, 1990), pp. 467–70.

23. King, *Why We Can't Wait*, p. 61.

24. Keith D. Miller, *Voice of Deliverance: The Language of Martin Luther King, Jr. and Its Sources* (New York: Free Press, 1992), p. 9.

25. King, *Strength to Love*, p. 121. For a perceptive analysis of King's tactic of reassuring whites, see August Meier, "On the Role of Martin Luther King," in Garrow, *Martin Luther King, Jr.*, vol. 3, pp. 636–39.

26. On the relationship of King's March on Washington speech to his prior oratory, see Fairclough, *To Redeem the Soul of America*, p. 155.

27. *TOH*, pp. 217–18.

28. Wills, *Under God*, p. 203; *TOH*, p. 219.

29. *TOH*, pp. 219–20.

30. *TOH*, p. 228.

31. James H. Cone, "Martin Luther King, Jr., Black Theology—Black Church," in Garrow, *Martin Luther King, Jr.*, vol. 1, p. 212.

32. *TOH*, p. 230.

33. To witness King's rhetorical achievement in this speech, see the film *Eyes on the Prize*, series 1 (Boston: Blackside, 1986), episode 6.

34. For criticisms of King as merely a "symbolic" leader, see Lewis, *King*, p. 213. James A. Colaico writes: "Though King would denounce the immoral practices recommended by Machiavelli for the successful politician, an analysis of his campaigns reveals that while he appeared to be the lamb, in reality his nonviolent method embodied much of the lion and the fox." Colaico, "Martin Luther King, Jr. and the Paradox of Nonviolent Direct Action," in Garrow, *Martin Luther King, Jr.*, vol. 1, p. 196.

35. KP, Series 3, box 1; King, *Stride toward Freedom*, p. 102.

36. KP, Series 3, box 2.

37. KPBU, box 52.

38. On Chief Pritchett, see Fairclough, *To Redeem the Soul of America*, pp. 101–2; and Branch, *Parting the Waters*, pp. 527, 604–7.

39. My argument here largely parallels that made by David J. Garrow, *Protest at Selma: Martin Luther King, Jr., and the Voting Rights Act of 1965* (New Haven: Yale University Press, 1978), pp. 220–32.

40. Young quoted in Henry Hampton and Steve Fayer, *Voices of Freedom: An Oral History of the Civil Rights Movement from the 1950s through the 1980s* (New York: Bantam Books, 1990), p. 214.

41. Baker quoted in Raines, *My Soul Is Rested*, p. 200; Abernathy, *And the Walls Came Tumbling Down*, p. 308.

42. *TOH*, p. 127.

43. Garrow, *Protest at Selma*, p. 225; King, *Why We Can't Wait*, p. 85.

44. KP, Series 3, box 2; Fairclough, *To Redeem the Soul of America*, p. 228.

45. John F. Kennedy, *Public Papers: 1963* (Washington, D.C.: Government Printing Office, 1964), p. 469; Johnson quoted in Stephen B. Oates, *Let the Trumpet Sound: The Life of Martin Luther King, Jr.* (New York: New American Library, 1983), p. 355.

46. Forman quoted in Garrow, *Bearing the Cross*, p. 423.

47. James Forman, *The Making of Black Revolutionaries* (New York: Macmillan Company, 1972), p. 255. On the SNCC approach to movement building, see Clayborne Carson, *In Struggle: SNCC and the Black Awakening of the 1960s* (Cambridge: Harvard University Press, 1981), pp. 45–174.

48. Martin Luther King, Jr., *Where Do We Go from Here: Chaos or Community?* (New York: Bantam Books, 1968), p. 186. Although King's celebrated Southern campaigns for the most part did not produce lasting local black organizations, another SCLC program, with which he was only marginally involved, did contribute effectively to the recruitment and training of indigenous black leadership. This was the SCLC Citizenship Education Program, run by Septima Clark. See Morris, *The Origins of the Civil Rights Movement*, pp. 236–39.

49. KP, Series 3, box 12.

50. KP, Series 3, box 6.

51. Morris, *The Origins of the Civil Rights Movement*, pp. 61–62.

52. For Cleveland Sellers's view of King, see Carson, *In Struggle*, p. 208.

53. Carson, *In Struggle*, p. 155.

54. Vincent Harding, "Re-calling the Inconvenient Hero: Reflections on the Last Years of Martin Luther King, Jr.," in Garrow, *Martin Luther King, Jr.*, vol. 2, p. 528.

55. KP, Series 3, box 14.

56. *TOH*, p. 194.

57. Young quoted in Garrow, *Bearing the Cross*, p. 437; KP, Series 1,

box 5; KP, Series 3, box 10; KP, Series 1, box 5.

58. KP, Series 1, box 5.

59. Alan B. Anderson and George W. Pickering, *Confronting the Color Line: The Broken Promise of the Civil Rights Movement in Chicago* (Athens: University of Georgia Press, 1986), p. 191.

60. KP, Series 3, box 11.

61. Young quoted in Hampton and Fayer, *Voices of Freedom*, p. 313; white participant quoted in Kathleen Connolly, "The Chicago Open-Housing Conference," in David J. Garrow, ed., *Chicago 1966: Open Housing Marches, Summit Negotiations, and Operation Breadbasket* (Brooklyn, N.Y.: Carlson Publishing, 1989), pp. 63–64; chants about King quoted in Anderson and Pickering, *Confronting the Color Line*, p. 228; King quoted in Oates, *Let the Trumpet Sound*, p. 413. Ralph Abernathy was another participant haunted by memories of Gage Park: "In Chicago we sometimes had the feeling that this huge sea of snarling white faces was going to sweep over us and kill every single black marcher." Abernathy, *And the Walls Came Tumbling Down*, pp. 379–80.

62. Chicago opened King's eyes to the depths of white racism in America. Yet he continued to believe that racism could be dealt with by civil rights legislation: "You know those people throwing rocks out there. . . . Do you know if the laws said Negroes had to live in Gage Park and the law was enforced and they knew that the law meant business. . . , those same people would be out there playing basketball with Negroes." KP, Series 3, box 11.

63. Connolly, "The Chicago Open-Housing Conference," in Garrow, *Chicago 1966*, p. 89. On the class composition of the marches, see Connolly, p. 65.

64. King quoted in John McKnight, "The Summit Negotiations: Chicago, August 17, 1966–August 26, 1966," in Garrow, *Chicago 1966*, pp. 120–21. McKnight, a participant in the negotiations, took detailed notes.

65. On the aftermath of the "summit agreement," see Anderson and Pickering, *Confronting the Color Line*, pp. 270–337.

66. Abernathy, *And the Walls Came Tumbling Down*, p. 395.

67. Ibid., p. 362.

68. From Johnson's "Hellhound on My Trail," quoted in Greil Marcus, *Mystery Train: Images of America in Rock 'n' Roll Music* (New York: E. P. Dutton, 1975), p. 28. "Hellhound on My Trail" copyright © by King of Spades Music.

69. King recounted how he agonized over his public stance on Vietnam to an SCLC staff retreat in May 1967. KP, Series 3, box 12.

70. King quoted in Garrow, *Bearing the Cross*, p. 554; KP, Series 3, box 12. On the reaction to King's Vietnam speech, see Garrow, pp. 553–54.

71. *TOH*, pp. 234, 236, 237.

72. *TOH*, pp. 240, 233.

73. KP, Series 3, box 12; King's speech before the California Democratic Council, Los Angeles, March 16, 1968. A tape of the latter speech is in the author's possession. I am grateful to Toni Ratner, Harriet Glickman, and Richard Glickman for providing me with this tape.

74. KP, Series 3, box 12.

75. KP, Series 3, box 5; KP, Series 3, box 13; KP, Series 3, box 12.

76. KP, Series 3, box 12; King, *Where Do We Go from Here*, p. 217; KP, Series 3, box 11.

77. KP, Series 3, box 11. In contrast to Elizabeth Cady Stanton, who temporarily dropped her universalistic principles during Reconstruction and derogated blacks in order to promote the cause of women, King steadfastly resisted the politics of exclusion. Recently dumped by the Congress of Racial Equality, Jim Peck, a white activist who had been savagely beaten during the Freedom Rides, sent a letter to King in June 1966, to thank him for not moving with the trend toward black separatism. "Despite the increasing clamor for 'black power' and 'self-defense,'" Peck wrote, "you adhere to the principles of equality and nonviolence—and this is admirable." KP, Series 1, box 19.

78. KP, Series 3, box 14.

79. KP, Series 3, box 14.

80. KP, Series 3, box 14.

81. Lewis, *King*, p. 355; Roche quoted in Garrow, *Bearing the Cross*, p. 554. On the 1968 FBI report about King, see Garrow, *The FBI and Martin Luther King, Jr.*, pp. 185–86.

82. Young quoted in Garrow, *Bearing the Cross*, p. 602.

83. KP, Series 3, box 13.

84. *TOH*, p. 286.

85. "To Redeem the Soul of America" was the motto of SCLC.

CHAPTER 10

Democracy and Leadership in America

1. On the New Left's problems in putting its ideal of participatory democracy into practice, see James Miller, *"Democracy Is in the Streets": From Port Huron to the Siege of Chicago* (New York: Simon and Schuster, 1987), pp. 157–328. See also Jane J. Mansbridge, "The Limits of Friendship," in John Arthur, ed., *Democracy: Theory and Practice* (Belmont, Calif.: Wadsworth Publishing Company, 1992), pp. 121–32.

2. Walter Lippmann, *Public Opinion* (1922; New York: Free Press, 1965).

3. Robert A. Dahl, *Who Governs? Democracy and Power in an American City* (New Haven: Yale University Press, 1961), p. 227; Bryan D. Jones,

"Causation, Constraint, and Political Leadership," in Jones, ed., *Leadership and Politics: New Perspectives in Political Science* (Lawrence: University Press of Kansas, 1989), p. 8. On the rational-choice approach to leadership, see also Morris P. Fiorina and Kenneth A. Shepsle, "Formal Theories of Leadership: Agents, Agenda Setters, and Entrepreneurs," in *Leadership and Politics*, pp. 17–40.

4. The waning of the debate over republicanism versus liberalism is expressed well by Isaac Kramnick, one of the principal figures on the neoliberal side:

> No one paradigm cleared the field in 1788 and obtained exclusive dominance in the American political discourse. Liberalism scored no watershed victory over republicanism. Both languages were heard during the "great national discussion." Other paradigms as well were available to the Framers' generation, such as the Protestant ethic and the ideals of sovereignty and power. So it has remained. American political discourse to this day tends, more often than not, to be articulated in all of these distinguishable idioms, however discordant they may seem to professors of history or political thought. (Kramnick, *Republicanism and Bourgeois Radicalism: Political Ideology in Late Eighteenth-Century England and America* [Ithaca, N.Y.: Cornell University Press, 1990], p. 294.)

5. Susan J. Carroll, "Feminist Scholarship on Political Leadership," in Barbara Kellerman, ed., *Leadership: Multidisciplinary Perspectives* (Englewood Cliffs, N.J.: Prentice-Hall, 1984), p. 142.

6. Not all American leaders fit neatly into one of these four types. Some are complex blends of several types. The typology of American leadership in this book is designed to be useful and suggestive, not definitive.

7. Alexis de Tocqueville, *Democracy in America* (1835, 1840; Garden City, N.Y.: Anchor Books, 1969), p. 197; C. Wright Mills, *The Power Elite* (New York: Oxford University Press, 1956), p. 361.

INDEX